Register Now f(
to You

SPRINGER PUBLISHING COMPANY
C(·)NNECT™

Your print purchase of *Internet Addiction in Children and Adolescents,*
includes online access to the contents of your book—increasing accessibility,
portability, and searchability!

Access today at:

**http://connect.springerpub.com/content/book/978-0-8261-3373-1
or scan the QR code at the right with your smartphone
and enter the access code below.**

VYDCS6KN

*Scan here for
quick access.*

LS

SPRINGER/ PUBLISHING COMPANY
View all our products at springerpub.com

INTERNET ADDICTION IN CHILDREN AND ADOLESCENTS

Kimberly S. Young, PsyD, is a licensed psychologist and an internationally known expert on Internet addiction. She founded the Center for Internet Addiction in 1995 and is a professor at St. Bonaventure University. She has published numerous articles and books, including *Caught in the Net*, the first to identify Internet addiction; *Tangled in the Web; Breaking Free of the Web;* and, with Dr. Nabuco de Abreu, *Internet Addiction: A Handbook and Guide to Evaluation and Treatment.* Her work has been featured in the *New York Times, Wall Street Journal, London Times, USA Today, Newsweek,* and *Time,* and in media outlets that include CNN, CBS News, Fox News, *Good Morning America,* and ABC's *World News Tonight.* She received the Psychology in the Media Award from the Pennsylvania Psychological Association and the Alumni Ambassador Award for Outstanding Achievement from Indiana University of Pennsylvania. She serves on the advisory board for The Internet Group in Toronto and the Japanese Ministry for the prevention and treatment of Internet addiction. She has testified for the Child Online Protection Act Congressional Commission and has been a keynote speaker at the European Union of Health and Medicine; the International Conference on Digital Culture in Seoul, Korea; the U.S. Army War College in Pennsylvania; and the First International Congress on Internet Addiction Disorders in Milan, Italy. She also served on the National Academy of Sciences panel for the Digital Media and Developing Minds colloquia.

Cristiano Nabuco de Abreu, PhD, is a psychologist who has a PhD in clinical psychology from the University of Minho in Portugal, with a post-doctoral fellowship in the Department of Psychiatry, Faculty of Medicine, Universidade of São Paulo. He coordinates the Internet Addicts Program of the Impulse Control Unit of the Institute of Psychiatry, Faculty of Medicine, University of São Paulo. Using a pioneering work method in Brazil and Latin America, the unit has offered therapy sessions and counseling to adults, adolescents, and their family members since 2005. He is the former president of the Brazilian Society of Cognitive Therapies and former vice president of Latina America Society of Cognitive Therapies. He has published numerous articles for various journals and 10 books on mental health, psychotherapy, and psychology, including *Internet Addiction: A Handbook and Guide to Evaluation and Treatment,* with Dr. Young; and *Clinical Handbook for Impulse Control Disorders.*

INTERNET ADDICTION IN CHILDREN AND ADOLESCENTS

Risk Factors, Assessment, and Treatment

Kimberly S. Young, PsyD
Cristiano Nabuco de Abreu, PhD
Editors

SPRINGER / PUBLISHING COMPANY
NEW YORK

Springer Publishing Company, LLC
11 West 42nd Street
New York, NY 10036
www.springerpub.com

Acquisitions Editor: Debra Riegert
Compositor: Newgen KnowledgeWorks

ISBN: 9780826133724
e-book ISBN: 9780826133731

17 18 19 20 21 / 5 4 3 2 1

Library of Congress Cataloging-in-Publication Data
Names: Young, Kimberly S., editor. | Abreu, Cristiano Nabuco de, editor.
Title: Internet addiction in children and adolescents : risk factors,
    assessment, and treatment / Kimberly S. Young, PsyD and Cristiano Nabuco
    de Abreu, PhD, editors.
Description: New York, NY : Springer Publishing Company, LLC, [2017] |
    Includes bibliographical references.
Identifiers: LCCN 2017007415 | ISBN 9780826133724 (paper back)
Subjects: LCSH: Internet addiction. | Internet and children—Health aspects.
    | Internet and teenagers—Health aspects.
Classification: LCC RC569.5.I54 I553 2017 | DDC 616.85/8400835—dc23
LC record available at https://lccn.loc.gov/2017007415

Printed in the United States of America by Gasch Printing.

CONTENTS

CONTRIBUTORS

Cristiano Nabuco de Abreu, PhD, Psychiatry Department Unit of Impulse Control Disorders, Medical School, University of São Paulo, São Paulo, Brazil

David L. Delmonico, PhD, Professor, School of Education, Counselor Education Program, Duquesne University, Pittsburgh, Pennsylvania

Tito De Morais, MD, Founder, Projecto MiudosSegurosNa.Net (KidsSafeOnThe.Net Project), Porto, Portugal

Victoria L. Dunckley, MD, Integrative Child, Adolescent and Adult Psychiatrist, Centre for Life, Los Angeles, California

Evelyn Eisenstein, MD, Associate Professor of Pediatrics and Adolescent Medicine, University of the State of Rio de Janeiro, Rio de Janeiro, Brazil

Elizabeth J. Griffin, MA, LMFT, Internet Behavior Consulting, LLC, Minneapolis, Minnesota

Marsali Hancock, MA, Chief Executive Officer, iKeepSafe.org, Washington, DC

Jill R. Kavanaugh, MLIS, Center on Media and Child Health, Division of Adolescent/Young Adult Medicine, Boston Children's Hospital, Boston, Massachusetts

Lawrence T. Lam, PhD, Professor of Public Health, Faculty of Health and Graduate School of Health, University of Technology, Sydney, Australia

Louis Leung, PhD, School of Journalism and Communication, The Chinese University of Hong Kong, Hong Kong, People's Republic of China

Tracy Markle, MA, LPC, Founder, Co-Director, Digital Media Treatment and Education Center, Boulder, Colorado

Debra Moore, PhD, Licensed Psychologist, Sacramento, California

Heather L. Putney, MS, LMFT, PhD Candidate, Duquesne University, Pittsburgh, Pennsylvania

Michael Rich, MD, MPH, Department of Pediatrics, Harvard Medical School, Director, Center on Media and Child Health, Boston Children's Hospital, Boston, Massachusetts

Yun Mi Shin, MD, Department of Psychiatry, Ajou University, School of Medicine, Suwon, South Korea

David Strayer, PhD, Professor of Psychology, University of Utah, Salt Lake City, Utah

Philip Tam, MA, MBBS, Child and Adolescent Psychiatrist, Sydney, Australia

Emmalie Ting, MD, Pediatric and Adolescent Health Chief of Staff, Clinica de Adolescentes, Rio de Janeiro, Brazil

Michael Tsappis, MD, Department of Psychiatry, Harvard Medical School, Division of Adolescent/Young Adult Medicine, Boston Children's Hospital, Boston, Massachusetts

Kimberly S. Young, PsyD, Professor, St. Bonaventure University, Alleghany, New York

Renwen Zhang, MPhil, School of Journalism and Communication, The Chinese University of Hong Kong, Hong Kong, People's Republic of China

PREFACE

How young is too young for children to go online? How much time is too much for children to spend online? What are the social implications for children who spend hours in isolation in front of screens? Will they become obese due to the lack of exercise because they spend hours playing video games with little real physical play? How will parents manage all these digital devices in their children's lives? What role do teachers play when they are encouraged to use technology in the classroom despite studies that have found these tools to be addictive among students? *Internet Addiction in Children and Adolescents: Risk Factors, Assessment, and Treatment* is the first book to address the new concerns people have about children who have early and easy access to the Internet and digital technologies.

Since the publication in 2010 of our previous book, *Internet Addiction: A Handbook and Guide to Evaluation and Treatment*, the inclusion of digital technology in everyday life has become even more prevalent. Now digital technologies highly interfere not only with the lives of young adults and adults but also—and mainly—with the lives of children and adolescents. We travel across the globe speaking about Internet and screen addictions only to find more questions about the impact of technology on children and adolescents. We hear from adolescent psychiatrists, pediatricians, child psychologists, school counselors, educators, and parents who are concerned about children's problem use of technology and devices.

Why does *screen time* matter? Although the use of technology as a learning tool holds much promise for our children, the misuse of technology can have the opposite effect. Research clearly shows that too much screen time is linked to a lack of school success: poor grades, lower reading scores, inattention, dulled thinking, and social problems. It is not hard to see how television, video games, and Internet activities might interfere with children's healthy eating and sleeping habits and getting their homework done. Less well known is how screen time can rob children of opportunities to develop essential learning skills. New research from the world of neuroscience shows that too much screen time—versus not enough *face time*—is wiring children's brains in ways that can make learning in the classroom, and getting along with teachers and other students, more difficult.

The impacts of this exposure are now more tangible because of the results of investigations carried out in different parts of the world, which show the potential consequences of uncontrolled online use and the observed effects of games and technology in our lives. These efforts resulted in the inclusion of Internet Gaming Disorder for further study in the American Psychiatric Association's *Diagnostic and Statistical Manual of Mental Disorders*, Fifth Edition (*DSM-5*). Independent of the platform on which studies are focusing, from excessive video gaming to social networking, texting, or any other applications, the results show that children's lives have become unmanageable and the implications of virtual experiences for the new generations can cause psychological, social, cognitive, and physical harm.

This book gathers exemplary professionals and researchers from around the world who, by working on the issue in an all-new way, have produced a wide-ranging and original reference, documenting a trove of research material. The chapters address a variety of components of virtual experiences from sexting to distracted driving to the impact of autism on Internet addiction in children, resulting in what are possibly the most comprehensive reference and guidance materials available today. Clinicians, pediatricians, investigators, professors, students, and even the lay public will find in it a rich, well-backed source of information to identify and treat screen addictions among children and adolescents.

This book identifies signs of problem Internet behavior among children, even at the earliest ages. For instance, does the child throw tantrums or become aggressive or agitated when asked to stop using screens? Does the child lie about screen use or sneak use of devices? Does the child show no interest in other things unless they are related to devices? Does the child prefer to spend time alone with screens rather than time with friends?

As children age, there is greater concern about screen time. Researchers estimate that 4% of adolescents in the United States meet the criteria for Internet addiction. The number is much higher in Hong Kong, where 17% to 26.8% of adolescents meet the criteria for addiction. The American adolescent nowadays has easy access to one or more mobile links to the Internet; 92% of teens go online every day, and 24% say they are online *almost constantly*.

Often, children and adolescents with Internet addiction are brought into therapy for other behavioral or psychiatric problems. Given the problems that co-occur with screen addictions, such as anxiety and depression, it is important for therapists who treat children and adolescents to develop a media use screening tool to measure and profile their media use (e.g., reach, time spent) across all relevant forms of media, including television, radio, and online portals. To help practitioners, this book presents standard tools, such as the Problematic and Risky Media Use in Children Checklist and the Parent–Child Internet Addiction Test, that effectively measure media use among children and adolescents and its impact. These tools address all media types and enable therapists, school counselors, pediatricians, and teachers to gain a great amount of information about media use from the responses, which provide a good idea of a child's level of risk for media-related problems.

For practitioners, this book also examines how to diagnose Internet addiction and differentiate it from other forms of adolescent psychiatric conditions. It explores evidence-based treatment approaches and how to define the problem accurately enough to distinguish pathology from normal development—an issue made more difficult by the rapid and enthusiastic adoption of these technologies in our schools, workplaces, and homes for communication, education, and entertainment. This book also serves as a clinical reference handbook for hospitals and clinics looking to create inpatient treatment programs and family therapy options to address Internet and screen addictions among children and adolescents.

Screens allow all of us to connect through texts, e-mails, and social media. They also allow children and adolescents who suffer from social phobias and anxieties, Asperger's syndrome, and autism to find a safe place to retreat. Studies show that psychiatric issues and dysfunctional family dynamics are closely associated with the development of screen addiction in young people. This book addresses the psychological, social, and family conditions for those most at risk and how to combat the use of technology that replaces important face-to-face social relationships.

The constant point-and-click scanning behavior associated with screen and tablet use has been shown to cause significant attentional problems in children. Among the issues cited are that our brains do not multitask as we would like to think and that technology use makes us easily bored with things that do not pop, beep, or scroll. Researchers studying the neuroscience of Internet addiction have found problems in the prefrontal cortex, the area of the brain most associated with judgment, decision making, and impulse control. This brain area undergoes major reorganization during adolescence and has been shown, in functional magnetic resonance imaging studies, to be weakened in Internet addicts. Thus, this book evaluates the effects of heavy screen use on the development of the adolescent's brain and the cognitive repercussions of excessive use of games and Internet platforms for mobile phones and tablets. More specifically, it explores the effects on executive function, impulse control (including emotion), and self-regulation.

Beyond the psychological, social, and cognitive concerns, this book addresses the physical risks that result from too much screen time and provides strategies to improve children's activities. Think of a child who slumps over a tablet and other devices all day. Early studies have found that users who spent more time on computers more likely suffered from back pain, eyestrain, carpel tunnel syndrome, repetitive injury disorders, and obesity.

Because school systems increasingly rely on technology, this book addresses school-based initiatives for administrators and teachers to develop Screen Smart Schools that employ policies and procedures designed to increase awareness among students (and their families) of how much time students spend in front of screens, and employ proper teacher training that helps instruct educators on early detection of students who misuse media or technology, as well as proper strategies of intervention and communication with parents.

Collectively, the book focuses on prevention before use of technology becomes a problem and emphasizes balancing screen time with activities for a healthy mind and body.

We hope you find this book a valuable guide and reference text.

Kimberly S. Young, PsyD
Cristiano Nabuco de Abreu, PhD

INTRODUCTION: THE EVOLUTION OF INTERNET ADDICTION

Kimberly S. Young and Cristiano Nabuco de Abreu

Internet Addiction in Children and Adolescents began as a pet project in a young researcher's one-bedroom apartment in Rochester, New York. I (KSY) was that young researcher. It was 1995, and I had a friend whose husband was seemingly addicted to AOL chat rooms, spending 40, 50, 60 hours online at a time when it was still $2.95 per hour to dial into the Internet. Not only did they suffer financial burdens but their marriage ended in divorce when he met women in online chat rooms (Young, 1996).

The first study on Internet addiction shortly followed as I collected more than 600 similar case studies of people who suffered from relationship problems, academic problems, financial problems, and job loss because they were unable to control their Internet use (Young, 1998). The research grew very quickly into a rapidly evolving new field. Psychologists such as Drs. David Greenfield and Marissa Hecht Orzack were early pioneers in the field (e.g., Greenfield, 1999; Orzack,1999). Their prolific writings in the late 1990s opened up new areas of research. Studies were carried out in China, Korea, and Taiwan in the early 2000s. Historically, this was a pivotal moment as the research led to the development of inpatient treatment facilities.

In 2006, the first inpatient center to treat Internet addiction opened in Beijing, China (Jiang, 2009). Asian countries seemingly had significant problems dealing with Internet use compared with the rest of the world, although that same year a national study in the United States found that one in eight Americans suffered from at least one criterion of problem Internet use (Aboujaoude, Koran, Gamel, Large, & Serpe, 2006). During this period, online applications such as Facebook and Twitter evolved, making technology an integral part of everyday life and blurring the distinction between addictive and functional Internet use.

By 2010, studies of this problem predominantly came from Asian cultures, which led to comprehensive prevention programs in some countries. For instance, Korea developed a master plan to prevent and treat Internet addiction, including national screening days to identify children at risk, early prevention programs offered in schools, and hundreds of inpatient units to treat Internet addiction (Koh, 2013). Comparatively, the United States had seemingly fallen behind, with no government-based or national intervention plans—such as screenings, prevention programs, or inpatient care—to deal with Internet addiction (Young, 2013).

Studies began to identify what were considered digitally potent online applications such as online role-playing games, online gambling, or online pornography that were more addictive than e-mail, PowerPoints, or texting. In 2013, Internet Gaming Disorder was singled out as the most potent problem categorized in the fifth edition of the *Diagnostic and Statistical Manual of Mental Disorders* (*DSM-5*) as a condition for further study (American Psychiatric Association, 2013). Later that year, the first inpatient hospital program for Internet addiction recovery opened in Pennsylvania (DeMarche, 2013), treating all forms of Internet addiction by applying concepts of digital diet and digital nutrition to find healthy ways of using technology, similar to approaches used in treating food addiction.

New statistical models also emerged that identified moderating factors such as coping styles and Internet expectancies that determined functional and dysfunctional Internet use among adult populations (Brand, Laier, & Young, 2014). Research on Internet addiction changed from clinical observation to more statistically and empirically grounded studies. Furthermore, a growing body of neurological and neuroimaging studies showed that the prefrontal cortex played a significant role in the development of Internet addiction (Brand, Young, & Laier, 2014), suggesting a biological causation for the disorder similar to other addictive syndromes.

In fact, neuropsychological and neuroimaging research on excessive and addictive use of the Internet is a rapidly growing scientific field, which has revealed a sum of very interesting results. The results show that an addictive use of the Internet is linked to functional brain changes involving parts of the prefrontal cortex, accompanied by changes in other cortical (e.g., temporal) and subcortical (e.g., ventral striatum) regions. Additionally, there are some hints for structural brain changes, which also may hurt one's executive functions in planning and reasoning and increase risk for impulsivity leading to a person's loss of control over Internet use.

Today, the question has shifted from how much time online is too much to how young is too young for children to go online. According to the Pew Internet Project (2013), more than 30% of children younger than 2 years have used a tablet or smartphone and 75% of those aged 8 years and younger live with one or more mobile devices in the home. Because technology is used so frequently in child play, the creativity and imagination of our youth are left idle, and studies suggest their opportunities to achieve optimal motor and sensory development are diminished (e.g., Dalbudak & Evren, 2014; Gentile, 2011; Rosenwald, 2013). Compounding the problem, children react with defiance, disobedience, and, in some cases, violence when parents try to limit or stop screen time.

These risks raise new concerns about technology addiction among children and adolescents, especially as technology use is encouraged at young ages. Already, the American Academy of Pediatrics (2014) warns against children younger than 2 years having any access to technology or any media and only limited amounts thereafter.

The United States could learn from countries like Korea that provide national screening days to identify children at young ages with problems related to Internet use, provide school-based prevention programs, and provide more Internet addiction inpatient programs, giving parents and families options for treatment. With greater awareness and prevention as children go online, we can intervene early, initiating ways to balance technology use without being consumed by it.

Realizing the emotional toll of technology addiction on children, adolescents, and families, the chapters in this book provide clinical, sociological, and developmental theories used in the evaluation and treatment of Internet addiction among children and adolescents. Looking ahead, this book builds on our earlier work (Young & Abreu, 2010) by focusing on the latest trends in treating children and adolescents. Our previous book minimally addressed adolescents, but now we see that digital addictions have spread dramatically into the lives of children and adolescents.

News stories constantly describe problems that children and teens have with social media, online gaming, Internet gambling, and sexting. The chapters that follow, written by content experts in their fields, incorporate theoretical models from the fields of psychiatry, psychology, communication, child development, education, and sociology to examine risk factors for addiction in children and adolescents, the most problematic online applications, ways of measuring problems, and strategies for prevention and recovery.

In outlining the content for this book, we sought to present information and expert perspectives that would be useful not only to individuals, families, teachers, and counselors but also to academics and mental health counselors from a variety of fields. Those specializing in social work, school counseling, psychology, psychiatry, child and family therapy, adolescent addiction services, and nursing will find evidence-based counseling approaches for treatment. Parents and teachers will find information on how to appropriately engage children and adolescents using technology, which is practically any child today. Educators concerned about the potential misuse of technology among children and adolescents, including teachers and school administrators, should use this book to identify potential risk factors in children in training and to develop prevention programs so that young people can better use this technology in a responsible and productive way. Finally, the chapters included here serve as a reference handbook for child and adolescent hospitals, adolescent recovery centers, community health agencies, and child and adolescent psychiatry units.

REFERENCES

Aboujaoude, E., Koran, L. M., Gamel, N., Large, M. D., & Serpe, R. T. (2006). Potential markers for problematic Internet use: A telephone survey of 2,513 adults. *CNS Spectrums*, *11*(10), 750–755.

American Academy of Pediatrics. (2014). Media and children guidelines. Retrieved from http://www.aap.org/en-us/advocacy-and-policy/aap-health-initiatives/Pages/Media-and-Children.aspx

American Psychiatric Association. (2013). *Diagnostic and statistical manual of mental disorders* (5th ed.). Arlington, VA: American Psychiatric Publishing.

Brand, M., Laier, C., & Young, K. S. (2014). Internet addiction: Coping styles, expectancies, and treatment implications. *Frontiers in Psychology: Psychopathology.* doi:10.3389/fpsyg.2014.01256

Brand, M., Young, K. S., & Laier, C. (2014). Prefrontal control and Internet addiction: A theoretical model and review of neuropsychological and neuroimaging findings. *Frontiers in Human Neuroscience, 8,* 375–390.

Dalbudak, E., & Evren, C. (2014). The relationship of Internet addiction severity with attention deficit hyperactivity disorder symptoms in Turkish university students; impact of personality traits, depression and anxiety. *Comprehensive Psychiatry, 55*(3), 497–503.

DeMarche, E. (2013, September 1). Pennsylvania hospital to open country's first inpatient treatment program for Internet addiction. Foxnews.com. Retrieved from http://www.foxnews.com/tech/2013/09/01/hospital-first-inpatient-treatment-internet-addiction

Gentile, D. (2011). The multiple dimensions of video game effects. *Child Development Perspectives, 5*(2), 75–81.

Greenfield, D. (1999). *Virtual addiction: Help for Netheads, cyberfreaks, and those who love them.* Oakland, CA: New Harbinger.

Jiang, J. (2009, January 28). Inside China's fight against Internet addiction. *Time.* Retrieved from http://content.time.com/time/world/article/0,8599,1874380,00.html

Koh, K. (2013, March 21). *A master plan for prevention and treatment of Internet addiction.* Keynote at the first International Congress on Internet Addiction Disorders, Milan, Italy.

Orzack, M. (1999). Computer addiction: Is it real or is it virtual? *Harvard Mental Health Letter, 15*(7), 8.

Pew Internet Project. (2013). Teens and technology 2013. Retrieved from http://www.pewinternet.org/files/oldedia/Files/Reports/2013/PIP_TeensandTechnology2013.pdf

Rosenwald, M. (2013, April 6). Serious reading takes a hit from online scanning and skimming, researchers say. *The Washington Post*. Retrieved from http://www.washingtonpost.com/local/serious-reading-takes-a-hit-from-online-scanning-and-skimming-researchers-say/2014/04/06/088028d2-b5d2-11e3-b899-20667de76985_story.html

Young, K. S. (1996, August 11). *Internet addiction: The emergence of a new clinical disorder*. Poster at the 104th Meeting of the American Psychological Association, Toronto, ON, Canada.

Young, K. S. (1998). Internet addiction: The emergence of a new clinical disorder. *CyberPsychology & Behavior, 1*(1), 237–244.

Young, K. S. (2013, March 21). *Understanding Internet addiction today*. Keynote at the first International Congress on Internet Addiction Disorders, Milan, Italy.

Young, K. S., & Nabuco de Abreu, C. (Eds.). (2010). *Internet addiction: A handbook and guide to evaluation and treatment*. New York, NY: Wiley.

RISK FACTORS AND IMPACT

PROBLEMATIC INTERACTIVE MEDIA USE AMONG CHILDREN AND ADOLESCENTS: ADDICTION, COMPULSION, OR SYNDROME?

Michael Rich, Michael Tsappis, and Jill R. Kavanaugh

THE PROBLEM

It begins benignly enough. Proud parents put a tablet in front of their infant and marvel at how smart he or she is. Toddlers are handed electronics to keep them quiet in restaurants. School-aged kids are given smartphones to stay in touch with parents—and use them to text each other. Tweens become masters at online video games, competing with and against gamers from around the world. High schoolers do their homework on laptops with multiple windows open, instant messaging friends, following and creating drama on social media, gaming and flaming, dating, and baiting each other. The digital revolution, with its rapid proliferation of electronic screen devices, has transformed not only how we communicate, educate, and entertain ourselves, but also how we behave, as individuals and in society. No group has been more profoundly affected than children and adolescents.

Parents encourage their children to become adept with digital technology, both to thrive in schools that assign increasing amounts of academic work online and to prepare them for the digital workplace of the future. At the same time, many parents worry that their children are more connected to their smartphones and laptops than to the "real world"—their academic work and sleep suffer, they do not play outside, pursue sports they love, or spend time with family and friends. Yet parents themselves are connected

24/7, bringing their smartphones to the dinner table and their laptops to bed. When parents voice concern, children feel that they are being held to a different standard—and, in most cases, ignore parental attempts to control their digital lives. In a recent survey, more than one third of parents revealed that they fought with their children over cell phone use, half of the youth and more than one quarter of their parents believed that they were addicted to their devices (Common Sense Media, 2016). Can young people develop addictions to interactive media use? Or is this a generation-dividing behavior that parents do not understand, as rock and roll was for earlier generations?

Pediatricians, as health professionals who oversee the well-being of children and adolescents through their developing years, may be "canaries in the coal mine" who are first presented with interactive media–related problems. Functioning as pragmatic child developmentalists, pediatricians translate biomedical and psychological science into practical guidance and problem solving for parents on a host of issues in children's lives, from nutrition to injury prevention to optimization of school performance. In recent years, pediatricians have been presented, in increasing numbers, with children and adolescents whose health and development have been affected by their use of smartphones, gaming, or the Internet. Although characterization of this condition (or conditions), diagnostic criteria, and effective intervention strategies are an active area of research and debate, pediatricians cannot wait for academics to complete deliberations. Pediatricians must understand, explain, and develop plans right now for children and adolescents who are impaired, whose developmental trajectories have been disturbed, and whose families have been disrupted.

Children and adolescents are especially at risk for problematic uses of interactive media, both because they are early and enthusiastic adopters of technology with which they are more facile than supervising adults, and because they have yet to develop executive brain functions such as impulse control, self-regulation, and future thinking. As a result, the onset of problematic use of interactive media from video games to smartphones occurs most frequently during childhood and adolescence. However, early signs of problematic interactive media use can go unnoticed or be seen as annoying rather than pathology requiring care—until the young person is impaired severely enough to have physical problems, academic failure, or social dysfunction.

In order to identify and care for children and adolescents at risk, it is important to define the problem accurately enough to distinguish pathology from normal developmental variants, an issue made more difficult by the rapid and enthusiastic adoption of these technologies in our schools, workplaces, and homes for communication, education, and entertainment. In 2015, 13- to 18-year-olds spent an average of 9 hours per day using screen media (Common Sense Media, 2016), one third of that time using two or more screens simultaneously; 91% of adolescents accessed the Internet through mobile devices (Lenhart et al., 2015). Tweens, aged 8 to 12 years, used screen media for 6 hours per day (Common Sense Media, 2016). Nine out of ten 5- to 8-year-olds and more than one half of 2- to 4-year-olds used screen media (Rideout, 2011). Ninety-seven percent of 0- to 4-year-olds used mobile interactive devices, most of them starting before the age of 1 year (Kabali et al., 2015).

Because of the rapid brain development during the first years of life, development that is exquisitely sensitive and responsive to the challenges presented by life experiences, the influences and outcomes of using interactive screen media during these early years remain to be seen. As with many environmental and educational stimuli, it is likely that we will find both positive and negative effects of using interactive media on the developing brain. In the immediate term, however, we must develop guidelines for clinical practice that can guide the healthy use of these devices; recognize emerging physical, mental, and social health problems that arise from technology use; and treat these problems in timely and effective ways.

DIAGNOSTIC DEFINITION

In the two decades since the concept of an addictive relationship with the Internet was suggested, first as Ivan Goldberg's tongue-in-cheek parody (Goldberg, 1996) of the complex diagnostic algorithms of the American Psychiatric Association's *Diagnostic and Statistical Manual of Mental Disorders* and later as a serious concern (Young, 1998b), technology has evolved dramatically. In the mid-1990s, those who responded (to Goldberg's surprise) that they met his fictitious diagnostic criteria were using clunky desktop computers communicating with each other via slow dial-up modems and displaying text-only on green or amber cathode-ray screens. Today's pocket-sized smartphones offer engaging graphics, videos, games, and social media through infant-accessible touchscreens many thousands of times faster.

Nearly every American adolescent now has easy access to one or more mobile links to the Internet; 92% go online every day and 24% say that they are online "almost constantly" (Lenhart et al., 2015). Our society has adopted these technologies so rapidly and has altered our lifestyles and behaviors so dramatically in that time that we have yet to determine what is normal use and what may be unhealthy. Any new technology, from the printing press to television, has been accompanied by a concern, rising to the level of hysteria in some quarters, that the technology will be misused or overused, irreversibly changing us and our society for the worse. Over time, as the nature of misuse or overuse becomes clear, this concern gives way to a reasoned understanding of a new norm that is healthy and productive. In part because we are not yet at that point of understanding about our digital behavior, the estimated prevalence of dysregulated or disabling uses of interactive media ranges from 0.8% in Italy (Poli & Agrimi, 2012) to 8.8% (Xu et al., 2012) and even as high as 14% in China (Wu et al., 2013). The range of these prevalence estimates reflects broad variations in clinical definitions and diagnoses of pathology as much as it reflects differences in culturally acceptable behaviors. However, even the lowest prevalence estimates represent hundreds of millions of individuals whose physical health, social–emotional functioning, and productivity may be impaired by their interactive media use.

Although pediatricians, child psychiatrists, and psychologists are asked to help increasing numbers of children and adolescents who struggle with dysfunctional uses of interactive technologies, the medical establishment has not yet agreed on a diagnosis for this problem. Two decades of research literature offer a diversity of nomenclature, definitions, and diagnostic criteria, reflecting that this is a problem recognized across scientific and clinical disciplines, but also revealing the siloed (and competitive) nature of academic inquiry. Names for this problem range from Internet Addiction Disorder (Young, 1998b) to Problematic Internet Use (Caplan, 2002), Pathological Internet Use (Byun et al., 2009), Compulsive Internet Use (Meerkerk, Van Den Eijnden, Vermulst, & Garretsen, 2009), and the only iteration that has, to date, entered the medical diagnostic lexicon, Internet Gaming Disorder (American Psychiatric Association [APA], 2013b). Each of these definitions captures key features of the condition, including uncontrolled interactive screen media use behaviors that impair an individual's physical, psychological, and/or social function. However, in our experience, none of these terminologies fully takes into account the nature of problematic interactive media use in the developing child and adolescent. As with most behavioral problems, the earlier the dysregulated interactive media use can be recognized and addressed, the easier it is to correct. However, because it is not yet identified as a health care problem, parents, teachers, and others who work with young people typically do not bring it to clinical attention until it has progressed far enough to cause severe dysfunction or disability and is much harder to treat.

Because the brain of the child and adolescent is a work in progress, some psychiatric diagnoses, such as personality disorders, cannot be reliably made until neurodevelopment is complete. Similarly, some dysregulated behaviors, such as temper tantrums, that are normal at one developmental stage represent pathology at another. The evolving nature of the child's developing brain makes it difficult to differentiate problem behaviors from normative behaviors with interactive screen media. During adolescence, interactive media provide a fertile environment for normative developmental tasks such as seeking life experience, exploring one's identity, establishing autonomy, and connecting with peers. Determining when a young person's interactive media use is problematic becomes more complex in a time of impulsivity, experimentation, and sensation seeking—and more critical because this is the period when executive functions such as self-regulation are developing.

Physical and psychological impairments from uncontrolled gambling, sex, and Internet use have been described as addiction by some researchers, but the term "addiction" is not universally accepted by the medical community. Although those who struggle with these issues demonstrate craving, increasing tolerance, inability to abstain, and diminished awareness of use-related problems, these behaviors do not feature the consistent, reproducible physiologic changes in heart and respiratory rates, blood pressure, and galvanic skin response seen with addictive use and withdrawal from substances such as narcotics, alcohol, and tobacco. Because of the absence of biomedical markers, many addiction medicine specialists do not characterize dysfunctional behaviors as equivalents of addiction to substances, preferring instead to characterize them as impulse control disorders. Although the *Diagnostic and Statistical Manual of Mental Disorders*, Fifth Edition (*DSM-5*; APA, 2013a), proposes establishing a category of behavioral addictions, currently it only recognizes Gambling Disorder as a diagnosis (APA, 2013c), with Internet Gaming Disorder included in an appendix of conditions requiring further study (APA, 2013b).

The lack of clinical consensus on description and diagnostic criteria presents a dilemma for practitioners who are being asked to care for increasing numbers of young people struggling with problematic interactive media use behaviors. Without an accepted diagnosis, these patients are invisible to the health care system as medical insurance does not cover treatment. If families cannot pay for care, they will not seek it. Those who can afford to pay for care out of pocket are vulnerable to a cottage industry of addiction treatment that offers them hope in their desperation, but shows little evidence of improved outcomes. As the legitimate health care system does not recognize this problem or bill for its care, there is little incentive to invest in research, clinical infrastructure, or training of clinicians to recognize and respond to the problem. Nevertheless, pediatric clinicians are being presented with increasing numbers of young people struggling with dysfunctional uses of interactive media and must respond now, based on the limited research specific to this problem and the broader medical and psychiatric evidence that can be brought to bear.

The predominant work of the pediatrician is to keep children and adolescents healthy. Pediatricians see young people regularly, monitoring their development, advising them on healthy lifestyles, immunizing them against preventable diseases, and providing anticipatory guidance for the next stage of their growth. In order to incorporate issues of problematic interactive media use in this process, it is critical to have an accessible description, normal benchmarks, and warning signs of impending problems that are observable by parents or the children themselves.

Although children and parents often present with the complaint that they are addicted to smartphones, video games, or the Internet, we have found that addiction terminology is not only medically inaccurate, but counterproductive in pediatric practice. The word "addiction" carries a stigma, often eliciting negative images of alcoholics and opioid abusers (American Medical Association [AMA] Task Force to Reduce Opioid Abuse, 2015); therefore, many parents do not recognize developing problems in their children's interactive media use unless and until their children's physical or mental health and/or their academic and social functions are severely affected. Recognizing the seeds of such problems and preventing or intervening early is much more effective than trying to correct a deeply ingrained habit in a child or adolescent who may have already sustained physical, psychological, or developmental harm. More subtly, perhaps because of our increasing understanding of inborn genetic or personality-based predispositions to opioid or alcohol addictions, use of terms such as Internet or videogame addiction directs the responsibility for the problem toward the device used in the compulsive behavior rather than the behavior itself.

In search of effective terminology to characterize this problem in the pediatric population, we reviewed existing diagnostic descriptions, which cover compulsive use of the Internet (Kuss, Griffiths, Karila, & Billieux, 2014; Lam, 2014; Moreno, Jelenchick, Cox, Young, & Christakis, 2011), video games (Kuss & Griffiths, 2011a; Lehenbauer-Baum et al., 2015; Potenza et al., 2011; Scharkow, Festl, & Quandt, 2014; Van Rooij, Schoenmakers, Vermulst, Van den Eijnden, & Van de Mheen, 2011), mobile phones (Foerster, Roser, Schoeni, & Röösli, 2015; R. Kim, Lee, & Choi, 2015; Lister-Landman, Domoff, & Dubow, 2015), online gambling (Abdi, Ruiter, & Adal, 2015; Floros et al., 2015), pornography (Doornwaard, van den Eijnden, Baams, Vanwesenbeeck, & ter Bogt, 2016; Laier, Pekal, & Brand, 2014; Levin, Lillis, & Hayes, 2012), social media (Hanprathet, Manwong, Khumsri, Yingyeun, & Phanasathit, 2015; Kuss & Griffiths, 2011b; Müller et al., 2016; Sriwilai & Charoensukmongkol, 2016; Tsitsika et al., 2014; Vernon, Barber, & Modecki, 2015), television/video (Orosz, Bőthe, & Tóth-Király, 2016; Sussman & Moran, 2013), and combinations thereof. We concluded that none of the proposed definitions is specific and inclusive enough to account for the key features of the behavioral aberrations we are seeing in children and adolescents. None of the nomenclature used was acceptable enough that both medical professionals and families will identify and address the problem as early in its progression as possible. As an example, the proposed diagnosis of Internet Gaming Disorder, although it avoids using the polarizing term addiction, fails to account for both compulsive electronic gaming on a console not connected to the Internet and nongaming Internet use behaviors ranging from pornography to social media use. Now that all media are available on many platforms, problematic behaviors are not confined to a single device, domain, or application. With respect to the considerable research required to generate these diagnostic descriptions, most were generated with populations that included adults, investigated in relation to a single device or application, and were often studying severely disabling behaviors over extended periods.

As a unifying description of the patients we have seen, we defined the syndrome as *Problematic Interactive Media Use* (PIMU; which, in an ironic case of the ancient speaking to the contemporary, can also be written in Greek as πμ). PIMU describes behaviors characterized by compulsive use of, increasing tolerance to, and negative reactions to being removed from interactive screen media use, which impair the individual's physical, mental, cognitive, and/or social function. These behaviors do not need to meet criteria for addiction (whatever one's definition of addiction may be) in order to require intervention, nor are they linked to a specific device, domain, or destination.

Although PIMU is a unifying description that can be accurately applied to different manifestations of compulsive interactive media use, it is not a diagnosis, but a syndrome, a collection of signs and symptoms. In our clinical experience with PIMU, there are four prominent presentations: gaming, social media, pornography, and information seeking (once known as surfing the web), which includes uncontrolled online searches of virtually any sort of textual or visual information, including binge-watching of short-form videos or television series (Dhir, Chen, & Nieminen, 2015).

Although each of these behaviors occurs on an interactive screen, the uses and gratifications of each are different (Grellhesl & Punyanunt-Carter, 2012; Sundar & Limperos, 2013; Whiting & Williams, 2013). Unlike substance abuse disorders, where abstinence from one substance may be followed by engagement with another, we have observed little crossover among the four variations of PIMU. Prevalence of these behaviors varies between populations. Uncontrolled gaming is more prevalent among boys, while more girls compulsively use social media, for example. Individual characteristics that predispose young people to each of these variations can be quite different. Social media can be very attractive to young people with social anxiety. Obsessive pornography use can be the result of or contribute to subsequent sexual dysfunction. Research is required to determine whether the variations in PIMU behavior that we observe are different manifestations of a single condition, separate conditions, or symptoms of established psychiatric diagnoses playing themselves out in the environment of interactive technology.

For the immediate practical purpose of getting patients to diagnosis and treatment and of building a care infrastructure for PIMU, we are currently diagnosing and treating PIMU patients under the conceptualization that these are symptoms of established psychiatric diagnoses manifesting themselves in the environment of interactive technology. Most commonly, PIMU patients whom we have evaluated suffer from attention deficit hyperactivity disorder (ADHD) or anxiety disorders (Chou, Liu, Yang, Yen, & Hu, 2015), including cyberchondria (Fergus & Dolan, 2014) and social anxiety (Ko et al., 2014). Oppositional defiant disorder (Bozkurt, Coskun, Ayaydin, Adak, & Zoroglu, 2013), substance use (Coeffec et al., 2015; Evren, Dalbudak, Evren, & Demirci, 2014; Rucker, Akre, Berchtold, & Suris, 2015), and depression (Bozkurt et al., 2013; Derbyshire et al., 2013; Fu, Chan, Wong, & Yip, 2010; Jang, Hwang, & Choi, 2008; King, Delfabbro, Zwaans, & Kaptsis, 2013; Ko et al., 2014; Lam & Peng, 2010; Lin et al., 2014; Messias, Castro, Saini, Usman, & Peeples, 2011; Tsitsika et al., 2011), with suicidal ideation or suicide attempts (Fu et al., 2010; Messias et al., 2011) may be preexisting or co-occurring. Medical outcomes of PIMU can include weight gain or loss (Canan et al., 2014; Kamal & Mosallem, 2013), nutritional deficiencies (Derbyshire et al., 2013; Gür, Yurt, Bulduk, & Atagöz, 2015; Y. Kim et al., 2010), musculoskeletal problems (Kamal & Mosallem, 2013), and sleep disturbances (Canan et al., 2013; Choi et al., 2009; King, Delfabbro, Zwaans, & Kaptsis, 2014; Stockburger & Omar, 2013). Social and emotional sequelae of PIMU frequently include school avoidance and academic failure, increasing conflicts with and isolation from peers, and family discord. The combined effects of the psychiatric condition, physical health status, and media use itself result in reductions in the young person's functional capacity.

ASSESSMENT

As with all dysfunctional behaviors, PIMU can be viewed as the consequence of traits unique to the individual's psychology and physiology as he or she develops and confronts environmental challenges. A comprehensive assessment of PIMU requires systematic history taking and thorough examination to develop a formulation of the problem that can be used to guide treatment planning. As information about the patient's medical and psychological history is obtained, consider how each of these experiences might have influenced the development of PIMU and how it may affect treatment.

It can be difficult to obtain accurate information about PIMU for two reasons. First, screen media cannot be abstained from or avoided completely, as recreational drugs or alcohol can. Interactive media are completely integrated, and often required, in young people's academic work, interpersonal communications, recreation, and entertainment. In home and school contexts where the norm may be adults and peers using interactive media frequently and often simultaneously, it can be very difficult for young people to have the perspective necessary to become aware that their use may have become problematic or pathological—and that is assuming that they will acknowledge PIMU if they recognize it in themselves.

Second, interactive media are rock and roll for many digital natives, the way that many youth distinguish their own culture from that of their parents. Getting one's own smartphone or social media presence is a coming of age ritual, a 21st-century visionquest, walkabout, or bar mitzvah. A key feature of adolescent autonomy-seeking is to protect the newly achieved independence from those in authority who might disapprove of or restrict activities that the adolescent has made his or her own. For many adolescents, the less acceptable the activity may be to adults, whether it be violent gaming or sexting, the more compelling it is (Bijvank, Konijn, Bushman, & Roelofsma, 2009). As a result, many young patients seen for suspected PIMU, like many patients struggling with substance abuse or eating disorders, are brought to care against their will, uncooperative, and nonverbal. They believe that they have nothing to gain from confessing their online behaviors to an authority figure that they suspect to be clueless about their lives and highly likely to restrict or prohibit them from their interactive media behaviors.

First, speak with the patient and parents about their concerns, establishing what they consider normative media use for themselves and their family. Obtain a full developmental and mental health history, including pregnancy and delivery, early temperament traits, bonding, and attachment (Moreau, Laconi, Delfour, & Chabrol, 2015). Note any delays in meeting developmental milestones, as well as problems with toilet training, sleep, or transitions. Ask about any previous psychiatric diagnoses, psychotherapy, medications, or other interventions. Assess for any past or present disordered eating, self-injury, suicidal thoughts or actions, and any other safety issues (Kaess et al., 2014). Any indication of a possible imminent safety concern must be responded to effectively, superseding any other assessment or treatment planning. Document previous or current medical conditions and treatments. Obtain a history of developmental stress, adversity, or trauma and ask if there are any previous or current legal concerns (Dalbudak, Evren, Aldemir, & Evren, 2014).

A primary concern for presenting families is often a decline in academic functioning, starting with poor-quality homework, missing homework, inattention, and sleepiness in class (Meena, Mittal, & Solanki, 2012; Tsitsika et al., 2011). Because PIMU behaviors often happen at night and can last all night, young people will begin to present to school late and eventually miss days of school altogether. Determine the timing of these changes in school function, sleep problems, depression, or secondary impairments in attention in relation to observed signs of PIMU. Because academic difficulties, particularly attention problems, can predispose youth to PIMU, detail the patient's educational history and any previous neuropsychological or educational testing. Explore potential behavioral issues at school, ranging from withdrawal to fighting with fellow students or teachers.

Because PIMU arises in family contexts, family structure and functioning, including family media use, must be fully explored. Assess who constitutes the patient's household or households, if in a dual-custody situation. If the patient moves between households, determine whether the relationship between households is harmonious or acrimonious, whether media use rules differ between households, and how much time the patient spends in each. Remain vigilant for any indications about member roles, subsystems, and maintenance of boundaries. A genogram can be helpful in organizing this information as it is obtained. It is helpful to learn of any medical or psychiatric conditions commonly experienced among members of the extended family, particularly if there is a family history of affective disorders, major mental illness, or any history of suicide.

Attitudes about and habits of media use vary widely. Assess baseline media-related behaviors of nuclear family members. Family functioning often changes in response to PIMU. Rules and expectations around media use may be stable, increasingly restrictive, or increasingly lax, and they may apply only to the young person exhibiting PIMU, to all children, or to all family members. It is common for the adolescent patient to exhibit increasing expression of emotional dysregulation, aggression, or suicidal ideation in response to caregiver efforts to limit unwanted behaviors (Young, 2009). After assessing for the presence of such reactive behaviors, the clinician should assess the impact of PIMU on power hierarchy within the family system.

After talking to the patient and parents together, it is critical to excuse the parents and establish a one-on-one dialogue with the patient, listening to his or her story with empathy and respect. If the patient can be reassured by the clinician's actions that the clinician can be the patient's partner and advocate rather than an agent of parental authority, the patient is more likely to share what attracts him or her to PIMU behaviors, how he or she feels about them, and whether and how he or she would like to change.

Explore the young person's interactive media use behaviors longitudinally from onset to the present, detailing frequency, duration, time of day, and context of use, multitasking with other media or activities. PIMU may occur in extended episodes, as with massively multiuser online role-playing games (MMORPGs) or intermittently, such as when teens constantly monitor and respond to text messages or social media posts. In a recent public opinion poll, more than three fourths of parents felt that their child was distracted from family conversations or activities by online exchanges; 72% of adolescents and 48% of their parents acknowledged that they felt the need to respond immediately to texts and social media (Common Sense Media, 2016). Inquire about which portion of the day is available to respond to such messages. Ask the patient to check his or her phone to see how many of such messages are exchanged throughout a given day and explore what else is going on at those times. Is the patient monitoring and responding to communications at school, during meals, at work, during health visits, or late at night?

There are validated research and/or clinical measures designed to assess the presence and severity of PIMU symptoms. Based on her foundational research, Young's Internet Addiction Test (IAT; Young, 1998a) was based on criteria for pathological gambling; Beard's proposed modifications (Beard & Wolf, 2001) focused the IAT more specifically on Internet use behaviors and resulting impairment. These were followed by the Chen Internet Addiction Scale (CIAS) out of China (Chen, Weng, Su, Wu, & Yang, 2003) and the Compulsive Internet Use Scale (CIUS) from the Netherlands (Meerkerk et al., 2009). In an attempt to standardize diagnostic criteria for Internet Addiction Disorder in a measure that is sensitive, specific, and short enough to implement as part of a comprehensive physical and mental health evaluation, Tao et al. (2010) proposed a 2 + 1 scale, where two cardinal criteria plus one of five other symptoms must be met.

In our experience, each of these scales is of limited usefulness because they do not assess the full range of PIMU behaviors seen in our pediatric population. Only the CIUS has been validated with adolescents (others have mixed pediatric and adult subjects), and only Tao et al.'s is concise enough for practical use in the clinic. Nevertheless, key features of PIMU behaviors can be addressed by versions of these scales modified to fit its broader definition: preoccupation with interactive media use; increasing tolerance; inability to control PIMU behaviors; social, academic, and/or psychological impairment; disregard of harmful consequences; withdrawal symptoms of dysphoria, anxiety, and/or irritability; and use of PIMU to alleviate feelings of anxiety, guilt, loneliness, or depression.

Inquiring about changes in physical health associated with PIMU can serve several purposes (Tazawa, Soukalo, Okada, & Takada, 1997). First, the clinician is asking about areas of discomfort with which he or she can help the patient, rather than interrogating the patient about "bad behavior." This establishes a therapeutic rapport, rather than the adversarial, punitive relationship that the patient may anticipate. Second, assessing whether there are medical conditions, such as asthma, which rightly or wrongly have predisposed the patient to an inactive, indoor lifestyle, can help elucidate the origins of PIMU and potential obstacles to recovery. Determining physical and physiological sequelae ranging from back pain to obesity can provide a better understanding of the timeframe and severity of PIMU, as well as the level of discomfort that the patient tolerates to maintain PIMU behaviors. As the patient and family describe the concrete physical health changes that have developed with PIMU, they may be able to recognize the impact of PIMU behaviors on their lives and the life of their family more clearly than when they relate the more gradual and often subjective changes seen with psychological dysfunction. This recognition can help both the patient and his or her family to accept that there is a problem and to promote their motivation to make the difficult changes that may be necessary to address it.

The basic domains of functioning are self-care, productivity, and relationships. Poor functioning is both a risk factor for and a consequence of PIMU. As a young person devotes increasing amounts of time to his or her media use, the individual often begins to show a decrease in self-care (Kamal & Mosallem, 2013). The assessment should include questions about personal hygiene, nutrition, physical activity, and sleep. Impaired sleep is a consistently demonstrated finding across various ages, genders, nationalities, and types of PIMU (An et al., 2014; Ekinci, Celik, Savaş, & Toros, 2014; King et al., 2014; Nuutinen et al., 2014). Ask about difficulty falling asleep, staying asleep, and early morning awakening, as well as excessive daytime sleepiness or difficulty waking in the morning. More subtle indicators of sleep deprivation to ask about include decreased concentration, poor memory, and irritability. If sleep problems are identified, determine whether the patient is forcing himself or herself to stay awake to text, game, or socialize online. Anxiety may drive fear of missing out (FOMO) or a self-defensive, hypervigilant monitoring of the virtual social environment for negative or threatening communications.

Productivity, for most children and youth, is measured by school performance. Ask how school is going for them, both academically and socially. Inquire about classroom behavior and homework habits. Assess relationships with fellow students and faculty. If there is a guidance counselor, homeroom teacher, or other adult at the school whom the patient identifies as an ally, ask to speak with that person as part of the initial evaluation.

Explore with the patient his or her social environment and baseline social functioning (Boies, Cooper, & Osborne, 2004; Kaczmarek & Drazkowski, 2014; Tsitsika et al., 2014). Are there any changes in social functioning? Is the patient retreating or isolating from previous social networks? Is there a new virtual social milieu developing? Is he or she using interactive media contact with others to explore romantic interests, to get closer to others or distance oneself, to create drama, or to harass or coerce? Is he or she attracted to boys, girls, or both? Gender or sexual orientation should be explored carefully and fully; minority status has been associated with an increased risk of PIMU as well as self-harming and suicidal behaviors (DeLonga et al., 2011). What is known about social contacts that have developed online? Has there been any face-to-face or virtual bullying, with the patient as perpetrator, victim, or both? Has there been any sexting or online seduction and, if so, has the patient met any online connections in person?

Evaluation of psychiatric illness underlying or comorbid with PIMU requires a systematic psychiatric review of symptoms with special attention to mood disorders, anxiety disorders, disruptive behavior such as opposition and defiance, and attention deficit/hyperactivity disorder (Bozkurt et al., 2013). Begin the assessment of each category of illness with open-ended questions. Follow any positive endorsement with a systematic assessment of that complaint, recording onset, course, signs, and symptoms, with special attention to their temporal relationship to PIMU symptoms. Obtaining syndrome-specific or general psychiatric rating scales such as the Patient Health Questionnaire (PHQ-9; Kroenke, Spitzer, & Williams, 2001) as well as collateral supports helps in detection and/or identification of severity of comorbid psychiatric illness.

The increased risk of substance use in individuals with PIMU can complicate both medical and psychiatric comorbidity (Ko, Yen, Yen, Chen, & Chen, 2012). Assuring confidentiality and avoiding judgmental language, assess which substances the patient uses or has used, beginning with caffeine, tobacco, and alcohol, and moving on to marijuana, cocaine, amphetamine, and opioids. Determine the age at which the patient first and most recently used each substance, frequency of use, typical quantity used, and longest period of secondary abstinence.

External physical signs of PIMU can be readily observable (Canan et al., 2014). Note the patient's personal hygiene as evidenced by lack of attention to grooming, hair care, body odor, halitosis, and clothing. Increased or decreased body mass index (BMI) may be reported or identified by longitudinal health records from primary care providers. Overweight and obesity increase risk of hypertension, dyslipidemia, insulin resistance, and musculoskeletal problems. Anorexia nervosa and bulimia nervosa can be discovered through the patient's creation or use of pro-ana and pro-mia sites, which promote eating disorders as lifestyle choices and political statements, rather than an illness. Eating disorders have the highest rate of fatality among psychiatric illnesses; they disrupt normal menses, increase the risk of fatal cardiac arrhythmias, and can cause long-term chronic problems from malnutrition to osteoporosis.

Because of the medical problems associated with PIMU, a comprehensive assessment should include a routine physical examination. If the clinician is not a medical provider, the most recent physical examination can be obtained from the primary care provider. Collect height, weight, and vital signs, including blood pressure and heart rate. Laboratory studies should include a complete blood count, basic metabolic panel, blood sugar, and fasting lipid panel. Additional laboratory tests or imaging may be indicated by findings on the physical examination. Examine for asymmetric musculature, repetitive strain injury, and decubitus skin changes. During the interview, note the level of patient and caregiver engagement and cooperation, patterns of eye contact, speech, and psychomotor activity. Integrate observations of the patient's affect with the patient's description of his or her mood. Evaluate the patient's thought process and content, including any recurrent worries, intrusive thoughts, delusions, abnormal perceptions, or thoughts to harm oneself or others. Assess the patient's cognitive function, insight into his or her presenting problem, and capacity to exercise sound judgment.

Frequently, full characterization of the patient's status and formulation of a diagnosis can take more than one visit, because of both the breadth of clinical data to be collected and the need to establish a trusting alliance with the patient and family, who are often at odds with each other. Because there is currently no established unifying diagnosis and we are only now building an evidence base of empirical data on PIMU, the final assessment can include one or more psychiatric and medical diagnoses. Integrate knowledge of the features of these diagnoses with unstated beliefs of the patient and family; social forces acting on involved parties at the time; reciprocal interactions of the patient's thoughts, feelings, and actions in response to evolving circumstances; effects of positive and negative developmental experiences in the patient's personal and family history; and the patient's own neurophysiology. Based on this formulation, the clinical team can construct an individualized treatment plan that is informed by and contributes to the ever-increasing library of evidence-based treatments for PIMU.

TREATMENT

Effective treatment planning for PIMU must respond to the comprehensive, accurate assessment of the patient's needs established in the clinical formulation. Because of the breadth of underlying problems presenting as PIMU, a multidisciplinary treatment team is often required to develop and implement an individualized treatment plan that is determined most likely to be effective based on current evidence, but flexible enough to adjust as the patient and family respond to that treatment. Depending on the specific presentation of a given case, a treatment team might include members from primary medical care, psychiatry, psychology, clinical social work, educational guidance, case management, and others, with close liaison and regular communication among them.

Unlike substance abuse or other conditions in which a dysfunctional behavior is repeated despite negative consequences, complete abstinence from electronics is unsustainable as a long-term goal of treatment. Alcohol or marijuana use is not necessary to everyday life. The chemical addiction patient can achieve complete abstinence from these substances without any significant change in expected daily routines. Interactive screen media have become so ubiquitous and integrated into virtually every aspect of daily living that the ability of young people to function in society depends on near-constant connectivity. For children and adolescents, technology is becoming required in school to access content, complete and submit homework, and communicate with teachers. They entertain and educate themselves with online information and videos. They connect and communicate via social media and text. Treatment for PIMU must build young people's capacity to use interactive media as tools, in focused, mindful ways, rather than abstain from their use. Recovery must occur in the context of our media-saturated environment, with the patient developing awareness and control of his or her interactive media use.

Effective treatment for problematic use of readily available electronic screen media begins with education. Explain and openly discuss the clinical assessment and treatment plan with the patient and his or her family, so that they and the treatment team can develop a shared roadmap to recovery. Conveying optimism and encouragement, connect elements of the assessment with specific components of the treatment plan, so that the patient and family proceed with a sense of understanding and investment in the proposed course of action. Acknowledge how difficult it will be to make the changes required by the treatment plan, connecting empathetically with the patient and avoiding any sense of shame or punishment. Encourage the patient to monitor himself or herself for PIMU behaviors. Because self-awareness and insight on one's behaviors can be blunted in PIMU, preprinted forms can be used to document those behaviors, antecedent circumstances and behaviors of others, thoughts and feelings experienced at the time of the behavior, and the personal and societal consequences of the behavior.

As with any compulsive behavior, PIMU can only be treated when the patient is ready to confront it. As treatment progresses, there will be resistance from the patient, the family, or both, as they confront difficult treatment tasks. Such resistance is integral and essential to recovery and it should not be opposed, but openly anticipated and discussed. Remain positive, empathetic, and workmanlike in affirming the patient's need to stick to the plan. If necessary, a sticking point in the treatment plan can be put on hold indefinitely, as the need to maintain alignment among the clinician, patient, and family takes precedence. As progress is achieved and alliance strengthens during the course of treatment, elements of the plan that have been put on hold can be revisited and addressed. Check with the patient and his or her family frequently to make sure that the understanding of the clinical formulation and proposed treatment is still shared. Provide clarification and further education when needed.

Meta-analysis of treatment strategies for PIMU indicates that psychotherapy shows promise for improving outcomes, at least in the short term (Winkler, Dorsing, Rief, Shen, & Glombiewski, 2013). The two most commonly used treatment modalities are counseling and cognitive behavioral therapy (CBT). Clinical evaluations of individual and family counseling programs showed decreases in prevalence and severity of PIMU among adolescents and young adults in Beijing (Liu et al., 2015), Hong Kong (Shek, Tang, & Lo, 2009), and Korea (Park, Kim, & Lee, 2014). Smaller positive effects on parenting attributes (Shek et al., 2009) and on parent–child communication (Liu et al., 2015; Park et al., 2014) were found. CBT helps patients confront and challenge maladaptive beliefs and fears in order to change their reflexive harmful reactions. CBT has demonstrated effectiveness in treating affective disorders, such as anxiety and depression, and behavioral pathology from eating disorders and self-harming to substance abuse and dependence (Beck, 2011). There is solid theoretical support for a cognitive behavioral model of PIMU (Davis, 2001), and CBT has been implemented in treating PIMU, showing biological results with postintervention resolution of prolonged latency of event-related potentials seen in both substance and interactive media dependence (Ge et al., 2011). A CBT pilot with adults in Germany showed significant reductions in psychopathology and psychosocial problems (Wolfling, Beutel, Dreier, & Müller, 2014). Chinese adolescents who received eight sessions of school-based group CBT showed significant decreases in Internet use and improvements in self-regulation; time management; and emotional, cognitive, and behavioral symptoms, both immediately and 6 months after the intervention (Du, Jiang, & Vance, 2010). In a U.S. trial with adults of Cognitive Behavioral Therapy for Internet Addiction (CBT-IA), a specialized variation of CBT designed to support recovery from PIMU and maintenance of healthy behaviors in a screen media–saturated world, more than 95% were able to manage PIMU symptoms after the 12-week treatment and 78% maintained their recovery at 6 months (Young, 2013).

Regardless of theoretical approach, psychotherapy seeks to improve the patient's self-awareness and insight. Self-monitoring is a critical tool in the patient's recovery. By systematically recording circumstances, events, thoughts, and feelings surrounding PIMU behaviors, the patient develops awareness of the behaviors, while providing further details and/or clarifying incomplete or incorrect elements of the clinical assessment. Provide PIMU calendars (modeled on menstrual calendars), so the patient can document dates and times of day for all interactive media activity. Use these records to discover antecedent PIMU triggers, contexts, and protective factors. Integrate identified protective factors into the treatment plan and follow changes in the frequency or expression of PIMU over time to evaluate the effectiveness of treatment strategies.

Behavior modification is central to treatment of PIMU. Explicit self-monitoring can result in the patient's increasing awareness of PIMU behaviors and what triggers those behaviors. As the patient's self-awareness improves, he or she will start to recognize thoughts and feelings associated with PIMU and develop insight on what needs are driving interactive media use. Help the patient create a list of functional and dysfunctional online activities and ideas for limiting or eliminating dysfunctional activities and overuse. Develop a list of the patient's offline interests and schedule technology-free activities and opportunities for socialization. In therapy, conduct thought experiments with the patient on distorted beliefs that perpetuate the problem. Keeping in mind the function of such beliefs, consider with the patient the evidence that supports the beliefs and construct alternative perspectives. Guide the patient to intentionally implement mental and behavioral exercises that challenge the emotional and behavioral illness process that triggers PIMU. Develop with the patient an internal script or *mantra* to rely on when maladaptive thoughts and behaviors occur.

Appreciate and applaud any positive changes documented in the patient's self-monitoring and encourage the patient's family to reinforce these desired behaviors.

Ideally, family therapy and education should be provided in parallel with individual therapy for PIMU. Identify and address predisposing contextual factors such as PIMU in parents or other family members, a permissive or an authoritarian stance on media use in the family, or previously unaddressed family conflicts (Cheung, Yue, & Wong, 2015). Family therapy provides a supportive setting for repair of the disruption of family function that occurs as a consequence of PIMU. Parents and family can be educated about PIMU; the needs, beliefs, and stressors giving rise to it in their child; the therapeutic strategies implemented with their child; and improved family communication. Family can be enlisted and supported as clinician extenders and guided to help the patient master skills learned during therapy and apply them in the real world. Finally, recognize and respond to the impact that PIMU has on the family system as a whole; understand how it affects siblings, parents, and interpersonal communication; and conceptualize treatment of the child's PIMU as a shared experience in support of family unity and healing.

Psychopharmacology can be helpful as an adjunctive intervention to support psychotherapy. Because there is no unifying psychiatric diagnosis, no medication has been approved by the Food and Drug Administration for the treatment of PIMU. Nevertheless, a limited number of studies have presented evidence to support specific medication protocols for PIMU. Because PIMU predominantly occurs with underlying or comorbid psychiatric conditions, clinicians have had success with medications that have been proven effective for those diagnoses. Stimulants (attention deficit disorder); selective serotonin reuptake inhibitors (SSRIs) and norepinephrine–dopamine reuptake inhibitors (anxiety and depression; tobacco, alcohol, and other substance use); benzodiazepines (anxiety); and antipsychotic medications have all been used to support psychotherapy for PIMU (Kuss & Lopez-Fernandez, 2016). Escitalopram, bupropion, and methylphenidate have specifically been demonstrated to improve behaviors associated with PIMU (Kuss & Lopez-Fernandez, 2016). However, as with many psychiatric conditions, including those most prevalent in PIMU patients, treating with medication alone is not supported by the evidence. A study from Korea, where PIMU is prevalent, compared CBT and bupropion, an atypical antidepressant that is also used to break dependence on tobacco, with bupropion treatment alone (S. M. Kim, Han, Lee, & Renshaw, 2012). After 8 weeks of treatment, patients in the CBT plus medication group showed a significant decrease in PIMU behaviors and improvements in their life satisfaction and school performance compared to the patients on medication alone. Anxiety was reduced in the CBT plus medication group, whereas it increased in the medication-only group.

It is likely that individuals affected by PIMU represent a diverse set of different subgroups, each with a different underlying psychopathology that is ultimately expressed as PIMU behavior. The task for the psychopharmacologist is to consider medication selection in the context of the patient's PIMU behavior and psychiatric comorbidities. The child with ADHD and associated disturbance of impulse control and attention regulation might experience an improvement in problematic video game playing if treated with methylphenidate, but not if treated with escitalopram. On the other hand, the adolescent with anxiety who remains awake at night repeatedly checking social media might experience the opposite medication response pattern. If these hypothesized differential treatment response patterns indeed exist, there is need for research to clarify specific interventions for individual subgroups within the larger PIMU population.

Finally, if we are to identify, care for, and prevent PIMU effectively, we must broaden our care infrastructure beyond individual clinicians or organizations with unique practice models. As with other conditions, PIMU manifests itself in a variety of presentations and has a great diversity of recovery patterns. If we are to care for even a conservative estimate of the numbers of young people who are struggling with or are at risk of PIMU, we must pool our collective experience and build a multilevel system of care similar to those for established behavioral conditions that affect young people's physical, mental, and social health, such as eating disorders or substance abuse. To that end, we must provide information and tools to teachers, guidance counselors, psychologists, primary care pediatricians, family practitioners, and others who are on the front lines with children and youth to recognize young people at risk for or struggling with PIMU. Child health clinicians must be prepared to give anticipatory guidance around PIMU and trained to assess and care for its different presentations. There is a great need for higher levels of care for PIMU. Inpatient pediatric psychiatric units are neither accessible nor effective at treating severe PIMU. In our experience, the most effective type of 24/7 care for severe PIMU in young people is wilderness therapy, where the patient confronts his or her issues with a trained therapist in a natural environment with no connectivity. Nature is calming and centering, but also implacable. Instead of simply reacting to external stimuli of pings and pokes, the young person must become active—building a fire, setting up a campsite, and becoming self-reliant. The young person must rediscover and rebuild his or her self, establish and sustain face-to-face communication and connection with others, and find capabilities and passions beyond the superficiality of the online world. When they complete wilderness therapy, many feel reborn. But the realities of reentry to the world in which they developed PIMU are harsh. Without sustained support by knowledgeable and skillful therapists and educators, many will backslide into familiar compensatory PIMU behaviors. This wraparound infrastructure of monitoring, identifying, treating, and supporting young people struggling with PIMU must include research and training components, so that it can respond to changes in technology and pathology by evolving with them and can train those who work with young people in various capacities to be mindful of the potential in human nature to fall into problematic behaviors with the media we use to educate, communicate, and recreate.

CONCLUSION

PIMU is a real and growing health problem among children and adolescents of the digital age. As child health clinicians, we must accept that reality and work together, across disciplines, to:

- Precisely define PIMU and standardize nomenclature so we can communicate effectively and accurately with fellow clinicians, parents, and society at large.

- Determine whether we are dealing with a single diagnosis or multiple diagnoses linked by the devices and domains where they occur, or syndromes of established diagnoses such as anxiety, depression, attention deficit disorder, or other psychopathologies that are presenting as PIMU behaviors in the interactive media environment.

- Establish assessment strategies that distinguish between normal child and adolescent behavior in the digital environment, and dysfunction that requires therapeutic intervention.

- Develop theoretically based, rigorously evaluated treatment strategies for PIMU.

- Build an infrastructure for delivering outpatient, inpatient, and residential care as determined by PIMU severity.

- Train clinical professionals in prevention, diagnosis, and treatment.

- Establish strategic plans for parents, educators, policy makers, and the technology sector to guide healthy use of interactive media and limit its problematic use.

In the digital age, we may have encountered a new pathology, or group of pathologies, to which we must develop a thoughtful, responsive, and structured systemic response. Children and adolescents are the sentinel cases of PIMU; they are early and enthusiastic adopters of new technologies and they have yet to develop self-regulating executive brain function. Building this clinical understanding and therapeutic strategy is necessary in any case, but at this point in our understanding of PIMU, it is equally possible that this is not new pathology, but "old wine in new bottles"—known pathologies that are playing themselves out in a new digital environment. Moving forward, we must continue to collect research and clinical evidence to determine whether we are seeing a new phenomenon that must be characterized and accepted by the medical establishment or syndromes of already accepted diagnoses of which the health care system needs to be made aware. As a pragmatic matter, we must now use the knowledge, tools, and infrastructure we have and care for these young people using accepted diagnoses and treatment strategies so that they are able to access, afford, and continue needed care.

REFERENCES

Abdi, T. A., Ruiter, R. A., & Adal, T. A. (2015). Personal, social and environmental risk factors of problematic gambling among high school adolescents in Addis Ababa, Ethiopia. *Journal of Gambling Studies, 31*(1), 59–72.

AMA Task Force to Reduce Opioid Abuse. (2015). Patients with addiction need treatment—not stigma. Retrieved from http://www.asam.org/magazine/read/article/2015/12/15/patients-with-a-substance-use-disorder-need-treatment-not-stigma

American Psychiatric Association. (2013a). *Diagnostic and statistical manual of mental disorders* (5th ed.). Arlington, VA: American Psychiatric Publishing.

American Psychiatric Association. (2013b). Internet gaming disorder. Retrieved from https://www.psychiatry.org/File%20Library/Psychiatrists/Practice/DSM/APA_DSM-5-Internet-Gaming-Disorder.pdf

American Psychiatric Association. (2013c). Substance-related and addictive disorders. In *Diagnostic and statistical manual of mental disorders* (5th ed., pp. 481–589). Arlington, VA: American Psychiatric Publishing.

An, J., Sun, Y., Wan, Y., Chen, J., Wang, X., & Tao, F. (2014). Associations between problematic Internet use and adolescents' physical and psychological symptoms: Possible role of sleep quality. *Journal of Addiction Medicine, 8*(4), 282–287.

Beard, K. W., & Wolf, E. M. (2001). Modification in the proposed diagnostic criteria for Internet addiction. *CyberPsychology & Behavior, 4*(3), 377–383.

Beck, J. S. (2011). *Cognitive behavior therapy: Basics and beyond.* New York, NY: Guilford Press.

Bijvank, M. N., Konijn, E. A., Bushman, B. J., & Roelofsma, P. H. (2009). Age and violent-content labels make video games forbidden fruits for youth. *Pediatrics, 123*(3), 870–876.

Boies, S. C., Cooper, A., & Osborne, C. S. (2004). Variations in Internet-related problems and psychosocial functioning in online sexual activities: Implications for social and sexual development of young adults. *CyberPsychology & Behavior, 7*(2), 207–230.

Bozkurt, H., Coskun, M., Ayaydin, H., Adak, I., & Zoroglu, S. S. (2013). Prevalence and patterns of psychiatric disorders in referred adolescents with Internet addiction. *Psychiatry and Clinical Neurosciences, 67*(5), 352–359.

Byun, S., Ruffini, C., Mills, J. E., Douglas, A. C., Niang, M., Stepchenkova, S., . . . Blanton, M. (2009). Internet addiction: Metasynthesis of 1996–2006 quantitative research. *CyberPsychology & Behavior, 12*(2), 203–207.

Canan, F., Yildirim, O., Sinani, G., Ozturk, O., Ustunel, T. Y., & Ataoglu, A. (2013). Internet addiction and sleep disturbance symptoms among Turkish high school students. *Sleep and Biological Rhythms, 11*(3), 210–213.

Canan, F., Yildirim, O., Ustunel, T. Y., Sinani, G., Kaleli, A. H., Gunes, C., & Ataoglu, A. (2014). The relationship between Internet addiction and body mass index in Turkish adolescents. *Cyberpsychology, Behavior, and Social Networking, 17*(1), 40–45.

Caplan, S. E. (2002). Problematic Internet use and psychosocial well-being: Development of a theory-based cognitive–behavioral measurement instrument. *Computers in Human Behavior, 18*(5), 553–575.

Chen, S. H. W. L., Weng, L., Su, Y., Wu, H., & Yang, P. (2003). Development of a Chinese Internet addiction scale and its psychometric study. *Chinese Journal of Psychology, 45*(3), 279.

Cheung, C. K., Yue, X. D., & Wong, D. S. W. (2015). Addictive Internet use and parenting patterns among secondary school students in Guangzhou and Hong Kong. *Journal of Child and Family Studies, 24*(8), 2301–2309.

Choi, K., Son, H., Park, M., Han, J., Kim, K., Lee, B., & Gwak, H. (2009). Internet overuse and excessive daytime sleepiness in adolescents. *Psychiatry and Clinical Neurosciences, 63*(4), 455–462.

Chou, W. J., Liu, T. L., Yang, P., Yen, C. F., & Hu, H. F. (2015). Multi-dimensional correlates of Internet addiction symptoms in adolescents with attention-deficit/hyperactivity disorder. *Psychiatry Research, 225*(1–2), 122–128.

Coeffec, A., Romo, L., Cheze, N., Riazuelo, H., Plantey, S., Kotbagi, G., & Kern, L. (2015). Early substance consumption and problematic use of video games in adolescence. *Frontiers in Psychology, 6*, 501.

Common Sense Media. (2016). Technology addiction: Concern, controversy, and finding balance. Retrieved from https://www.commonsensemedia.org/sites/default/files/uploads/research/csm_2016_technology_addiction_research_brief_0.pdf

Dalbudak, E., Evren, C., Aldemir, S., & Evren, B. (2014). The severity of Internet addiction risk and its relationship with the severity of borderline personality features, childhood traumas, dissociative experiences, depression and anxiety symptoms among Turkish university students. *Psychiatry Research, 219*(3), 577–582.

Davis, R. A. (2001). A cognitive-behavioral model of pathological Internet use. *Computers in Human Behavior, 17*(2), 187–195.

DeLonga, K., Torres, H. L., Kamen, C., Evans, S. N., Lee, S., Koopman, C., & Gore-Felton, C. (2011). Loneliness, internalized homophobia, and compulsive Internet use: Factors associated with sexual risk behavior among a sample of adolescent males seeking services at a community LGBT center. *Sexual Addiction & Compulsivity, 18*(2), 61–74.

Derbyshire, K. L., Lust, K. A., Schreiber, L. R., Odlaug, B. L., Christenson, G. A., Golden, D. J., & Grant, J. E. (2013). Problematic Internet use and associated risks in a college sample. *Comprehensive Psychiatry, 54*(5), 415–422.

Dhir, A., Chen, S., & Nieminen, M. (2015). Predicting adolescent Internet addiction: The roles of demographics, technology accessibility, unwillingness to communicate and sought Internet gratifications. *Computers in Human Behavior, 51* (Pt. A), 24–33.

Doornwaard, S. M., van den Eijnden, R. J., Baams, L., Vanwesenbeeck, I., & ter Bogt, T. F. (2016). Lower psychological well-being and excessive sexual interest predict symptoms of compulsive use of sexually explicit Internet material among adolescent boys. *Journal of Youth Adolescence, 45*(1), 73–84.

Du, Y. S., Jiang, W., & Vance, A. (2010). Longer term effect of randomized, controlled group cognitive behavioural therapy for Internet addiction in adolescent students in Shanghai. *The Australian and New Zealand Journal of Psychiatry, 44*(2), 129–134.

Ekinci, Ö., Celik, T., Savaş, N., & Toros, F. (2014). Association between Internet use and sleep problems in adolescents. *Nöropsikiyatri Arşivi—Archives of Neuropsychiatry, 51*(2), 122–128.

Evren, C., Dalbudak, E., Evren, B., & Demirci, A. C. (2014). High risk of Internet addiction and its relationship with lifetime substance use, psychological and behavioral problems among 10(th) grade adolescents. *Psychiatria Danubina, 26*(4), 330–339.

Fergus, T. A., & Dolan, S. L. (2014). Problematic Internet use and Internet searches for medical information: The role of health anxiety. *Cyberpsychology, Behavior and Social Networking, 17*(12), 761–765.

Floros, G., Paradisioti, A., Hadjimarcou, M., Mappouras, D. G., Karkanioti, O., & Siomos, K. (2015). Adolescent online gambling in Cyprus: Associated school performance and psychopathology. *Journal of Gambling Studies, 31*(2), 367–384.

Foerster, M., Roser, K., Schoeni, A., & Röösli, M. (2015). Problematic mobile phone use in adolescents: Derivation of a short scale MPPUS-10. *International Journal of Public Health, 60*(2), 277–286.

Fu, K. W., Chan, W. S., Wong, P. W., & Yip, P. S. (2010). Internet addiction: Prevalence, discriminant validity and correlates among adolescents in Hong Kong. *The British Journal of Psychiatry, 196*(6), 486–492.

Ge, L., Ge, X., Xu, Y., Zhang, K., Zhao, J., & Kong, X. (2011). P300 change and cognitive behavioral therapy in subjects with Internet addiction disorder: A 3-month follow-up study. *Neural Regeneration Research, 6*(26), 2037–2041.

Goldberg, I. (1996). Internet addiction disorder. Retrieved from https://blogs .scientificamerican.com/mind-guest-blog/internet-addiction-real-or-virtual-reality

Grellhesl, M., & Punyanunt-Carter, N. M. (2012). Using the Uses and Gratifications Theory to understand gratifications sought through text messaging practices of male and female undergraduate students. *Computers in Human Behavior, 28*(6), 2175–2181.

Gür, K., Yurt, S., Bulduk, S., & Atagöz, S. (2015). Internet addiction and physical and psychosocial behavior problems among rural secondary school students. *Nursing & Health Sciences, 17*(3), 331–338.

Hanprathet, N., Manwong, M., Khumsri, J., Yingyeun, R., & Phanasathit, M. (2015). Facebook addiction and its relationship with mental health among Thai high school students. *Journal of the Medical Association of Thailand, 98*(Suppl. 3), S81–S90.

Jang, K. S., Hwang, S. Y., & Choi, J. Y. (2008). Internet addiction and psychiatric symptoms among Korean adolescents. *Journal of School Health, 78*(3), 165–171.

Kabali, H. K., Irigoyen, M. M., Nunez-Davis, R., Budacki, J. G., Mohanty, S. H., Leister, K. P., & Bonner, R. L. (2015). Exposure and use of mobile media devices by young children. *Pediatrics, 136*(6), 1044–1050.

Kaczmarek, L. D., & Drazkowski, D. (2014). MMORPG escapism predicts decreased well-being: Examination of gaming time, game realism beliefs, and online social support for offline problems. *Cyberpsychology, Behavior and Social Networking, 17*(5), 298–302.

Kaess, M., Durkee, T., Brunner, R., Carli, V., Parzer, P., Wasserman, C., . . . Wasserman, D. (2014). Pathological Internet use among European adolescents: Psychopathology and self-destructive behaviours. *European Child & Adolescent Psychiatry, 23*(11), 1093–1102.

Kamal, N. N., & Mosallem, F. A. (2013). Determinants of problematic Internet use among El-Minia high school students, Egypt. *International Journal of Preventive Medicine, 4*(12), 1429–1437.

Kim, R., Lee, K. J., & Choi, Y. J. (2015). Mobile phone overuse among elementary school students in Korea: Factors associated with mobile phone use as a behavior addiction. *Journal of Addictions Nursing, 26*(2), 81–85.

Kim, S. M., Han, D. H., Lee, Y. S., & Renshaw, P. F. (2012). Combined cognitive behavioral therapy and bupropion for the treatment of problematic on-line game play in adolescents with major depressive disorder. *Computers in Human Behavior, 28*(5), 1954–1959.

Kim, Y., Park, J. Y., Kim, S. B., Jung, I. K., Lim, Y. S., & Kim, J. H. (2010). The effects of Internet addiction on the lifestyle and dietary behavior of Korean adolescents. *Nutrition Research and Practice, 4*(1), 51–57.

King, D. L., Delfabbro, P. H., Zwaans, T., & Kaptsis, D. (2013). Clinical features and axis I comorbidity of Australian adolescent pathological Internet and video game users. *The Australian and New Zealand Journal of Psychiatry, 47*(11), 1058–1067.

King, D. L., Delfabbro, P. H., Zwaans, T., & Kaptsis, D. (2014). Sleep interference effects of pathological electronic media use during adolescence. *International Journal of Mental Health and Addiction, 12*(1), 21–35.

Ko, C. H., Liu, T. L., Wang, P. W., Chen, C. S., Yen, C. F., & Yen, J. Y. (2014). The exacerbation of depression, hostility, and social anxiety in the course of Internet addiction among adolescents: A prospective study. *Comprehensive Psychiatry, 55*(6), 1377–1384.

Ko, C. H., Yen, J. Y., Yen, C. F., Chen, C. S., & Chen, C. C. (2012). The association between Internet addiction and psychiatric disorder: A review of the literature. *European Psychiatry, 27*, 1–8.

Kroenke, K., Spitzer, R. L., & Williams, J. B. (2001). The PHQ-9: Validity of a brief depression severity measure. *Journal of General Internal Medicine, 16*(9), 606–613.

Kuss, D. J., & Griffiths, M. D. (2011a). Internet gaming addiction: A systematic review of empirical research. *International Journal of Mental Health and Addiction, 10*(2), 278–296.

Kuss, D. J., & Griffiths, M. D. (2011b). Online social networking and addiction—A review of the psychological literature. *International Journal of Environmental Research and Public Health, 8*(9), 3528–3552.

Kuss, D. J., Griffiths, M. D., Karila, L., & Billieux, J. (2014). Internet addiction: A systematic review of epidemiological research for the last decade. *Current Pharmaceutical Design, 20*(25), 4026–4052.

Kuss, D. J., & Lopez-Fernandez, O. (2016). Internet addiction and problematic Internet use: A systematic review of clinical research. *World Journal of Psychiatry, 6*(1), 143.

Laier, C., Pekal, J., & Brand, M. (2014). Cybersex addiction in heterosexual female users of Internet pornography can be explained by gratification hypothesis. *Cyberpsychology, Behavior and Social Networking, 17*(8), 505–511.

Lam, L. T. (2014). Risk factors of Internet addiction and the health effect of Internet addiction on adolescents: A systematic review of longitudinal and prospective studies. *Current Psychiatry Reports, 16*(11), 508.

Lam, L. T., & Peng, Z. W. (2010). Effect of pathological use of the Internet on adolescent mental health: A prospective study. *Archives of Pediatrics & Adolescent Medicine, 164*(10), 901–906.

Lehenbauer-Baum, M., Klaps, A., Kovacovsky, Z., Witzmann, K., Zahlbruckner, R., & Stetina, B. U. (2015). Addiction and engagement: An explorative study toward classification criteria for Internet gaming disorder. *Cyberpsychology, Behavior and Social Networking, 18*(6), 343–349.

Lenhart, A., Duggan, M., Perrin, A., Stepler, R., Rainie, H., & Parker, K. (2015). Teens, social media & technology overview 2015. Retrieved from http://www.pewinternet.org/files/2015/04/PI_TeensandTech_Update2015_0409151.pdf

Levin, M. E., Lillis, J., & Hayes, S. C. (2012). When is online pornography viewing problematic among college males? Examining the moderating role of experiential avoidance. *Sexual Addiction & Compulsivity, 19*(3), 168–180.

Lin, I. H., Ko, C. H., Chang, Y. P., Liu, T. L., Wang, P. W., Lin, H. C., . . . Yen, C. F. (2014). The association between suicidality and Internet addiction and activities in Taiwanese adolescents. *Comprehensive Psychiatry, 55*(3), 504–510.

Lister-Landman, K. M., Domoff, S. E., & Dubow, E. F. (2015, October 5). The role of compulsive texting in adolescents' academic functioning. *Psychology of Popular Media Culture.* Advance online publication. doi:10.1037/ppm0000100

Liu, Q. X., Fang, X. Y., Yan, N., Zhou, Z. K., Yuan, X. J., Lan, J., & Liu, C. Y. (2015). Multi-family group therapy for adolescent Internet addiction: Exploring the underlying mechanisms. *Addictive Behaviors, 42*, 1–8.

Meena, P. S., Mittal, P. K., & Solanki, R. K. (2012). Problematic use of social networking sites among urban school going teenagers. *Industrial Psychiatry Journal, 21*(2), 94–97.

Meerkerk, G. J., Van Den Eijnden, R. J., Vermulst, A. A., & Garretsen, H. F. (2009). The Compulsive Internet Use Scale (CIUS): Some psychometric properties. *CyberPsychology & Behavior, 12*, 1–6.

Messias, E., Castro, J., Saini, A., Usman, M., & Peeples, D. (2011). Sadness, suicide, and their association with video game and Internet overuse among teens: Results from the Youth Risk Behavior Survey 2007 and 2009. *Suicide & Life-Threatening Behavior, 41*(3), 307–315.

Moreau, A., Laconi, S., Delfour, M., & Chabrol, H. (2015). Psychopathological profiles of adolescent and young adult problematic Facebook users. *Computers in Human Behavior, 44*, 64–69.

Moreno, M. A., Jelenchick, L., Cox, E., Young, H., & Christakis, D. A. (2011). Problematic Internet use among US youth: A systematic review. *Archives of Pediatrics & Adolescent Medicine, 165*(9), 797–805.

Müller, K. W., Dreier, M., Beutel, M. E., Duven, E., Giralt, S., & Wölfling, K. (2016). A hidden type of Internet addiction? Intense and addictive use of social networking sites in adolescents. *Computers in Human Behavior, 55*, 172–177.

Nuutinen, T., Roos, E., Ray, C., Villberg, J., Valimaa, R., Rasmussen, M., . . . Tynjala, J. (2014). Computer use, sleep duration and health symptoms: A cross-sectional study of 15-year olds in three countries. *International Journal of Public Health, 59*(4), 619–628.

Orosz, G., Bőthe, B., & Tóth-Király, I. (2016). The development of the Problematic Series Watching Scale (PSWS). *Journal of Behavioral Addictions, 5*(1), 144–150.

Park, T. Y., Kim, S., & Lee, J. (2014). Family therapy for an Internet-addicted young adult with interpersonal problems. *Journal of Family Therapy, 36*(4), 394–419.

Poli, R., & Agrimi, E. (2012). Internet addiction disorder: Prevalence in an Italian student population. *Nordic Journal of Psychiatry, 66*(1), 55–59.

Potenza, M. N., Wareham, J. D., Steinberg, M. A., Rugle, L., Cavallo, D. A., Krishnan-Sarin, S., & Desai, R. A. (2011). Correlates of at-risk/problem Internet gambling in adolescents. *Journal of the American Academy of Child & Adolescent Psychiatry, 50*(2), 150–159.

Rideout, V. (2011). Zero to eight: Children's media use in America. Retrieved from https://www.commonsensemedia.org/file/zerotoeightfinal2011pdf-0/download

Rucker, J., Akre, C., Berchtold, A., & Suris, J. C. (2015). Problematic Internet use is associated with substance use in young adolescents. *Acta Paediatrica, 104*(5), 504–507.

Scharkow, M., Festl, R., & Quandt, T. (2014). Longitudinal patterns of problematic computer game use among adolescents and adults—A 2-year panel study. *Addiction, 109*(11), 1910–1917.

Shek, D. T., Tang, V. M., & Lo, C. Y. (2009). Evaluation of an Internet addiction treatment program for Chinese adolescents in Hong Kong. *Adolescence, 44*(174), 359–373.

Sriwilai, K., & Charoensukmongkol, P. (2016). Face it, don't Facebook it: Impacts of social media addiction on mindfulness, coping strategies and the consequence on emotional exhaustion. *Stress Health, 32*(4), 427–434.

Stockburger, S. J., & Omar, H. A. (2013). Internet addiction, media use, and difficulties associated with sleeping in adolescents. *International Journal of Child & Adolescent Health, 6*(4), 459–463.

Sundar, S. S., & Limperos, A. M. (2013). Uses and grats 2.0: New gratifications for new media. *Journal of Broadcasting & Electronic Media, 57*(4), 504–525.

Sussman, S., & Moran, M. B. (2013). Hidden addiction: Television. *Journal of Behavioral Addictions, 2*(3), 125–132.

Tao, R., Huang, X., Wang, J., Zhang, H., Zhang, Y., & Li, M. (2010). Proposed diagnostic criteria for Internet addiction. *Addiction, 105*(3), 556–564.

Tazawa, Y., Soukalo, A. V., Okada, K., & Takada, G. (1997). Excessive playing of home computer games by children presenting unexplained symptoms. *Journal of Pediatrics, 130*(6), 1010–1011.

Tsitsika, A., Critselis, E., Louizou, A., Janikian, M., Freskou, A., Marangou, E., . . . Kafetzis, D. (2011). Determinants of Internet addiction among adolescents: A case-control study. *Scientific World Journal, 11*, 866–874.

Tsitsika, A. K., Tzavela, E. C., Janikian, M., Olafsson, K., Iordache, A., Schoenmakers, T. M., . . . Richardson, C. (2014). Online social networking in adolescence: Patterns of use in six European countries and links with psychosocial functioning. *The Journal of Adolescent Health, 55*(1), 141–147.

Van Rooij, A. J., Schoenmakers, T. M., Vermulst, A. A., Van den Eijnden, R. J., & Van de Mheen, D. (2011). Online video game addiction: Identification of addicted adolescent gamers. *Addiction, 106*(1), 205–212.

Vernon, L., Barber, B. L., & Modecki, K. L. (2015). Adolescent problematic social networking and school experiences: The mediating effects of sleep disruptions and sleep quality. *Cyberpsychology, Behavior and Social Networking, 18*(7), 386–392.

Whiting, A., & Williams, D. (2013). Why people use social media: A uses and gratifications approach. *Qualitative Market Research: An International Journal, 16*(4), 362–369.

Winkler, A., Dorsing, B., Rief, W., Shen, Y., & Glombiewski, J. A. (2013). Treatment of Internet addiction: A meta-analysis. *Clinical Psychology Review, 33*(2), 317–329.

Wolfling, K., Beutel, M. E., Dreier, M., & Müller, K. W. (2014). Treatment outcomes in patients with Internet addiction: A clinical pilot study on the effects of a cognitive-behavioral therapy program. *BioMed Research International, 2014*, 425924.

Wu, X., Chen, X., Han, J., Meng, H., Luo, J., Nydegger, L., & Wu, H. (2013). Prevalence and factors of addictive Internet use among adolescents in Wuhan, China: Interactions of parental relationship with age and hyperactivity-impulsivity. *PLOS ONE, 8*(4), e61782. doi:10.1371/journal.pone.0061782

Xu, J., Shen, L. X., Yan, C. H., Hu, H., Yang, F., Wang, L., . . . Shen, X. M. (2012). Personal characteristics related to the risk of adolescent Internet addiction: A survey in Shanghai, China. *BMC Public Health, 12*, 1106.

Young, K. S. (1998a). *Caught in the net: How to recognize the signs of Internet addiction—and a winning strategy for recovery.* New York, NY: Wiley.

Young, K. S. (1998b). Internet addiction: The emergence of a new clinical disorder. *CyberPsychology & Behavior, 1*(3), 237–244.

Young, K. S. (2009). Understanding online gaming addiction and treatment issues for adolescents. *The American Journal of Family Therapy, 37*(5), 355–372.

Young, K. S. (2013). Treatment outcomes using CBT-IA with Internet-addicted patients. *Journal of Behavioral Addictions, 2*(4), 209–215.

2 SMARTPHONE ADDICTION IN CHILDREN AND ADOLESCENTS

Yun Mi Shin

A smartphone is a novel technology that combines the features of a mobile phone with those of other mobile devices, such as a personal digital assistant, media player, Global Positioning System (GPS) navigation, and many more applications. Most importantly, the key difference between smartphones and previous mobile phones is the full-featured Internet access, which enables users to e-mail, search the web, check the weather, and do much more, whenever and wherever. Furthermore, smartphones offer unique opportunities for maintaining unrestricted and spontaneous contact with others through voice communication, messaging, video call, and social network services (Sarwar & Soomro, 2013). Owing to its wide range of functions, a smartphone is now considered a handheld computer rather than a simple phone. Smartphones changed children's and adolescents' patterns of electronic media consumption profoundly. First, with access to wireless Internet, smartphones allow communication with others even without having a contract with a telecommunication company. Second, smartphones' superior handiness enables children's and adolescents' ubiquitous use of smartphones. This is important because with smartphones it is much easier to dodge adult supervision than with other devices such as televisions or personal computers (PCs). The wide use of smartphones raises a multitude of new and complex issues. Because of their connectivity with the Internet, smartphone addiction is highly likely to cause physical and psychosocial problems similar to Internet addiction.

THE GROWTH OF SMARTPHONE USAGE

Smartphones are becoming widely popular, and the number of users is increasing significantly with more than 1.08 billion users around the world in

2012 (Mok et al., 2014). The smartphone penetration rate reached more than 50% in the United States and more than 65% in South Korea in 2013, and these percentages are continuously increasing (H. Ahn, Wijaya, & Esmero, 2014).

The increased use of smartphones among adolescents has surpassed a healthy standard. In Switzerland, the ownership of a smartphone of 12- to 19-year-olds was 47% in 2010 but increased by 32% in 2012 (Lemola, Perkinson-Gloor, Brand, Dewald-Kaufmann, & Grob, 2015). Figures in 2013 showed that nearly half of 5- to 15-year-olds in the United Kingdom owned mobile phones. Studies have shown that as the age of subjects increases, so does the proportion of preferred devices being smartphones, reaching as high as 62% for 12- to 15-year-olds. In the United States, the figures have shown a similar trend. Ninety-five percent of 12- to 17-year-olds have access to the Internet, with 74% of them using mobile devices. In Korea, the ownership rate of smart devices has shown a staggering increase in youth aged 6 to 19 years. In 2011, it was 21.4%, whereas in 2012 it increased to 64.5%. By 2013 the rate had nearly quadrupled to 74.1%.

DEFINITION OF SMARTPHONE ADDICTION

The World Health Organization (1964) defines addiction as dependence; the continuous use of something for the purpose of relaxation, comfort, or stimulation, which often accompanies cravings when it is absent (World Health Organization, 2006). Addiction was once considered limited to drugs or substances, but recently, behavioral addictions have been proposed as a new diagnostic entity in the current *Diagnostic and Statistical Manual of Mental Disorders*, Fifth Edition (*DSM-5*; American Psychiatric Association, 2013). Similar to substance addiction, behavioral addiction is best understood as a habitual drive or compulsion to continue to repeat a behavior despite its negative impact on one's well-being (Roberts & Pirog, 2012). Loss of control over the behavior is an essential element of any addiction.

The only category of behavioral addiction included in the *DSM-5* is pathological gambling. A scientific debate is currently taking place to consider compulsive use of the Internet, mobile phone or smartphone, gaming, shopping, and eating as addictive behaviors (J. H. Kim, 2006). Smartphone addiction appears to be the latest behavioral addiction to emerge. In behavioral science, all entities or activities capable of stimulating a person are considered to be potentially addictive (Alavi et al., 2012). While the reliance on the benefits of this technology continues to increase, so does the potential risk of being addicted to such convenient devices.

PREVALENCE OF SMARTPHONE ADDICTION

The Korean government was the first in the world to develop a national policy to manage the problems of Internet addiction (J. Ahn, 2012). As South Korea prides itself on being the global leader in high-speed Internet and advanced mobile technology, it is not unusual that Korea's rate of smartphone ownership and addiction is among the highest in the world (Alam et al., 2014; U. Lee, Lee, et al., 2014). Based on the results of a 2013 Korean survey in adolescents, 25.5% of 10- to 19-year-olds were considered to be in the smartphone addiction risk group. This number had more than doubled from 11.4% in 2011. Middle school–aged students were most at risk, with 29.3%, followed by high schoolers (23.6%) and elementary school students (22.6%). This report clearly shows that addiction to smartphones among youth is getting serious.

Smartphone-addicted users spent an average of 5.4 hours using their smartphones for social networking purposes (40.6%), news searches (17.6%), or for gaming (8.3%).

In Korea, school students are required to hand over their mobile phones and smartphones at the beginning of the school day, which in turn is returned at the end of the day. This is done not only for restricting addiction but also to maintain the students' concentration on their studies. In the United States, many school districts prohibit cell phones or smartphones in schools, because they can be disruptive to the class.

The mobile phone addiction problem is by no means confined to Korean adolescents. The prevalence rates of young adults at risk of smartphone addiction were estimated to be 16.9%, 12.8%, and 21.5% in Switzerland, Spain, and Belgium, respectively (Haug et al., 2015; Lopez-Fernandez, 2017). In a study of 5,049 Taiwanese adolescents, it was revealed that 10.54% had a problematic mobile phone use. The prevalence of smartphone addiction in 11- to 14-year-olds in Britain was 10% (Lopez-Fernandez, Honrubia-Serrano, Freixa-Blanxart, & Gibson, 2014). In Indian adolescents, smartphone addiction was reported to be 39% to 44% (Davey & Davey, 2014). In addition, 21.4% of Iranian youth and 27.4% of adolescents in Hong Kong have been classified as mobile phone addicts (Babadi-Akashe, Zamani, Abedini, Akbari, & Hedayati, 2014).

RISK FACTORS

A diverse number of risk factors have been identified through many studies. Because the cortical development of children and adolescents is not yet fully achieved, self-control regarding device use is also underdeveloped, leading to high vulnerability to smartphone addiction (Gogtay et al., 2004). Moreover, children's body functions are not fully developed and these may be adversely affected if they are exposed too much to smartphone use. Regular checking of their smartphone for peer contact has become an uncontrollable routine, sometimes taken for granted. To date, several studies on smartphone addiction in adults and youth have been performed, but few attempts to study the risk and protective factors in children have been made. Therefore, the following sections explain the risk factors of adolescents and young adults.

Sociodemographic Factors

Previous studies have shown that the younger the age, the more time spent using a mobile phone, as well as the more problems related to mobile phone use (Bianchi & Phillips, 2005; Smetaniuk, 2014). It is not surprising that younger people are more eager to embrace the new technology compared to older people, because younger people would be more familiar with the rather complex functions of the mobile phone. Furthermore, younger people are used to immediate rewards and feedback, with less self-regulation (Howe & Strauss, 2009). Physical limitations may also play a role. Age-related changes in vision and manual dexterity could prevent older people from using smartphones for long periods at a time (Bianchi & Phillips, 2005).

In a study of 164 U.S. college undergraduates, females spent significantly more time on their phones per day than males (Roberts, Yaya, & Manolis, 2014). Furthermore, in a study of 463 Korean college students, females were associated with higher smartphone addiction scores, whereas males were associated with higher Internet addiction scores (Choi et al., 2015). In general, gender differences were revealed in the content and purpose of smartphone usage. Females spent more time texting, sending e-mails, and using social network services, whereas males spent more time in gaming (Heo, Oh, Subramanian, Kim, & Kawachi, 2014). Therefore, females can engage in their favorite Internet-based activities more conveniently with smartphones, but males would probably prefer PCs over smartphones when gaming (Choi et al., 2015). This is most likely the reason why smartphone addiction seems higher in females.

In a study of 197 Korean adults, it was reported that those with a lower education level were more at risk of smartphone addiction (Kwon et al., 2013). In a study of 281 Spanish adults, the unemployed group showed significantly more problems related to smartphone overuse compared to the control groups (Lopez-Fernandez, 2017).

No association between excessive smartphone use and tobacco or alcohol use has been revealed to date. This is of particular interest, as studies on Internet addiction have shown its association with alcohol problems (Hwang, Choi, et al., 2014). Adolescents who come from families with a high income showed a tendency to spend more time on their smartphones. As new devices are frequently released along with numerous updated applications ready for purchase, keeping up with the quick changes has been noticed more in this socioeconomic group (Castells, Fernandez-Ardevol, Qiu, & Sey, 2009).

Psychological Factors

It has been suggested that preexisting factors increase the chances of one becoming addicted to smartphones. Previous studies have shown that excessive use of electronic devices exhibits psychological traits such as stress, loneliness, depression, or anxiety. Negative emotion is the evocation of one's unpleasantness or unhappiness, with negativity expressed as depression, anxiety, loneliness, and anger. Evidence to support that there is a correlation between negative emotion and mobile phone addiction levels has been rapidly accumulated in recent years. A study by Beranuy, Oberst, Carbonell, and Chamarro (2009) found that loneliness, anxiety, and depression in problematic mobile phone users were high. A 2014 Korean study by Baek, Shin, and Shin on smartphone addiction in elementary school students revealed statistically significant differences in gender, usage time, ownership, and internalization symptoms (somatization, anxiety/depression, and withdrawal) between the excessive user group and control group.

After reviewing several articles, Billieux (2012) came to the conclusion that the exact etiology of mobile phone addiction is currently unknown due to insufficient theoretical framework and differences among psychological variables in the articles. Based on a synthesis of these studies, Billieux drew up an integrative model to describe the pathways to problematic mobile phone use (e.g., addiction symptoms). The adopted title is pathway model (PM); it has four pathways: (a) the impulsive pathway, (b) the relationship maintenance pathway, (c) the extraversion pathway, and (d) the cyber addiction pathway. The final outcome variable is negative affect (e.g., depressive symptoms, anxiety). It is not yet conclusive whether mobile phone addiction affects depressive symptoms or depression is the reason for mobile phone addiction.

A few studies on the co-relationship between mobile phone addiction and depressive symptoms as well as other psychological factors such as chronic stress among adolescents have been carried out (Augner & Hacker, 2012; Sánchez-Martínez & Otero, 2009; Thomée, Härenstam, & Hagberg, 2011). A few Korean studies on mobile phone addiction and adolescent stress have revealed that this has been brought on by depression (Koo & Kwon, 2014). Severe depressive symptoms have been shown to be caused by academic stress and peer relationship difficulties, resulting in mobile phone addiction. This trend has also been put forth in a study by Yen et al. (2009) on adolescents in southern Taiwan, whereas Toda and Ezoe (2013) from Japan stated that depressive symptoms independently influence the degree of mobile phone dependency among Japanese youth.

Smartphone users with a higher level of social interaction anxiety demonstrated a higher level of smartphone addiction (Y.-K. Lee, Chang, Lin, & Cheng, 2014).

Previous studies have shown that lonely and anxious individuals prefer online interaction, because social anxiety is less online than in real life. Most individuals strive for a social relationship where they are accepted. If there is a discrepancy between one's desired social relationships and one's actual social relationships, it may lead to a feeling of loneliness. Although the Internet and smartphones could improve one's existing social relationships, they worsen loneliness if one lacked prior social relationships (Reid & Reid, 2007).

Low self-esteem is one of the characteristics of the addictive personality (Marlatt, Baer, Donovan, & Kivlahan, 1988). Individuals who do not value themselves highly are more likely to bow to peer pressure, which makes them vulnerable to engaging in addictive behaviors (Zimmerman, Copeland, Shope, & Dielman, 1997). Furthermore, lack of self-worth can keep people trapped in addiction (Marlatt et al., 1988). In case of smartphone addiction, low self-esteem has been proposed to be a predictor of mobile phone and smartphone addiction (Ha, Chin, Park, Ryu, & Yu, 2008). In a study that examined the profiles of smartphone addicts, low self-esteem, fear of rejection, and need for approval were found to be important characteristics of smartphone addicts (Lapointe, Boudreau-Pinsonneault, & Vaghefi, 2013).

Lower levels of self-regulation have been found to predict higher risk of smartphone addiction (van Deursen, Bolle, Hegner, & Kommers, 2015). Deficient self-regulation is controlled by emotions and automatic processes steered by impulses. Lack of self-control leads to various types of problem behaviors and social maladaptation, including impulsive, insensitive, and risky behaviors. A study by S. M. Kim et al. (2014) showed that impulsivity is a significant risk factor for smartphone addiction as well.

Many studies have revealed a close relationship between aggression and Internet addiction. In terms of specific contents, online chatting, pornography, online gaming, and online gambling were all found to be associated with aggressive behavior (Ko, Yen, Liu, Huang, & Yen, 2009; Yang, Yen, Ko, Cheng, & Yen, 2010). It can be postulated that because smartphones enable one to access the Internet more easily and more frequently, the impact of aggression via a smartphone could be even greater than that via the Internet.

The authors argue that online anonymity may lead to personal responsibility and individuation being decreased. Therefore, online aggressive behavior may end up being transferred into the real world and may have significant negative consequences both for the addicted individual and his or her interpersonal relations online and offline. Online disinhibition because of online anonymity may lead to deindividuation and can bring on aggressive behavior. This process may be particularly problematic for adolescents as their cognitive control capabilities may not have fully developed.

Familial Factors

Lack of parental intervention has been proven to have some association with the vulnerability of unwanted cyber attention. The nature of parental involvement can be further clarified: Law, Shapka, and Olson (2010) linked adolescent online aggression to lack of parental involvement.

Similarly, with the aid of a questionnaire, Toda et al. (2008) studied a sample population of 155 Japanese female students to investigate the associations between mobile phone dependence and perceived parental rearing attitudes. In relation to maternal rearing attitudes, respondents revealed a statistically significant difference in scores between those who fell in the categories of high care/high protection and low care/low protection. This study concludes that mobile phone dependency is closely related to the childhood relationship to the mother.

SOCIAL NETWORKING SERVICES VERSUS GAMES (CONTENT TYPE)

Smartphones are used for various purposes, including information searching, entertainment, and social relations. Activities that are potentially high-risk factors for smartphone addiction are game use and social networking. Owing to the small screen of a smartphone when compared to that of a computer, one's interest, presence, enjoyment, and full experience while playing games may be reduced (Hou, Nam, Peng, & Lee, 2012). These findings suggest that although gaming on smartphones is addictive, it cannot be compared to computer gaming and, therefore, may not be completely substituted. Take social networking for example; 85% of Facebook users access their accounts from mobile devices. Goggin (2014) suggested that social media have gained a lot since the smartphone and social media devices were developed, because of their infinite access and connectivity. In a study of 164 college students in the United States, the time spent by smartphone users on various social networking sites was a good indicator of a potential smartphone addiction (Roberts et al., 2014). For instance, although females spent more time on Facebook, it was Pinterest and Instagram that significantly drove their smartphone addiction. Facebook use was a relatively strong indicator of a smartphone addiction among males.

It is likely that with the enhanced accessibility of social network sites via smartphones, susceptibility to such addiction may also be on the rise. Matthews, Pierce, and Tang (2009) have provided some initial evidence to support the fact that smartphone users have greater potential for developing addiction to web-based social interactions. Although social network sites allow for relationship building in a brand new format, their usage can be excessive, or even compulsive in some cases. For example, Subrahmanyamam, Reich, Waechter, and Espinoza (2008) found that some college respondents spent up to four or more hours on social network sites every day. Problematic use of these sites is also related to a host of negative psychosocial outcomes, such as decreased real-life community involvement, poorer academic performance, and more relationship problems (Blaszczynski, 2006; Kuss & Griffiths, 2011).

CONSEQUENCES OF SMARTPHONE ADDICTION

Smartphone addiction can affect one's physical, psychological, and social well-being. Adverse results caused by smartphone addiction are easily identified. Children and adolescents who are distracted because of their smartphones are in danger of getting struck by vehicles while crossing the street because of not checking the traffic signals, and elementary school–aged children cannot concentrate in class.

Physical Health

Motor Vehicle Crash

Driver distraction is a risk factor for motor vehicle crash injury and death, and smartphones or mobile phones are a major cause of such distraction (Wilson & Stimpson, 2010). An estimated 75% of college students are reported to use their mobile phones while driving (Cook & Jones, 2011). Many studies provide evidence that the mechanism underlying such a dangerous behavior is related to response to smartphone-related stimuli (Atchley & Warden, 2012; O'Connor et al., 2013).

Musculoskeletal Disorders

Excessive smartphone use may produce considerable stress on the cervical spine, thus changing the cervical curve and resulting in neck–shoulder pain (Park et al., 2015). When using a smartphone, people tend to flex their neck downward to stare at the lowered object and maintain the head in a forward position. Maintenance of a head-forward posture can cause musculoskeletal disorders, such as "upper crossed syndrome" (Moore, 2004). Furthermore, it can lead to a forward head posture, or a turtle neck posture, which decreases cervical lordosis of the lower cervical vertebrae and creates a posterior curve in the upper thoracic vertebrae to maintain balance (Kang et al., 2012).

Eye Disorders

Prolonged use of smartphones can lead to eye and visual problems such as ocular discomfort, eyestrain, dry eye, headache, blurred vision, and even double vision. In a study of 288 children in Korea, longer durations of smartphone use was associated with increased risk of dry eye disease (Moon, Lee, & Moon, 2014).

Electromagnetic Radiation

Smartphones produce nonionizing radiation, but at a low frequency level. However, radiation can be found in all other aspects of our technological lives as well, such as radios, TVs, microwaves, and the like. There is no conclusive evidence at this stage to state that the radiation from smartphones can directly harm our health. Still, the World Health Organization categorizes mobile phone radiation emissions as "possible human carcinogens." Children face a greater risk of bodily damage from radiation because their brain tissues are more absorbent, their skulls are thinner, and their relative size is smaller (Morgan, Kesari, & Davis, 2014).

People with a relatively small body size are at a higher risk of radiation damage, especially children who also have an added higher risk because of more absorbent brain tissues and thinner skulls.

Cancer, specifically brain cancer, and its correlation with phone use, is an ongoing investigation. There are many variables that affect the likelihood of hosting cancerous cells, which include how long and how frequently people use their phones. There has been no definitive evidence linking cancer and phone use if phones are used moderately. Although a relationship has not yet been fully established, research is continuing based on leads from changing patterns of mobile phone use over time and habits of phone users.

Infection

Germs are everywhere and, considering the numerous times people interact with their smartphones under different circumstances and places, smartphones may act as reservoirs of microorganisms and could play a role in dissemination of diseases (Badr, Badr, & Ali, 2012; Repacholi, 2001). Ulger et al. (2009) stated that 94.5% of phones showed evidence of bacterial contamination and the isolated microorganisms were similar to hand isolates. They found that 49% of phones grew one bacterial species, 34% grew two different species, and 11.5% grew three or more different species. Many studies reported the rate of mobile phone contamination as high as 96.5% (Elkholy & Ewees, 2010; Tambekar, Gulhane, Dahikar, & Dudhane, 2008).

Mental Health

During the child and adolescent period, sleep and quality of sleep are considered a key element for learning and memory, as well as for emotional regulation (Dewald, Meijer, Oort, Kerkhof, & Bögels, 2010). Poor sleep quality has been associated with problems in memory performance, as well as poor concentration, which logically ascertains poor academic performance (Gradisar, Terrill, Johnston, & Douglas, 2008). Smartphones may lead to overexcitement and interfere or shorten sleep time (Van den Bulck, 2010). Although this is true for all media including TV, PCs, and the like, a smartphone is the most convenient device to use right before going to sleep, probably after lights out. Children and adolescents especially can easily use a smartphone without their parents knowing. Therefore, the impact of smartphones on sleep quality and duration could be greater than that of other media and devices.

In a study of 300 Egyptians, 29.5% reported sleep disturbance, which correlated with longer total use per day of mobile phones (Salama & Abou El Naga, 2004). In a Finnish study, intense mobile phone usage among 7,292 adolescents was associated with negative sleep effects and increased daytime fatigue (Punamäki, Wallenius, Nygård, Saarni, & Rimpelä, 2007).

In a study of 94,777 Japanese adolescents, calling and/or text messaging after lights out was associated with shorter sleep duration, poorer subjective sleep quality, insomnia, and excessive daytime sleepiness (Munezawa et al., 2011).

A number of mechanisms by which media use can impact sleep quality or quantity have been proposed. The possible mechanisms are: (a) usage directly displaces sleep and causes an unstructured time schedule; (b) usage causes increased mental, emotional, and physiological arousal, because of smartphone excitement (music, drama, cartoons, etc.) and anticipation (incoming calls, messages) stimuli; and (c) bright light exposure delays the circadian rhythm and leads to delayed melatonin release (Cain & Gradisar, 2010). The demand to be available or reachable, regardless of time and space, could give great stress to individuals. A study in Sweden found an association between reports of mental health and the perceived stress of being accessible, which is defined as the possibility to be disturbed at any moment of day or night (Thomée, Härenstam, & Hagberg, 2011). For employees, work-related communications outside of regular working hours can greatly enhance one's distress (Schieman & Young, 2013). Children and adolescents can experience consistent close monitoring and supervision from their parents, resulting in a lack of autonomy.

Furthermore, nomophobia, an abbreviation for *no-mobile-phone phobia*, refers to the discomfort or anxiety caused by the nonavailability of a mobile phone, PC, or other devices (Bragazzi & Del Puente, 2014). It is the pathological fear of remaining out of touch with technology. People with smartphone addiction tend to feel guilty if they do not reply to all calls and messages. Adolescents can become very anxious when they do not feel connected, or feel alienated from their friends and information. Phantom vibration syndrome (a pseudo-sensation that a mobile phone is vibrating) and ringxiety (anxiety due to mobile phone ringing) are some new terminologies about distress caused by excessive smartphone usage (Alam et al., 2014).

Social Relationships

Smartphones facilitate communication by enabling people to overcome barriers such as spatial proximity and immobility. However, these new technologies, characterized by the absence of face-to-face communication, can also interfere with social interactions, causing disturbed behaviors and bad feelings, leading to social isolation and a certain degree of alienation (Bragazzi & Del Puente, 2014). Individuals who constantly use smartphones may experience a decrease in the amount of time they have for other social relations, especially activities that involve face-to-face interactions. As a result, social interactions in real life are ignored, whereas more anonymous online interactions increase (Whang, Lee, & Chang, 2003). Although smartphones are used as communication tools, their excessive use causes individuals to become addicted and isolated.

Excessive smartphone use has significantly increased the odds of one becoming a perpetrator or victim of cyberbullying (Englander, 2013). Once a cyberbullying act is propelled, it "snowballs" out of the perpetrator's control. Slonje, Smith, and Frisén (2013) stated that publicly made cyberbullying intended for someone else is forwarded to others as well as back to the intended victim by others to bully him or her further.

In other words, a single act made by one person is repeated by others and experienced over and over by the victim. In contrast to traditional bullying, where one may experience short-term physical intimidation or pain, cyberbullying has an ongoing effect because of its never-ending widespread nature, which has been reported in some studies to cause suicidal thoughts (e.g., Hinduja & Patchin, 2010).

Academic Achievement and Functioning

Smartphone addiction has been linked to the disruption and decrease of one's academic performance because of multitasking behaviors, such as frequently or habitually interacting with one's smartphone. Students spend precious time sending and replying to messages, listening to music, or watching movies during class lectures as well as during examinations (David, Kim, Brickman, Ran, & Curtis, 2015; Hwang, Kim, & Jeong, 2014; Junco, 2012).

CONCLUSION

Use of smartphones by children and adolescents has sharply increased. Evidence-based risk factors are as follows: personality factors (negative emotion, low self-esteem, loneliness), social factors (lack of parental support), and digital factors (screen size, gaming, social networking). Mobile phone- and smartphone-related harmful events are growing, especially among children and adolescents. Because of a child's or adolescent's inability to self-regulate, he or she is at risk of spending prolonged time using these devices. Parents and teachers are a young person's bridge to healthy use of the Internet and electronic devices. To stimulate this ability it would be ideal to provide parents and teachers with appropriate training.

Because the majority of parents were born in an Internet-less generation, their children trump their knowledge and skills about this new technology. Some early warning signs of smartphone addiction:

- Frequently checking the phone without reason
- Feeling anxious or restless at the thought of being without the phone
- Favoring smartphone time to social interaction
- Constantly waking up during the night to check the smartphone
- Lowered academic performance
- Being easily distracted by e-mails or smart apps

REFERENCES

Ahn, H., Wijaya, M. E., & Esmero, B. C. (2014). A systemic smartphone usage pattern analysis: Focusing on smartphone addiction issue. *International Journal of Multimedia Ubiquitous Engineering*, 9(6), 9–14.

Ahn, J. (2012). *Broadband policy in South Korea: The effect of government regulation on Internet proliferation* (pp. 20–23). PTC 12 (Pacific Telecommunications Council) Proceedings, Honolulu, HI.

Alam, M., Qureshi, M. S., Sarwat, A., Haque, Z., Salman, M., Masroor, M. A. M., . . . Ehtesham, S. A. (2014). Prevalence of phantom vibration syndrome and phantom ringing syndrome (ringxiety): Risk of sleep disorders and infertility among medical students. *International Journal of Advanced Research*, 2(12), 688–693.

Alavi, S. S., Ferdosi, M., Jannatifard, F., Eslami, M., Alaghemandan, H., & Setare, M. (2012). Behavioral addiction versus substance addiction: Correspondence of psychiatric and psychological views. *International Journal of Preventive Medicine*, 3(4), 290–294.

American Psychiatric Association. (2013). *Diagnostic and statistical manual of mental disorders* (5th ed.). Arlington, VA: American Psychiatric Publishing.

Atchley, P., & Warden, A. C. (2012). The need of young adults to text now: Using delay discounting to assess informational choice. *Journal of Applied Research in Memory and Cognition*, 1(4), 229–234.

Augner, C., & Hacker, G. W. (2012). Associations between problematic mobile phone use and psychological parameters in young adults. *International Journal of Public Health, 57*, 437–441.

Babadi-Akashe, Z., Zamani, B. E., Abedini, Y., Akbari, H., & Hedayati, N. (2014). The relationship between mental health and addiction to mobile phones among university students of Shahrekord, Iran. *Addiction & Health, 6*(3–4), 93–99.

Badr, R. I., Badr, H. I., & Ali, N. M. (2012). Mobile phones and nosocomial infections. *International Journal of Infection Control, 8*(2), 1–5. doi:10.3396/ijic.v8i2.9933

Baek, H. W., Shin, Y. M., & Shin, K. M. (2014). Emotional and behavioral problems related to smartphone overuse in elementary school children. *Journal of Korean Neuropsychiatric Association, 53*(5), 320–326.

Beranuy, M., Oberst, U., Carbonell, X., & Chamarro, A. (2009). Problematic Internet and mobile phone use and clinical symptoms in college students: The role of emotional intelligence. *Computers in Human Behavior, 25*(5), 1182–1187.

Bianchi, A., & Phillips, J. G. (2005). Psychological predictors of problem mobile phone use. *Cyberpsychology & Behavior: The Impact of the Internet, Multimedia and Virtual Reality on Behavior and Society, 8*(1), 39–51.

Billieux, J. (2012). Problematic use of the mobile phone: A literature review and a pathways model. *Current Psychiatry Reviews, 8*, 299–307.

Blaszczynski, A. (2006). Internet use: In search of an addiction. *International Journal of Mental Health and Addiction, 4*, 7–9.

Bragazzi, N. L., & Del Puente, G. (2014). A proposal for including nomophobia in the new DSM-V. *Psychology Research and Behavior Management, 7*, 155–160.

Cain, N., & Gradisar, M. (2010). Electronic media use and sleep in school-aged children and adolescents: A review. *Sleep Medicine, 11*(8), 735–742.

Castells, M., Fernandez-Ardevol, M., Qiu, J. L., & Sey, A. (2009). *Mobile communication and society: A global perspective*. Cambridge, MA: MIT Press.

Choi, S. W., Kim, D. J., Choi, J. S., Ahn, H., Choi, E. J., Song, W. Y., . . . Youn, H. (2015). Comparison of risk and protective factors associated with smartphone addiction and Internet addiction. *Journal of Behavioral Addictions, 4*(4), 308–314.

Cook, J. L., & Jones, R. M. (2011). Texting and accessing the web while driving: Traffic citations and crashes among young adult drivers. *Traffic Injury Prevention, 12*(6), 545–549.

Davey, S., & Davey, A. (2014). Assessment of smartphone addiction in Indian adolescents: A mixed method study by systematic-review and meta-analysis approach. *International Journal of Preventive Medicine, 5*(12), 1500–1511.

David, P., Kim, J.-H., Brickman, J. S., Ran, W., & Curtis, C. M. (2015). Mobile phone distraction while studying. *New Media & Society, 17*(10), 1661–1679.

Dewald, J. F., Meijer, A. M., Oort, F. J., Kerkhof, G. A., & Bögels, S. M. (2010). The influence of sleep quality, sleep duration and sleepiness on school performance in children and adolescents: A meta-analytic review. *Sleep Medicine Reviews, 14*(3), 179–189.

Elkholy, M. T., & Ewees, I. E. (2010). Mobile (cellular) phone contamination with nosocomial pathogens in intensive care units. *Medical Journal of Cairo University, 78*(2), 1–5.

Englander, E. K. (2013). *Understanding cyberbullying in 8-to-10 year olds: New research.* Paper presented at the 2013 AAP National Conference and Exhibition, Orlando, FL.

Goggin, G. (2014). Facebook's mobile career. *New Media & Society, 16,* 1068–1086.

Gogtay, N., Giedd, J. N., Lusk, L., Hayashi, K. M., Greenstein, D., Vaituzis, A. C., . . . Thompson, P. M. (2004). Dynamic mapping of human cortical development during childhood through early adulthood. *Proceedings of the National Academy of Sciences of the United States of America, 101*(21), 8174–8179.

Gradisar, M., Terrill, G., Johnston, A., & Douglas, P. (2008). Adolescent sleep and working memory performance. *Sleep and Biological Rhythms, 6*(3), 146–154.

Ha, J. H., Chin, B., Park, D. H., Ryu, S. H., & Yu, J. (2008). Characteristics of excessive cellular phone use in Korean adolescents. *Cyberpsychology & Behavior: The Impact of the Internet, Multimedia and Virtual Reality on Behavior and Society, 11*(6), 783–784.

Haug, S., Castro, R. P., Kwon, M., Filler, A., Kowatsch, T., & Schaub, M. P. (2015). Smartphone use and smartphone addiction among young people in Switzerland. *Journal of Behavioral Addictions, 4*(4), 299–307.

Heo, J., Oh, J., Subramanian, S. V., Kim, Y., & Kawachi, I. (2014). Addictive Internet use among Korean adolescents: A national survey. *PLOS ONE, 9*(2), e87819. doi:10.1371/journal.pone.0087819

Hinduja, S., & Patchin, J. W. (2010). Bullying, cyberbullying, and suicide. *Archives of Suicide Research: Official Journal of the International Academy for Suicide Research, 14*(3), 206–221.

Hou, J., Nam, Y., Peng, W., & Lee, K. M. (2012). Effects of screen size, viewing angle, and players' immersion tendencies on game experience. *Computers in Human Behavior, 28*(2), 617–623.

Howe, N., & Strauss, W. (2009). *Millennials rising: The next great generation.* New York, NY: Vintage.

Hwang, J. Y., Choi, J. S., Gwak, A. R., Jung, D., Choi, S. W., Lee, J., . . . Kim, D. J. (2014). Shared psychological characteristics that are linked to aggression between patients with Internet addiction and those with alcohol dependence. *Annals of General Psychiatry, 13*(1), 6.

Hwang, Y., Kim, H., & Jeong, S.-H. (2014). Why do media users multitask?: Motives for general, medium-specific, and content-specific types of multitasking. *Computers in Human Behavior, 36,* 542–548.

Junco, R. (2012). In-class multitasking and academic performance. *Computers in Human Behavior, 28*(6), 2236–2243.

Kang, J. H., Park, R. Y., Lee, S. J., Kim, J. Y., Yoon, S. R., & Jung, K. I. (2012). The effect of the forward head posture on postural balance in long time computer based worker. *Annals of Rehabilitation Medicine, 36*(1), 98–104.

Kim, J. H. (2006). Currents in Internet addiction. *Journal of the Korean Medical Association, 49*(3), 202–208.

Kim, S. M., Huh, H. J., Cho, H., Kwon, M., Choi, J. H., Ahn, H. J., . . . Kim, D. J. (2014). The effect of depression, impulsivity, and resilience on smartphone addiction in university students. *Journal of Korean Neuropsychiatric Association, 53*(4), 214–220.

Ko, C. H., Yen, J. Y., Liu, S. C., Huang, C. F., & Yen, C. F. (2009). The associations between aggressive behaviors and Internet addiction and online activities in adolescents. *The

Journal of Adolescent Health: Official Publication of the Society for Adolescent Medicine, *44*(6), 598–605.

Koo, H. J., & Kwon, J.-H. (2014). Risk and protective factors of Internet addiction: A meta-analysis of empirical studies in Korea. *Yonsei Medical Journal, 55*, 1691–1711.

Kuss, D. J., & Griffiths, M. D. (2011). Online social networking and addiction—A review of the psychological literature. *International Journal of Environmental Research and Public Health, 8*, 3528–3552.

Kwon, M., Lee, J. Y., Won, W. Y., Park, J. W., Min, J. A., Hahn, C., . . . Kim, D. J. (2013). Development and validation of a Smartphone Addiction Scale (SAS). *PLOS ONE, 8*(2), e56936. doi:10.1371/journal.pone.0056936

Lapointe, L., Boudreau-Pinsonneault, C., & Vaghefi, I. (2013). *Is smartphone usage truly smart? A qualitative investigation of IT addictive behaviors.* Paper presented at the 2013 46th Hawaii International Conference on System Sciences (HICSS), Wailea, HI.

Law, D. M., Shapka, J. D., & Olson, B. F. (2010). To control or not to control? Parenting behaviours and adolescent online aggression. *Computers in Human Behavior, 26*, 1651–1656.

Lee, U., Lee, J., Ko, M., Lee, C., Kim, Y., Yang, S., . . . Song, J. (2014). *Hooked on smartphones: An exploratory study on smartphone overuse among college students.* Paper presented at the Proceedings of the 32nd Annual ACM Conference on Human Factors in Computing Systems, Toronto, ON, Canada.

Lee, Y.-K., Chang, C.-T., Lin, Y., & Cheng, Z.-H. (2014). The dark side of smartphone usage: Psychological traits, compulsive behavior and technostress. *Computers in Human Behavior, 31*, 373–383.

Lemola, S., Perkinson-Gloor, N., Brand, S., Dewald-Kaufmann, J. F., & Grob, A. (2015). Adolescents' electronic media use at night, sleep disturbance, and depressive symptoms in the smartphone age. *Journal of Youth and Adolescence, 44*(2), 405–418.

Lopez-Fernandez, O. (2017). Short version of the Smartphone Addiction Scale adapted to Spanish and French: Towards a cross-cultural research in problematic mobile phone use. *Addictive Behaviors, 64*, 275–280.

Lopez-Fernandez, O., Honrubia-Serrano, L., Freixa-Blanxart, M., & Gibson, W. (2014). Prevalence of problematic mobile phone use in British adolescents. *Cyberpsychology, Behavior and Social Networking, 17*(2), 91–98.

Marlatt, G. A., Baer, J. S., Donovan, D. M., & Kivlahan, D. R. (1988). Addictive behaviors: Etiology and treatment. *Annual Review of Psychology, 39*, 223–252.

Matthews, T., Pierce, J, & Tang, J. (2009). *No smart phone is an island: The impact of places, situations, and other devices on smart phone use* (IBM Research Report #RJ10452). Austin, TX: IBM Research.

Mok, J. Y., Choi, S. W., Kim, D. J., Choi, J. S., Lee, J., Ahn, H., . . . Song, W. Y. (2014). Latent class analysis on Internet and smartphone addiction in college students. *Neuropsychiatric Disease and Treatment, 10*, 817–828.

Moon, J. H., Lee, M. Y., & Moon, N. J. (2014). Association between video display terminal use and dry eye disease in school children. *Journal of Pediatric Ophthalmology and Strabismus, 51*(2), 87–92.

Moore, M. K. (2004). Upper crossed syndrome and its relationship to cervicogenic headache. *Journal of Manipulative and Physiological Therapeutics, 27*(6), 414–420.

Morgan, L. L., Kesari, S., & Davis, D. L. (2014). Why children absorb more microwave radiation than adults: The consequences. *Journal of Microscopy and Ultrastructure, 2*(4), 197–204.

Munezawa, T., Kaneita, Y., Osaki, Y., Kanda, H., Minowa, M., Suzuki, K., . . . Ohida, T. (2011). The association between use of mobile phones after lights out and sleep disturbances among Japanese adolescents: A nationwide cross-sectional survey. *Sleep, 34*(8), 1013–1020.

O'Connor, S. S., Whitehill, J. M., King, K. M., Kernic, M. A., Boyle, L. N., Bresnahan, B. W., . . . Ebel, B. E. (2013). Compulsive cell phone use and history of motor vehicle crash. *The Journal of Adolescent Health: Official Publication of the Society for Adolescent Medicine, 53*(4), 512–519.

Park, J., Kim, J., Kim, J., Kim, K., Kim, N., Choi, I., . . . Yim, J. (2015). The effects of heavy smartphone use on the cervical angle, pain threshold of neck muscles and depression. *Advanced Science and Technology Letters, 91*, 12–17.

Punamäki, R. L., Wallenius, M., Nygård, C. H., Saarni, L., & Rimpelä, A. (2007). Use of information and communication technology (ICT) and perceived health in adolescence: The role of sleeping habits and waking-time tiredness. *Journal of Adolescence, 30*(4), 569–585.

Reid, D. J., & Reid, F. J. (2007). Text or talk? Social anxiety, loneliness, and divergent preferences for cell phone use. *Cyberpsychology & Behavior: The Impact of the Internet, Multimedia and Virtual Reality on Behavior and Society, 10*(3), 424–435.

Repacholi, M. H. (2001). Health risks from the use of mobile phones. *Toxicology Letters, 120*(1–3), 323–331.

Roberts, J. A., & Pirog, S. F. (2012). A preliminary investigation of materialism and impulsiveness as predictors of technological addictions among young adults. *Journal of Behavioral Addictions, 2*(1), 56–62.

Roberts, J. A., Yaya, L. H., & Manolis, C. (2014). The invisible addiction: Cell-phone activities and addiction among male and female college students. *Journal of Behavioral Addictions, 3*(4), 254–265.

Salama, O. E., & Abou El Naga, R. M. (2004). Cellular phones: Are they detrimental? *The Journal of the Egyptian Public Health Association, 79*(3–4), 197–223.

Sánchez-Martínez, M., & Otero, A. (2009). Factors associated with cell phone use in adolescents in the community of Madrid (Spain). *CyberPsychology & Behavior, 12*, 131–137.

Sarwar, M., & Soomro, T. R. (2013). Impact of smartphones on society. *European Journal of Scientific Research, 98*(2), 216–226.

Schieman, S., & Young, M. C. (2013). Are communications about work outside regular working hours associated with work-to-family conflict, psychological distress and sleep problems? *Work & Stress, 27*(3), 244–261.

Slonje, R., Smith, P. K., & Frisén, A. (2013). The nature of cyberbullying, and strategies for prevention. *Computers in Human Behavior, 29*(1), 26–32.

Smetaniuk, P. (2014). A preliminary investigation into the prevalence and prediction of problematic cell phone use. *Journal of Behavioral Addictions, 3*(1), 41–53.

Subrahmanyam, K., Reich, S. M., Waechter, N., & Espinoza, G. (2008). Online and offline social networks: Use of social networking sites by emerging adults. *Journal of Applied Developmental Psychology, 29*, 420–433.

Tambekar, D., Gulhane, P., Dahikar, S., & Dudhane, M. (2008). Nosocomial hazards of doctor's mobile phones in hospitals. *Journal of Medical Sciences, 8*(1), 73–76.

Toda, M., & Ezoe, S. (2013). Multifactorial study of mobile phone dependence in medical students: Relationship to health-related lifestyle, Type A behavior, and depressive state. *Open Journal of Preventive Medicine, 3*, 99–103.

Thomée, S., Härenstam, A., & Hagberg, M. (2011). Mobile phone use and stress, sleep disturbances, and symptoms of depression among young adults—A prospective cohort study. *BMC Public Health, 11*, 66.

Ulger, F., Esen, S., Dilek, A., Yanik, K., Gunaydin, M., & Leblebicioglu, H. (2009). Are we aware how contaminated our mobile phones with nosocomial pathogens? *Annals of Clinical Microbiology and Antimicrobials, 8*, 7.

Van den Bulck, J. (2010). The effects of media on sleep. *Adolescent Medicine: State of the Art Reviews, 21*(3), 418–429, vii.

van Deursen, A. J., Bolle, C. L., Hegner, S. M., & Kommers, P. A. (2015). Modeling habitual and addictive smartphone behavior: The role of smartphone usage types, emotional intelligence, social stress, self-regulation, age, and gender. *Computers in Human Behavior, 45*, 411–420.

Yen, C.-F., Tang, T.-C., Yen, J.-Y., Lin, H.-C., Huang, C.-F., Liu, S.-C., & Ko, C.-H. (2009). Symptoms of problematic cellular phone use, functional impairment and its association with depression among adolescents in Southern Taiwan. *Journal of Adolescence, 32*, 863–873.

Whang, L. S., Lee, S., & Chang, G. (2003). Internet over-users' psychological profiles: A behavior sampling analysis on Internet addiction. *Cyberpsychology & Behavior: The Impact of the Internet, Multimedia and Virtual Reality on Behavior and Society, 6*(2), 143–150.

Wilson, F. A., & Stimpson, J. P. (2010). Trends in fatalities from distracted driving in the United States, 1999 to 2008. *American Journal of Public Health, 100*(11), 2213–2219.

World Health Organization. (1964). *WHO Expert Committee on Drug Dependence: Thirteenth Report* (WHO Technical Report Series 273). Geneva, Switzerland: Author.

World Health Organization. (2006). *WHO Expert Committee on Drug Dependence: Thirty-fourth report* (WHO Technical Report Series 942). Geneva, Switzerland: Author.

Yang, Y. S., Yen, J. Y., Ko, C. H., Cheng, C. P., & Yen, C. F. (2010). The association between problematic cellular phone use and risky behaviors and low self-esteem among Taiwanese adolescents. *BMC Public Health, 10*, 217.

Zimmerman, M. A., Copeland, L. A., Shope, J. T., & Dielman, T. E. (1997). A longitudinal study of self-esteem: Implications for adolescent development. *Journal of Youth and Adolescence, 26*(2), 117–141.

3 NARCISSISM AND SOCIAL MEDIA USE BY CHILDREN AND ADOLESCENTS

Louis Leung and Renwen Zhang

Social media are defined as "a group of Internet-based applications that build on the ideological and technological foundations of Web 2.0 and that allow the creation and exchange of user generated content" (Kaplan & Haenlein, 2010, p. 61). Kaplan and Haenlein (2010) classified social media into six types: blogs (e.g., WordPress), social network sites (SNSs; e.g., Facebook), content communities (e.g., YouTube), collaborative projects (e.g., Wikipedia), virtual game worlds (e.g., World of Warcraft), and virtual social worlds (e.g., Second Life). Riding the crest of Web 2.0, social media have seeped into the everyday lives of people across the world. Young people are in the vanguard of social networking practice and are more expert in social media use than their older counterparts are. The mania for access to social media, however, has raised considerable concerns. Children and adolescents have been found to spend excessive amounts of time on SNSs and virtual game worlds, and they are susceptible to online risks, such as cyberbullying, online game addiction, sexting, antisocial behavior, and privacy invasion (Livingstone & Helsper, 2007).

Among the large number of predictors of social media use, narcissism is a fascinating yet often downplayed factor. Previous research has found narcissism to be positively related to online social interaction and self-promoting content (Buffardi & Campbell, 2008; Leung, 2013). Individuals with narcissistic traits generally report a greater number of online friends, wall posts, and photos (Ong et al., 2011), and they are more likely to be addicted to massive multiplayer online role-playing games (MMORPG; Kim, Namkoong, Ku, & Kim, 2008). The maladaptive aspects of narcissism, such as exploitativeness and entitlement, have been found to be predictors of physical aggression (Reidy, Zeichner, Foster, & Martinez, 2008), antisocial behaviors on Facebook (Carpenter, 2012), and cyberbullying among children and teens (Ang, Tan, & Mansor, 2011).

This chapter synthesizes the previous research on narcissism and social media use among children and adolescents. As a personality trait, narcissism is systematically reviewed in terms of its definition, origins, and assessment. Specific narcissistic traits such as exhibitionism and exploitativeness/entitlement have been mapped in the online behaviors of children and adolescents by drawing on empirical research in psychology and communication. By uncovering early socialization experiences that cultivate narcissism, this chapter also provides insights into intervention and treatment in order to curtail narcissistic development at an early age.

SOCIAL MEDIA, CHILDREN, AND ADOLESCENTS

Social Media Penetration Across the World

Although young adults aged 18 to 24 years have been found to be the main consumers of social media, both children and adolescents have increasingly incorporated new technologies into their daily lives. According to the most recent national survey in the United States, 90% of teenagers used some form of social media, and 75% of teenagers currently have a profile on a SNS (Lenhart et al., 2015). Studies also showed that 50% of all teens in the United States visited SNSs daily, and more than one third of them visited SNSs several times a day (Common Sense Media, 2012). In Europe, the use of SNSs among children aged 9 to 16 years increased from 44% in 2010 to 63% in 2014 (Livingstone, Haddon, Vincent, Mascheroni, & Ólafsson, 2014). In Singapore in 2015, 51% of children aged 14 years and younger had used social media, and 62% of them starting using social media between the ages of 7 and 10 years; 13% started earlier at the age of 6 years or younger (Lee, 2015).

Within this overall picture, Facebook remains a dominant force in teens' social media ecosystems, with 71% of American teens aged 13 to 17 years using the site, followed by Instagram (52%), Snapchat (41%), and Twitter (33%; Lenhart et al., 2015). Teens also have diversified their social media use, which was indicated by the finding that 71% of teens reported using more than one SNS (Lenhart et al., 2015). In Europe, Facebook is used by 43% of 9- to 16-year-olds, overshadowing Instagram (19%), YouTube (18%), and Twitter (14%; Livingstone et al., 2014). In Singapore, Facebook, YouTube, and Instagram are the top three most popular social media platforms among children aged 14 years and younger. Interestingly, YouTube is the most commonly used social media platform for children aged 6 years and younger. In China, 90.7% of children younger than 18 years use instant messaging services such as WeChat, 40.7% have a microblog account, and 17% visit forums or bulletin board system (BBS; CNNIC, 2015). Online games are also exceedingly popular among children in China, attracting 67.9% of 6- to 18-year-olds.

Benefits of Social Media Use

Much of the frenzy for access to social media is driven by the unique traits of childhood and adolescence. A distinct feature that compels children to engage with social media is their strong eagerness to learn. At the age of cognitive development, children are as open to learning from social media as they are from other sources. Watching videos on YouTube not only entertains children but also helps them learn new things and explore the unknown. Students could also benefit from sharing and discussing schoolwork with their peers via SNSs. In their study on a high school science-mentoring project, Pollara and Zhu (2011) found that students who frequently interacted with their peers and mentors via Facebook engaged in project collaboration more actively and had closer relationships with their mentors than those who did not. In line with this finding, the results of a longitudinal study also showed that heavy Facebook use had a positive effect on overall grades, but the heavy use of blogs and online games led to grade impairment (Leung, 2015).

Adolescence, however, is often characterized as a time of challenge and turbulence. Despite their dramatic physical changes, teens are faced with increased independence and growing self-discovery. The emerging yet immature sense of self motivates teens to experiment with a variety of behaviors and to explore their identity, which is highly social in nature. Through their interactions with other people in different occasions, teens gradually make sense of and integrate different facets of themselves. Therefore, SNSs have become the venue for teens to express and actualize their identities via self-disclosure (Livingston, 2008), which was shown in the finding that teen bloggers regarded LiveJournal as a digital space for self-expression and self-theorizing (Davis, 2010; Leung, 2011). In their study, Valkenburg, Schouten, and Peter (2005) found that half of children aged 9 to 18 years had pretended to be someone else online.

It is important to note that social media satisfy teens' need to stay connected (Kuss & Griffiths, 2011). In the essential period of socialization, children and adolescents have a greater tendency to connect with their peers than people in other age groups do. Hartup and Stevens (1997) found that, on average, teens spent up to one third of their time with friends. Interacting with friends via SNSs helps teens to make social connections, seek social support, and exchange ideas. Children and teens may sometimes feel compelled to maintain their social networks, which results in excessive SNS use or SNS addiction.

Risks and Concerns About Social Media Use

Despite the benefits of social media, parents and educators have expressed concerns about their disadvantages to the developmental challenges young people face today, including risk taking (Gullone & Moore, 2000), peer delinquency (Haynie, 2002), puberty, and sexual development (J. D. Brown, Halpern, & L'Engle, 2005). The first risk concerns the potential influence of social media on adolescents' attitudes to risky behaviors. Although youth are more *tech savvy* than adults are, they bring less real-world knowledge and experience to the online environment and thus are more easily swayed by the risky behaviors displayed by their peers on social media (Strasburger, Wilson, & Jordan, 2009). Litt and Stock (2011) found that adolescents who perceived alcohol use to be normative based on others' Facebook profiles had more interest in initiating alcohol use. Similarly, adolescents were more inclined to post references to sexual behavior if a peer had posted similar references on Facebook (Dunton, Liao, Intille, Spruijt-Metz, & Pentz, 2011).

Parents and teachers are also concerned about cyberbullying and sexting. The anonymity and reduced nonverbal cues in the online environment offer perpetrators the cloak of disguise, reducing their risk of being condemned and punished and thus intensifying their bullying behaviors. A survey by the Pew Research Center showed that 32% of adolescents reported having experienced some form of online harassment, such as aggressive behavior, insults, denigration, and exclusion. Social media also make children and teens more vulnerable to sexting because sexual messages and images are rapidly distributed through SNSs, blogs, and forums. Temple et al. (2012) found that 28% of high school students had sent a sext, and 31% had asked someone else for a sext.

Another risk arises from the exposure of children's privacy. The term *privacy exposed* refers to the inability to control the information about one-self over the Internet, in this case social media, especially regarding who has access to that information. Livingstone and Helsper (2007) contended that interacting with friends online was potentially risky because children and teenagers, intentionally or unintentionally, give out personal or private information, such as phone numbers, home addresses, and e-mail addresses. The prevalence of mobile devices, such as smartphones and tablets, has also increased youth's exposure to online risks, which was indicated in the data collected in 2010 and 2014 by EU Kids Online (Livingstone, Haddon, Görzig, & Ólafsson, 2010; Livingstone et al., 2014).

NARCISSISM: ORIGINS AND ASSESSMENT

Narcissism as a Predictor of Social Media Use

Because of the potential risks of social media use, scholars have devoted considerable attention to examining its antecedents and predictors. Personality traits and psychological status, such as extroversion, self-esteem, narcissism, and loneliness, have been consistently documented as factors that influence the behaviors of children and teens on social media (Correa, Hinsley, & De Zuniga, 2010; Kuss & Griffiths, 2011; Leung, 2013). Among all these predictors, narcissism plays a significant yet often downplayed role in affecting online behaviors.

People with higher levels of narcissism tend to have a greater number of friends on SNSs, update more wall posts and photos, and find SNSs more gratifying than non-narcissists do (Mo & Leung, 2015; Ong et al., 2011; Poon & Leung, 2011). These results consolidate the argument that the self-presentational nature of SNSs empowers adolescents with narcissistic tendencies to present themselves favorably online and construct their ideal selves in cyberspace (Buffardi & Campbell, 2008; Mehdizadeh, 2010). Before discussing the relationship between narcissism and social media use, we briefly review the definition, origins, and construct of narcissism, and we delineate the assessment of narcissistic personality.

Defining Narcissism and Its Origins

The personality trait of narcissism is marked by a grandiose and inflated self-concept (Buffardi & Campbell, 2008). Individuals with a narcissistic personality possess a sense of superiority, feelings of entitlement, strong self-focus, and exhibitionism (Campbell & Foster, 2007; Emmons, 1984). Narcissists attach great importance to gaining admiration and establishing dominance over others, and they constantly protect and promote their esteem using self-regulatory strategies (Morf & Rhodewalt, 2001). Simultaneously, however, the grandiose sense of self is vulnerable and highly contingent on the appraisals of others (Thomaes, Stegge, Bushman, Olthof, & Denissen, 2008). Narcissists are dependent on obtaining affirmation from their interpersonal relationships, and thus they gain and lose self-worth quickly depending on how others view them. The vulnerable aspect of narcissism makes it distinct from self-esteem, which involves a positive evaluation of self-worth that is relatively stable and independent of the appraisals of others (R. P. Brown & Zeigler-Hill, 2004).

A complex construct, narcissism has been investigated in clinical theory, social/personality psychology, and psychiatric diagnoses in past decades. Although psychiatrists regard narcissism as a personality disorder and first included it in the *Diagnostic and Statistical Manual of Mental Disorders, Third Edition* (*DSM-III*; American Psychiatric Association [APA], 1980), clinical and psychological researchers focus on narcissism as a trait that varies in the general population (Raskin & Terry, 1988). Clinical theorists, such as Kohut (1971) and Kernberg (1975), conceptualized narcissism as a normal aspect of self-development that evolves as the individual matures, thereby maintaining self-cohesion and self-esteem. Pathological narcissism is likely to develop when there is a defect in the normal progression of self-development. Social and personality psychologists, however, primarily assess *subclinical narcissism* in nonclinical contexts, contending that normal narcissism reflects the strategies used to promote a positive self-image and facilitate agency (Paulhus & Williams, 2002; Wallace & Baumeister, 2002).

Individual differences in narcissism first emerge in late childhood at around the ages of 7 to 12 years (Barry, Frick, & Killian, 2003; Thomaes et al., 2008). At these ages, children form a sense of self and are able to develop self-views based on social comparisons, which are more realistic than those of younger children, who find it hard to differentiate their actual self-views from their ideal self-views (Harter, 2006). Varied levels of narcissism have been found among children (Hughes, Cavell, & Grossman, 1997). Although the empirical evidence on origins of narcissism is scarce, clinical theorists have suggested that narcissism often grows out of either excessive parental admiration (Millon, 1981) or the lack of parental warmth (Kernberg, 1975; Kohut, 1971). In their most recent longitudinal study, Brummelman et al. (2015) found that narcissism was predicted by parental overvaluation rather than the lack of parental warmth; that is, children develop narcissism, in part, by internalizing their parents' inflated views of them. These findings can be applied to early socialization experiences that cultivate narcissism, which may provide insights into interventions to curtail narcissistic development at an early age.

Dimensional Structure and Assessment of Narcissism

The Narcissistic Personality Inventory (NPI; Raskin & Hall, 1979) is the most widely used instrument to measure individual differences in narcissism among the nonclinical population. Although the self-report items on the NPI were derived from the *DSM-III* criteria for narcissistic personality disorder (NPD; APA, 1980), these behaviors are actually reflective of narcissism as a normal personality trait unless they are exhibited in extreme forms (Emmons, 1984; Raskin & Terry, 1988). Originally including 223 items, this inventory was later condensed to a 40-item measure that has been used predominantly in research on narcissistic personality traits for more than two decades (Raskin & Terry, 1988).

A considerable amount of research has explored the underlying structure of the NPI item pool. Emmons (1984) conducted a factor analysis of the NPI scores and proposed a four-component solution: exploitativeness/entitlement, leadership/authority, superiority/arrogance, and self-absorption/self-admiration. Raskin and Terry (1988), however, clustered these items into seven dimensions: authority, exhibitionism, superiority, vanity, exploitativeness, entitlement, and self-sufficiency. More recently, Ackerman et al. (2011) proposed a robust three-dimensional model of narcissism: leadership/authority, grandiose exhibitionism, and entitlement/exploitativeness. According to Ackerman et al. (2011), leadership/authority represents adaptive aspects of personality that reflect high self-esteem, extraversion, and social potency, whereas grandiose exhibitionism and entitlement/exploitativeness capture socially toxic elements of personality, which Barry et al. (2003) called *maladaptive narcissism*. They suggested that researchers should conduct subscale analyses in order to gain more precise psychological insights into the correlations and consequences of narcissism.

Despite the prevalent usage of the NPI, scholars have acknowledged its limitations in measuring narcissism in children and adolescents (Ang & Yusof, 2006; Thomaes et al., 2008). Given that the NPI was developed to assess adults, some items are either beyond children's cognitive and linguistic abilities or too abstract to fit their social reality. Against this backdrop, Thomaes et al. (2008) developed a short but comprehensive self-report measure of childhood narcissism—the Childhood Narcissism Scale (CNS). This 10-item scale was validated by subsequent empirical studies (Thomaes et al., 2008; Thomaes, Bushman, de Castro, Cohen, & Denissen, 2009). Other scales include the Narcissistic Personality Questionnaire for Children (NPQC; Ang & Yusof, 2006) and the revised version of NPQC (NPQC-R; Ang & Raine, 2009). The two self-report scales were designed to measure narcissism as a normal personality trait in children, which could be generalized to all school-going children and youth (Ang & Yusof, 2006).

NARCISSISM AND SELF-PRESENTATION ON SNSs

Narcissism and Self-Promotion

Central to most theoretical models of narcissism in social and personality psychology is the use of social relationships to regulate self-esteem and self-image (Campbell, Brunell, & Finkel, 2006; Morf & Rhodewalt, 2001). Narcissists often use self-regulatory strategies, such as relationship management and identity construction, to make themselves appear and feel special, important, and successful (Bergman, Fearrington, Davenport, & Bergman, 2011). Therefore, narcissists are passionate about initiating relationships and employing social connections for the purpose of self-enhancement, such as bragging about themselves and performing well in public places (Buffardi & Campbell, 2008; Buss & Chiodo, 1991; Wallace & Baumeister, 2002).

SNSs serve as a fertile ground for narcissists to promote themselves and regulate their narcissistic esteem. On the one hand, the public display of social connections on SNSs allows individuals to view and traverse their social networks and interactions, which enables narcissists to appear and feel popular by maintaining a large number of superficial friendships (Buffardi & Campbell, 2008). Studies found that narcissism, particularly grandiose exhibitionism, was related to Facebook behaviors that afforded extensive self-presentation to a wide audience through attaining large numbers of friends, posting status updates, and uploading photos (Carpenter, 2012; Ong et al., 2011). On the other hand, the controllability of online environments renders users complete control over self-presentation on social media (Vazire & Gosling, 2004). Narcissists can use their personal homepage to display achievements, wealth, and attractive photographs of themselves, which largely satisfies their eagerness for self-promotion and desire for public glory (Buss & Chiodo, 1991; Wallace & Baumeister, 2002). Mo and Leung (2015) supported this finding by demonstrating that narcissism was positively related to intensity and the gratification obtained from microblog use.

Grandiose Exhibitionism and Body Image

Narcissists are exhibitionistic, attention-seeking, and acutely concerned about their physical appearance (Vazire, Naumann, Rentfrow, & Gosling, 2008). They make great efforts to look well groomed and fashionable, and they tend to overestimate their attractiveness (Bleske-Rechek, Remiker, & Baker, 2008). Therefore, narcissists are likely to share more photos of themselves on SNSs and edit their selfies to maximize their attractiveness in order to affirm their illusions of physical desirability and convey their perceived superiority to others (Jonason, Lyons, Baughman, & Vernon, 2014). Fox and Rooney (2015) found that narcissism predicted the number of selfies posted and the frequency of editing photos posted on SNSs.

Indulging in posting and editing one's photos on SNSs might lead to problematic Internet use and body dissatisfaction. Studies have shown that higher appearance-related Internet use was associated with lower weight satisfaction and the higher drive for thinness in 15-year-old girls (Tiggemann & Miller, 2010). The exposure of adolescent and preadolescent girls to the Internet was also correlated with the internalization of appearance ideals and body surveillance (Tiggemann & Slater, 2013, 2014). Specifically, posting self-images on SNSs exposed females to greater peer scrutiny of appearance and competition, which may increase body dissatisfaction and body concerns. In the same vein, engagement in photo-based Facebook activities was correlated with greater thin-ideal internalization, self-objectification, and the drive for thinness, whereas overall Facebook and Internet use was unrelated to body image (Meier & Gray, 2014).

NARCISSISM, ADDICTION, AND CYBERBULLYING

Pathological Narcissism and Aggression

Specific narcissistic traits such as exploitativeness and entitlement were found to be predictors of proactive aggression and bullying (Reidy et al., 2008; Washburn, McMahon, King, Reinecke, & Silver, 2004). According to Ackerman et al. (2011), exploitativeness/entitlement includes "a sense of deserving respect and a willingness to manipulate and take advantage of others" (p. 6). People high in this trait feel entitled to their wants and tend to exploit others to achieve social goals without empathy and regard for others (Emmons, 1984; Werner, Bumpus, & Rock, 2010). Therefore, narcissists are likely to employ aggression and bullying as a means of dominating others in order to attain their desired goals and maintain their grandiose sense of self (Salmivalli, 2001; Washburn et al., 2004).

Previous studies have documented an association between narcissism and aggressive behavior of children and teens (Barry et al., 2003). In their survey of 698 Asian adolescents, Seah and Ang (2008) found that narcissism was correlated with proactive aggression and not reactive aggression, which corroborated Salmivalli's (2001) argument regarding the construct of narcissism in relation to reactive–proactive aggression. Reactive aggression is characterized by hostile and defensive responses to threats to one's inflated self-view, whereas proactive aggression refers to exploitative acts executed for self-enhancement and self-gain (Bushman & Baumeister, 1998; Salmivalli, 2001). Although evidence suggests that narcissists tend to react aggressively when their fragile egos are threatened (Stucke & Sporer, 2002), it is more likely that their aggression stems from the motivation to dominate and control others to attain their desired goals, which is accompanied by the exploitative and unempathetic nature of the narcissistic personality.

In taking this study one step further, Kauten and Barry (2014) found that self-reported pathological narcissism significantly predicted self-reported, but not peer-reported, aggression among U.S. adolescents. It seems that adolescents with high levels of narcissism were not concerned about portraying themselves as aggressive because they deemed aggression acceptable (Ang et al., 2011). However, adolescents with pathological narcissism were more skilled at concealing their aggressive behaviors from peers than nonpathological narcissists were, and nonpathological narcissism has been found to be a predictor of peer-nominated aggression (Golmaryami & Barry, 2009). Therefore, children and adolescents may find it hard to recognize and avoid those with pathological narcissism.

Narcissism and Online Game Addiction

The aggressive tendency of pathological narcissists also compels them to engage in online game playing. Previous studies demonstrated that individuals with narcissistic traits were more likely to be addicted to MMORPG, especially those of an aggressive nature (Kim et al., 2008). Within the social setting of MMORPG, excellent players receive recognition and attention from others, and they gain power and status as they collect valuable prizes and upgrade their skills in the game. These achievements largely satisfy their grandiose sense of self-importance and their fantasies of success, which motivates them to increase their wealth and strength at any cost and invest more time in online games than other players do (Kim et al., 2008). The violent content of online games also appeals to narcissists because it provides them with a virtual space to dominate and control others without being blamed.

Furthermore, Eksi (2012) found a positive correlation between narcissism and Internet addiction. The results showed that narcissistic entitlement significantly predicted *deprivation* and *controlling difficulty* in Internet addiction, whereas superiority was related to *social isolation* in Internet addiction. This finding, however, was not supported by Odacı and Çelik (2013), who found no significant correlation between problematic Internet use and narcissism. These inconsistent findings might be because they examined the entire construct of narcissism and focused on total NPI scores instead of considering each dimension of narcissism separately. Because aggression emerged as an antecedent of problematic Internet use, further research that examines the risk factors for Internet addiction should consider the maladaptive aspects of narcissism (Odacı & Çelik, 2013).

Cyberbullying and Antisocial Behaviors on SNSs

The Internet also opens up new possibilities for narcissists to execute aggressive and bullying behaviors. The anonymity and reduced contextual cues in cyberspace could exacerbate adolescents' sense of disregard for others and their belief that aggression is acceptable and justifiable. Specifically, the anonymity on the Internet can result in deindividuation by reducing self-awareness, which weakens the individual's ability to regulate his or her behavior (Zimbardo, 1969). In a similar vein, limited social and contextual cues in cyberspace are likely to activate adolescents' belief about the legitimacy of aggression, leading to disinhibited online behavior (Hinduja & Patchin, 2008).

Recent studies have documented a positive relationship between narcissism and cyberbullying among adolescents and adults (Ang et al., 2011; Carpenter, 2012). Stover (2006) contended that adolescents used SNSs such as Facebook and MySpace to gain social status by opposing people with higher social status and speaking ill of others or ostracizing them. Ang et al. (2011) found that narcissistic exploitativeness was significantly and positively associated with cyberbullying among Asian adolescents, and the relationship was partially mediated by normative beliefs about aggression. Such beliefs about the acceptability of aggression have been shown to be one of the mechanisms by which narcissistic exploitativeness influences cyberbullying. Goodboy and Martin (2015) further substantiated the relationship between narcissism and cyberbullying by demonstrating that the Dark Triad—Machiavellianism, psychopathy, and narcissism—was positively related to both visual- and text-based cyberbullying reports, although psychopathy was the strongest predictor of cyberbullying tendency.

Narcissism also has been blamed for causing antisocial behaviors on SNSs. Carpenter (2012) found that narcissistic entitlement/exploitativeness was correlated with antisocial behaviors on Facebook, such as retaliating against mean comments and seeking greater social support from others. Grandiose exhibitionism, however, was found to be a predictor of anger when the individual did not receive comments on his or her status updates. These findings corroborate previous research that suggested that the maladaptive aspects of narcissism disrupt communal orientations to social interaction and lead to interpersonal deviance (Ackerman et al., 2011).

INTERVENTIONS AND TREATMENT

Parental-Training Interventions

Because of the deleterious impact of narcissism in engendering Internet addiction, cyberbullying, and antisocial behaviors in social media, certain interventions and treatment should be promoted at an early age to curtail narcissistic development. Understanding the origins of narcissism serves as the starting point for providing appropriate interventions. Previous studies found evidence that parental overvaluation and the lack of parental warmth were the roots of narcissism (Brummelman et al., 2015; Kohut, 2013; Millon, 1983). According to social learning theory, children are likely to grow up to be narcissistic if their parents regard them as more special and more entitled to privileges than other children are (Millon, 1983). Such children might internalize a sense of superiority and entitlement as they grow up, thus becoming narcissistic. Moreover, the psychoanalytic theory holds that the lack of parental warmth molds children into narcissists because they might try to obtain from others the approval and appreciation that they did not receive from their parents (Kernberg, 1985; Kohut, 2013).

An alternative explanation for parental overvaluation is that parents who overvaluate their children are narcissistic themselves. Narcissistic parents project their inflated self-views onto their children, who might mimic or inherit their narcissistic levels (Brummelman et al., 2015). Therefore, parental-training interventions might be effective in curtailing narcissistic development at an early age. Parents should be instructed to convey affection and appreciation to their children without making them feel that they are superior to others. However, providing parental warmth helps to raise children's self-esteem and reduce narcissism, and lavishing children with praise and special treatment might spoil them and promote narcissism. Parents should strike a balance between appreciation and overvaluation in raising their children, and they should educate children appropriately when they display narcissistic tendencies.

Moreover, parents with high levels of narcissism should take the initiative to engage in the therapeutic process. Despite the scarce evidence on the effectiveness of interventions to prevent narcissism in youth, previous research has found some psychotherapeutic options for narcissistic parents. For example, parent–infant psychotherapeutic interventions have been found to be an effective approach to evaluate the nature of *problems of parenthood* and the quality of parental narcissism (Espasa, 2004). During the intervention session, a therapist attempts to explore the effects of the parents' childhood experiences—particularly the relationship with their parents—on their parental style. The therapist works with the parents to show them how their past experiences are now affecting their relationship with their children and helps parents find the best way to counter these effects.

Treatment of Childhood Narcissism

Although parental-training interventions may be effective in curbing the development of narcissism at an early age, research has found that narcissism is difficult to treat after it has developed. Narcissists are notoriously resistant to change, and they regard any feedback from others as criticism (Campbell, Reeder, Sedikides, & Elliot, 2000; Sedikides, Rudich, Gregg, Kumashiro, & Rusbult, 2004). However, evidence has shown that narcissists do change. Theoretically, narcissists can be changed by adding communal traits (e.g., warmth, morality, caring) to their personality, which is defined as a *communal shift* (Campbell & Foster, 2007, p. 132). In one study on married couples, narcissists who reported that their partners made them feel more caring and warm actually became better partners over time (Campbell & Foster, 2007).

Recent advances have been made in the clinical treatment of narcissism. Researchers and practitioners have found self-control regulation/interpersonal psychotherapy (SCRIPT) to be a potent therapeutic approach to eliciting psychological changes in individuals suffering from NPD. This approach helps narcissists reevaluate their behaviors with regard to individual goals. For example, if a narcissistic teenage girl spends excessive time posting her photos on Facebook in order to gain admiration and compliments from her peers, the clinician would ask her to think of the drawbacks of such behaviors and then find an alternative way of achieving her goals, such as getting high scores at school. According to Campbell and Foster (2007, p. 132), "Over time, the narcissist will ideally shape his or her behavior to be consistent with his or her goals and develop some awareness of the detrimental effects of his or her narcissism." Although these approaches seem promising, it is imperative that future research develops new strategies for minimizing narcissism and its effects.

CONCLUSION

Narcissism has a fascinating yet often downplayed influence on social media use and addiction among children and adolescents. People with higher levels of narcissism tend to have a greater number of friends on SNSs, update more wall posts and photos, and find SNSs more gratifying than nonnarcissists do. Moreover, the maladaptive aspects of narcissism, such as grandiose exhibitionism and exploitativeness/entitlement, might lead to problematic photo-based SNS use, online game addiction, body dissatisfaction, physical aggression, antisocial behavior, and cyberbullying. Early socialization experiences cultivate narcissism; thus, parental-training interventions and psychotherapy at an early age can help to curb the development of narcissism. Strategies for improving self-esteem, which focus on a child's receiving positive evaluations from others and expecting such positive feedback, could be potentially harmful. Instead, interventions should also help children cope with negative feedback from others.

REFERENCES

Ackerman, R. A., Witt, E. A., Donnellan, M. B., Trzesniewski, K. H., Robins, R. W., & Kashy, D. A. (2011). What does the Narcissistic Personality Inventory really measure? *Assessment, 18*(1), 67–87.

American Psychiatric Association. (1980). *Diagnostic and statistical manual of mental disorders* (3rd ed.). Washington DC: Author.

Ang, R. P., & Raine, A. (2009). Reliability, validity and invariance of the Narcissistic Personality Questionnaire for Children-Revised (NPQC-R). *Journal of Psychopathology and Behavioral Assessment, 31*(3), 143–151.

Ang, R. P., Tan, K. A., & Mansor, A. B. (2011). Normative beliefs about aggression as a mediator of narcissistic exploitativeness and cyberbullying. *Journal of Interpersonal Violence, 26*, 2619–2634.

Ang, R. P., & Yusof, N. (2006). Development and initial validation of the Narcissistic Personality Questionnaire for Children: A preliminary investigation using school-based Asian samples. *Educational Psychology, 26*(1), 1–18.

Barry, C. T., Frick, P. J., & Killian, A. L. (2003). The relation of narcissism and self-esteem to conduct problems in children: A preliminary investigation. *Journal of Clinical Child and Adolescent Psychology, 32*(1), 139–152.

Bergman, S. M., Fearrington, M. E., Davenport, S. W., & Bergman, J. Z. (2011). Millennials, narcissism, and social networking: What narcissists do on social networking sites and why. *Personality and Individual Differences, 50*(5), 706–711.

Bleske-Rechek, A., Remiker, M. W., & Baker, J. P. (2008). Narcissistic men and women think they are so hot—but they are not. *Personality and Individual Differences, 45*(5), 420–424.

Brown, J. D., Halpern, C. T., & L'Engle, K. L. (2005). Mass media as a sexual super peer for early maturing girls. *Journal of Adolescent Health, 36*(5), 420–427.

Brown, R. P., & Zeigler-Hill, V. (2004). Narcissism and the non-equivalence of self-esteem measures: A matter of dominance? *Journal of Research in Personality, 38*(6), 585–592.

Brummelman, E., Thomaes, S., Nelemans, S. A., De Castro, B. O., Overbeek, G., & Bushman, B. J. (2015). Origins of narcissism in children. *Proceedings of the National Academy of Sciences, 112*(12), 3659–3662.

Buffardi, E. L., & Campbell, W. K. (2008). Narcissism and social networking web sites. *Personality and Social Psychology Bulletin, 34*, 1303–1314.

Bushman, B. J., & Baumeister, R. F. (1998). Threatened egotism, narcissism, self-esteem, and direct and displaced aggression: Does self-love or self-hate lead to violence? *Journal of Personality and Social Psychology, 75*(1), 219.

Buss, D. M., & Chiodo, L. M. (1991). Narcissistic acts in everyday life. *Journal of Personality, 59*(2), 179–215.

Campbell, W. K., Brunell, A. B., & Finkel, E. J. (2006). Narcissism, interpersonal self-regulation, and romantic relationships: An agency model approach. In K. D. Vohs & E. J. Finkel (Eds.), *Self and relationships: Connecting intrapersonal and interpersonal processes* (pp. 57–83). New York, NY: Guilford Press.

Campbell, W. K., & Foster, J. D. (2007). The narcissistic self: Background, an extended agency model, and ongoing controversies. In C. Sedikides & S. J. Spencer (Eds.), *The self* (pp. 115–138). New York, NY: Psychology Press.

Campbell, W. K., Reeder, G. D., Sedikides, C., & Elliot, A. J. (2000). Narcissism and comparative self-enhancement strategies. *Journal of Research in Personality, 34*, 329–347.

Carpenter, C. J. (2012). Narcissism on Facebook: Self-promotional and anti-social behavior. *Personality and Individual Differences, 52*(4), 482–486.

CNNIC. (2015). Online behaviors among Chinese children and adolescents in 2014. Retrieved from http://www.cnnic.cn/hlwfzyj/hlwxzbg/qsnbg/201506/P02015060 3434893070975.pdf

Common Sense Media. (2012). *Social media, social life: How teens view their digital lives.* Washington, DC: Author. Retrieved from https://www.commonsensemedia.org/research/social-media-social-life-how-teens-view-their-digital-lives

Correa, T., Hinsley, A. W., & De Zuniga, H. G. (2010). Who interacts on the web? The intersection of users' personality and social media use. *Computers in Human Behavior, 26*(2), 247–253.

Davis, K. (2010). Coming of age online: The developmental underpinnings of girls' blogs. *Journal of Adolescent Research, 25*(1), 145–171.

Dunton, G. F., Liao, Y., Intille, S. S., Spruijt-Metz, D., & Pentz, M. (2011). Investigating children's physical activity and sedentary behavior using ecological momentary assessment with mobile phones. *Obesity, 19*(6), 1205–1212.

Eksi, F. (2012). Examination of narcissistic personality traits' predicting level of internet addiction and cyber bullying through path analysis. *Educational Sciences: Theory and Practice, 12*(3), 1694–1706.

Ellison, N. B., & Boyd, D. (2013). Sociality through social network sites. In W. Dutton (Ed.), *The Oxford handbook of Internet studies* (pp. 151–172). Oxford, UK: Oxford University Press.

Emmons, R. A. (1984). Factor analysis and construct validity of the Narcissistic Personality Inventory. *Journal of Personality Assessment, 48*(3), 291–300.

Espasa, F. P. (2004). Parent–infant psychotherapy, the transition to parenthood and parental narcissism: Implications for treatment. *Journal of Child Psychotherapy, 30*(2), 155–171.

Fox, J., & Rooney, M. C. (2015). The Dark Triad and trait self-objectification as predictors of men's use and self-presentation behaviors on social networking sites. *Personality and Individual Differences, 76,* 161–165.

Golmaryami, F. N., & Barry, C. T. (2009). The associations of self-reported and peer-reported relational aggression with narcissism and self-esteem among adolescents in a residential setting. *Journal of Clinical Child & Adolescent Psychology, 39*(1), 128–133.

Goodboy, A. K., & Martin, M. M. (2015). The personality profile of a cyberbully: Examining the Dark Triad. *Computers in Human Behavior, 49,* 1–4.

Gullone, E., & Moore, S. (2000). Adolescent risk-taking and the five-factor model of personality. *Journal of Adolescence, 23*(4), 393–407.

Harter, S. (2006). The self. In W. Damon & R. M. Lerner (Eds.), *Handbook of child psychology* (pp. 505–570). New York, NY: Wiley.

Hartup, W. W., & Stevens, N. (1997). Friendships and adaptation in the life course. *Psychological Bulletin, 121*(3), 355–370.

Haynie, D. L. (2002). Friendship networks and delinquency: The relative nature of peer delinquency. *Journal of Quantitative Criminology, 18*(2), 99–134.

Hinduja, S., & Patchin, J. W. (2008). Cyberbullying: An exploratory analysis of factors related to offending and victimization. *Deviant Behavior, 29*(2), 129–156.

Hughes, J. N., Cavell, T. A., & Grossman, P. B. (1997). A positive view of self: Risk or protection for aggressive children? *Development and Psychopathology, 9*(1), 75–94.

Jonason, P. K., Lyons, M., Baughman, H. M., & Vernon, P. A. (2014). What a tangled web we weave: The Dark Triad traits and deception. *Personality and Individual Differences, 70,* 117–119.

Kaplan, A. M., & Haenlein, M. (2010). Users of the world, unite! The challenges and opportunities of social media. *Business Horizons, 53*(1), 59–68.

Kauten, R., & Barry, C. T. (2014). Do you think I'm as kind as I do? The relation of adolescent narcissism with self- and peer-perceptions of prosocial and aggressive behavior. *Personality and Individual Differences, 61,* 69–73.

Kernberg, O. F. (1975). A systems approach to priority setting of interventions in groups. *International Journal of Group Psychotherapy, 25*(3), 251–275.

Kernberg, O. F. (1985). *Borderline conditions and pathological narcissism.* New York, NY: Rowman & Littlefield.

Kim, E. J., Namkoong, K., Ku, T., & Kim, S. J. (2008). The relationship between online game addiction and aggression, self-control and narcissistic personality traits. *European Psychiatry, 23*(3), 212–218.

Kohut, H. (1971). *The analysis of the self.* Chicago, IL: University of Chicago Press.

Kohut, H. (2013). *The analysis of the self: A systematic approach to the psychoanalytic treatment of narcissistic personality disorders.* Chicago, IL: University of Chicago Press.

Kuss, D. J., & Griffiths, M. D. (2011). Online social networking and addiction—A review of the psychological literature. *International Journal of Environmental Research and Public Health, 8*(9), 3528–3552.

Lee, P. (2015). Kids in Singapore accessing social media tools "even before P1." Retrieved from http://www.straitstimes.com/singapore/kids-in-singapore-accessing-social-media-tools-even-before-p1

Lenhart, A., Duggan, M., Perrin, A., Stepler, R., Rainie, H., & Parker, K. (2015). Teens, social media & technology overview 2015. Retrieved from http://www.pewinternet.org/2015/04/09/teens-social-media-technology-2015

Leung, L. (2011). Loneliness, social support, and preference for online social interaction: The mediating effects of identity experimentation online among children and adolescents. *Chinese Journal of Communication, 4*(4), 381–399.

Leung, L. (2013). Generational differences in content generation in social media: The roles of the gratifications sought and of narcissism. *Computers in Human Behavior, 29*(3), 997–1006.

Leung, L. (2015). A panel study on the effects of social media use and internet connectedness on academic performance and social support among children and adolescents. *International Journal of Cyber Behavior, Psychology, & Learning, 5*, 1–16.

Litt, D. M., & Stock, M. L. (2011). Adolescent alcohol-related risk cognitions: The roles of social norms and social networking sites. *Psychology of Addictive Behaviors, 25*(4), 708–713.

Livingstone, S. (2008). Taking risky opportunities in youthful content creation: Teenagers' use of social networking sites for intimacy, privacy and self-expression. *New Media & Society, 10*(3), 393–411.

Livingstone, S., Haddon, L., Görzig, A., & Ólafsson, K. (2010). Risks and safety on the internet: The perspective of European children: Full findings and policy implications from the *EU Kids Online* survey of 9–16 year olds and their parents in 25 countries. Retrieved from http://www.lse.ac.uk/media%40lse/research/EUKidsOnline/EU%20Kids%20II%20(2009-11)/EUKidsOnlineIIReports/D4FullFindings.pdf

Livingstone, S., Haddon, L., Vincent, J., Mascheroni, G., & Ólafsson, K. (2014). *Net children go mobile: The UK report.* London: London School of Economics and Political Science.

Livingstone, S., & Helsper, E. J. (2007). Taking risks when communicating on the internet: The role of offline social-psychological factors in young people's vulnerability to online risks. *Information, Communication & Society, 10*(5), 619–644.

Mehdizadeh, S. (2010). Self-presentation 2.0: Narcissism and self-esteem on Facebook. *Cyberpsychology, Behavior, and Social Networking, 13*(4), 357–364.

Meier, E. P., & Gray, J. (2014). Facebook photo activity associated with body image disturbance in adolescent girls. *Cyberpsychology, Behavior, and Social Networking, 17*(4), 199–206.

Millon, T. (1981). *Disorders of personality: DSM-III, axis II*. New York, NY: Wiley.

Millon, T. (1983). *Modern psychopathology: A biosocial approach to maladaptive learning and functioning*. Prospect Heights, IL: Waveland Press.

Mo, R., & Leung, L. (2015). Exploring the roles of narcissism, gratifications of microblog use, and affinity-seeking on social capital. *Asian Journal of Social Psychology, 18*(2), 152–162. doi:10.1111/ajsp.12087

Morf, C. C., & Rhodewalt, F. (2001). Unraveling the paradoxes of narcissism: A dynamic self-regulatory processing model. *Psychological Inquiry, 12*(4), 177–196.

Odacı, H., & Çelik, Ç. B. (2013). Who are problematic internet users? An investigation of the correlations between problematic internet use and shyness, loneliness, narcissism, aggression and self-perception. *Computers in Human Behavior, 29*(6), 2382–2387.

Ong, E. Y., Ang, R. P., Ho, J. C., Lim, J. C., Goh, D. H., Lee, C. S., & Chua, A. Y. (2011). Narcissism, extraversion and adolescents' self-presentation on Facebook. *Personality and Individual Differences, 50*(2), 180–185.

Paulhus, D. L., & Williams, K. M. (2002). The dark triad of personality: Narcissism, Machiavellianism, and psychopathy. *Journal of Research in Personality, 36*(6), 556–563.

Pollara, P., & Zhu, J. (2011). Social networking and education: Using Facebook as an edusocial space. In M. Koehler & P. Mishra (Eds.), *Proceedings of Society for Information Technology & Teacher Education International Conference 2011* (pp. 3330–3338). Chesapeake, VA: Association for the Advancement of Computing in Education (AACE).

Poon, D. C. H., & Leung, L. (2011). Effects of narcissism, leisure boredom and gratification sought on net-generation user-generated content. *International Journal of Cyber Behavior, Psychology & Learning, 1*(3), 1–14.

Raskin, R., & Hall, C. S. (1979). A narcissistic personality inventory. *Psychological Reports, 45*(2), 590.

Raskin, R., & Terry, H. (1988). A principal-components analysis of the Narcissistic Personality Inventory and further evidence of its construct validity. *Journal of Personality and Social Psychology, 54*(5), 890–902.

Reidy, D. E., Zeichner, A., Foster, J. D., & Martinez, M. A. (2008). Effects of narcissistic entitlement and exploitativeness on human physical aggression. *Personality and Individual Differences, 44*(4), 865–875.

Salmivalli, C. (2001). Feeling good about oneself, being bad to others? Remarks on self-esteem, hostility, and aggressive behavior. *Aggression and Violent Behavior, 6*(4), 375–393.

Seah, S. L., & Ang, R. P. (2008). Differential correlates of reactive and proactive aggression in Asian adolescents: Relations to narcissism, anxiety, schizotypal traits, and peer relations. *Aggressive Behavior, 34*(5), 553–562.

Sedikides, C., Rudich, E. A., Gregg, A. P., Kumashiro, M., & Rusbult, C. (2004). Are normal narcissists psychologically healthy? Self-esteem matters. *Journal of Personality and Social Psychology, 87*, 400–416.

Stover, D. (2006). Treating cyberbullying as a school violence issue. *Education Digest: Essential Readings Condensed for Quick Review, 72*(4), 40–42.

Strasburger, V. C., Wilson, B. J., & Jordan, A. B. (2009). *Children, adolescents, and the media*. Thousand Oaks, CA: Sage.

Stucke, T. S., & Sporer, S. L. (2002). When a grandiose self-image is threatened: Narcissism and self-concept clarity as predictors of negative emotions and aggression following ego-threat. *Journal of Personality, 70*(4), 509–532.

Temple, J. R., Paul, J. A., van den Berg, P., Le, V. D., McElhany, A., & Temple, B. W. (2012). Teen sexting and its association with sexual behaviors. *Archives of Pediatrics & Adolescent Medicine, 166*(9), 828–833.

Thomaes, S., Bushman, B. J., de Castro, B. O., Cohen, G. L., & Denissen, J. J. (2009). Reducing narcissistic aggression by buttressing self-esteem: An experimental field study. *Psychological Science, 20*(12), 1536–1542.

Thomaes, S., Stegge, H., Bushman, B. J., Olthof, T., & Denissen, J. (2008). Development and validation of the Childhood Narcissism Scale. *Journal of Personality Assessment, 90*(4), 382–391.

Tiggemann, M., & Miller, J. (2010). The Internet and adolescent girls' weight satisfaction and drive for thinness. *Sex Roles, 63*(1–2), 79–90.

Tiggemann, M., & Slater, A. (2013). NetGirls: The Internet, Facebook, and body image concern in adolescent girls. *International Journal of Eating Disorders, 46*(6), 630–633.

Tiggemann, M., & Slater, A. (2014). NetTweens: The Internet and body image concerns in pre-teenage girls. *The Journal of Early Adolescence, 34*(5), 606–620.

Valkenburg, P. M., Schouten, A. P., & Peter, J. (2005). Adolescents' identity experiments on the Internet. *New Media & Society, 7*(3), 383–402.

Vazire, S., & Gosling, S. D. (2004). e-Perceptions: Personality impressions based on personal websites. *Journal of Personality and Social Psychology, 87*(1), 123–132.

Vazire, S., Naumann, L. P., Rentfrow, P. J., & Gosling, S. D. (2008). Portrait of a narcissist: Manifestations of narcissism in physical appearance. *Journal of Research in Personality, 42*(6), 1439–1447.

Wallace, H. M., & Baumeister, R. F. (2002). The performance of narcissists rises and falls with perceived opportunity for glory. *Journal of Personality and Social Psychology, 82*(5), 819–834.

Washburn, J. J., McMahon, S. D., King, C. A., Reinecke, M. A., & Silver, C. (2004). Narcissistic features in young adolescents: Relations to aggression and internalizing symptoms. *Journal of Youth and Adolescence, 33*(3), 247–260.

Werner, N. E., Bumpus, M. F., & Rock, D. (2010). Involvement in internet aggression during early adolescence. *Journal of Youth and Adolescence, 39*(6), 607–619.

Zimbardo, P. G. (1969). The human choice: Individuation, reason, and order versus deindividuation, impulse, and chaos. *Nebraska Symposium on Motivation, 17*, 237–307.

4

SEXTING AND THE @ GENERATION: IMPLICATIONS, MOTIVATIONS, AND SOLUTIONS

David L. Delmonico, Heather L. Putney, and Elizabeth J. Griffin

The world of technology has provided numerous advantages to upcoming generations; however, it has also added a venue of concern when it comes to the sexual and psychological development of youth. One such concern is sexting behavior. Sexting among adolescents has proved to be a complex and concerning issue for those who are responsible for the welfare of children, including family members, schools, churches, the legal system, and mental health professionals. This chapter explores sexting behavior among youth, including various typologies and strategies for assessment and prevention.

One of the challenges is the lack of a consistent definition in the literature for sexting-related behaviors. Although sexting may occur at any age, including adulthood, for the purposes of this chapter, sexting is defined as youth-produced (under 18 years of age) sexually explicit images/videos, which are transmitted to others who are also younger than 18 years. The images/videos may include nude or partially nude youth (younger than 18 years), and may or may not meet the legal definition of child pornography. These images/videos can be exchanged using a variety of technologies, including social media, text messaging, cell phone apps (e.g., Snapchat, Instagram), webcams, digital cameras, and so forth.

Klettke, Hallford, and Mellor (2014) stated, "It is difficult to accurately estimate the prevalence of sexting behaviors at this time. This is due to the variance in definitions and sampling techniques which results in large differences in estimates across studies . . . " (p. 51). Keeping this caveat in mind, Klettke et al. (2014) conducted a systematic review of 31 studies and estimated that

12% of the youth admitted to sending sexual images/videos to other youth, and 16% reported receiving such images. A number of other studies estimate the prevalence of sexting among youth to be approximately 15% for sending sexting images, and 35% for receiving such images (Fleschler et al., 2013; Kopecký, 2012; Strassberg, McKinnon, Sustaíta, & Rullo, 2013; Temple et al., 2012).

Klettke et al. (2014) also found that: (a) sexting is more prevalent among adults than adolescents; (b) older adolescents are more likely to engage in sexting behavior than younger children; (c) it is more common to receive rather than send sexts; (d) sexting behavior is associated with many behavioral, psychological, and social factors; (e) females are more likely to send images whereas males are more likely to be the receivers of sexts; (f) although not causal, sexting is associated with an increase in sexually risky behaviors such as unprotected sex, drinking, or using alcohol before sexual behavior, adult pornography use, and web-based chatting; and (g) sexting is most likely to occur in the context of a committed relationship.

Rice et al. (2014) examined sexting as it is related to middle school–aged students. Results from the research indicated that youth aged 11 to 13 years who text at least 100 times per day had an increased likelihood to report both receiving and sending text messages with sexual content, and are more likely to report real-life sexual activity with others. Similar results were reported in a study by Houck et al. (2014) who reported that a group of at-risk middle school students (aged 12–13 years) who engaged in any form of sexting behavior were more likely to be engaged in a variety of sexual activities with others in real life. Those students who sent sexualized photos/videos (as opposed to sexualized text messages) were at an even higher risk to engage in sexual behaviors with others in real life.

Goggin and Crawford (2011) suggested that individuals often have different explanations for sexting behavior and his or her motivations for such behavior. The research indicates that some of these motivations include: (a) sexual curiosity, (b) sexual flirtation, (c) foreplay, (d) satisfying a partner's fantasies, and (e) staying romantically connected to a long-distance partner. Research also suggests that there may be other motivations that are not developmentally appropriate and may include revenge against past sexual partners or the sexual exploitation of others (Wolak & Finkelhor, 2011). Albury, Crawford, Byron, and Mathews (2013) reported that other individuals are motivated to engage in sexting behavior because they believe it is humorous or a great way to prank their peers.

The research shows that motivation for engaging in sexting behavior differs for males and females (Englander, 2012). More often than males, females reported feeling an increased pressure to send sexts as the primary motivator for the behavior (Englander, 2012; Henderson, 2011). Although males may feel the pressure to engage in sexting, it appears to be more related to *showing off* to their male peers rather than to please their romantic partners.

Albury et al. (2013) indicated that youth do not always comprehend the full range of the potential consequences associated with sexting behaviors, especially serious legal consequences. Furthermore, Strohmaier, Murphy, and DeMatteo (2014) reported that most youth believed that sexting was a common practice among their peers and had few concerns about the legal and psychological implications.

Media attention has been focused on the self-production/receipt of self-produced sexual images and the consequent risk of prosecution of these cases under the child pornography laws. Between 2008 and 2009, U.S. law enforcement agencies handled approximately 3,477 cases of youth-produced sexual images (Wolak, Finkelhor, & Mitchell, 2012). Based on their findings, the percentage of youth who appear in and/or create sexually explicit photos or videos that meet the legal definition of child pornography is about 1%. Although this number may seem small, 1% of the youth population who use digital media translates into a large number of youth who are engaging in illegal behavior. It is important to remember that a broader definition of sexting would include more youth who were sending or receiving nude/seminude images that would not necessarily meet the legal definition of child pornography.

The majority of youth who produce and/or distribute sexting images are not arrested for their behavior; however, there are a number of exceptions. W. A. Walsh, Wolak, and Finkelhor (2013) interviewed 236 prosecutors who were asked about the percentage of sexting cases among minors that resulted in legal charges; 59% said that "all or nearly all" of their sexting cases did not result in criminal charges; however, 21% said that "most or all" of their sexting cases resulted in criminal charges. When criminal charges were filed, the prosecutors indicated that it was likely because of the circumstances related to malicious intent, harassment, distribution of illegal images, significant age differences, and violent/explicit images. Zhang (2010) argues that our attempts to protect youth through prosecution have failed miserably and relegated them to far worse, including lifetime consequences for what may be a developmentally normal exploration of sexuality. It is important that the clinicians working with sexting behaviors should be familiar with their state's definition and mandated reporting requirements. In cases where sexting behavior is involved, the mandated reporting laws may require a report to be filed with the relevant agency.

The studies that examined the psychological impact of sexting-related behaviors had mixed results. For example, two studies found that there was no difference in the measures of self-esteem between groups of youth who sexted versus those who did not (Gordon-Messer, Bauermeister, Grodzinski, & Zimmerman, 2013; Hudson, 2011, as cited in Klettke et al., 2014). Furthermore, Englander (2012) found that youth who sexted were less prone to depression than their non sexting counterparts; however, he also reported that when the youth felt pressured to engage in sexting behaviors by a peer or partner, they had higher levels of anxiety, and reported higher incidences of dating violence than those who did not engage in sexting. Dake, Price, Maziarz, and Ward (2012) found that youth who had engaged in sexting behaviors were more likely to experience hopelessness and/or suicidal ideation or attempts than those who did not engage in sexting behavior. Finally, Mitchell, Finkelhor, Jones, and Wolak (2012) found that 21% of the youth who sent sexting messages and 25% of those who received sexting messages reported feeling "extremely emotionally upset, embarrassed, or afraid" among other negative emotions.

Given the mixed results of the research, it is understandable that there is a divide among professionals as to how sexting behavior should be addressed. There are individuals who believe that sexting among youth is a trend that causes significant and long-term developmental, psychological, and sexual issues, while others take a "kids will be kids" attitude and believe that sexting is an extension of many juvenile games such as Spin the Bottle or Truth or Dare. Although individuals in this group may admit that sexting is not necessarily a good decision on the part of youth, they believe it is just another way for youth to explore relationships and sexuality. This group is often dismissive of the legal consequences and support laws that would allow sexting behaviors among age-appropriate peers, while the first group is often influenced by media accounts and becomes paranoid about the possibility of dire consequences. Neither extreme is a useful way of conceptualizing sexting, as a balanced and thoughtful approach is needed.

The truth is both groups are right. Examining the motive for a youth's sexting behavior is a critical step in determining the appropriateness of the behavior as well as the consequences of such behavior. The literature on sexting provides a typology that is helpful in differentiating youth who are sexually exploitive versus those who are developmentally curious.

SEXTING TYPOLOGIES

All youth who engage in sexting behaviors are not the same. Wolak and Finkelhor (2011) developed a typology for understanding the differences among youth who engage in sexting behavior. Their review of more than 550 legal cases involving "youth-produced sexual images" obtained from a national survey of law enforcement agencies resulted in two main categories, "aggravated" versus "experimental."

Aggravated cases involved criminal or abusive components including:

1. Adult involvement through solicitation/receipt of sexted images from minors

2. Criminal or abusive behavior among minors such as sexual abuse, extortion, deception, or threats

When criminal or abusive sexting behaviors occur among youth, there are two possible explanations for such behavior. First, the individual sharing the images intends to cause significant harm to another individual. This intent to harm may range from a tumultuous breakup of an interpersonal relationship (revenge), blackmailing, threatening, or deceiving others, and/or intentional sexual abuse/exploitation by juvenile offenders. The second explanation may be related to reckless misuse of sexting images, which involves photographs/videos being taken or sent without the knowledge or willingness (consent) of the youth. Reckless misuse cases differ from malicious intent and frequently involve poor judgment and impulsive behaviors without real intent to harm. An example of reckless misuse is when a youth has a pool party and someone films the people at the party swimming in the nude, and then shares it with others who were not at the party. Albury and Crawford (2012) found that consent was the defining feature that made the difference between the youth's positive or negative experiences of sexting. The negative experiences were primarily characterized by an unauthorized or unintended distribution of images.

Intuitively, people worry that sexting behavior, especially *aggravated sexting*, sets the stage for a future sexual offense; however, few methodologically strong studies regarding adolescent sexual offending are available. The research that is available is limited and is somewhat dated. In fact, no one has directly looked at the impact of technology on sexual offending behaviors in youth. One study linked texting about antisocial behaviors to a predicted increase in aggressive behavior and rule breaking (Ehrenreich, Underwood, & Ackerman, 2014) and suggested that peers may reinforce or instruct such behaviors.

According to Wolak and Finkelhor (2011), experimental sexting may have several motivations. Romantic purposes were by far the most common context for sexting among youth. Most youth indicated that they were either in a committed relationship with the person they sexted with or trusted that individual with their photos/videos. In addition to sexting when already in a romantic relationship, youth also use sexting behaviors to flirt or express general sexual interest in potential romantic partners. Youth may take a sexualized photo/video of themselves and text it to someone they are interested in sexually to see whether the feelings are mutual. This is slightly riskier because the person receiving the sext may not have desired it, or may be more likely to share the image with unintended recipients. Finally, youth may engage in sexting behaviors in an attempt to show off to other youth, or while engaging in games, pranks, or jokes with other youth. Youth may also take images of themselves without the initial intent to share those images, or younger children may exchange their images as a way to appear "older and cool" among their peers. Experimental sexting appears to be part of a youth's typical development, including his or her sexual curiosity, creating sexual interest, finding romantic partners, and/or getting attention from other youth.

PSYCHOLOGY OF THE INTERNET

Wallace (1999) introduced the concept "psychology of the Internet," and suggested that the Internet creates a unique environment, which alters the way people think, feel, and behave. Suler (2004) researched the unique psychological characteristics of the Internet among typically developing individuals and found that the online environment was a frequent catalyst for online risk taking and boundary crossing behaviors. Suler (2004) called this phenomenon the "online disinhibition effect." Online disinhibition provides a context for understanding why some youth push boundaries and take risks with their sexting behavior, even when they know that such behavior may not be appropriate. The main tenets of Suler's (2004) online disinhibition theory include:

- *You Don't Know Me* and *You Can't See Me* are concepts that combine together to give individuals the sense that they are anonymous and in a digital environment where there are no boundaries or rules associated with their online behavior. This phenomenon has existed in social psychology since Zimbardo (1969) discussed the concept of *deindividuation*. It is not surprising that the concepts of anonymity and deindividuation play a role in youth sexting behavior.

- *See You Later*—The Internet allows users to easily *escape* situations online, thereby, making it more likely to engage in risk-taking behaviors. When an online user engages in questionable or risky behavior such as sexting, in the moment after the behavior there does not appear to be any consequences related to it. Although consequences may eventually result, they are most effective at deterring future behavior when they come immediately after the negative behavior. Sexting behavior often has a delayed consequence—it may take days, weeks, or months, but this ability to avoid consequences is one aspect of the digital world that allows the sexting to continue.

- *It's All in My Head* and *It's Just a Game* give the illusion that the online world only operates in fantasy, and that no one is harmed by our online ventures. The line between fantasy and reality can be easily blurred as there are many online activities that are fantasy based. This idea that the digital world is a fantasy-based game also leads many to the conclusion that the rules of the real world do not apply to the online world. The belief that there are no rules or consequences is a dangerous combination for potentially problematic online behaviors, including sexting behaviors.

- *We're Equals* and *We're All Friends* create the illusion that everyone online is equal and friends with one another; therefore, the rules that dictate appropriate interactions between different groups (e.g., adults and children) in the real world can be ignored online. Hierarchies that are built into society to establish roles and boundaries can be easily dismissed. As a result, sexting behavior between adults and adolescents may not feel as inappropriate as real-life sexual interactions.

The online disinhibition effect combines with the previously mentioned motivations, and creates an environment that facilitates youth sexting behavior. Both the experimental and the aggravated groups of youth who engage in sexting behavior can be significantly influenced by the online disinhibition effect.

ASSESSMENT

In order to determine the typologies and influence of the psychology of the Internet, a comprehensive assessment should be conducted. The main goals of assessing youth who engage in sexting behavior are to determine whether they best fit into the "aggravated" or "experimental" group, and to identify any underlying mental health issues that should be addressed. In order to conduct a valid and reliable clinical opinion, all youth who are referred for sexting behavior should be thoroughly interviewed and given objective measures of their mental health and personality. Although it may seem excessive to do this for each sexting case, it is far too easy to develop impressions and judgments based on our biases and assumptions about a youth and/or their history without having solid data to support such impressions and judgments. The next two sections discuss the two aspects of a comprehensive assessment: (a) the psychosocial–sexual assessment and (b) psychological testing and standardized questionnaires.

Psychosocial–Sexual Assessment

Conducting a complete psychosocial–sexual assessment is the first step in the process. The common components of a psychosocial–sexual assessment include both historical and current information about an individual's:

- Home and family life
- Academic/work performance and behavior
- Sexual knowledge and behaviors
- Addictive/compulsive behaviors (e.g., substances, gaming, pornography)
- Social skills and friendships
- Mental health concerns
- Abusive or traumatic events

- Suicidal thoughts, plans, or attempts
- Digital world interactions (e.g., gaming, social media, sexuality)
- Extracurricular activities (e.g., sports, band, church)

Klein, Goldenring, and Adelman (2014) developed a standardized questionnaire to assist in conducting a psychosocial–sexual interview with adolescents, named HEEADSSS 3.0. This questionnaire can be extremely useful for gathering standardized information across clients, including the bullet points listed earlier. It is equally important to gather collateral information from those individuals who have knowledge about the youth's current and past thoughts, feelings, and behaviors. Interviews may include parents/guardians, close family members, past counselors, teachers/school counselors, and so forth. This information can be useful in validating the self-report data from the youth.

Psychological Testing and Standardized Questionnaires

Psychological testing and standardized questionnaires are important sources of objective data, which help to increase the validity and reliability of clinical impressions formed during the psychosocial–sexual interview. Some of the common tests and questionnaires that may be helpful in sexting cases are discussed in the following sections. Clinicians should be reminded that many psychological tests require specialized training and competency in interpretation.

Internet Sex Screening Test—Adolescent

The Internet Sex Screening Test–Adolescent (ISST-A) was developed by two of this chapter's authors (Delmonico and Griffin), and can be used to conduct a quick-screen of the digital media use of adolescents. While the ISST-A has no psychometric data associated with it, the items can be used as a follow-up to the clinical interview. Inherent in the ISST-A are questions that would help determine if an adolescent may have addictive or compulsive behaviors related to their online behavior, including sexting behavior (e.g., Have you made efforts to stop your digital behavior? Do you feel your digital behavior is out of control? Have you suffered consequences as a result of your behavior?). A copy of the ISST-A is provided in Figure 4.1.

Minnesota Multiphasic Personality Inventory—Adolescent

Minnesota Multiphasic Personality Inventory–Adolescent (MMPI-A; Williams, Butcher, Ben-Porath, & Graham, 1992) was published in 1992 and was the first of the MMPI family to assess adolescents between the ages of 14 and 18 years. The MMPI-A is a self-report instrument used to assess for a wide range of clinical conditions, including mood disorders, personality

---

FIGURE 4.1 Internet Sex Screening Test–Adolescent

Directions: Read each statement carefully. If the statement is mostly TRUE, place a check mark on the blank next to the item number. If the statement is mostly FALSE, skip the item and place nothing next to the item number.

____ 1. I have some sexual sites in my Favorites/Bookmarks.

____ 2. I spend more than 5 hr/wk using my digital devices/computer for sexual purposes.

____ 3. I have searched online for pornography or other sexual material (e.g., apps, games).

____ 4. Online sex has sometimes interfered with certain aspects of my life.

____ 5. I have participated in sexually related texts, chats, videochats, and so forth.

____ 6. I have a sexualized username or nickname that I use online.

____ 7. I have masturbated while using my digital devices/computer.

____ 8. I have accessed online sexual material in places other than my own house.

____ 9. No one knows I use my digital devices/computer for sexual purposes.

___ 10. I have tried to hide my online sexual behavior so that others cannot see it.

___ 11. I have accessed online sexual material on my digital device/computer after midnight.

___ 12. I experiment with different aspects of sexuality (e.g., bondage, homosexuality, cross-dressing) while online.

___ 13. I have made promises to myself to stop using my digital devices/computer for sexual purposes.

___ 14. I sometimes use online sex as a reward for accomplishing something (e.g., finishing a project, stressful day).

___ 15. When I am unable to access sexual material online, I feel anxious, angry, or disappointed.

___ 16. I have increased the risks I take online (give out name and phone number, meet people offline).

___ 17. I have punished myself when I use technology for sexual purposes (e.g., time-out from cell phone, stop using Xbox).

___ 18. I have met someone face to face whom I met online for romantic/sexual purposes.

___ 19. I have engaged in sexting behavior.

___ 20. I have seen sexual pictures of other kids or teenagers online.

___ 21. I believe I am an online sex addict.

___ 22. I have posted/viewed sexual photos or information on social media.

___ 23. I have used online sexual hookup apps to find someone who may want to have sex with me.

___ 24. I have stored sexualized photos on my hard drive or on the cloud somewhere.

___ 25. I have posted/viewed sexualized videos online.

---

traits/disorders, psychopathic deviance (antisocial), drug/alcohol, immaturity, and other mental disorders. This instrument has been standardized on typical developing youth, as well as those with mental health concerns. The MMPI-A is a general instrument that should be administered to all youth referred for their sexting behavior to help determine whether the motivation was more "aggravated" or "experimental."

Desistence for Adolescents Who Sexually Harm

The Desistence for Adolescents who Sexually Harm (DASH-13) is a checklist of 13 factors that may be related to the desistence (decrease) of adolescent sexual offending (Worling, 2013). Seven factors are related to future sexual health, while six factors are related to the general prosocial functioning. Although many sexting cases should not be considered sexual offense behavior, the DASH-13 provides valuable information for those who have crossed sexual boundaries with others and can help identify protective factors that could help the prevention of such boundary crossings in the future. For that reason, the DASH-13 is a checklist that would be appropriate for both the aggravated and experimental sexting scenarios.

Jesness Inventory—Revised

The Jesness Inventory–Revised (JI-R) is a comprehensive, self-report measure of personality and psychopathology that is applicable to children and adolescents with more severe behavioral problems (Jesness, 2003). The JI-R is particularly useful in discriminating between social maladjustment of a typical youth, and more severe emotional disturbances. Given that the JI-R is for better understanding the more severe behavioral problems, it may not be appropriate to give to all youth who have engaged in sexting behavior. It can be useful in cases where clinicians are still unsure whether the sexting was experimental or aggravated, or to determine if there are more serious concerns behind the sexting behavior. While trying to determine whether or not to administer the JI-R, it is important to review the results of other psychological testing administered to the youth during the assessment process.

Other Considerations

There is a lack of research related to the underlying psychological issues that may be related to sexting behavior. A review of the adult literature related to problematic online sexual behavior indicates that several common comorbid mental health issues are often present, including: (a) mood disorders, (b) addictive disorders, (c) attentional disorders, (d) autism spectrum disorder (ASD), and (e) sexual abuse victimization. Other issues may include intellectual and developmental disabilities. Not all youth who engage in sexting behavior have an underlying mental health issue; however, screening for the possibility that an underlying issue exists is an important part of the assessment process. There is not enough space in this chapter to address screening for each of these issues, but clinicians should practice within their competence or employ someone to screen for such issues in sexting-related cases.

At the start of the assessment section, it was stated that the goals of assessment in sexting cases are to determine whether the individual engages in aggravated or experimental sexting behavior, and/or whether there are any underlying mental health issues related to the sexting. This is best accomplished by reviewing the assessment data for patterns of behavior that may be indicative of deeper issues (e.g., truancy, antiauthority attitudes, drug/alcohol issues, impulsivity, Internet or sexual addictions). Much of the assessment process is to rule out the more significant mental health or behavioral issues that may be related to sexting behavior. A comprehensive assessment should assist clinicians in developing strategies for primary, secondary, and tertiary prevention.

PREVENTION

There are three basic levels to all forms of prevention: (a) primary, (b) secondary, and (c) tertiary. Primary prevention provides basic and general education about a topic to everyone who may be affected. Secondary prevention is for individuals who have not yet engaged in the target behavior (e.g., sexting), but have certain underlying issues that place them at high risk for engaging in the behavior. Secondary prevention builds on the information provided during primary prevention, but works to address those underlying issues placing the individual at risk of the target behavior. Tertiary prevention focuses on individuals who are currently engaging in or have consequences as a result of the target behavior. Tertiary prevention works to both stop the behavior and prevent future occurrences of it. Tertiary prevention is essentially a psychological treatment as it typically involves a myriad of affective and behavioral issues.

Primary Prevention

Primary prevention provides a baseline of educational information and should be the foundation for secondary and tertiary prevention strategies. Prevention strategies that include youth in the dialogue and respect their current development level work best. Primary prevention should provide youth with information about sexting behavior and its consequences that assist them in making appropriate decisions. Sexting, and other uncomfortable topics, are often avoided in the settings that most often deliver the primary prevention programs (e.g., schools, churches); however, in order to assist youth with these issues it is critical that organizations develop a more tolerant and open attitude in discussing such topics. One way to discuss sexting behavior is to incorporate the topic into other related issues. Primary prevention programs that could incorporate sexting include digital health/citizenship, Internet safety, antibullying, and other sex education–related topics.

The following paragraphs describe the topic areas that should be addressed as part of a primary prevention program on sexting behavior.

Motivation for Sexting

Often youth engage in negative online behaviors without considering their motivation for such behaviors. It is important to help them understand that the motivation behind a negative behavior is a first step in preventing it from occurring. For example, asking youth about why an individual might engage in sexting behavior can not only uncover possible motivations (e.g., sexual interest, seeking affirmation, pressure from others, revenge against an ex-boy/girlfriend, or a joke/prank), but also assist them in developing alternative behaviors that may also satisfy the motivation. Engaging youth in dialogue regarding their decision-making process and teaching them to develop alternatives to negative behaviors are more successful than simply telling them what to do.

Psychology of the Internet

Another aspect of primary prevention is educating youth about how the psychology of the Internet influences their online and offline behaviors. Educating youth about the online disinhibition effect can assist them in understanding how they may be predisposed to engaging in online behaviors that they may have never imagined agreeing to in the offline world (e.g., sexting behavior). Once youth can identify how the psychology of the Internet influences them, they can then begin to develop strategies for preventing it from leading them into high-risk/high-consequence behavior.

Psychological and Long-Term Consequences

Youth have the most difficulty in recognizing the psychological and long-term consequences of their sexting behavior (Albury et al., 2013). Even when they are consensually participating in sexting behavior, their naiveté often prevents them from anticipating the possible psychological long-term consequences. Research has demonstrated that the brain is not fully developed until around 25 years of age, and as a result, youth often have difficulty in anticipating the potential psychological impact and consequences of their behavior (D. Walsh, 2014). Primary prevention strategies should focus on filling in the gaps for youth about the psychological and long-term consequences, which they may not be able to fully anticipate.

These long-term consequences may include an unintended audience viewing the images (e.g., strangers, parents, employers, colleges), the inability to anticipate feelings years into the future (e.g., when married, when they have children), the permanence of the images, and the possible regret that they cannot retrieve the sexting images. Some of the most significant long-term consequences include potential legal ramifications of sexting behavior. Primary prevention strategies should educate youth about possible legal consequences in order for them to make informed choices about their sexting behavior.

Although there is no research that supports that sexting behavior is associated with long-term psychological consequences, youth may feel anxious, embarrassed, or depressed about their sexting behavior, especially if they feel pressured to send sexting images/videos. Other situations may also lead to short-term psychological reactions, including sext images/videos taken without the consent of one of the partners (e.g., locker-room shower, unknown recording of sexual behavior), or when these images are shared among peers without the person's explicit permission. Helping youth take the perspective of others and realize the impact that sexting may have on others (empathy) is an important part of a primary prevention program.

Sexuality and Relationship Education

Sexting behavior, especially among the experimental group, may be an artifact of a youth's naive attempt in negotiating an intimate and romantic relationship with others. One of the main developmental goals of an adolescent is learning how to negotiate romantic and sexual relationships. Broader conversations about sexuality and relationships are an important aspect of primary prevention, because the youth may not comprehend why sexting behavior may be viewed as inappropriate by society. As youth develop a better understanding of healthy courtship in physical/sexual relationships, they also learn how and why sexting images may not be the best foundation on which to build relationships with others.

Using existing resources, such as the ones found at www.tes.com, a quick search for "sexting" provides a lesson plan with multiple activities for age-appropriate youth. Lessons include topics such as respect in relationships, boundaries, privacy, exploitation in partnerships, and so forth. The lesson plan also specifies the learning style matched to the activities.

Activities

When working with youth, it is important to remember that engaging them in the prevention and treatment process requires creative strategies. Creative strategies often incorporate activities, movement, movies, multimedia, books, and so forth. In using these creative strategies, not only are youth more likely to retain the information, the activities can also be useful to address various learning styles. The following paragraphs provide some examples of activities that could be used to assist youth in thinking about primary prevention.

Psychology of the Internet Activity

Ask for a single volunteer from a large group. Divide the large group into four smaller groups. Each small group represents one aspect of the online disinhibition effect: (a) anonymity, (b) escape consequences, (c) it is just a fantasy world, and (d) we are equals/we are friends. Instruct the single volunteer to act as though he or she is thinking about engaging in sexting behavior and that each small group tries to convince him or her to do it. His or her job is to resist the temptation by telling the small groups why their arguments are not convincing. For example, the *anonymity* group may say, "No one will know if you just take a picture of your penis and not your face." The single volunteer might respond, "People may still figure it out through my screen name or IP address." The purpose of this activity is to help youth understand how difficult it is to resist the influence of the psychology of the Internet. *Individual therapy adaptation*: The therapist could play the role of the various aspects of the online disinhibition effect and have the youth respond.

Consequences Activity

Print an image on an 8.5 × 11 inch piece of paper. The image can be of anything that would be easily recognized by youth (e.g., hot air balloon, tree, dog). Ask for a youth volunteer to come forward and show him or her the image. Fold the paper in half and hand it to the youth. Instruct him or her to give the paper to one person in the room without letting anyone else see the image. The volunteer then picks another youth from across the room. The person holding the paper must pass it from one side of the room to the other while remaining seated. Instruct everyone who passes it to keep the paper folded and NOT to look at the image. Repeat the passing of the paper once or twice. At the end of the activity, ask the large group to raise their hand if they know what is printed on the paper. Most, if not all, in the room likely know what is printed on the paper. Now process with the group the difficulty in keeping messages private when using technology, and the way they might feel if this was a sexted image.

Secondary Prevention (At-Risk Youth)

Secondary prevention should include and build on all of the educational elements of primary prevention. There is no research that has identified specific characteristics of youth that may make them more susceptible to engaging in sexting behavior. Based on the adult literature and clinical intuition, it could be hypothesized that the underlying comorbid psychological issues would increase the vulnerability of youth for engaging in sexting behavior. For this reason, a comprehensive assessment of youth who are referred for other issues is critical, especially youth who have features of mood disorders, addictive disorders (substance and behavioral), attentional disorders, ASD, and past sexual abuse victimization. Additionally, research even reports an association between youth who engage in offline sexual behavior and sexting behavior. This relationship is not causal and therefore it is not possible to know which began first—offline sexual behavior or sexting.

Given the potential consequences of sexting behavior, including the legal ramifications, it is recommended that the topic of sexting behavior should be addressed with all youth referred for psychological counseling. Even if the youth do not present a high-risk for engaging in sexting behavior, the topics mentioned in the primary prevention section are applicable and appropriate. Research indicates that primary prevention alone appears to decrease the frequency of sexting behaviors among minors who are at the greatest risk (Dir, Cyders, & Coskunpinar, 2013).

Tertiary Prevention (Treatment)

To date, there are no empirically supported tertiary intervention/treatment strategies. It is important to remember that many sexting cases involve the experimental group and may not be indicative of more problematic behaviors. Using the primary prevention strategies mentioned earlier it is likely enough to assist the experimental group with addressing their sexting behavior.

For the limited number of cases in the aggravated group, it may be appropriate to review the models of treatment for juvenile sex offenders, as the issues of boundaries, empathy toward others, and the need for accountability (including technology use) are concerns for this group. It is also important to remember that the aggravated group may have the most significant underlying mental health issues, and these issues need to be addressed as part of the comprehensive tertiary prevention/intervention process. The primary prevention strategies mentioned earlier would also be useful in building a solid foundation of knowledge and skills related to technology use and sexting behavior. Although legal consequences should be a last resort, it is important that youth who engage in aggravated sexting behavior should receive consequences commensurate with their behavior. This may include developmentally appropriate legal consequences if the behavior involved the victimization of others.

CONCLUSION

Sexting behavior among youth includes various typologies that require individualized strategies for assessment and prevention. Through a review of the current literature on sexting behavior, and anecdotal clinical experiences, the following conclusions and implications can be made.

The definition of sexting behavior varies widely in the literature and by the individual. Clinicians should be aware of these definitions when reading the literature and/or discussing sexting behavior with a client. The professional literature indicates that there are many motivations as to why youth engage in sexting behavior, many of which are developmentally appropriate. Assessing the motivation of a youth who sexts is an important clinical task to develop appropriate primary, secondary, and/or tertiary prevention strategies. Legal consequences for sexting behavior vary by jurisdiction; therefore, it is important for clinicians to understand the mandated reporting laws related to sexting behavior, and the potential legal consequences for youth who engage in sexting behavior.

Although the percentage of youth who engage in sexting behaviors is somewhat small, it remains an important and relevant area for research and prevention. An estimated 1% of the youth who engage in sexting behavior send or receive images/videos that would qualify as illegal child pornography. Clinicians should not assume that sexting images are illegal; however, the risk and impact of illegal images should be discussed among all youth. There is no research that indicates that sexting behavior leads to long-term psychological consequences. Given the lack of research, the best approach in working with youth involved in sexting cases is to follow their lead and pay close attention to signs and symptoms that may be indicators of potential psychological concerns.

Youth who engage in sexting behavior can be divided into two main groups: experimental or aggravated. Clinicians should use the assessment tools mentioned herein to assist in determining the typology of the youth involved in sexting behavior. This determination is critical because prevention/intervention for these two groups vary greatly. A comprehensive assessment is critical to determine the typology of sexting behavior, as well as to determine whether there are underlying psychological issues that need to be addressed.

Primary prevention strategies establish an important foundation for all youth, including those who have not yet engaged in sexting behavior, those who are at risk of sexting, and those who have already engaged in it. The four main areas of primary prevention suggested in this chapter include: (a) motivation for sexting, (b) psychology of the Internet, (c) psychological and long-term consequences, and (d) sexuality and relationship education.

The issue of sexting behavior among youth is complicated and only promises to become more complicated as technology advances. While some sexting behavior may be experimental and developmentally appropriate, other forms can be exploitive and cross significant boundaries. Clinicians should work with all youth to provide accurate and critical information about it. In addition, when indicated, creative and engaging assessment and intervention strategies should be employed. Clinicians should neither overreact nor underreact to youth sexting cases. Creating a trusting environment where youth can honestly discuss their thoughts, feelings, and behaviors related to sexting is the essential foundation for prevention at all levels.

REFERENCES

Albury, K., & Crawford, K. (2012). Sexting, consent and young people's ethics: Beyond Megan's Story. *Continuum, 26*(3), 463–473.

Albury, K., Crawford, K., Byron, P., & Mathews, B. (2013). Young people and sexting in Australia: Ethics, representation, and the law. ARC Centre for Creative Industries and Innovation/ Journalism and Media Research Centre, University of New South Wales, Australia. Retrieved from http://www.cci.edu.au/sites/default/files/Young_People_ And_Sexting_Final.pdf

Dake, J. A., Price, J. H., Maziarz, L., & Ward, B. (2012). Prevalence and correlates of sexting behavior in adolescents. *American Journal of Sexuality Education, 7*, 1–15. doi:10.1080/ 15546128.2012.650959

Dir, A. L., Cyders, M. A., & Coskunpinar, A. (2013). From the bar to the bed via mobile phone: A first test of the role of problematic alcohol use, sexting, and impulsivity-related traits in sexual hookups. *Computers in Human Behavior, 29*(4), 1664–1670.

Ehrenreich, S. E., Underwood, M. K., & Ackerman, R. (2014). Adolescents' text message communication and growth in antisocial behavior across the first year of high school. *Journal of Abnormal Child Psychology, 42*, 251–264. doi:10.1007/s10802-013-9783-3

Englander, E. (2012). Low risk associated with most teenage sexting: A study of 617 18-year-olds. Retrieved from http://vc.bridgew.edu/marc_reports/6

Fleschler, P. M., Markham, C. M., Addy, R. C., Shegog, R., Thiel, M., & Tortolero, S. R. (2013). Prevalence and patterns of sexting among ethnic minority urban high school students. *Cyberpsychology, Behavior, and Social Networking, 16*(6), 454–459.

Goggin, G., & Crawford, K. (2011). Generation disconnections: Youth culture and mobile communication. In R. Ling & S. W. Campbell (Eds.), *Mobile communication: Bringing us together and tearing us apart*. New Brunswick, NJ: Transaction.

Gordon-Messer, D., Bauermeister, J. A., Grodzinski, A., & Zimmerman, M. (2013). Sexting among young adults. *Journal of Adolescent Health, 52*(3), 301–306.

Henderson, L. (2011). Sexting and sexual relationships among teens and young adults. *McNair Scholars Research Journal, 7*(1), 9.

Houck, C. D., Barker, D., Rizzo, C., Hancock, E., Norton, A., & Brown, L. K. (2014). Sexting and sexual behavior in at-risk adolescents. *Pediatrics, 133*(2), e276–e282.

Jesness, C. F. (2003). *Jesness Inventory–Revised*. North Tonawanda, NY: Multi-Health Systems.

Klein, D. A., Goldenring, J. M., & Adelman, W. P. (2014). HEEADSSS 3.0: The psychosocial interview for adolescents updated for a new century fueled by media. *Contemporary Pediatrics*. Retrieved from http://contemporarypediatrics.modern medicine.com/contemporary-pediatrics/content/tags/adolescent-medicine/ heeadsss-30-psychosocial-interview-adolesce?page=full

Klettke, B., Hallford, D. J., & Mellor, D. J. (2014). Sexting prevalence and correlates: A systematic literature review. *Clinical Psychology Review, 34*(1), 44–53.

Kopeckỳ, K. (2012). Sexting among Czech preadolescents and adolescents. *The New Educational Review, 28*(2), 39–48.

Mitchell, K. J., Finkelhor, D., Jones, L. M., & Wolak, J. (2012). Prevalence and characteristics of youth sexting: A national study. *Pediatrics, 129*(1), 13–20.

Rice, E., Gibbs, J., Winetrobe, H., Rhoades, H., Plant, A., Montoya, J., & Kordic, T. (2014). Sexting and sexual behavior among middle school students. *Pediatrics, 134*(1), e21–e28. doi:10.1542/peds.2013–2991

Strassberg, D. S., McKinnon, R. K., Sustaíta, M. A., & Rullo, J. (2013). Sexting by high school students: An exploratory and descriptive study. *Archives of Sexual Behavior, 42*(1), 15–21.

Strohmaier, H., Murphy, M., & DeMatteo, D. (2014). Youth sexting: Prevalence rates, driving motivations, and the deterrent effect of legal consequences. *Sexuality Research and Social Policy, 11*(3), 245–255.

Suler, J. (2004). The online disinhibition effect. *Cyberpsychology & Behavior, 7*(3), 321–326.

Temple, J. R., Paul, J. A., van den Berg, P., Le, V. D., McElhany, A., & Temple, B. W. (2012). Teen sexting and its association with sexual behaviors. *Archives of Pediatrics & Adolescent Medicine, 166*(9), 828–833.

Wallace, P. (1999). *The psychology of the internet.* Cambridge, UK: Cambridge University Press.

Walsh, D. (2014). *Why do they act that way?—Revised and updated: A survival guide to the adolescent brain for you and your teen.* New York, NY: Simon & Schuster.

Walsh, W. A., Wolak, J., & Finkelhor, D. (2013). *Sexting: When are state prosecutors deciding to prosecute? The Third National Juvenile Online Victimization Study (NJOV-3).* Durham: University of New Hampshire, Crimes Against Children Research Center.

Williams, C. L., Butcher, J. N., Ben-Porath, Y. S., & Graham, J. R. (1992). MMPI-A content scales: Assessing psychopathology in adolescents. Retrieved from http://psycnet.apa.org/psycinfo/1992-98640-000

Wolak, J., & Finkelhor, D. (2011). *Sexting: A typology.* Durham: University of New Hampshire, Crimes Against Children Research Center.

Wolak, J., Finkelhor, D., & Mitchell, K. J. (2012). How often are teens arrested for sexting? Data from a national sample of police cases. *Pediatrics, 129*(1), 4–12.

Worling, J. R. (2013). DASH-13: Desistence for adolescents who sexually harm. Retrieved from https://www.ncjrs.gov/App/Publications/abstract.aspx?ID=266954

Zhang, X. (2010). Charging children with child pornography—Using the legal system to handle the problem of "sexting." *Computer Law & Security Review, 26*(3), 251–259.

Zimbardo, P. G. (1969). The human choice: Individuation, reason, and order versus deindividuation, impulse, and chaos. *Nebraska Symposium on Motivation, 17*, 237–307.

5 | INTERNET AND GAMING ADDICTION IN YOUTH ON THE AUTISM SPECTRUM: A PARTICULARLY VULNERABLE POPULATION

Debra Moore

Recent research has found that youth on the autism spectrum are especially prone to developing problematic Internet gaming behaviors (Finkenauer, Pollmann, Begeer, & Kerkhof, 2012; Mazurek & Engelhardt, 2013; Romano, Osborne, Truzoli, & Reed, 2013). Although this is not surprising considering the biological, emotional, and social characteristics of this population, the problem is not yet widely recognized by parents, educators, or clinicians. As the number of affected youth rise, it is vital that awareness grows and therapeutic interventions begin to include the specific needs of this group. This chapter reviews the key diagnostic markers of autism, explains how they relate to an increased vulnerability to Internet gaming disorder (IGD), introduces ways to proactively decrease this susceptibility, and proposes specific modifications to current treatment protocols.

DESCRIPTION OF THE PROBLEM

The number of youth diagnosed with autism spectrum disorder (ASD) has risen dramatically in the past decade. The Centers for Disease Control and Prevention (CDC) now estimates that one out of every 68 children meets the diagnostic criteria (CDC, 2014). This is 120% higher than the estimate of 15 years ago. About 50,000 youth with autism exit high school each year, and about a half million will enter adulthood over the next decade (Roux, Shattuck, Rast, Rava, & Anderson, 2015). Both parents and professionals are belatedly realizing that many autistic children, teens, and young adults are so glued to their computer screens that they are not successfully transitioning to their next developmental stage (Cash & McDaneil, 2008). Children and teens with ASD are involved in screen-based activities more often than any other leisure activity on both weekdays and weekends (Orsmond & Kuo, 2011). Although some youth on the autism spectrum become compulsive about researching their special interests, or replaying their favorite videos or shows, the larger problem is an addiction to online video games. For males on the autism spectrum, the most popular genre of games is massive multiplayer online role-playing games (MMORPGs). Females tend to prefer games involving animals or puzzles.

Parents of children and teens with autism report more problematic electronics use than parents of nonautistic youth. These parents also note that their children started using the Internet, electronic devices in general, and video games in particular at an earlier age than parents of neurotypical (NT) children report. The only online arena where youth with autism became involved at a later age than their peers was social media (MacMullin, Lanky, & Weiss, 2015).

One study examined 169 boys aged 8 to 18 years who had a diagnosis of autism. It found that compulsive gaming was associated with both attention problems and oppositional behaviors, with the greatest levels of defiant behavior correlated with MMORPGs in particular (Engelhardt & Mazurek, 2014).

Another study compared the habits of 202 children and teens with ASD to 179 typically developing siblings. Those with ASD spent more than 60% of their time in screen activities than in nonscreen activities. Boys with autism were the greatest users and averaged about 2.5 hours per day just on video games, whereas their NT brothers spent about an hour less per day (Mazurek & Wenstrup, 2013).

The study participants also completed the Problem Video Game Playing Test, which assesses behavioral addiction to video games. The children and teens with autism had greater rates of addictive levels of play, as well as related problems including poor anger management and social isolation.

Most professionals I have spoken with have grave concerns about ASD youth getting involved with video games. Dr. Temple Grandin, herself autistic and an international advocate and speaker on autism (as well as a professor of animal science), believes that she would become an addict if she allowed herself to play video games. She reports that alarmed parents are, with an increasing frequency, approaching her at conferences and relating stories of their addicted children. They feel helpless, telling her, "He's 21 and he won't leave the bedroom" (T. Grandin, personal communication, July 7, 2015).

Christopher Mulligan, a therapist who works with high functioning autistic teens and young adults, is also highly troubled by the pervasiveness and frequency of video gaming in this population. He has found that

90% of his clients (he has worked with more than 500 ASD clients in the past 12 years) grew up playing video games. He also found that 97% of those aged 18 years and older are unemployed. He believes that excessive gaming is a major contributor to this statistic. He also thinks that compulsive gaming has resulted in increasingly less interest in real-life relationships. "I have never seen a kid go through the process of courtship or dating that resulted in a long-term committed relationship. The long-term committed relationships they have are with their games" (C. Mulligan, personal communication, June 25, 2015).

AN OVERVIEW OF AUTISM CHALLENGES

ASD is, by definition, a diagnosis that encompasses a range of capacities and impairments, and individuals who meet the diagnostic criteria are rated within three levels of severity (American Psychiatric Association [APA], 2013). Two primary categories of deficits and behaviors are common across all these levels.

The first category pertains to the social arena. Children and teens with autism show persistent deficits in social communication and interaction across multiple contexts. These deficits fall into three areas: (a) social–emotional reciprocity; (b) nonverbal ways of communicating; and (c) developing, maintaining, and understanding relationships. Struggles in social–emotional reciprocity may include failure to initiate social contact (or unusual initiation behaviors), failure to engage in typical back-and-forth conversation, and less sharing of interests, emotions, or affects compared to their NT peers. Often, communication is restricted to special interests and is characterized by one-sided imparting of information, with little or no awareness of the other person's responses to it.

Nonverbal differences may include absent, restricted, or unusual facial expressions. Both fine and gross motor coordination may be poorly developed. Gestures, eye contact, posture, and movements may appear odd. Nonverbal behaviors may not accurately mirror verbal communication, which may confuse others and further impede social understanding.

Some individuals with autism show no interest in creating social bonds, while others who do desire friends or romantic relationships face daunting challenges in creating and maintaining them. Typical challenges include poor ability to read social cues, misinterpreting the social intent, not understanding the communication that involves humor, sarcasm or idioms, and taking everything literally. Especially during later childhood and adolescence, a time when NT teens often engage in bonding via cliques and a culture of shared music, clothing, and language, youth with autism may be painfully aware of not knowing how to fit in. When anxiety is present, social challenges are further magnified.

The second primary category of deficits and behaviors necessary for the diagnosis of ASD is a pattern of restricted, repetitive behavior, interests, or activities. These can include motor activities, daily routines, rituals, thinking patterns, interests, and atypical reactions to sensory input.

Some individuals with autism exhibit unusual or repetitive movements, either of their own bodies or of objects. Perseveration can also appear in language, with a penchant for repetition of words or idiosyncratic, pedantic phrases. Repetitive behavior seems to serve a calming purpose and is very resistant to interruption.

Most youth on the autism spectrum greatly prefer sameness to novelty. From infancy on, they may show extreme distress when routines are changed or when they have to transition from one situation to another. Even as teenagers, when prevented from engaging in their preferred activities, they may regress and exhibit emotional meltdowns of an intensity and flavor that are more typical of toddlers.

In addition to favoring sameness, the child or teen on the autism spectrum may also show an extraordinary passion for their preferred activities. Both the intensity of their attention to these pursuits, as well as the length of time they can sustain that attention, may greatly surpass that of a NT peer. When channeled into productive ventures, this can result in impressive positive results. When directed to destructive activities, however, their intense focus and repetition may result in an addiction.

Those on the autism spectrum often have unusual and seemingly contradictory reactions to incoming sensory data. At times they show indifference to the input that others would find aversive—when engrossed in a preferred activity, they may not notice temperature, hunger, or pain. They may continue to engage in the activity long past the time when a NT peer would have needed to eat, sleep, or simply use the bathroom.

At other times, those on the spectrum are unusually reactive to specific sensory experiences, becoming intensely upset by certain sounds, smells, or textures. Yet they may become particularly activated and captivated by other sounds or visual stimuli such as patterns of light or repetitive movement. Some individuals on the spectrum have a need to repeatedly touch items or repeat other actions that result in pleasurable sensory stimulation.

AUTISM CHALLENGES OVERLAP WITH ONLINE GAMING

The two defining characteristics of autism—social deficits and a preference for restricted, repetitive interests and behaviors—uniquely overlap with the world of online gaming.

Engaging in video games is a virtual, ultimately solitary activity that involves interaction with a screen and avatars. A player can be quite successful without having social understanding, skills, or grace. Video games are carefully and intentionally designed to be intensely engrossing by involving the player in repetitive cycles of effort and reward that occur within the context of a highly restricted and rule bound environment. In our current technology-centric world, it is difficult to imagine a more perfect fit for a child or teen on the autism spectrum. As Christopher Mulligan (personal communication, June 25, 2015), the therapist cited earlier, says, "If one were to sit down and design a form of environmental stimulation that would be toxic or damaging to the ASD brain by virtue of exacerbating the core neurological deficits, that stimulation is 21st century technology."

In the world before screens and video games, the characteristic deficits of autism still lent themselves to a solitary lifestyle and avoidance of novelty. The flip side of these deficits, however—intense passion for special interests and activities, and the ability to sustain narrowly focused attention for long periods of time—could manifest as strengths under the right circumstances, without the distraction of online gaming. These interests had a greater chance of resulting in creative, useful theories and inventions. In contrast, online gaming poses the very real danger of both reinforcing the deficits and sabotaging the potential gifts of autism.

ONLINE GAMES AND AUTISTIC PROCESSING PATTERNS

The two diagnostic deficits of autism are the observable manifestations of how the information is processed by the brain of someone on the spectrum. When researchers compare brain scans of those with autism to NT individuals, they see consistent differences in how energy is allocated to complete the cognitive tasks. Given identical problems to solve, the image from the person with autism shows higher levels of activity concentrated within a smaller area (Grandin & Panek, 2013). This correlates with relatively greater efficiency in solving problems that are concrete and do not require integration of multiple neural networks.

We know that brain circuitry is *plastic*—it can be modified and powerfully shaped by repetitive experiences. MRI scans of London taxi drivers show obvious changes in both the function and the actual structure of their brains in the area of spatial navigation (Maguire, Woollett, & Spiers, 2006). Scans of expert violinists show that the part of their brain corresponding to the control of their left fingers has expanded over their years of playing (Elbert, Pantey, Wienbruch, Rockstroh, & Taub, 1995).

Brain scans of gamers also look different than that of nongamers. They have been likened to those of the addicts in general, with lower neural activation in the prefrontal cortex, and less volume of gray matter in general compared to nongamers. Greater degrees of shrinkage in compulsive gamers was correlated with a greater number of errors made on memory and decision-making tests (Brand, Young, & Christian, 2014; Wang et al., 2015).

One of the key sets of brain operations found to be compromised in individuals with autism is what is called executive functioning. This set of skills—often compared to the skill set required in a good CEO—involves initiating action, integrating data from multiple sources, planning ahead, organizing, and prioritizing data, being able to remember data even when interrupted or multitasking, and shifting attention from one task to another in a flexible manner. In contrast to this proactive and "big picture" thinking, the cognitive strengths of those with autism are more often reflected in a deep understanding of specialized interests. They may also perform best when asked to react to concrete information rather than generate abstract ideas.

Individuals with autism are born with brain circuitry that is wired to default to repeatedly process specialized, restricted interests. Extra effort is usually required in order for them to strengthen underdeveloped skills that help them to successfully navigate the NT world. Parents and professionals often have youth on the spectrum practice cognitive flexibility and executive functioning tasks in the hopes that they develop greater ability to handle complex social, educational, and vocational tasks. When these youth are involved in addictive gaming, however, these efforts may prove ineffectual. Their brain circuitry may have become too locked into repetitive, inflexible patterns.

"They become all thumbs," says Dr. Andrew Doan, co-author of *Hooked on Games* (Doan & Strickland, 2012). Dr. Doan goes so far as to say that autism and video games should never be combined. His belief is strong: "If you are autistic, and game, you will become addicted." He uses a hand as a metaphor to describe how he proposes that gaming impacts the brain of someone on the spectrum. In his analogy the thumb represents cortical areas associated with the benefits of video gaming and the use of technology— quicker reflexes and hand–eye coordination, and perhaps an improvement in analytical skills. The index finger represents brain areas that are associated with verbal communication with others. The middle finger represents social bonding. The ring finger represents empathy, and the little finger symbolizes cortical areas associated with self-control.

He says that although higher executive functions are biologically based, they will not have a chance to develop without proper practice and feedback. He believes that when gaming becomes addictive, those with autism become "all thumbs" in their functioning; they possess quick analytical skills and reflexes, but are not as developed in communication skills, having few bonds with others, exhibiting less empathy, and showing minimal self-control (Doan & Strickland, 2012).

Social Challenges of Gaming and Autism

Screen activities have sometimes been used successfully to improve social functioning of those on the autism spectrum. These activities include games that require children to guess the feelings of online characters or to predict social story lines. Individuals with autism often prefer online learning for several reasons—they usually have a natural affinity for computers, and they are able to adjust the learning environment to meet their needs. For instance, they can control the timing of learning (often preferring later in the day or at night), sensory input (they do not have to interact with other students or contend with noxious lighting or noise), and they can work at their own pace.

Thus, social skills, under certain circumstances, can benefit from technology-based activities. Massive multiplayer online games, however, are unlikely to improve real-life social skills. No research has systematically studied this question. Many therapists, including myself, have found that these games in particular increase social isolation. However, as they are designed to never end (players keep advancing levels as they improve, but never reach a set goal that "wins" the game), such games suck players into long periods of play and detract from the already limited time that autistic youth give to building real friendships.

There are reasons why autistic youth neglect real social relationships even if they desire them. Many individuals with autism have been traumatized by bullying, or have been overwhelmed by social situations that bombarded and overwhelmed their senses. They have also repeatedly experienced feeling alienated from their peers as a result of having atypical interests, unique styles of thinking, and indifference or disdain for popular culture. Many individuals have reacted by giving up on trying to make friends.

Internet gaming may represent a seemingly safe and brilliant alternative. In this remarkably stimulating world, autistic youth's attention to detail, natural tendencies to hyper-focus for extremely long periods on areas of special interest, and preference for being alone and interfacing with objects instead of people all come together magnificently. The sense of mastery, belonging, and comfort that results is understandably compelling.

For perhaps the first time, autistic youth are receiving positive attention and accolades. Other players judge them by their game scores rather than by their awkward physical presence, or their unusual use of language, or their clumsy social skills. Social reciprocity, a primary deficit in autism, is not necessary in gaming.

In real life, NT youth learn to improve social competence by adjusting their voices, facial expressions, words, and actions in response to the reactions from another person. In Internet gaming, with identities hidden behind avatars and fake names, there is no feedback loop that provides cues that can help a person build social skills; neither are there natural consequences to poor social behavior. Rather, there may be an indirect reinforcement of social incompetence and inappropriateness. The anonymity of online gaming lends itself to crude comments and insults on many online forums. For nonautistic children and teens, this is regrettable, but they have many other opportunities to observe positive social interactions. For autistic youth, this may not be the case.

The power of the virtual world is apparent in brain scan research that found compulsive gamers emotionally identify more strongly with their avatar than with their biological self. These same gamers also had better memory for their avatars than for other people in their lives. This behavior increased the more they played (Gnash, van Schie, de Lange, Thompson, & Wigboldus, 2012).

Family life has often been the only consistent positive social arena in the world of the child or teen with autism. When Internet addiction disorder takes hold, however, even this previously stable support breaks down. Parents are now regarded as obstacles to gaming. Siblings, often already struggling with a mix of both protectiveness and resentment of the extra attention garnered by their brother or sister on the spectrum, may find the increase in family tension to be the tipping point in their sibling relationship. Whereas in the past, activities, meals, and even meaningful conversations may have been shared, now the Internet is the only recipient of the gamer's attention.

Gaming Worsens Autism's Biological Challenges

There are three basic biological functions that frequently have different *rhythms* or patterns in those with autism. These are sleep, appetite, and mobility. From infancy on, many on the autism spectrum show disrupted or unusual patterns in these areas. These differences can result in negative impacts to their energy levels and health. IGD usually significantly exacerbates each of these problems.

In one study, 70% to 90% of those diagnosed with Asperger's disorder (a diagnosis now subsumed under ASD) reported frequent insomnia (Tani et al., 2003). Children with ASD are also more likely to have disturbed circadian rhythms, sometime to the point of a reversal in their wake/sleep cycle, which may result from an abnormal melatonin regulation. We know that computer screens and other electronics emit light that interferes with melatonin production and regulation. A review of 36 research papers that examined the relationship between sleep and electronic media in children and teens found that delayed bedtime and shorter total sleep were consistently related to media use (Cain & Gradisar, 2010). These were studies of NT children who did not report baseline sleep disturbance. It is reasonable to hypothesize that the effects on children with autism are more pronounced.

A second biological function, which is often dysregulated or atypical in ASD, is appetite. Parents of infants on the spectrum frequently encounter feeding difficulties, sometimes accompanied by gastrointestinal problems. As these children begin to eat solid food, they may be abnormally picky eaters who insist on rigid eating patterns that are extreme enough to compromise adequate caloric intake. They may refuse many foods, recoiling from certain colors or textures or smells. They may have meltdowns if two different foods touch each other on the plate, and may insist on eating only at specific times.

Those who become addicted to Internet gaming frequently further restrict their eating habits to accommodate their play. Food becomes secondary, meals are missed, and junk food and caffeinated sodas consumed while playing replace adequate nutrition. Some players develop secondary caffeine or stimulant addictions from their attempts to stay awake for extended periods, as any break in play jeopardizes their score ranking. This phenomenon has become known as *digital doping* and the Electronic Sports League began routine drug testing in 2015 after a leading competitive player acknowledged pervasive and regular stimulant abuse among eSport competitors (Turtle Entertainment, 2015). While all youth can suffer from unhealthy diets, children and teens with autism are susceptible to more severe damage because they often have less healthy eating patterns to begin with.

Finally, IGD involves extended periods of sitting in the same position, often hunched over with the neck hyperextended. The amount of time spent playing and gross motor movement are inversely related, eventually resulting in a decline in muscle tone. Youth with autism are often born with hypotonia, a condition of low muscle mass. Usually preferring nonphysical special interests, they often get almost no exercise. As with sleep and appetite, IGD increases disturbances in this biological realm.

In all three areas—sleep, appetite, and mobility—damage to the NT child may be moderate. Damage to the child with autism may tip the child into a health crisis.

Gaming Reinforces Restricted, Repetitive Behaviors

Before developing their addiction, most NT children and teens likely engaged in a variety of interests and activities. However, youth with autism exhibit, by definition, pervasive patterns of restricted or repetitive interests or behaviors. One of the greatest challenges for parents and professionals is how to channel the special interests of autistic youth into productive expression, while also developing sufficient proficiency in additional, nonpreferred activities. A related major challenge is to increase the child's flexible thinking and his or her willingness to try novel experiences.

Once Internet addiction takes hold, these challenges become much more daunting. Now other interests and activities are totally neglected. For NT children, this can be reversed after successful treatment. For youth on the spectrum, this is much more difficult even well into recovery. NT children had built a broader repertoire of interests and experiences before their addiction, and they can fall back on these once recovery begins. In addition, NT children do not typically suffer from severe anxiety and resistance to novelty that children with autism usually experience. As a result, they can more readily build new, healthier lifestyles posttreatment.

As youth on the spectrum may have nothing to turn to as a replacement for gaming, alternative activities must be specifically built into the treatment plans for these children and teens. This aspect of a treatment program requires the extensive participation and input of parents or others to succeed.

Gaming Exacerbates Autism's Emotional Challenges

Anxiety and depression commonly coexist with autism. Studies have found that up to 70% of those diagnosed on the spectrum also experience at least one accompanying psychiatric condition, with depression occurring in 53%, anxiety in 50%, and obsessive-compulsive disorder in 24% (Hofvander et al., 2009). Although they infrequently verbalize suicidal thoughts, many autistic youth, if asked, acknowledge having them, especially during their teens and early adult years.

Adolescence is often a period of increased emotional distress for all teens, but this is commonly greater in those on the spectrum. In both populations, mood disorders and other psychiatric conditions are most likely to initially manifest in late adolescence. Anxiety and depression often worsen when puberty and hormonal swings begin. These internal struggles can start even before the physical signs of puberty appear.

Children and teens on the autism spectrum may be especially sensitive to the changes in their body. They hate feeling out of control and often do not share the excitement of NT teens about exploring their sexuality. They may not care about being viewed as physically attractive, and may have no interest in flirting or dating. Their apathy about this aspect of adolescence may set them further apart from their peers and increase feelings of alienation and isolation.

While experiencing multiple shifts in their emotions and bodies, autistic teens have the added challenge of changes in their physical environment. Most of their day is spent at school, and as they move into junior and senior high school, this world becomes more complex and intense. Classes are larger, hallways and cafeterias are noisier, and academic tasks become more abstract and demanding. This may result in exhaustion by day's end. They may have a tremendous desire to retreat into the world of online gaming as soon as they arrive home. They need to replace the chaos of school and social interactions with the predictable, codified, and structured boundaries of fantasy games.

Many report that playing these games relaxes them and makes them feel better. Research indicates otherwise, and parents can attest to the heightened reactivity of their children who compulsively turn to gaming for distraction from distress.

Internet addiction is linked to moderate to severe rates of depression (Young & Rodgers, 1998). There is also evidence that the greater the degree of addiction, mood plummets more strikingly after only 15 minutes of exposure to the Internet (Romano et al., 2013). This can create a vicious cycle—youth go online, rapidly feel worse, do not have the capacity to consciously self-reflect and identify their mood shift, and stay online longer chasing the dopamine rushes that they interpret as "feeling better." Instead, their heart rate significantly escalates.

Autistic youth are often perfectionists, and if their performance or scores do not meet their high standards, they usually become very frustrated. If they encounter glitches in the game (and they are highly adept at finding them), they may angrily ruminate about these errors for days. I have had to redirect many counseling sessions with males on the spectrum who came to their appointments highly agitated and wanting only to talk obsessively about how stupid a particular game developer was. They get caught in the classic repetitive thinking that is an integral part of the way someone with autism often processes information.

Male gamers who play the greatest number of hours per week started playing at earlier ages and experience more severe depression and social phobia. Female gamers, even though they start later and play fewer hours, develop even worse depression and social phobia, plus more somatic issues such as pain, the longer they play (Wei, Chen, Huang, & Bai, 2012).

TREATMENT AND FAMILY DYNAMICS

Children and teens on the autism spectrum were often introduced to technology at an earlier age than their NT peers. Parents of autistic youth have understandably turned to computers and other screen devices for multiple reasons. Their children were often precociously preoccupied with technology. They may have demanded to play repetitive loops of television shows, cartoons, movies, online programs, or video games. Those who were intellectually gifted or had special interests that could be investigated online would often engage in Internet surfing for many hours.

Autistic toddlers and children are notorious for unpredictable and intense meltdowns. Some parents found that technology—handing their child a particular device or allowing access to screen time—was the only consistent way to interrupt these violent storms. Unfortunately, that intervention usually created a vicious cycle that the parent soon found intractable to change. As their children aged, addictive video gaming may have replaced repetitive viewing of cartoons or other childhood activities. The parents, however, are locked into allowing limitless Internet access because of the fear of their child blowing up if interrupted.

Although most parents of all addicted youth fear the consequences of blocking their child's addiction, it is wise for professionals to understand that this dread is often heightened for parents of autistic youth. They know from experience that standing in the way of their child's special interest can cause meltdowns that include violence to property, self, or others. Thus, a first step in treatment must be a significant education of parents, siblings, extended family, and anyone else who has meaningful contact with or influence on the child. If other professionals are involved—speech therapists, occupational therapists, behavioral coaches—they should be informed of and included in the treatment whenever possible.

A pretreatment step especially important for autistic youth is to also assess for Internet addiction in their parents. Although the causes of autism are likely multiple and complex, numerous studies have found patterns in paternal DNA that link to the presence of autism. The same neurological, emotional, and social factors that increase the risk for youth may also apply to parents, especially fathers. If a child's parent is also on the spectrum, and especially if their vocation or special interest involves technology, they may not view their child's behavior as an addiction. Although it may be tempting for professionals to bypass this admittedly delicate and highly charged discussion, ignoring it may well cause the treatment to later derail.

Treatment and Information Processing in Autism

Therapeutic interventions with youth on the spectrum are most effective if they incorporate styles of thinking that are familiar and naturally appealing to the autistic brain. Children and teens with autism may not respect or engage in attempts to *establish rapport*. They may dismiss any appeal to their emotions. A collaborative, cognitive behavioral approach with clearly verbalized logic works better. Expectations and consequences must be explicit and should be written down, as many on the spectrum process and remember information visually rather than verbally.

Many autistic youth have had the experience of being more fully informed on subjects of special interest than the adults in their lives, including teachers and therapists. As the Internet and gaming are their special interest, they may regard themselves as the clear expert in these areas. Parents, educators, or therapists who work with autistic youth with Internet addiction disorder must become as fully informed as possible about the child's world before attempting to enter it. Most youth on the spectrum do not suffer fools gladly.

The interpersonal style of many therapists is very different than that of most people on the autism spectrum. If a team treatment approach is being used, such as in an inpatient or residential unit, it is wise to choose a primary therapist who has a style similar to the client's. Generally, this would be someone who is verbally nimble and speaks in a concise, literal, logical manner. They should expect some of the children and teens they work with to question them as relentlessly as an expert trial attorney. If a NT client did this, "calling them out" on their defensive mannerisms may be appropriate. With an autistic youth, this is simply their style of communicating and learning, and any interpretation of it is likely to lead to greater resistance instead of progress.

The physical therapeutic environment may be more important in the treatment of an autistic child than a NT one. Sensory sensitivity can sabotage the otherwise appropriate treatment. Autistic youth cannot attend to another person or process information if they are shut down as a result of aversive or overwhelming stimuli. Whereas NT children and teens may prefer and benefit from stimulating colors, sounds, or touch, autistic youth may become overloaded quickly. They do not generally think to verbalize their distress, but instead act it out via a mix of withdrawal and agitation.

Treating Autistic Youth With NT Children

I am not aware of any research that compares the outcome of addiction treatment of autistic youth alongside NT children versus treatment limited to clients on the spectrum. To date, few structured treatment programs exist for Internet addiction disorder. Those programs that do, whether they realize it or not, are most likely serving many youth with undiagnosed ASD.

Some programs, however, have recognized the significant prevalence of this population. Dr. Hilarie Cash, one of the founders of ReStart, a residential program for gaming addicts, says that while most kids come for treatment with a diagnosis of attention deficit disorder (ADD), obsessive-compulsive disorder (OCD), anxiety, depression, or oppositional defiant disorder (ODD), she believes these are often the result of gaming, not the cause (Cash & McDaneil, 2008). She has come to think that 50% of the kids are actually on the autism spectrum but have gone undiagnosed because they were bright and high functioning (H. Cash, personal communication, June 18, 2015).

An important factor in considering whether to put autistic youth into treatment groups with NT members is how capable they are of socially integrating with others. Some youth on the spectrum may be able to fit in, but others are more likely to stick out as odd and simply not have the skills to compensate for this. Addiction counselors working with autistic youth must be vigilant to prevent further damage to a vulnerable child's self-perception as defective or "weird." It may be impossible for that child to successfully complete treatment if that happens.

The group leader should also be aware of the personalities of each NT member and consider whether they are likely to bully those with autism. Bullying outside of the formal treatment time is unfortunately reasonably likely to occur unless monitored carefully by staff. It should not be allowed to detract from the primary tasks of group therapy.

Outside of formal treatment time, NT youth may enjoy spending their free time engaged in very different activities than their peers with autism. The latter group is much more likely to need time alone to recover from what to them were probably highly stimulating and exhausting therapeutic exercises. Although total isolation should be prohibited, staff are advised to recognize that autistic youth have much greater legitimate needs for quiet, alone time. They rarely recharge in the company of others.

The staff should also keep in mind what professionals who routinely work with autistic children and teens call the *1/3 rule*. This formula assumes that many autistic youth, in social and emotional areas, are about one third less mature than their chronological age would predict. As a result, they are often more successful in interacting with younger children versus their peers. Some are more comfortable with adults. Mixing them into groups with same-aged peers without the recognition of this disparity puts them at risk for alienation and even trauma.

Assuming that no treatment programs are available specifically for autistic youth, staff meetings should highlight these special needs and they should be reinforced in writing in client charts. Additionally, social interactions should be closely observed and coaching should be provided as appropriate to assist the autistic client to communicate effectively and create social bonds.

When inept or detrimental social behavior is noted, staff should provide private assistance in the form of detailed, written guidelines followed by repeated modeling and role-playing of appropriate interactions. With this added support, it is possible that integrated treatment programs can work well and even provide additional benefits.

PREVENTION STRATEGIES SPECIFIC TO YOUTH WITH AUTISM

We now know how particularly vulnerable autistic youth are to becoming addicted to technology, and realize that the amount of Internet exposure sufficient to lead to an addiction may be much less for them as compared to their NT peers. Therefore, generally accepted guidelines for screen time may need to be adjusted downward. They may also need to be modified so that technology use is primarily limited to educational programs or recreational ones that involve at least one other real, in per-son, participant.

Children with autism need more guidance than most of their NT peers in finding healthy recreational outlets. Parents, teachers, and other adults can help by proactively exposing spectrum youth to activities and interests they would not seek out on their own. These are best piggybacked off the special interests of the child, so that they have a chance of leading to long-lasting hobbies or even eventual vocational pursuits. When individuals on the spec-trum were interviewed about how to help spectrum kids become successful adults, they all cited at least one influential adult who took an interest in them and helped them discover new passions and absorptions (Grandin & Moore, 2016).

Autistic youth also need informed, early assistance in maintaining moti-vation, hope, and self-esteem. In the face of bullying (I have never met a single individual with autism who did not report being bullied), and chronically feeling different, extra steps must to taken to offset the grow-ing distress and alienation. If left unaddressed, these conditions, along with a natural propensity for technology, pose a high risk for the development of an addiction. Involvement in counseling, volunteer work (which can be as informal as regularly helping an elderly or ill neighbor), having routine household chores, and frequently scheduled family activities are all good prevention strategies.

Attention to academic needs, creating individualized educational plans as necessary, and preparing for eventual employment are also crucial. With vocational training no longer a standard part of most school districts, parents must seek out opportunities for learning preemployment foun-dations. These basics include learning to drive (or use public transport if intellectually or physically unable to drive), knowing how to interview appropriately, being able to communicate in public (asking for directions, conducting simple transactions such as shopping, being aware of and responding at least minimally to social signals), and knowing how to do basic household tasks such as simple cooking, cleaning, laundry, and bill paying.

Although these activities and skills are important resilience builders for all youth, they are extraordinarily important for those with autism.

CONCLUSION

Children and teens on the autism spectrum, especially males, have a higher risk of developing Internet addiction disorder. The key diagnostic markers of autism—social deficits and restricted, repetitive interests and behaviors—lend themselves to early preoccupation with technology to an extent that can result in compulsions or addictions.

Children and teens with autism process information differently than their NT peers. Excessive Internet activities, especially online role-playing games, may heighten these neurological differences. In autistic youth, social struggles and emotional distress may correlate with gaming addiction risk, and may become even more pronounced in the presence of excessive online activities.

The biological functions of sleep, appetite, and mobility are often compromised in autistic youth. Online activities can dangerously add to the disruption in all three areas. Adolescence can be especially challenging for teens on the spectrum. Parents, educators, and other professionals' awareness of this can increase the odds of successful navigation of this developmental stage, and help prevent the development of addictions in response to this added stress.

Family members of autistic youth should be assessed and engaged before beginning the treatment of an Internet addiction disorder. Treatment should recognize information-processing patterns typical of an autistic youth, and match staff and interventions to those styles. Youth with autism are often socially and emotionally significantly less mature than their NT peers. Their ability to handle stress is less developed and their emotional breakdowns may be more intense and regressive in nature. During the treatment phase of acute withdrawal, they may require closer monitoring.

Treatment programs likely include many undiagnosed children and teens on the autism spectrum. If autistic youth are treated alongside NT youth, special precautions should be taken to prevent bullying and alienation, and coaching should be provided as needed to add the benefit of improved social functioning. Strategies to prevent addiction can be started early and intentionally. They optimally include building emotional, social, and vocational skills and resiliency.

REFERENCES

American Psychiatric Association. (2013). *Diagnostic and statistical manual of mental disorders* (5th ed.). Arlington, VA: American Psychiatric Publishing.

Brand, M., Young, K. S., & Laier, C. (2014). Prefrontal control and Internet addiction: A theoretical model and review of neuropsychological and neuroimaging findings. *Frontiers in Human Neuroscience, 8*(375), 1–12.

Cain, N., & Gradisar, M. (2010). Electronic media use and sleep in school-aged children and adolescents: A review. *School of Psychology.* Adelaide, SA: Flinders University. doi: 10.1016/j.sleep.2010.02.006

Cash, H., & McDaneil, K. (2008). *Video games & your kids: How parents stay in control.* Enumclaw, WA: Issues Press.

Centers for Disease Control and Prevention. (2014). Media press release. Retrieved from http://www.cdc.gov/media/releases/2014/p0327-autism-spectrum-disorder.html

Doan, A., & Strickland, B. (2012). *Hooked on games: The lure and cost of video game and internet addiction*. Ontario, CN: FEP International [Kindle].

Elbert, T., Pantey, C., Wienbruch, C., Rockstroh, B., & Taub, E. (1995). Increased cortical representation of the fingers of the left hand in string players. *Science, 270,* 305–307.

Engelhardt, C. R., & Mazurek, M. O. (2014). Video game access, parental rules, and problem behavior: A study of boys with autism spectrum disorder. *Autism, 18*(5), 529–553.

Finkenauer, C., Pollmann, M. M., Begeer, S., & Kerkhof, P. (2012). Brief report: Examining the link between autistic traits and compulsive internet use in a non-clinical sample. *Journal of Autism and Developmental Disorders, 42,* 14–65.

Gnash, S., van Schie, H. T., de Lange, F. P., Thompson, E., & Wigboldus, D. H. (2012). How the human brain goes virtual: Distinct cortical regions of the person-processing network are involved in self-identification with virtual agents. *Cerebral Cortex, 22*(7), 1577–1585.

Grandin, T., & Moore, D. (2016). *The loving push: How parents and professionals can help spectrum kids become successful adults.* Arlington, TX: Future Horizons.

Grandin, T., & Panek, R. (2013). *The autistic brain.* New York, NY: Harcourt.

Hofvander, B., Delorme, R., Chaste, P., Nydén, A., Wentz, E., Ståhlberg, O., . . . Leboyer, M. (2009). Psychiatric and psychosocial problems in adults with normal-intelligence autism spectrum disorders. *BMC Psychiatry, 9,* 35.

MacMullin, J. A., Lanky, Y., & Weiss J. A. (2015). Plugged in: Electronics use in youth and young adults with autism spectrum disorder. *Autism, 18,* 1–10.

Maguire E. A., Woollett, K., & Spiers, H. J. (2006). London taxi drivers and bus drivers: A structural MRI and neuropsychological analysis. *Hippocampus, 16*(12), 1091–1101.

Mazurek, M. O., Shattuck, P. T., Wagner, M., & Cooper, B. P. (2012) Prevalence and correlates of screen-based media use among youths with autism spectrum disorders. *Journal of Autism and Developmental Disorders, 42*(8), 1757–1767.

Mazurek, M. O., & Wenstrup, C. (2013). Television, video game and social media use among children with ASD and typically developing siblings. *Journal of Autism and Developmental Disorders, 43*(6), 1258–1271.

Mulligan, C. (2013). The toxic relationship: Autism and technology. Retrieved from http://www.groupworkswest.com/the-toxic-connection-autism-and-technology

Orsmond, G. I., & Kuo, H.-Y. (2011). The daily lives of adolescents with an autism spectrum disorder. *Autism, 15,* 579–599.

Romano, M., Osborne, L. A., Truzoli, R., & Reed, P. (2013). Differential psychological impact of internet exposure on internet addicts. *PLOS ONE, 8*(2), e55162. doi:10.1371/journal.pone.0055162

Roux, A. M., Shattuck, P. T., Rast, J. E., Rava, J. A., & Anderson, K. A. (2015). *National Autism Indicators Report: Transition into young adulthood.* Life Course Outcomes Research Program. Philadelphia, PA: Drexel University.

Tani, P., Lindberg, N., Nieminen-von Wendt, T., von Wendt, L., Alanko, L., & Porkka-Heiskanen, T. (2003). Insomnia is a frequent finding in adults with Asperger syndrome. *BMC Psychiatry, 3*, 12.

Turtle Entertainment. (2015). Esports industry leader ESL joins forces with Sportradar. Retrieved from https://www.turtle-entertainment.com/news/esports-industry-leader-esl-joins-forces-with-sportradar

Wang, H., Jin, C., Yuan, K., Shakir, T. M., Mao, C., Niu, X., . . . Zhang, M. (2015). The alteration of gray matter volume and cognitive control in adolescents with internet gaming disorder. *Frontiers in Behavioral Neuroscience, 20*(9), 1–7.

Wei, H. T., Chen, M. H., Huang, P. C., & Bai, Y. M. (2012). The association between online gaming, social phobia, and depression: An Internet survey. *BMC Psychiatry, 12*(92), 1–7.

Young, K. S., & Rodgers, R. C. (1998). The relationship between depression and Internet addiction. *CyberPsychology & Behavior, 1*, 25–28.

6

UNDERSTANDING THE COGNITIVE IMPACT OF INTERNET ADDICTION ON ADOLESCENTS

Cristiano Nabuco de Abreu

Our increasingly easy access to technology has produced undeniable effects on all domains of our lives. Some investigators have suggested that the quantity of information circulating on the web in the next 2 years will be larger than all the knowledge accumulated throughout human history. It is no surprise that this avalanche of information has had a number of cerebral and cognitive consequences.

Over the past two decades, research studies have shown that the use of electronic media—and, more specifically, the Internet—affects adolescents' brain structures responsible for cognitive information processing and other functions. In addition, an important change has occurred toward more super-ficial forms of mental functioning, characterized by so-called *quick scanning*, as well as substantial changes in memory contemplation and consolidation functions. Similarly, information exchange occurs in increasingly quicker and more reduced forms in today's adolescents (Young & Abreu, 2010). This virtual way of living and thinking has led to what I call *digital cognition*, meaning the use of newly created skills in mental functioning that are clearly distinct from those of previous generations that did not use today's devices. It is becoming clear that these devices, used to excess, do not promote an advance in the developing adolescent's brain skills.

Electronic media as a whole (television, computers, Internet games, and mobile phones) is so strongly present in everyday life that it is widely and unrestrictedly consumed by children and adolescents worldwide. The impli-cations of this trend have been a focus of research for more than 20 years. Consider that almost 100% of 9- to 16-year-olds studied in 2000 were TV viewers (Beentjes, Koolstra, Marseille, & Voort, 2001). The differences in behaviors and ways of thinking between this generation of young adults, termed Millennials (or the Me Generation), and former generations are huge—a result of their contact with technology and virtual media since birth.

This chapter details the effects of this use on the development of the adolescent's brain and reports some of the cognitive repercussions of the excessive use of games, TV, the Internet, and other platforms available for mobile phones and tablets. Although the concept of cognition is diverse and has multiple understandings, I believe cognition should be construed as the result of conscious mental activities executed by a person; that is, a concept through which the activities of thinking, understanding, learning, and remembering occur as a whole in our brain. Therefore, in this chapter, cognition is addressed as a connector, directly impacted by excessive technology use.

THE ADOLESCENT BRAIN

It is well known that adolescents often engage in risky, fearless, and aggressive behavior, and the plasticity (rather than the growth as previously thought) of the networks connecting the brain regions is critical to understand this stage of life. Strictly speaking, such bold behaviors should not be taken by adults as a result of senselessness, defiance, or even an indirect result of behavioral or emotional problems (Giedd, 2015). In fact, such demeanors can be better understood as coming from short-range thinking, that is, resulting from the still unfinished process of brain maturation.

Because the brain does not mature at the same speed as it expands, but rather matures when the interconnectivity of its different components is enhanced, the elapse of time is a critical element to ensure the maintenance of a person's balance and well-being. For example, magnetic resonance imaging scans show that, as time goes by, the quantity of connections increases, which is corroborated by the increase of white matter volumes in the brain. In fact, this white matter results from a lipid material called myelin that, by coating and insulating the filamentous extension called the axon, is spread throughout the neuron with the purpose of facilitating the electrical conductivity.

The myelination or formation of this fat *sheath* continues from childhood to adulthood, considerably accelerating the conduction of nerve impulses between neurons. Myelinated axons convey signals up to 100-fold faster than the nonmyelinated ones. Myelination also accelerates information processing by helping axons to rapidly recover after having been triggered, which allows them to be primed and ready to send new messages in a shorter time. A quicker recovery may mean a 30-fold increase in the information transmission frequency (Giedd, 2015). And the combination of faster transmission and quicker recovery results in a 3,000-fold increase of the observed brain's computing bandwidth capacity from the beginning of childhood up to adulthood—which creates a more complex interconnectivity. This results in better functioning across the brain networks, providing higher variety and ability of execution of cognitive tasks—*long-range thinking* in opposition to short-range thinking.

Stated another way, the brain maturation process is nothing but an exponential increase of the myelination (or communication) process across different neuronal groups, making the young person better skilled to accomplish distinct activities, with a higher level of complexity and function, as time goes by. This occurs mainly in those brain regions involved in judgment, social interactions, and long-term planning—vital functions for a better individual and social well-being (Baron & Hoekstra, 2010).

BRAIN MATURATION

As the white matter develops (and thickens), another process called selective elimination takes place. The frequently used connections are naturally reinforced and widened, whereas the connections left unused are eliminated.

Those unused brain cell connections start to be eliminated, thereby reducing the brain's gray matter. This gray matter is composed of materials such as cellular bodies, dendrites, and some nonmyelinated axons. The brain's gray matter expands during childhood, reaches its peak at around 10 years of age, and decreases during adolescence. Then, it stabilizes in adulthood and when individuals become elderly it starts decreasing again. This elimination process occurs throughout life, but it is more intense during adolescence (Giedd, 2015; Simons & Lyons, 2013).

Although the quantity of gray matter reaches its peak during puberty, the full development of the different regions only occurs later on. Therefore, we could state that adolescence is marked by changes in the white and gray matter, and together, they slowly transform the brain regions, leading to the full maturation of the brain structure at approximately 21 years of age.

EMOTIONAL REGULATION

As time goes by, another important process also comes into play. As connections become enhanced because of the repeated execution of a set of behaviors, there are new possibilities of brain maturation starting to take place. The limbic system, fully functioning since the first days of life and responsible for emotional functioning—which not only mediates learning and memory functions, but also creates an emotional scenario for the adolescent's experiences—signals to the body through emotions the threatening, dangerous situations coming from the environment and prepares the body for action.

This is how the amygdala takes over the triggering of emotions (fear, sadness, and anxiety) and empowers the body for fight-or-flight behaviors by giving the body an enhanced ability for action in the environment. This primitive mechanism of emotional functioning is understood as being based on biology, and leads to a more intense emotional behavior in the first stages of life. It stimulates mammalian adolescents (of any species) to leave the group's—or, in the case of humans, the family's—comfort to look for new environments to mate, and in doing so, to ensure a genetically healthier offspring by diminishing the chances of endogamy, as well as to look for new environments to hunt and reside, thereby reducing the competitiveness among the group members.

In this attempt to explore and be differentiated, adolescents share everything via social media—from selfies to where they are and what they are doing, wearing, or eating, to their opinion about anything. According to some authors, this has contributed to the emergence of a narcissistic generation. The U.S. National Institutes of Health (NIH) found that the presence of narcissistic personality disorder among 20-year-olds is today three times higher than in previous generations who are now 65 years and older.

Another important area is the cerebral cortex, which has a role in the emotional control and regulation process. By acting as the headquarters of reasoning and impulse control, it keeps a close relationship with the limbic system, making the crude emotions emerging in the amygdala refined and balanced by the conscious brain (Giedd, 2015; Greenberg & Paivio, 2003). And when the limbic system and prefrontal cortex "talk," they emit the emotions (understanding of threatening situations) on one side, and on the other side, they plan for action, creating a highly important mechanism for adaptation.

However, the cerebral cortex does not mature in line with the development of the limbic system; in the first two decades of life, emotions are broader, but the reasoning functions delay the full capacity of emotional regulation in adolescents for almost one decade, creating a biologic misstep. That is why adolescents are more prone to adopt dangerous, fearless behaviors than children or even adults, partly because of the maturation gap between the limbic and prefrontal systems, which inhibits emotions and dangerous behaviors, and only starts consolidating after 21 years of age. This creates uneven maturation and leaves adolescents more prone to risky behaviors, such as alcohol and drug abuse, excessive use of technology, and the like (Giedd, 2015; Greenberg & Paivio, 2003).

The so-called *behavioral constraint* still works partially, thereby creating a number of vulnerabilities (Tavares, Abreu, Seger, Mariani, & Filomensky, 2015).

However, we should remember that the maturity of a person, group, or society mostly occurs through vertical relationships, with people of all ages and education levels, and the role models of older people to whom we are exposed, such as parents and other relatives, teachers and professors, employers, leaders, and the like. The discomfort of what is unfamiliar to us is what has the capability to expose us and induce us to think in a different manner; therefore, we can only grow when our convictions are challenged. The one-million-dollar question is, "Do the Millennials have the chance to live this whole process or are they being spared?"

If we consider that the Internet encourages young people to take a more horizontal model of communication, exposure, and exchange, it is possible that Millennials have been experiencing a deep immersion with people having similar interests and affinities. They live in a highly customized environment that increasingly mirrors their personal or group values, which makes them more impermeable to knowledge that is out of their bubble, as described by Eli Pariser (2011).

On the other hand, there has never been so much access to information and if well used, our youth have in their hands the opportunity to cause the most important social changes in centuries. Don Tapscott (2009), author of the book *Grown Up Digital*, says that, for the first time in history, young people are the authorities in something really important, because they have the power to change virtually every aspect of our society—from the classrooms to the halls of Congress.

TECHNOLOGY AND CHILDREN

The effects of exposure to electronic media (TV, DVD, computer programs) have been reported for a long time. For example, there are both theoretical and empirical reasons to believe that the effects of electronic media on children's development are more likely to be adverse before the age of about 30 months than afterward. However, survey data involving large samples are scarce; so I will use the information available.

Some studies suggest that about 90% of parents say that their children younger than 2 years watch some sort of digital media during the day. This is because watching TV or playing with electronic gadgets makes the house quieter and leaves parents unworried while they are doing activities such as preparing dinner, eating their meals, or even relaxing during their leisure time (Council on Communications and Media & Brown, 2011).

Records show that children at this age watch TV for 1 to 2 hours a day on average, while there are reports of as many as 4 hours a day. More recent studies found that 64% to 100% of all infants and toddlers watch TV before the age of 2 years (Zimmerman, Christakis, & Meltzoff, 2007). Although the access is the same for different socioeconomic levels, the *consumption* tends to be substantially higher in less-favored groups; this means that the higher the caregivers' education level, the more exposed their children become to TV. The same is true for broken homes with only one of the parents living with the children.

With regard to the educational programs that children watch, there is a lot of discussion about their importance, such as the positive effects of increasing social skills and language. What is not generally known, though, is that three quarters of the educational programs supposedly designed for children were actually never duly assessed and effectively proven to promote such skills. We should be reminded that, for some effect to be verified, young children would need to have minimum cognitive skills (such as attention or memory), skills that in fact are still out of operation in this age group. Added to that, it is well known that young children still have a significant difficulty to determine where the events introduced to them come from, that is, whether it is from a video or if it originates from the reality in their environment (as a result of the interaction between two people, for example); such events remain undifferentiated.

Children's attention will only show significant changes when they reach 18 to 30 months; however, we should take into account that there are exceptions (some children can be even slower), which would nullify any educational assumptions for programs with these purposes. This means that 1-year-old or younger children will not be able to follow a conversation among adults or a sequence of TV or video images, as their attention is not totally developed yet. Two studies revealed that the famous TV show Sesame Street had, in fact, negative effects on the language development of children younger than 2 years.

The longer the interaction between children and their caregivers, the better their vocabulary level. Therefore, in homes where TV and tablets vie for the attention of the parents, the interference with language development will be higher, just because parents talk little with their children, and this would impact their development. A child's vocabulary is known to increase in a direct proportion to the time spent by his or her parents in conversations with the child.

A study evaluating children at 1, 24, and 36 months of age found that the background sound of the TV not only hinders and reduces their playing, but also directly affects their attention, as they head for another activity at each interruption. In addition, the shows that parents watch are often not designed for children, and they end up producing background noise, also making them interrupt their playtime, which equally produces a reduction of their attention.

It is important to stress that today, in addition to TV, the exposure to gadgets has played a key role in children's education process. While in the past TV was restricted to a single room in the home, gadgets can be carried everywhere today, and this creates an even greater exposure and an impact that may be more devastating.

Passive media are now in the same position as active media, and the results may not be so beneficial. Children who live in households where there is heavy exposure to media (TV, videos, and digital platforms) spend between 25% (for 3- to 4-year-olds) and 38% (for 5- to 6-year-olds) less time reading or having books read to them. These children have a lower likelihood of being able to read when compared with their peers living in homes with low media use. What is known is that unstructured playtime is critical to learning problem-solving skills and improving creativity at this period of life (Rideout & Hamel, 2006). Therefore, children living in homes where there is intense exposure to media show lower judgment capacity, decreased creative skills, and poorer learning of problem solving when compared with those not exposed to such a level. Despite the small number of studies on this topic, we can imagine the potential outcomes.

Additionally, the exposure to modern media contained in laptops is also associated with an increase of obesity, sleep problems, mood swings, aggressive behaviors, and behaviors related to lack of attention at school. And this is not all: Specifically related to language development in young children (up to 16 months), the exposure to media recorded significant delays in this population (Linebarger & Walker, 2005). Although the long-term effects remain unknown, the short-term effects are considered to be worrisome, mainly for the executive functions developed by the brain.

EXECUTIVE FUNCTION

As previously described, because brain maturation does not end in adulthood, some consequences of excessive use of technology can be observed in cognitive functioning, and having some understanding of executive functions is critical when analyzing its impacts on children and adolescent cognition.

The term *executive function* is not the simplest to define. There are different definitions, and it is generally understood to be a concise way to describe a set of complex processes. The executive processes are seen as the mental abilities required to formulate goals and adequately put execution plans into practice. With this in mind, these functions may be defined as a set of metacognitive abilities that allow individuals to notice the stimuli coming from their own environment, respond in an adaptive manner with good flexibility for change, anticipate future goals, and finally, adequately evaluate the consequences of their actions and behaviors. Executive function could be better explained as a construct consisting of multiple competences or skills that are interrelated. Some processes emerge as underlying factors to these functions: inhibition and disinhibition, working memory, and selective attention. Together, these processes are responsible for emotional self-regulation, impulse control, and mainly problem-solving activities. Behind an adolescent's academic and social success is executive function, as it is the basis for skills such as problem solving and goal directing. It consists of three key components: working memory, inhibitory control, and attention flexibility.

The working and learning memories are critical for processing information. Both are the building blocks of knowledge, with the former being responsible for the acquisition of new knowledge and the latter for retaining the new information. It is known that working memory is the foundation of learning, as it determines the ability to process information, follow instructions, and keep up with activities such as those presented in a classroom. Working memory is used to perform tasks requiring reasoning, such as mathematical operations, reading, text interpretation, and the like.

In turn, inhibitory control prevents inadequate responses or actions that halt the effective course of a given activity, or even inhibits actions that compromise the execution of a goal—which is generically called *self-control*. The lower an adolescent's inhibitory control, the lower is his or her ability to fully perform a task. What can we say, then, about digital-generation adolescents, who are constantly distracted with their mobile phones?

Attention flexibility is being aware that the interpretations of some stimuli may, at some point, be reviewed because it introduces stimuli that allow for the construction and perception of other meanings, thereby enabling the body to have a higher response capacity.

In addition to the body's capacity of functioning in a correct manner, some findings have already pointed to the existence of a close correlation between the development of executive functions and the family environment; that is, as a child grows, his or her brain remains open to and in close dialogue with the environment, responding either better or worse to these stimulations. It is well known that the executive function can be *transmitted* through parental styles; that is, depending on the acceptance consistency and level and the support offered by parents to their children, different coping skills can be attained. For example, disorganized and unpredictable family environments where parents educate in an inconsistent, disorganized manner may disrupt the development of the executive function. In contrast, parents who are sensitive and responsive are more likely to create an emotionally interactive context that helps children feel comfortable, which allows good internalization and self-regulation.

Because the exposure to media always takes place in an environment—that is, it does not occur in a vacuum—we understand the need to analyze its impacts from the point of view of the consequences of the environmental influences. Therefore, interpersonal relationships are not only sensitive to the exposure to media, but also to the environmental factors; they are both to be considered when analyzing the media effect on people and their family units.

Findings show that parents participating in their children's exposure to media by supervising the time (level) and quality of exposure considerably reduce the risks of a not-very-adequate development of the executive functions, which would probably lead to a more moderate and healthier use of technology. Therefore, a more positive and consistent family presence at home will result in a better self-regulation capacity on the part of the children.

Let us think of those homes where technology plays the role of distracting and occupying children's attention while parents are absent (Linebarger, Barr, Lapierre, & Piotrowski, 2014). Children who are constantly stimulated by sounds, such as those from a television or any other background media in the environment, interact little with their parents, and when they do, the quality of the relationship is poor (Kirkorian, Pempek, Murphy, Schmidt, & Anderson, 2009). This effect is minimized in environments where parents have higher education, and by ensuring a controlled and better quality exposure; children receive more benefits from this sort of exposure.

Another important issue for the development of executive functions is notably seen during class—one of the major environments for the excessive, uncontrolled use of technology. Carrying portable and multifunctional smart devices, the digital generation behaves differently in the classroom when compared with older generations. For example, research studies have reported that students today send text messages, navigate the web, or use some other electronic media during some school activities. Researchers investigated the impacts of multitasking on classroom learning, considering a 20-minute class for the experiment. They found that multitasking with gadgets when compared with pen-and-pencil note taking led to a poorer recall of the material that was presented by teachers. Comparisons revealed the obvious: Students who did not use any technology performed better than those using it (Wood et al., 2012).

To test the impacts of multitasking, the researchers exposed participants to an everyday condition in which multitasking is usually observed: TV watching and computer (or smartphone) usage. Without any specific guidance, the individuals switched from TV to computer and vice versa at an average rate of four switches per minute and an average of 120 switches throughout the 30-minute experiment. So, for students engaged in media use during classroom learning, the brain activity necessary for efficiency can be compromised (Rosen, Mark, & Cheever, 2013).

The simultaneous occurrence of two tasks was evaluated for the impact on the brain. Two studies investigated the neural correlates through an activity involving the simultaneity of stimuli. Another study addressed the distraction caused by media while individuals were stimulated by other activities. Findings revealed that dual tasking led to a 37% decrease in parietal brain activations when compared with controls; this means that the individuals had losses and made more disadvantageous and risky choices when doing two things at the same time.

Analyses suggested that Internet-addicted individuals were less likely to account for probability and outcome magnitude in these decisions. Internet-addicted individuals were strongly driven by immediate rewards for their actions, even in situations where the probabilities of loss were concrete and evident. This would partly explain the reason why Internet-addicted individuals, in face of imminent losses, still exhibit their maladaptive behaviors of abusive use of the Internet, yet in clear, transparent awareness of the risks (Schweizer et al., 2013).

INFORMATION PROCESSING

Although the Internet is an efficient means for knowledge distribution and access, its excessive use creates a type of rapid cognitive processing of information that is quite distinct from that used when reading a book, for example. Marked by rapid, nonlinear attention shifts, scanning behavior, selective reading, decreased information retention, and other attributes, the navigation demands new mental skills.

As a result, the deeper forms of cognitive processing (such as the analytical reasoning that leads to deeper reflections) significantly deteriorate in the learning process as a whole. Because much of the digital content is presented as embedded hyperlinks or fragmented pieces of information, a more detailed content analysis becomes unnecessary. The hyperlinks, then, demand an extra effort from visual processing before the individual decides where to go next in searching for the information he or she wants, thereby creating a major lack of pace in memory consolidation. Less time is dedicated to the execution of associative tasks, which is responsible for the fixation of knowledge in the form of long-term memories, which impacts data preservation and subsequent recovery.

The fact that they are constantly connected to the web significantly compromises the Millennials' ability to learn new things, and as a result, their process of thinking about some subject is seriously impaired. When compared to previous generations, they exhibit a minimum level of social knowledge, in spite of having access to all sorts of information, as there is no anchoring of such information.

Content can only be retained when assimilated gradually and in such a way that allows comparing (and *anchoring*) it with the content already in store—also referred to as *cognitive anchoring*. Therefore, the access to online information makes adolescents quickly rely on the Internet for knowledge retrieval and makes them better at recalling where to retrieve information rather than the information itself. For example, when one takes a picture of an object, which is different from observing it, this leads to a poorer recall of the object's characteristics and properties. Thus, knowing that we can access this record later, the effort that our cognition makes when processing or analyzing its details is lower, which would otherwise lead to better remembering in the future (Henkel, 2014).

In the same line of reasoning, people were found to be highly prone to misinterpret information they accessed when they looked for information online. So, the Internet is understood as an important *transactive memory*. As such, instead of remembering the complete information, people only focus on remembering *where* and *how* to access that knowledge. Individuals, then, end up being less responsible and less committed to that information (Ward, 2013). Therefore, the Internet became a powerful tool for information access, while reducing the need for effortful processing and remembering of information. However, it is not new that human beings make use of external resources to facilitate their memorization. The examples are numerous and may be similar to calendars, shopping lists, notes, and Post-it notes that we so commonly use. When we excessively count on this external information source (*off-sourcing*), some cognitive effects may be not so productive.

The shift toward shallow information processing can disrupt the development of deep reading skills. We should, however, remember that these skills (such as inferential reasoning, reflection, or critical analysis) are not innate but progressively acquired throughout life. And in disrupting deep reading, the Internet-induced shallow information processing can affect the development of these brain circuitries (Loh & Kanai, 2016).

SELF-CONTROL AND NEURAL CORRELATES

Internet-addicted individuals also show poor skills in controlling or inhibiting their responses. According to research studies using the Stroop Test (which measures executive functions and concentration), participants with Internet addiction tend to make more mistakes than their controls. And by using the Go/No-Go task (that evaluates two processing components responsible for response flexibility and inhibition in which the participants are invited to answer positively to a stimulus with *go* and negatively with *no-go*), researchers found that Internet-addicted participants, when compared with controls, reacted faster and had similar mistake rates in *go* trials, but had more mistakes in *no-go* trials (Dong, Lin, Zhou, & Lu, 2014). Other investigations showed the percent decrease of successful *no-go* trials in participants with Internet addiction. And individuals diagnosed with Internet addiction showed poorer results of response inhibition, which was further aggravated in the presence of Internet-related cues (Li et al., 2014; Loh & Kanai, 2016).

Based on the preceding, research studies have often suggested that Internet-addicted individuals are highly driven by instant rewards in their decisions even when they have losses and in spite of the low possibilities of success and gain. Studies also suggest that, from the cognitive perspective, they are worse at inhibiting their responses, particularly when there are Internet-related cues. And "these findings provide an important link between excessive Internet use and impaired reward-processing and self-control abilities" (Loh & Kanai, 2016, p. 9).

With regard to the neural mechanisms, studies have consistently revealed that Internet-addicted individuals show enhanced neural activations toward

Internet-related cues (Brewer & Potenza, 2008). For example, a study compared the regional gray matter density differences between frequent and infrequent Internet gamers and found that frequent gamers had higher gray matter density in the left ventral striatal region. They suggested that the increased striatal volume was due to the increased dopamine release as a result of the continuous use of online games (Ko et al., 2009; Kühn et al., 2011; Loh & Kanai, 2016).

Internet-addicted individuals also show changes in their neural self-control mechanisms. When compared with control groups, they show decreased gray matter density in the frontal–parietal structures of their brains, which are those directly involved in the cognitive control operations (Hong et al., 2013). Other research studies showed, via voxel-based morphometry (VBM), a reduction of gray matter volumes in the anterior cingulate cortical activation, precuneus, supplementary motor area, superior parietal cortex, and dorsolateral prefrontal cortex in Internet-dependent individuals (H. Wang et al., 2015). It is important to stress that the decreased activation volume of the cingulate cortex was correlated with lower Stroop Test scores (Loh & Kanai, 2016).

Some neurobiological studies revealed a decreased dopamine transporter expression and reduced D2 receptors in the striata of Internet-addicted individuals (the two main dopamine receptors are D1 and D2), with both being associated with a decreased dopamine regulation. Even more interesting is the finding that the activation of the same striatal region (indicating dopamine release) increased even when the individuals experienced losses. This could underlie the existence of tendencies to persist in addictive behaviors even when confronted with negative consequences (Hou et al., 2012; Loh & Kanai, 2016).

Internet-addicted individuals show great activation of the superior frontal gyrus even when repeatedly losing and failing. In the investigation, when compared with the control group, they showed increased reward anticipation in both situations—when either losing or winning. In face of losses, Internet-addicted individuals had a reduction of the anterior and posterior cingulate cortical activation, when compared with controls, which suggests reduced sensitivity to loss (Dong, Hu, & Lin, 2013; Dong, Huang, & Du, 2011).

The neurobiological mechanisms and their implications for the Internet dependence are more specifically addressed in the following sections.

Neurobiological Mechanisms

It is well known that the prefrontal cortex and striatum are implicated in Internet-addicted individuals. The prefrontal cortex is often classified as a multimodal association cortex because extremely processed information from various sensory modalities is integrated here in a precise fashion to form the physiologic constructs of memory, perception, and various cognitive processes. Human neuropsychological studies also support the notion of different functional operations within the prefrontal cortex. The specification of the component of *executive* processes and their location at particular regions of the prefrontal cortex have been implicated in a wide variety of psychiatric disorders (Li et al., 2014).

In contrast, the striatum is a structure involved in functionally segregated corticostriatal circuits related to cognitive functions. For example, by parceling caudate and putamen in three regions, patterns of corticostriatal functional circuits that are involved in affective, motivational, cognitive, and motor processes are delineated (Di Martino et al., 2008). Many studies have shown functionality/effectivity between the striatum and cortex that are reduced in Internet-addicted adolescents.

Additionally, research studies have already confirmed the reduction of gray matter densities and volumes when compared with controls (Weng et al., 2013), as well as cortical thickness (Yuan et al., 2013), changes in glucose metabolism (Tian et al., 2014), and altered brain activation in the prefrontal cortex—specifically the dorsolateral, orbitofrontal, and anterior cingulate cortices (Ko et al., 2014). Studies even show low levels of dopamine D2 receptors (Hou et al., 2012) and altered glucose metabolism in the striatum (Park et al., 2010). All of these findings are consistent with the pathophysiological model and the significant role of the prefrontal cortex and striatum in addiction disorder models (Limbrick-Oldfield, van Holst, & Clark, 2013).

Resting-state functional connectivity, measuring interregional correlations of spontaneous brain activity via blood oxygen level–dependent functional magnetic resonance imaging (fMRI), has been used to assess the functional brain. Using these procedures, evidence emerged indicating that corticostriatal functional circuits are critical to compulsive behaviors, such as addictive behaviors and reward-seeking and novelty-seeking behaviors in Internet-addicted individuals (Loh & Kanai, 2016; Shepherd, 2013). Altered corticostriatal functional circuits were also found in many other psychiatric disorders. For instance, disrupted corticostriatal functional circuits have been found in patients with reward-related and addictive behaviors (Kühn & Gallinat, 2014).

Another study pointed to the occurrence of reduced connectivity between the nucleus accumbens/inferior ventral striatum and the caudal head, which implies changed reward-related functions in Internet-addicted individuals, indicating that they prefer smaller immediate rewards (i.e., immediate euphoric effects) in detriment to larger rewards that occur in the future, such as good health, good relationships, or occupational success. Therefore, the results demonstrated impairment of corticostriatal functional circuits involving affective and emotional processing and cognitive control, which also suggested that Internet addiction disorder in adolescents may share psychological and neural mechanisms with other types of impulse control disorders and substance addiction (Lin et al., 2015).

Another interesting research study that is worth describing investigated in more detail the features involved in the basal ganglia and striatum and habit formation processes. Using an animal model, the researchers trained healthy mice to form sugar habits of varying severity levels by pressing a lever (to receive sweets). The animals that became addicted kept pressing the lever even after the treats were removed (O'Hare et al., 2016). Then, the researchers compared the brains of mice that had formed a habit with the ones in the control group and studied the electrical activity in the basal ganglia.

Basal ganglia are a network of brain areas (the dorsal striatum, ventral striatum, globus pallidus, ventral pallidum, substantia nigra, and subthalamic nucleus) that controls motor actions and compulsive behaviors (including drug addiction). They are primarily involved in action selection and help determine the decision on which among the several possible behaviors to execute at any given moment. More specifically, the basal ganglia's primary function is likely to control and regulate activities of the motor and premotor cortical areas so that voluntary movements can be performed. Experimental studies show that they exert an inhibitory influence on a number of motor systems, and that releasing this inhibition allows the motor system to become active.

The well-known *behavior switching* that takes place within the basal ganglia is influenced by signals from many parts of the brain, including the prefrontal cortex, which plays a key role in executive function. In addition, there are two main types of paths carrying opposite messages during the behavior: The first path carries a *go* signal that spurs an action, whereas the other one makes a *stop* signal. The stop signal equally ramps up in the habit brain, because it has been traditionally viewed as the factor that helps prevent a behavior.

The animal study mentioned here showed that the stop and go pathways were both more active in the sugar-habit mice, and researchers found that the timing of activation changes in both pathways; that is, in mice that formed a habit, the go pathway turned on before the stop pathway. In nonhabit brains, the stop signal preceded the go signal.

These changes in the brain circuitry were so long lasting and obvious that it was possible for the group to predict which mice had formed a habit just by looking at isolated pieces of their brains. The scientists had previously noticed that these opposing basal ganglia pathways seem to be in *competition*, though no one has shown that a habit gives the go pathway a head start. The group observed that changes in go-and-stop activity occurred across the entire region of the basal ganglia while they were studying specific subsets of brain cells, which may pressure a patient to be more likely to engage in other unhealthy habits or addictions. In order to break a habit, the researchers encouraged the mice to change their behavior by only rewarding them if they stopped pressing the lever. The mice that were the most successful at quitting had weaker go cells.

To have more clues about the compulsive behaviors and offer new possibilities of intervention on the abusive use of technology we will have to wait until the experiment is extrapolated to human models.

The "Distraction" Effect

Another aspect that deserves mention is the lack of attention. The constant lack of attention produced by the Internet results in a phenomenon that some have explained as "distracted from distraction by distraction." According to Carr (2011), the cacophony of stimuli in the form of short circuits provided by continuous stimulation prevents our minds from thinking either deeply or creatively. "Our brains turn into simple signal-processing units, quickly shepherding information into consciousness and then back again" (p. 119), which creates a massive remodeling resulting from the disorganized, almost unnatural exposure. Although in the past our cognition used to be trained to evaluate the stimuli from the environment in a correct and adaptive manner, today the macro-stimulation requires new ways of cognitive functioning, which, therefore, would create major neurological consequences.

There is an important neuroscience metaphor that goes "neurons that fire together, wire together," meaning that, as our brain is stimulated, the functions and operations that are mentally activated somehow tend to connect. However, Carr says that "neurons that *do not* fire together, *do not* wire together." He means that, as users spend their time rapidly scanning web pages, deciding which direction to take, what to follow, and where to go next, in a navigation based on continuous and unspecific attention, the circuits that support those intellectual functions and pursuits weaken and begin to break apart and, ultimately, cause extensive brain changes.

Research studies suggest that people who are constantly online activate regions associated with language, memory, and visual processing in a lower intensity, that is, they do not display much activity in the prefrontal area. We should be reminded that the activities involving memory fixation require a certain amount of time for mental operation, as the brain needs some seconds to coordinate and evaluate the merit of the next actions. However, when one navigates the web, the mental operation is switched from a careful *analysis* to a judgment about the relevance of the contents, and as this operation is frequently repeated, it eventually prevents the understanding and retention operations.

"We revert to being 'mere decoders of information,' because our ability to make rich mental connections that are formed when we are concentrated remains largely disengaged, and such an intense exercise makes us lose our primary model of thought" (Carr, 2011, p. 125). Therefore, excessive users of technology progressively lose their ability to perform deeper mental operations, and as this process is strengthened, it becomes a key gear in this vicious cycle with not only psychological, but also neurobiological, impacts, resulting in a substantial change in the adolescents' cognitive functioning.

Impact of Excessive Media on Memory and Sleep Patterns

To date, we have reported a number of possibilities in which the cognition may be affected by the abusive use of technology that are mainly about the processes triggered during wakefulness—or full consciousness. However, we cannot refrain from mentioning that the effects of abusive use of the Internet in adolescents—which, by the way, can also be observed as a result of the modified periods of sleep or rest—are a result of a *more technological* routine. Therefore, the rest deprivation also interferes with the cognitive processes.

It is well documented that sleeping is vital to maintaining one's balance and well-being, and it also plays a fundamental role in the consolidation and performance of learning and memory. For example, video games considerably increase some metabolic and physiological variables, including a significant stimulation of the central nervous system. Unlike other platforms in which the interaction is more relaxed, in games an increase of the heart rate, blood pressure, breathing, momentary suppression of some digestive processes, and the like are reported, which interfere with the subsequent quality of sleep (X. Wang & Perry, 2006). And it is well known that the vast majority of adolescents spend a considerable part of their day (or, more accurately, night) playing video games and using electronic gadgets of all kinds in the privacy of their rooms, even when lying down, which significantly delays getting into the sleep cycle, allowing a variety of problems to manifest.

Some conceptions interpret that a high level of emotions—as those experienced when playing online games—may compromise the learning process. Because the knowledge acquired during the wakefulness period is still under the consolidation process, the emotional intensity resulting from the stimulation may significantly interfere with it. Because games produce challenges, surprises, excitement, and mainly frustration, the changes are followed by major physiological changes.

Positron emission tomography scans showed significant dopamine and norepinephrine release during the use of video games—which are, by the way, the same neurotransmitters involved in the learning process and present in emotions and sensory–motor coordination of memory processing. In a study of 10- to 14-year-old children, evidence shows that as little as one night with sleep restrictions would be enough to impair the cognitive functions. Using the Wisconsin Card Sorting Test (WCST), a difficulty to learn new abstract concepts in the group with less total sleep time was found when compared with the group with complete sleep duration (Radazzo, Muehlback, Schweitertzer, & Walsh, 1998).

During the sleep stages of rapid eye movement (REM) and slow-wave sleep (SWS), there is the consolidation of the process in which explicit memory is fixed. Therefore, the low acetylcholine (ACh) levels during SWS would facilitate the information from the hippocampus back to the cortex (ACh is a cholinergic system's neurotransmitter that is widely distributed in the autonomic nervous system as well as in certain brain regions). In turn, the high acetylcholine levels during REM sleep would allow the neocortex to undergo a process of reanalysis, thereby developing new feed-forward representations for behavior (Hasselmo, 1999).

Once video games reduce the quantity of SWS, memory consolidation is impaired (Dworak, Schierl, Bruns, & Strüder, 2007). Additionally, because more time spent playing video games means less time dedicated to physical activities (one of the consequences being that it negatively affects the brain structures), this time reduction could also affect the adolescents' physical health by increasing their tiredness while reducing attention promptness.

The findings of the study mentioned earlier are consistent with previous studies in which the inappropriate use of TV and video games during the middle school years was associated with a negative impact on academic achievements (Christakis, Zimmerman, DiGiuseppe, & McCarty, 2004; Sharif & Sargent, 2006).

TWO SIDES OF THE SAME COIN

As described previously, we know for a fact that the changes occurring in the brain, triggered by novel interactions, are also the root cause of the cognitive understanding of the world by adolescents. As already mentioned, the current generation is involved in a highly customized environment, and we can easily notice that the information out of this customized model is naturally filtered or blocked.

As a result, these young people are probably not disturbed by things that do not please them, as they only access websites that draw their attention, sign up to receive RSS feeds about things they care about, and participate in groups discussing subjects that interest them; they participate in what stimulates them and avoid what does not give them satisfaction. The risk is to become a generation closed in their own world, concentrated on their own values, with little awareness and a narrow view of the world.

While Don Tapscott (2009) offers us an optimistic perspective of our youth, by considering that they have in hand the opportunity to cause the most important social changes ever and by highlighting that changes in the brain structure bring some positive impacts, some see it from a more pessimistic point of view, by forecasting that this generation threatens future generations because it is not necessarily turning the information into knowledge. Mark Bauerlein (2008), author of the book *The Dumbest Generation*, argues that this generation is living with one of the highest alienation levels, with narrow horizons and incompetence levels that have never been seen before. He says that "21st century young people will not be the 'next great generation.'"

The truth is that the core of almost all compulsive behavior is not only based on free will, but also on new pathways of neurological wiring that inevitably create a deep change in the human cognition (Brewer & Potenza, 2008). Internet addicts suffer permanent physical neurological change in their brains and nervous systems. Once the new neurological pathways are established, they do not just disappear.

In my clinical practice with these adolescents, the future does not seem very promising. However, we will have to wait for the outcomes as well as for further, deeper research studies on this topic.

CONCLUSION

While cognitive operations are often responsible for significant changes in cerebral activation patterns (either for better or for worse), they also bring about the development of new mental processing habits, which have allowed adolescents to have better and more effective skills to decode the virtual world's environments and information.

The downside is that, while new skills are developed, the long-range thinking and the assimilation of information are at stake, since this new ability to *decode* the world leaves the brain area responsible for the cognitive information processing and other functions working less. With regard to Internet dependence, studies have already demonstrated that it is not only based on emotional or social aspects, but also on the physical dependence created by altered neurotransmitter balances, driven by thousands of new neurological pathways that have been established to sustain the condition in the addict's brain (Koepp et al., 1998).

The use of the Internet can make a highly stimulating and rewarding environment available around the clock—an environment that includes things that are inherently pleasant, such as social networks, videos, songs, games; provides easy access to activities such as video games, shopping, and chatting; and does not require physical presence. For adolescents and young people, this is an extremely seductive environment.

Adolescents stay online for increasingly longer, sustained periods because they want to keep up with everything that belongs in the virtual world. Always vigilant, they receive with huge satisfaction each (expected and unexpected) news item that appears in their Facebook page, Instagram, blog, and the like, often giving higher emotional magnitude to online life situations than real-life experiences.

This continuous reinforcement process makes the rewarding part of cerebral mechanisms very active all the time, which perpetuates and invigorates the behaviors of imperative connection and may frequently lead to the emergence of compulsive behaviors, thereby increasing the disease prevalence statistics, not to mention other disorders that might come up—and has already been verified—as a consequence of this new way of living.

The cognition (as well as the mental functioning) in adolescents today is certainly trained in a distinct manner, and they exhibit functioning traits and characteristics that are very distinct from those of previous generations.

Although some advantages can be obtained with this new mental *training* (such as more cognitive agility, more focus, rapid decision making, multitasking, etc.), as extensively advertised by the nonprofessional media, we should keep in mind that the consequences should be evaluated in the long term. More mental skills are not always translated into better quality of functioning—and there are research studies to prove this point of view. "Scores of common tests designed to measure intellectual skills seem to be stagnant or declining" (Carr, 2011, p. 145).

Thus, we should be attentive to the continuous, indiscriminate use of the Internet by our adolescents, as the perspectives are not among the most promising ones. As health care professionals, we must be prepared to help adolescents reestablish control, sometimes of their entire lives, mainly to help restore a healthy mental and psychological functioning model in order to allow their mental skills to continue to develop, with preservation of the future generations in mind.

Today, as digital immigrants, we still manage to bring some of our past experiences into play and bridge the knowledge to the current generations. But I ask myself: How will the children of our children be? How will the mind and cognition of our digital grandchildren be formatted? We better be alert and take action.

ADDITIONAL READING

Gupta, R. K., Saini, D. P., Acharya, U., & Miglani, N. (1994). Impact of television on children. *Indian Journal of Pediatrics, 61*(2), 153–159.

Internet World Stats Usage and Population Statistics. (2017). Internet usage statistics. Retrieved from http://www.internetworldstats.com/stats.htm

Johnson, J. G., Cohen, P., Smailes, E. M., Kasen, S., & Brook, J. S. (2002). Television viewing and aggressive behavior during adolescence and adulthood. *Science, 295*, 2468–2471.

REFERENCES

Baron, W., & Hoekstra, D. (2010). On the biogenesis of myelin membranes: Sorting, trafficking and cell polarity. *FEBS Letters, 584*(9), 1760–1770.

Bauerlein, M. (2008). *The dumbest generation: How the digital age stupefies young Americans and jeopardizes our future (or, don't trust anyone under 30).* New York, NY: Jeremy P. Tarcher/ Penguin.

Beentjes, J. W., Koolstra, C. M., Marseille, N., & Voort, T. H. (2001). Children's use of different media: How long and why? In S. Livingstone & M. Bovill (Eds.), *Children and their changing media environment: A European comparative study* (pp. 85–112). Mahwah, NJ: Erlbaum.

Brewer, J. A., & Potenza, M. N. (2008). The neurobiology and genetics of impulse control disorders: Relationships to drug addictions. *Biochemical Pharmacology, 75*(1), 63–75.

Carr, N. (2011). *The shallows: What the Internet is doing to our brains.* New York, NY: Norton.

Christakis, D. A., Zimmerman, F. J., DiGiuseppe, D. L., & McCarty, C. A. (2004). Early television exposure and subsequent attentional problems in children. *Pediatrics, 113*(4), 708–713.

Council on Communications and Media & Brown, A. (2011). Media use by children younger than 2 years. *Pediatrics, 128*(5), 1040–1045.

Di Martino, A., Scheres, A., Margulies, D. S., Kelly, A. M., Uddin, L. Q., Shehzad, Z., . . . Milham, M. P. (2008). Functional connectivity of human striatum: A resting state fMRI study. *Cerebral Cortex, 18*(12), 2735–2747.

Dong, G., Hu, Y., & Lin, X. (2013). Reward/punishment sensitivities among internet addicts: Implications for their addictive behaviors. *Progress in Neuro-Psychopharmacology & Biological Psychiatry, 46*, 139–145.

Dong, G., Huang, J., & Du, X. (2011). Enhanced reward sensitivity and decreased loss sensitivity in Internet addicts: An fMRI study during a guessing task. *Journal of Psychiatric Research, 45*(11), 1525–1529.

Dong, G., Lin, X., Zhou, H., & Lu, Q. (2014). Cognitive flexibility in Internet addicts: fMRI evidence from difficult-to-easy and easy-to-difficult switching situations. *Addictive Behaviors, 39*(3), 677–683.

Dworak, M., Schierl, T., Bruns, T., & Strüder, H. K. (2007). Impact of singular excessive computer game and television exposure on sleep patterns and memory performance of school-aged children. *Pediatrics, 120*(5), 978–985.

Giedd, J. N. (2015). The amazing teen brain. *Scientific American, 158*, 28–33.

Greenberg, L. S., & Paivio, S. C. (2003). *Working with emotions in psychotherapy.* New York, NY: Guilford Press.

Hasselmo, M. E. (1999). Neuromodulation: Acetylcholine and memory consolidation. *Trends in Cognitive Sciences, 3*(9), 351–359.

Henkel, L. A. (2014). Point-and-shoot memories: The influence of taking photos on memory for a museum tour. *Psychological Science, 25*(2), 396–402.

Hong, S. B., Kim, J. W., Choi, E. J., Kim, H. H., Suh, J. E., Kim, C. D., . . . Yi, S. H. (2013). Reduced orbitofrontal cortical thickness in male adolescents with internet addiction. *Behavioral and Brain Functions: BBF, 9*, 11.

Hou, H., Jia, S., Hu, S., Fan, R., Sun, W., Sun, T., & Zhang, H. (2012). Reduced striatal dopamine transporters in people with Internet addiction disorder. *Journal of Biomedicine & Biotechnology, 2012*, 854524.

Kirkorian, H. L., Pempek, T. A., Murphy, L. A., Schmidt, M. E., & Anderson, D. R. (2009). The impact of background television on parent-child interaction. *Child Development, 80*(5), 1350–1359.

Ko, C.-H., Hsieh, T.-J., Chen, C.-Y., Yen, C.-F., Chen, C.-S., Yen, J.-Y., . . . Liu, G.-C. (2014). Altered brain activation during response inhibition and error processing in subjects with Internet gaming disorder: A functional magnetic imaging study. *European Archives of Psychiatry and Clinical Neuroscience, 264*(8), 661–672.

Ko, C.-H., Liu, G.-C., Hsiao, S., Yen, J.-Y., Yang, M.-J., Lin, W.-C., . . . Chen, C.-S. (2009). Brain activities associated with gaming urge of online gaming addiction. *Journal of Psychiatric Research, 43*(7), 739–747.

Koepp, M. J., Gunn, R. N., Lawrence, A. D., Cunningham, V. J., Dagher, A., Jones, T., . . . Grasby, P. M. (1998). Evidence for striatal dopamine release during a video game. *Nature, 393*(6682), 266–268.

Kühn, S., & Gallinat, J. (2014). Brain structure and functional connectivity associated with pornography consumption: The brain on porn. *JAMA Psychiatry, 71*(7), 827–834.

Kühn, S., Romanowski, A., Schilling, C., Lorenz, R., Mörsen, C., Seiferth, N., . . . Gallinat, J. (2011). The neural basis of video gaming. *Translational Psychiatry, 1*, e53.

Li, B., Friston, K. J., Liu, J., Liu, Y., Zhang, G., Cao, F., . . . Hu, D. (2014). Impaired frontal-basal ganglia connectivity in adolescents with internet addiction. *Scientific Reports, 4*, 5027.

Limbrick-Oldfield, E. H., van Holst, R. J., & Clark, L. (2013). Fronto-striatal dysregulation in drug addiction and pathological gambling: Consistent inconsistencies? *NeuroImage: Clinical, 2*, 385–393.

Lin, F., Zhou, Y., Du, Y., Zhao, Z., Qin, L., Xu, J., & Lei, H. (2015). Aberrant corticostriatal functional circuits in adolescents with Internet addiction disorder. *Frontiers in Human Neuroscience, 9*, 356.

Linebarger, D. L., Barr, R., Lapierre, M. A., & Piotrowski, J. T. (2014). Associations between parenting, media use, cumulative risk, and children's executive functioning. *Journal of Developmental and Behavioral Pediatrics, 35*(6), 367–377.

Linebarger, D. L., & Walker, D. (2005). Infants' and toddlers' television viewing and languages outcomes. *American Behavioral Science, 48*(5), 624–645.

Loh, K. K., & Kanai, R. (2016). How has the Internet reshaped human cognition? *The Neuroscientist, 22*(5), 506–520.

O'Hare, J. K., Ade, K. K., Sukharnikova, T., Van Hooser, S. D., Palmeri, M. L., Yin, H. H., & Calakos, N. (2016). Pathway-specific striatal substrates for habitual behavior. *Neuron, 89*(3), 472–479.

Pariser, E. (2011). *The filter bubble: What the Internet is hiding from you.* London, UK: Viking/ Penguin.

Park, H. S., Kim, S. H., Bang, S. A., Yoon, E. J., Cho, S. S., & Kim, S. E. (2010). Altered regional cerebral glucose metabolism in Internet game overusers: A 18F-fluorodeoxyglucose positron emission tomography study. *CNS Spectrums, 15*(3), 159–166.

Radazzo, A. C., Muehlback, M. J., Schweitertzer, P. K., & Walsh, J. K. (1998). Cognitive function following acute sleep restriction in children ages 10–14. *Sleep, 21*, 861–868.

Rideout, V. J., & Hamel, E. (2006). *The media family: Electronic media in the lives of infants, toddlers, preschoolers, and their parents.* Menlo Park, CA: Kaiser Family Foundation.

Rosen, L. D., Mark, C. L., & Cheever, N. A. (2013). Facebook and texting made to me: Media induced task-switching while studying. *Computers in Human Behavior, 29*, 948–958.

Schweizer, T. A., Kan, K., Hung, Y., Tam, F., Naglie, G., & Graham, S. J. (2013). Brain activity during driving with distraction: An immersive fMRI study. *Frontiers in Human Neuroscience, 7*, 53.

Sharif, I., & Sargent, J. D. (2006). Association between television, movie, and video game exposure and school performance. *Pediatrics, 118*(4), e1061–e1070.

Shepherd, G. M. (2013). Corticostriatal connectivity and its role in disease. *Nature Reviews. Neuroscience, 14*(4), 278–291.

Simons, M., & Lyons, D. A. (2013). Axonal selection and myelin sheath generation in the central nervous system. *Current Opinion in Cell Biology, 25*(4), 512–519.

Tapscott, D. (2009). *Grown up digital: How the net generation is changing your world*. New York, NY: McGraw-Hill.

Tavares, H., Abreu, C. N. de, Seger, L., Mariani, M. C. M., & Filomensky, T. (2015). *Psiquiatria, Saúde Mental e a Clínica da Impulsividade*. São Paulo, Brazil: Manole.

Tian, M., Chen, Q., Zhang, Y., Du, F., Hou, H., Chao, F., & Zhang, H. (2014). PET imaging reveals brain functional changes in Internet gaming disorder. *European Journal of Nuclear Medicine and Molecular Imaging, 41*(7), 1388–1397.

Wang, H., Jin, C., Yuan, K., Shakir, T. M., Mao, C., Niu, X., . . . Zhang, M. (2015). The alteration of gray matter volume and cognitive control in adolescents with internet gaming disorder. *Frontiers in Behavioral Neuroscience, 9*, 1–7.

Wang, X., & Perry, A. C. (2006). Metabolic and physiologic responses to video game play in 7- to 10-year-old boys. *Archives of Pediatrics & Adolescent Medicine, 160*(4), 411–415.

Ward, A. F. (2013). Supernormal: How the internet is changing our memories and our minds. *Psychological Inquiry, 24*, 341–348.

Weng, C. B., Qian, R. B., Fu, X. M., Lin, B., Han, X. P., Niu, C. S., & Wang, Y. H. (2013). Gray matter and white matter abnormalities in online game addiction. *European Journal of Radiology, 82*(8), 1308–1312.

Wood, E., Zivcakova, L., Gentile, P., Archer, K., De Pasquale, D., & Nosko, A. (2012). Examining the impact of off-task multitasking with technology on real-time classroom learning. *Computers & Education, 58*, 365–374.

Young, K. S., & Abreu, C. N. de (Eds.). (2010). *Internet addiction: A handbook and guide to evaluation and treatment*. New York, NY: Wiley.

Yuan, K., Cheng, P., Dong, T., Bi, Y., Xing, L., Yu, D., . . . Tian, J. (2013). Cortical thickness abnormalities in late adolescence with online gaming addiction. *PLOS ONE, 8*(1), e53055. doi:10.1371/journal.pone.0053055

Zimmerman, F. J., Christakis, D. A., & Meltzoff, A. N. (2007). Television and DVD/video viewing in children younger than 2 years. *Archives of Pediatrics & Adolescent Medicine, 161*(5), 473–479.

7 PARENTAL MENTAL HEALTH AND INTERNET ADDICTION IN ADOLESCENTS

Lawrence T. Lam

"I don't have much to do, just chat with my friends on WhatsApp, upload my pics to the Instagram, and tweet a bit." This was how a 13-year-old boy described what he usually does after school during a group discussion on adolescent social life in a local school. When I asked how much time he usually spends on doing all those, he said, "Not much, about 6 hours every day." I then asked about his parents, and he said: "My father is a businessman and he spends most of his time working and traveling, but when he is at home we seldom talk. We just WhatsApp [each other]. I know that he is not happy about a lot of things and does not talk about them.
He just watches movies online until late at night. I think I am a bit like him."

The preceding scenario is common in the East Asia region, as well as many other areas of the developed and developing world. The Internet has become an essential part of our lives and has grown to be a dominant force in shaping our daily lives. Although the Internet offers tremendous convenience, in many ways improving our lives, there is a down side, as reflected in the remarks from this 13-year-old adolescent.

This chapter explores the issue of parental involvement in the Internet addiction of their adolescent children. Of particular focus is the relationship between parental mental health and adolescent Internet addiction. My own research suggests that parental mental health plays an important role in the Internet addiction of their children. There is also a significant association between parent and child Internet addiction after controlling for the effect of the child's mental health status. In considering possible mediating effects of the child's mental health status and parental Internet addiction, a further study showed that this relationship is rather complex. Results suggest that the effect of parental mental health, particularly depression, on adolescent

Internet addiction is mainly mediated by adolescent mental health as well as parental Internet addiction.

These complex relationships can be understood in the light of well-established psychosocial theories, such as stress, appraisal, and coping, which may have direct implications on clinical assessment and treatment. Possible assessment and treatment approaches have been suggested that aim to address different factors involved in the complex relationship between parental mental health and Internet addiction in adolescents.

FAMILIAL FACTORS CONTRIBUTING TO ADOLESCENT INTERNET ADDICTION

Over the past 7 years, familial and parental factors of adolescent Internet addiction have gained much attention, with a growing volume of literature in this particular area of research. In terms of the factors being studied, an array of different variables is identified from the literature. These included: family satisfaction (Lam, Peng, Mai, & Jing, 2009; Yen, Yen, Chen, Chen, & Ko, 2007); family conflict or cohesion (Park, Kim, & Cho, 2008; Siomos et al., 2012; Wu et al., 2013; Yen et al., 2007); family communication and relationship (Liu, Fang, Deng, & Zhang, 2012; Park et al., 2008; Van den Eijnden, Spijkerman, Vermulst, & Van Rooij, 2010); parental attitudes toward excessive Internet use (Park et al., 2008; Yen et al., 2007); parenting styles (Durkee et al., 2012; Huang, Zhang, Li, Wang, Zhang, & Tao, 2010; Kalaitzaki & Birtchnell, 2014; Xu et al., 2014; Yang, Sato,Yamawaki, & Miyata, 2013); parental drinking (Jang & Ji, 2012; Yen et al., 2007); and family dysfunction (Tsitsika et al., 2011; Xu et al., 2014; Yen et al., 2007).

Family satisfaction was the first familial factor that drew the attention of researchers. Back in 2007, Yen et al. had already started exploring family satisfaction as one of the possible risk factors of Internet addiction among Asian adolescents (Yen et al., 2007). Although the interest in family satisfaction and Internet addiction was further extended in the East Asia region, researchers in Europe cast their eyes on the same topic in 2012 (Siomos et al., 2012). In the 2007 study, Yen et al. used the APGAR family index score as the assessment of family satisfaction, and this study found a negative association between the family index score and Internet addiction among Taiwanese adolescents (Yen et al., 2007). Similarly, Lam and colleagues had conducted a population-based cross-sectional survey among adolescents in the city of Guangzhou and found that family dissatisfaction was significantly associated with Interact addiction as assessed by the Young Internet Test. The results suggested that adolescents who were addicted to the Internet are about two and a half times as likely to be dissatisfied with their family (odds ratio [OR] = 2.4,

95% confidence interval [CI] = 1.3–4.3) when compared to normal users (Lam et al., 2009). Family conflict and lack of cohesion are also potential risk factors of Internet addiction in adolescents of different cultural backgrounds. For example, in the study by Yen et al., a positive relationship between parent–adolescent conflict and Internet addiction was identified (Yen et al., 2007). In South Korea, Park et al. assessed family cohesion and communication among adolescents using a 10-item Likert scale. Results obtained from the regression analysis indicated a negative association between family cohesion and communication scores and Internet addiction (Park et al., 2008). Similar results were also obtained in a later study in Europe among Greek adolescents. In a longitudinal study of a cohort of Greek adolescents, Siomos et al. revealed that adolescents who indicated a closer bond to their parents at baseline were less likely to be addicted to the Internet at the follow-up measure 2 years later (Siomos et al., 2012). Furthermore, results from a study among adolescents in China also showed that addicted Internet users scored significantly lower on parental relationships (Wu et al., 2013).

Communication within the family is an essential and integral part of the family life and is closely related to family satisfaction. Good family communications on specific matters would help resolve issues such as the excessive use of the Internet in children or sometimes even in parents. In terms of the relationship between family communication and Internet addiction in adolescents few studies have been found. As mentioned, Park et al. had studied family cohesion and communication and Internet addiction among Korean adolescents, and found a negative correlation between family communication and Internet addiction (Park et al., 2008). In Europe, Van den Eijnden et al. also examined the relationship between family communication and Dutch adolescents in two separate studies: a large-scale population-based, cross-sectional survey of nearly 4,500 parent–child dyads and a smaller longitudinal study of about 500 such dyads (Van den Eijnden et al., 2010). Results from both studies provided evidence that qualitatively good parent–adolescent communication regarding Internet use could prevent the development of compulsive Internet use in adolescents. Moreover, a bidirectional relationship between parent and child indicated that compulsive Internet use in adolescents also predicted a reduction in the frequency of parent and child communication regarding Internet use (Van den Eijnden et al., 2010). These results are also echoed in the study by Liu et al. (2012). In their study among Chinese youth, Liu et al. also identified a negative association between Internet addiction and the parent–adolescent relationship in general.

An important aspect of parental communication with their children regarding Internet use is the parent's own attitude toward excessive Internet use. In an earlier study by Yen and colleagues, it was found that parental attitudes toward addictive behavior had a direct influence on the actual behavior of adolescents. A more positive attitude toward addictive behavior was associated with Internet addiction among Taiwanese adolescents (Yen et al., 2007). Park et al. (2008) also revealed that a negative parental attitude toward excessive Internet use was associated with a lesser likelihood for Korean adolescents to be addicted to the Internet. Verbal communication could have some influence on the perception of adolescents toward addiction. However, parental supervision and monitoring may have a more direct effect on the actual behavior. For example, in a study by Lin, Lin, and Wu (2009) among Taiwanese adolescents, it was found that participative and supportive parental monitoring reduced the likelihood of adolescent Internet addiction. Similarly, Kwon, Chung, and Lee (2011) found a negative relationship between parental supervision and Internet gaming addiction. On the other hand, a recent study by Yang et al. among older adolescents suggested otherwise (Yang et al., 2013). In a survey of Chinese and Japanese university students, it was revealed that students who were problematic Internet users tended to perceive their parents as more overcontrolling in comparison to normal Internet users (Yang et al., 2013). The discrepancies in these results may be because of the differences in the age of respondents. Parental intervention may be more effective for younger adolescents as they are more likely to be teachable and willing to comply with parental requests than older adolescents. Hence, the timing of parental intervention may be a crucial factor for a successful strategy in reducing and preventing Internet addiction in young people.

Closely related to parent-and-child communication is parenting style. Researchers have only recently started examining the relationship between parenting style and adolescent Internet addiction (Durkee et al., 2012; Huang et al., 2010; Kalaitzaki & Birtchnell, 2014; Xu et al., 2014; Yang et al., 2013). Huang et al. (2010) investigated the relationship in 2010 and reported that adolescents who exhibited symptoms of Internet addiction had rated maternal and parental rearing practices as "insufficient in emotional warmth," "overinvolvement," "rejecting," and "punitive." In a large-scale study in Europe involving many countries of the European Union, the research group found an association between low parental involvement in the life of adolescents and problematic Internet use. In the aforementioned study by Yang et al. (2013) that evaluated the differences in problematic Internet use between Chinese and Japanese adolescents, mother's care was identified as one of the mediators explaining the differences. Kalaitzaki and Birtchnell (2014) studied the relationship between parental bonding and problematic Internet use behavior in more than 750 Greek adolescents. They discovered indirect associations between optimality of parenting styles and subsequent Internet addiction through "negatively relating to others" and "sadness." In addition, a study conducted in high school students in Shanghai by Xu et al. suggested that the quality of the parent–adolescent relationship was closely associated with the development of Internet addiction. Adolescents who were addicted to the Internet were about four times as likely to have a poor mother-and-child relationship (OR = 3.79, 95% CI = 2.22–6.48) and about two times as likely to have a poor father-and-child relationship when compared to normal users (Xu et al., 2014).

In terms of environmental risk factors for Internet addiction among young adolescents, family dysfunction has also been identified as a potential risk factor. Yen et al. (2007) identified a positive relationship between high parent–adolescent conflict and Internet addiction among Taiwanese adolescents. Similarly, in a case–control study Tsitsika et al. (2011) reported that dysfunctional familial relationships and divorced parents were more likely to be found among adolescents with Internet addiction than in the control group. In the study by Xu et al. (2014) results also indicated that there was a positive association between "parents being married but separated" and Internet addiction symptoms in Chinese adolescents. An increased occurrence of fathers or mothers who were heavy users of alcohol among young problematic Internet users in comparison to normal users was also found in the study by Yen et al., (2007). The effect of parental drinking problems on adolescent Internet addiction was further studied by Jang and Ji (2012). It was found that parental problematic drinking had a positive but indirect effect on Internet addiction via anxiety, depression, and aggression in male adolescents. However, among female adolescents, the positive effect of parental alcohol drinking on Internet addiction was mediated through family function and aggression (Jang & Ji, 2012).

A recent study reviewed 42 studies from English and Chinese literature on family factors of Internet addiction among adolescents. Of these 42 studies, 24 were in the English language and a range of different familial and parental variables were investigated including most of the aforementioned factors. Results suggested that adolescent Internet addiction was significantly associated with divorced parents, single-parent households, and being the only child in the family. Adolescents having these familial and parental characteristics were more likely to exhibit Internet addiction in comparison to those without (Li, Garland, & Howard, 2014). However, methodological shortcomings in the studies included in the review were identified by the authors of the report. Additionally, the review study only focused on Internet addiction among Chinese youth, presenting some limitations to the findings. Moreover, all these studies suffered from the same drawback of parental information being collected through the report of the child, not from the parents per se (Li et al., 2014).

PARENTAL MENTAL HEALTH AND ADOLESCENT INTERNET ADDICTION

In terms of the mental health aspect of adolescent Internet addiction, a number of studies have reported that mental health problems, such as attention deficit disorder, obsessive-compulsive disorder, depression, anxiety, and hostility, are comorbidities of Internet addiction among adolescents (Huang et al., 2010; Ko, Yen, Yen, Chen, & Chen, 2012; Yen et al., 2008). However, in seeking to identify the parental risk or protective factors of Internet addiction, the relationship between parental mental health and adolescent Internet addiction has scarcely been studied.

In order to bridge the gap of knowledge, the author conducted a parent-and-child dyad study with the specific aim of exploring the association between parental mental health and their children's Internet addiction (Lam, 2015). Moreover, to address the methodological weakness in many of the previously reported studies, information on parental mental health and other related variables, including their own Internet usage, was collected from parents themselves and not based on the report of adolescents. By the same token, information pertaining to adolescent Internet addiction and related variables, including their own mental health, was also collected from adolescents themselves. The results obtained from the study indicated a significant association between parental mental health and adolescent Internet addiction. After adjusting for potential confounding factors, including the mental health of the child, adolescents in the moderate to severe Internet addiction group were three times (OR = 3.03, 95% CI = 1.67–5.48) as likely to have parents classified with moderate to severe depression when compared to those in the mild or normal group (Lam, 2015). However, no significant relationship between parental anxiety, as well as stress, and adolescent Internet addiction was found. Considering the effect of parental behaviors on the behaviors of their children, parental Internet use may also be an influential factor on the Internet usage of their children. Hence, another secondary analysis study was conducted by the author to investigate the relationship between parental Internet addiction and the Internet addiction of their children, taking into consideration adolescent mental health (Lam & Wong, 2015). The results suggested a significant parent-and-adolescent Internet addiction relationship in the group of adolescents with low stress levels (OR = 3.18, 95% CI = 1.65–6.14), but not in the high stress group. Combining the results from these studies suggests that the relationship between parental mental health and their children's Internet addiction is complex, and other factors, such as parental Internet addiction and the mental health status of the child, are also involved. The involvement of these factors may be more of a mediating nature than of an interactive nature as suggested by the results of the two previous studies. Furthermore, the gender of the parent and child may also play an important role in these complex relationships, especially in behavioral modeling.

The author has further explored the relationship between parental mental health and their children's Internet addiction taking into consideration parental Internet addiction, the mental health of the children, as well as the genders of parent and child using a structural equation modeling approach (Lam, 2015). The inclusion of the genders of parent and child is based on the established significant association between parent-and-child mental health, and the evidence that different offspring genders may have different levels of susceptibility to their parent's problems depending on the gender of the parent (Bennett, Brewer, & Rankin, 2012; Chen & Weitzman, 2005). This study obtained the following outstanding results:

- The effect of parental mental health, particularly depression, on their child's Internet addiction was mainly mediated through the child's mental health problems such as depression and stress.

- The aforementioned effect was manifested more prominently in gender-matched parent-and-child dyad (i.e., father-and-son and mother-and-daughter match).

- The effect of parental depression on their child's Internet addiction, to a lesser extent, was also mediated through the parent's Internet addiction.

THEORETICAL UNDERSTANDING OF THE RESULTS OBTAINED

The results obtained from these recent studies on the relationship between parental mental health and adolescent Internet addiction provide a new perspective on adolescent Internet addiction as a whole. Although the efforts of establishing mental health problems as comorbidities of adolescent Internet addiction are still ongoing (Huang et al., 2010; Ko et al., 2012), the results of this study has shed some light on the possible pathway for the relationship between parent-and-child mental health and adolescent Internet addiction. Previous studies also highlighted that adolescents might indulge in excessive Internet use as a means to alleviate the burden of their mental health problems, such as depression and stress (Lam, 2015). The findings of the current study further suggest that there exists a possible mediating pathway between parental depression, adolescent depression and stress, and adolescent Internet addiction. These results suggest that the parental mental health problems may, in some ways, exert an influence on the mental health status of their children. The mental health issues of the children, in turn, motivate them to seek a way out and the Internet can provide such an easy exit.

The relationship between parental, particularly maternal, depression and the depression of the offspring has long been established with evidence on the causal pathway between mother and child (Mendes et al., 2012;

Weissman & Jensen, 2002). Moreover, the findings of the current study further highlight that the mediating pathway is more prominent in same-sex parent-and-child dyads such that boys tend to be more affected by their fathers' than their mothers' mental health problems. In the same token, girls are also more affected by their mothers' mental health problems than that of their fathers'. This in turn results in a higher risk of Internet addiction. These results echo the phenomena observed in the adolescent mental health problem of eating disorders, where there is a strong mother–daughter gender match effect in the development of the problem (Cooley, Toray, Wang, & Valdez, 2007; Jacobs et al., 2009).

These results could be interpreted in light of the stress, appraisal, and coping theory proposed by Lazarus and Folkman (1984). This theory stipulates that, as a response to a stressor or any stressful situation, a cognitive appraisal process is evoked in the individual who is under stress. This process consists of two stages: the primary and the secondary appraisal. Primary appraisal refers to an evaluation of whether the stressor poses a threat and is harmful, or is simply a challenge to the individual. On the completion of the primary appraisal, the secondary appraisal follows with an assessment of whether the individual has enough internal or external resources to handle or cope with the stressor effectively (Lazarus & Folkman, 1984). The result of the appraisal, incorporating the usual way of coping for the individual, determines whether the stressor can be successfully handled. A positive appraisal coupled with an effective coping strategy results in a positive outcome, while a negative appraisal and an ineffective coping strategy results in a negative outcome. Family problems such as parental mental health issues may trigger a stress reaction in adolescents in the form of distress, depression, or stress. While appraising that the mental health issues of the parent may not be a threat but still cause a certain amount of distress, adolescents may not have the knowledge, understanding, and skills to handle their own distress and depressed mood. With easy access to the Internet through all sorts of mobile devices at any time, the cyber world becomes an ever-ready *safe refuge* for adolescents to escape to in order to alleviate their distress. To bear witness to this point, often in the school setting, counselors and social workers could counter a scenario similar to the case presented subsequently.

> During a counseling session with Debby, a junior high school student, for her rapid decline in her school performance, the counselor found that one of the reasons of the poor school performance was that she had been spending far too much time tweeting with her online friends and could not manage herself. On further prompting, the counselor also discovered that the student exhibited some depressive symptoms. Further discussions on the

family situation of the teenagers revealed that her mother had been on antidepressants for some time because of an episode of severe clinical depression related to incidents at work a few years ago. The girl said: "My mum and I are very close and I hate to see her like that but I cannot do anything. I feel so unhappy and I get online to talk to my friends. I feel better when I am online and gradually that becomes a must-do thing for me."

Furthermore, the parental Internet behavior could also become a model coping method for their children, such that adolescents adopt it as an acceptable behavior when facing stressful situations. To illustrate this, Theresa would be a good example.

Theresa is a 39-year-old executive officer of an academic institute with an 8-year-old daughter, Annmarie. There have been some ongoing relationship issues with Theresa's own parents, both retirees, such that they are seeking a divorce. This has caused Theresa a considerable amount of stress. During a group session on stress management at work, Theresa shared with the group that whenever she has to face up to her parents' problem, she will go to her smartphone, call up a game, and start playing. However, she also expressed her concern that she had realised Annmarie also did the same when she was preparing for her piano grade examination. Whenever Annmarie had been reminded to practice for the examination, she went straight to her phone and started playing games.

The finding on the gender-matched results further lends support to this understanding. It is possible that, while looking for a role model as part of their natural psychosocial development during periods of growth, adolescents usually adopt the parent of their own sex as an example, resulting in their being more affected by that parent than the parent of the opposite sex. Hence boys are more affected by their fathers' mental health and coping behaviors while girls are more affected by their mothers'.

The following is a vivid example. Another mother of about 40 years, who is a professional working in a high stress environment, shared the following during a focus group interview:

At the beginning, I just want to take my mind off things when I am in a bad mood so I start browsing the Net for something interesting and enjoyable to help me feel better. Unknowingly, it has grown on me and it seems that I cannot do anything else. I can see that my 10-year-old girl is also doing that too.

ASSESSMENT OF FAMILY DYNAMICS

There are many suitable instruments for assessing parent-and-child mental health problems and Internet addiction, as well as their ways of coping. The following are suggested mainly because they satisfy the established scientific merits of reliability and validity, as well as possessing predictive power of the problems they address. These instruments are not meant to be used as clinical diagnostic assessment tools.

To assess the mental health status of both the adolescent and the parent, there is a wealth of well-designed and validated instruments that can be used. Interested parties can consult the PsycTESTS® section of the American Psychological Association (APA, 2016) website. Some of the included tools are clinically based and others are for more generic assessments. For the purpose of screening and research on common mental health problems, the Depression, Anxiety, Stress Scale (DASS) is proposed as a useful tool (Antony, Bieling, Cox, Enns, & Swinson, 1998). As a fully validated and commonly used instrument, the DASS has been designed for the assessment of stress, depressive symptoms, and anxiety with good psychometric properties including strong reliability and validity (Antony et al., 1998). The authors of the scale emphasize the fact that as the DASS had been designed as a quantitative measure of distress along three axes, it is not meant to be a categorical assessment of clinical diagnosis (Antony et al., 1998). Nevertheless, it could be used for identifying individuals who are at high risk of mental health problems with high scores in the subscales indicating a greater likelihood of depression, anxiety, or stress. As the validity of DASS among adults has been demonstrated, it has also been recommended for use among children and adolescents (Antony et al., 1998; Szabó & Lovibond, 2006). In terms of its clinical application, it is commonly used as an initial screen tool for its high predictive power of mental health problems. For example, in the clinic of Dr. Harvey, a fictitious general practitioner at a multipurpose medical center in Sydney, Australia, patients are invited to complete the DASS before each consultation visit. He would use the general cutoff points recommended by the original authors of the instrument for gauging the current mental health status of his patients. For the depression scale, a score between 0 and 4 represents a normal level of depressive behavior manifestation, 5 and 6 mild, 7 and 10 moderate, 11 and 13 severe, and 14 or higher extremely severe. Similarly for the anxiety scale, a score between 0 and 3 represents a normal level of anxious behavior manifestation, 4 and 5 mild, 6 and 7 moderate, 8 and 9 severe, and 10 or more extremely severe. For the stress scale, the cutoffs are: 0 and 7, 8 and 9, 10 and 12, 13 and 16, and 17 and above. As the medical center practices family medicine, Dr. Harvey has been collating the mental health profile of his patient families for a period of time. This could provide him with very useful and important information on all members of families under his care. He can make use of the information obtained to understand the health condition of the family as a whole, exploring possible causes, making diagnoses, and designing treatment plans or referrals for the family. In his exploration of the family health problems, he could also examine the Internet use of family members.

For the measure of Internet addiction, the Internet Addiction Test (IAT) designed and developed by Young is suggested for assessing the risk of addictive Internet use for both adolescents and parents (Young, 2016). Based on the concepts and behaviors exhibited by pathological gamblers as defined by the *Diagnostic and Statistical Manual of Mental Disorders*, 4th Edition (*DSM-IV*; American Psychiatric Association, 1994) diagnostic criteria, the IAT was designed as a 20-item self-report scale. Questions included in the scale specifically reflect typical behaviors of addiction relating to Internet use. An example question is: "How often do you feel depressed, moody, or nervous when you are offline, which goes away once you are back online?" Respondents are asked to indicate the propensity of their responses on a Likert scale ranging from 1 (rarely) to 5 (always). The IAT was validated with good reliability of Cronbach's alpha values ranging from 0.54 to 0.82 for various factors (Widyanto & McMurran, 2004). A total score could be calculated with possible scores ranging from a minimum of 20 to a maximum of 100. In comparison to the original eight-item Young's Diagnostic Questionnaire for Internet Addiction (YDQ; Young, 1996), the IAT has been considered a more comprehensive scale with better utilities and is the most commonly used instrument in the field (Frangos, Frangos, & Sotiropoulos, 2012). As part of the overall assessment of the family dynamics that may have an impact of the physical and mental health conditions of the family, Dr. Harvey could also examine the specific issue of Internet use among parents and children. The IAT would be a handy tool in providing useful information on whether members of the family become addicted to the Internet or not. A simple screening procedure using the IAT would provide indicative information of the Internet addiction status. Using the 20-item IAT, a cutoff of 0 to 30 suggests a normal range in terms of addictive behavior toward the Internet, 31 to 49 suggest a mild range, 50 to 79 moderate, and 80 or more severe. The test could be applied to the whole family including adolescents aged 13 years or older. The reason for the age limit of 13 years or older is merely based on the lowest age range of the IAT application in the literature. On obtaining this information and if Internet addiction has been identified in the children, Dr. Harvey could make use of the mental health screening results and examine the family dynamics with his family therapy colleagues. They could explore whether the parental mental health issues, if there are any, are affecting the mood state of the children and would in turn motivate the children to use the Internet as a means for coping with the family difficulties. The clinical team could also investigate how the family as a whole copes with different difficult situations in order to gain a better insight into the family dynamics. A simple assessment using a validated tool would provide insightful information on the ways of coping of the various family members.

For ways of coping, the Ways of Coping–Revised (WOC-R) Questionnaire designed by Folkman and Lazarus in 1985 is recommended (Folkman & Lazarus, 1985; Folkman, Lazarus, Dunkel-Schetter, DeLongis, & Gruen, 1986). The design of this questionnaire is based on the original Ways of Coping Checklist developed by the same authors in 1980. As suggested by the authors, the main purpose of the WOC-R is not to be used as an instrument to assess coping styles or traits of individuals. The WOC-R consists of 66 items that describe a wide range of thoughts and acts that people use to deal with internal and/or external demands in a specific stressful situation. The questionnaire is meant to assess the process of coping in response to specific stressors. Psychometric studies suggest that the questionnaire consists of eight distinct factors that can be formatted into eight subscales with good internal consistency for each subscale having Cronbach's alpha coefficients ranging from 0.61 to 0.79. These eight subscales capture different ways of coping that respondents could employ as a means to handle the distress evoked by a specific stressful encounter. These ways of coping include: confronting, distancing, self-controlling, seeking social support, accepting responsibilities, escape and avoidance, problem solving, and positive reappraisal. Based on the conceptual framework of stress and coping, other similar questionnaires have also been developed. These include the Coping Scale for Adults (CSA) and the Adolescent Coping Scale (ACS; Fredenberg & Lewis, 2000). As Dr. Harvey and his family therapy colleagues explore the family dynamics and the potential relationship between parents' mental health issues and the Internet addiction of the children as well as the parents' own, assessing the ways of coping of individual members of the family is also important. It would provide valuable insight into whether the Internet addiction problem of the child would be a negative means of handling his or her depressive mood or the stress encountered within or outside the family. A quick assessment using the ACS would reveal the predominant ways of coping by the child with a high score on the subscales indicating a higher tendency for adopting the strategy as a means of coping with difficult situations. For example, a young person who scores high on the problem-solving scale would take things in his or her own hands, face up to the difficulties, and try to resolve them. He or she is likely to initiate action plans aiming to address the problems at hand. Most adolescents do not employ only one way of coping with stress and difficulties. However, it is very likely that among the different ways of coping, there are one or two more prominent than the others. Understanding the ways of coping of individual adolescents is important as it provides the counselor or therapist insight into the coping mechanisms of the individual. The therapist is then able to explore alternative coping mechanisms for excessive Internet use.

TREATMENTS

In terms of implications for clinical treatment, the results can be applied directly to the design of family therapy, such as the brief strategic family therapy (BSFT) introduced by Dr. Kimberly Young in Chapter 13. As highlighted in the BSFT, diagnosis is an important step that "not only investigates gaming behavior and its abstinence but it must assess the way the family functions and engages in treatment activities. Therapists should evaluate how the family externalizes problem behaviors, the level of prosocial activities the family engages in, family communication styles, and the overall level of family functioning" (Young, Chapter 11 of this book). In addition to the main areas of diagnosis, it would also be prudent to assess the mental health status of both parents and children given that the problematic Internet behaviors of the child could be a result of his or her mental health issue which is, in some way, influenced by the same-sex parent. In the actual therapeutic treatment and management process, it would also be beneficial to provide therapy for the mental health problems of both parents and children. Moreover, it is important to understand that Internet addiction may not just be the problem of the child, but also a problem of the parents. Hence, during the family therapy process, it could be good practice to have full and complete diagnoses on Internet addiction for all family members including both parents and other siblings.

To enhance family therapy, clinicians could also pay attention to the ways of coping within the family as a whole and individually by parents and children. Debate on the dichotomization of coping mechanisms into straightforward positive and negative categories is ongoing. However, in the process of coping with a stressful situation, an individual may employ different means through which to face a difficult situation. In providing a more comprehensive treatment, it is also prudent for clinicians to explore this aspect of the family function in order to gain a deeper insight into the root of the Internet addiction problems within the family. For example, while facing the mother's depression with episodes of certain mood swing, the teenage child may find it difficult and feel helpless. In order to cope with the situation, he or she may turn to his or her games or other online activities that could provide the teenager a respite and sense of stability. An assessment of the ways of coping of the adolescent, in this case, could provide valuable insight into the mechanism used, and whether these ways of coping would be useful or harmful to the problems and situation the family is facing. Should any ineffective or *negative* means of coping, such as using the Internet as a refuge, be identified either in the parents or children, clinicians could provide support and guidance through psychoeducation and counseling as part of the treatment regime.

CONCLUSION

Adolescent Internet addiction may not be an aspect only of the individual. Parental involvement may play an important role in the onset, development, and maintenance of the addictive behavior. Of particular importance is the mental health status of parents that may contribute to the addictive behavior of their children through impacting on the mental health of the children. Hence, the mental health problems of adolescents, such as depression and stress, are not only comorbidities of the addiction but may actually be one of the causes as well as a maintaining factor of the behavior. The family therapy approach should be considered as a front-line treatment option in handling adolescent Internet addiction. Particular attention should also be paid to the identification and treatment of any mental health issues within the family including parents and children. Ineffective ways of coping with stress and the mood state of adolescents may serve as a conduit between the mental health problems and their addictive behavior. This may apply to parents as well. Assessment of the ways of coping by individuals within the family structure would provide insightful information on the dynamics of the family that may, in turn, help to identify the root problems of the adolescent Internet addiction.

REFERENCES

American Psychiatric Association. (1994). *Diagnostic and statistical manual of mental disorders* (4th ed.). Washington, DC: Author.

American Psychological Association. (2016). PsycTESTs. Retrieved from http://www.apa.org/pubs/databases/psyctests

Antony, M. M., Bieling, P. J., Cox, B. J., Enns, M. W., & Swinson, R. P. (1988). Psychometric properties of the 42-item and 21-item versions of the Depression Anxiety Stress Scales in clinical groups and a community sample. *Psychological Assessment, 10*, 176–181.

Bennett, A. C., Brewer, K. C., & Rankin, K. M. (2012). The association of child mental health conditions and parent mental health status among U.S. children, 2007. *Maternal and Child Health Journal, 16*, 1266–1275.

Chen, Y.-Y., & Weitzman, E. R. (2005). Depressive symptoms, *DSM-IV* alcohol abuse and their comorbidity among children of problem drinkers in a national survey: Effects of parent and child gender and parent recovery status. *Journal of Study on Alcohol, 66*, 66–73.

Cooley, E., Toray, T., Wang, M. C., & Valdez, N. N. (2008). Maternal effects on daughters' eating pathology and body image. *Eating Behaviors, 9*, 52–61.

Durkee, T., Kaess, M., Carli, V., Parzer, P., Wasserman, C., Floderus, B., . . . Wasserman, D. (2012). Prevalence of pathological internet use among adolescents in Europe: Demographic and social factors. *Addiction, 107*, 2210–2222.

Folkman, S., & Lazarus, R. S. (1985). If it changes it must be a process: Study of emotion and coping during three stages of a college examination. *Journal of Personality and Social Psychology, 48*, 150–170.

Folkman, S., Lazarus, R. S., Dunkel-Schetter, C., DeLongis, A., & Gruen, R. (1986). The dynamics of a stressful encounter: Cognitive appraisal, coping and encounter outcomes. *Journal of Personality and Social Psychology, 50*, 992–1003.

Frangos, C. C., Frangos, C. C., & Sotiropoulos, I. (2012). A meta-analysis of the reliability of Young's Internet Addiction Test. In S. Ao, L. Gelman, D. Hukins, A. Hunter, & A. Korsunsky (Eds.), *World Congress on Engineering 2012* (Vol. 1., pp. 368–371). London, UK: The International Association of Engineers.

Fredenberg, E., & Lewis, R. (2000). *The Coping Scale for Adults: Construct validity and what the instrument tells us* (pp. 24–28). Paper presented at the Annual Meeting of the American Educational Research Association, New Orleans, LA.

Huang, X., Zhang, H., Li, M., Wang, J., Zhang, Y., & Tao, R. (2010). Mental health, personality, and parental rearing styles of adolescents with Internet addiction disorder. *Cyberpsychology, Behavior, and Social Networking, 13*, 401–406.

Jacobs, M. J., Roesch, S., Wonderlich, S. A., Crosby, R., Thornton, L., Wilfley, D. E., . . . Bulik, C. M. (2009). Anorexia nervosa trios: Behavioral profiles of individuals with anorexia nervosa and their parents. *Psychological Medicine, 39*, 451–461.

Jang, M. H., & Ji, E. S. (2012). Gender differences in associations between parental problem drinking and early adolescents' internet addiction. *Journal of Special Pediatric Nursing, 17*, 288–300.

Kalaitzaki, A. E., & Birtchnell, J. (2014). The impact of early parenting bonding on young adults' Internet addiction, through the mediation effects of negative relating to others and sadness. *Addictive Behaviors, 39*, 733–736.

Ko, C.-H., Yen, J.-Y., Yen, C.-F., Chen, C.-S., & Chen, C.-C. (2012). The association between Internet addiction and psychiatric disorder: A review of the literature. *European Journal of Psychiatry, 27*, 1–8.

Kwon, J.-H., Chung, C.-S., & Lee, J. (2011). The effects of escape from self and interpersonal relationship on the pathological use of Internet games. *Community Mental Health Journal, 47*, 113–121.

Lam, L. T. (2015). Parental mental health and Internet addiction in adolescents. *Addictive Behaviors, 42*, 20–23.

Lam, L. T., Peng, Z. W., Mai, J. C., & Jing, J. (2009). Factors associated with Internet addiction among adolescents. *Cyberpsychology and Behavior, 12*, 551–555.

Lam, L. T., & Wong, E. M. Y. (2015). Stress moderates the relationship between problematic Internet use by parents and problematic Internet use by adolescents. *Journal of Adolescent Health, 56*, 300–306.

Lazarus, R. S., & Folkman, S. (1984). *Stress, appraisal, and coping.* New York, NY: Springer Publishing Company.

Li, W., Garland, E. I., & Howard, M. O. (2014). Family factors in Internet addiction among Chinese youth: A review of English- and Chinese-language studies. *Computer and Human Behaviors, 31,* 392–411.

Lin, C.-H., Lin, S.-L., & Wu, C.-P. (2009). The effects of parental monitoring and leisure boredom on adolescents' Internet addiction. *Adolescence, 44,* 993–1004.

Liu, Q.-X., Fang, X.-Y., Deng, L.-Y., & Zhang, J.-T. (2012). Parent-adolescent communication, parental Internet use and Internet-specific norms and pathological Internet use among Chinese adolescents. *Computer and Human Behaviors, 28,* 1269–1275.

Mendes, A. V., Loureiro, S. R., Crippa, J. A., de Meneses Gaya, C., García-Esteve, L., & Martín-Santos, R. (2012). Mothers with depression, school-age children with depression? A systematic review. *Perspective in Psychiatric Care, 48,* 138–148.

Park, S. K., Kim, J. Y., & Cho, C. B. (2008). Prevalence of Internet addiction and correlations with family factors among South Korean adolescents. *Adolescence, 43,* 895–909.

Siomos, K., Floros, G., Fisoun, V., Evaggelia, D., Farkonas, N., Sergentani, E., . . . Geroukalis, D. (2012). Evolution of Internet addiction in Greek adolescent students over a two-year period: The impact of parental bonding. *European Child and Adolescence Psychiatry, 21,* 211–219.

Szabó, M., & Lovibond, P. F. (2006). Anxiety, depression and tension/stress in children. *Journal of Psychopathology and Behavioral Assessment, 28,* 195–205.

Tsitsika, A., Critselis, E., Louizou, A., Janikian, M., Freskou, A., Marangou, E., . . . Kafetzis, D. (2011). Determinants of Internet addiction among adolescents: A case-control study. *Scientific World Journal, 11,* 866–874.

Van den Eijnden, R. J., Spijkerman, R., Vermulst, A. A., & Van Rooij, A. J. (2010). Compulsive Internet use among adolescents: Bidirectional parent-child relationships. *Journal of Abnormal Child Psychology, 38,* 77–89.

Weissman, M. M., & Jensen, P. (2002). What research suggests for depressed women with children. *Journal of Clinical Psychiatry, 63,* 641–647.

Widyanto, L., & McMurran, M. (2004). The psychometric properties of the Internet Addiction Test. *Cyberpsychology and Behaviors, 7,* 443–450.

Wu, X., Chen, X., Han, J., Meng, H., Luo, J., Nydegger, L., & Wu, H. (2013). Prevalence and factors of addictive Internet use among adolescents in Wuhan, China: Interactions of parental relationship with age and hyperactivity-impulsivity. *PLOS ONE, 8,* e61782. doi:10.1371/journal.pone.0061782

Xu, J., Shen, L.-X., Yan, C.-H., Hu, H., Yang, F., Wang, L., . . . Shen, X.-M. (2014). Parent-adolescent interaction and risk of adolescent internet addiction: A population-based study in Shanghai. *BMC Psychiatry, 14,* 112.

Yang, C. Y., Sato, T., Yamawaki, N., & Miyata, M. (2013). Prevalence and risk factors of problematic Internet use: A cross-national comparison of Japanese and Chinese university students. *Transcultural Psychiatry, 50,* 263–279.

Yen, J.-Y., Ko, C.-H., Yen, C.-F., Chen, S.-H., Chung, W.-L., & Chen, C.-C. (2008). Psychiatric symptoms in adolescents with Internet addiction: Comparison with substance use. *Psychiatry and Clinical Neuroscience, 62,* 9–16.

Yen, J.-Y., Yen, C.-F., Chen, C.-C., Chen, S.-H., & Ko, C.-H. (2007). Family factors of Internet addiction and substance use experience in Taiwanese adolescents. *Cyberpsychology and Behavior, 10*, 323–329.

Young, K. S. (1996, August). *Internet addiction: The emergence of a new clinical disorder*. Paper presented at the 104th annual meeting of the American Psychological Association, Toronto, Canada.

Young, K. S. (2016). Parent-Child Internet Addiction Test. Retrieved from https://www.healthyplace.com/addictions/center-for-internet-addiction-recovery/parent-child-internet-addiction-test

II | PREVENTION AND TREATMENT

8 | ASSESSMENT ISSUES WITH INTERNET-ADDICTED CHILDREN AND ADOLESCENTS

Kimberly S. Young

This chapter describes the growing impact of Internet addiction on children and adolescents as new users of this technology. It views Internet addiction in terms of technology overuse and compulsive tendencies related to a child's use of digital devices. It focuses on assessment methods that practitioners working with this population can use to measure and assess the behavior. It also focuses on how practitioners can develop their own screening tools of media use for children and adolescents. Finally, looking at parents who are the primary caregivers of technology at home, this chapter outlines comprehensive parenting guidelines based on the developmental age of the child to best integrate technology at home.

SCREEN ADDICTION IS UP

A survey of 350 parents in Philadelphia published by the American Academy of Pediatrics (AAP; Kabali et al., 2015) found that three quarters of their children had been given tablets, smartphones, or portable media players of their own by the age of 4 years and had used the devices without supervision. The study also noted that one third of the parents of 3- and 4-year-olds said that their children liked to use more than one device at the same time. Seventy percent of the parents reported allowing their children, aged 6 months to 4 years, to play with mobile devices while the parents did housework, and 65% said that they had done so to pacify a child in public. One quarter of the parents said that they left children with devices at bedtime and it was not clear how often the parents had bequeathed old devices as digital hand-me-downs or had bought new ones.

The survey was not nationally representative and relied on self-reported data from parents, but the surprising result adds to growing evidence that the use of electronic devices has become deeply woven into the experience of childhood. According to the results of a large-scale nationwide survey by Common Sense Media, 72% of children aged 8 years or younger used a mobile device in 2013, for example, compared with 38% in 2011. Within 2 years, they found that children's media environments and behaviors had changed and children were more likely to use mobile interactive media such as smartphones and tablets at younger ages.

Common Sense Media is a nonprofit organization that tracks children and their use of technology. In their latest study in 2015, they surveyed more than 2,600 teenagers (aged 13–18 years) and tweens (aged 8–12 years). Their findings showed that tweens spent almost 6 hours a day on *entertainment media*, which included things like listening to music or watching online videos. For teenagers, that number spiked to almost 9 hours. The study suggested that kids spent more time with media and technology than they did with their parents, at school, or for any other activity. They also found that 60% of teens said that they texted while doing homework and nearly two thirds of them said that it did not affect the quality of their work. However, in practice, the behavior actually results in a greater number of mistakes and less retention of what is done.

Earlier studies on Internet gaming disorder had found that nearly one in 10 youth gamers (aged 8–18 years) were classified as pathological gamers or addicted to video gaming (Gentile, 2009). Compared to nonpathological gamers, pathological gamers were significantly more likely to play for more years, play more frequently and for more time, be more familiar with video-game rating symbols, have worse grades in school, have difficulties with attention and attention deficit hyperactivity disorder (ADHD), have more health problems, and have friends who were addicted to games.

The data show that children at young ages are using media and mobile devices and little has been done in terms of prevention or treatment of what may be considered a serious problem. For instance, the AAP (2015) recommends that children between the ages of 6 and 18 years should only be allowed to use technology devices up to 2 hours per day. Before age 2 years, children should not be exposed to any electronic media, the pediatrics academy maintains, because a child's brain develops rapidly during these first years, and young children learn best by interacting with people, not screens, but lately it has softened its stance. It now advises setting time limits, prioritizing what it calls unplugged play, and not using devices as pacifiers to calm toddlers. However, as the data show, a lack of parental supervision may be more worrisome than the use of mobile devices by the very young.

This may be the age at which children engage in sensory–motor activities that encourage free use of their imaginations at play. Although children who are heavy users of electronics may become adept at multitasking, there is also a concern that they can lose the ability to focus on what is most important, a trait critical to deep thought and problem solving needed for many jobs and other endeavors later in life. Some data show that heavy use of electronic media, or what has been called screen addiction, can also have significant negative effects on children's attention, health, and social behavior.

Screen Addiction and Attention

Due to the constant point- and click-scanning behavior associated with screen and tablet use, several studies have found that children have developed significant attentional problems due to screen use (e.g., C.-F. Yen, Chou, Liu, Yang, & Hu, 2014; Yoo et al., 2004). The issues cited are that our brains do not multitask as we would like to think and that technology use makes us easily bored with things that do not pop, beep, or scroll (Sharma, 2014). The neuroscience of Internet addiction has found problems in the prefrontal cortex, or the area of the brain most associated with judgment, decision making, and impulse control; it undergoes major reorganization during adolescence, and has been shown to be weakened in functional MRI (fMRI) studies among Internet addicts (Brand, Young, & Laier, 2014). Studies also show that playing video games floods the pleasure center of the brain with dopamine (e.g., Han et al., 2007; Liu & Luo, 2015).

Imaging studies have found less efficient information processing and reduced impulse inhibition (Dong, Devito, Du, & Cui, 2012), increased sensitivity to rewards and insensitivity to loss (Dong, Hu, & Lin, 2013), and abnormal spontaneous brain activity associated with poor task performance (Yuan et al., 2013). With repeated use of screens, studies support that children are more likely to have an aversion to delayed reward whereas rapid response, immediate reward, and multiple windows with different activities characterized Internet behavior, reducing feelings of boredom or delayed aversion. This creates problems with skills that require concentration on single tasks such as reading books, which are linear and more line by line and page by page.

Screen Addiction and Health

Health can be considered on two levels, psychological health and physical health. When considering psychological health, issues of screen time impact a child's moods and feelings. Earlier studies have shown that the use of technology has been found to alleviate depression through social support, achievement, pleasure of control, and a virtual world to escape into from emotional difficulties (e.g., Young & Rodgers, 1998). However, too much Internet use can worsen the symptoms of depression and make depressed children particularly vulnerable to developing an Internet addiction (Chou, Liu,Yang, Yen, & Hu, 2015). High levels of depression and suicidal ideation (Park, Hong, Park, Ha, & Yoo, 2013) along with ADHD symptoms, depression, social phobia, and hostility were high among adolescents with Internet addiction in Taiwan (Ha et al., 2006; J.-Y. Yen, Ko, Yen, Wu, & Yang, 2007).

As with depression, children and adolescents who suffer from anxiety, especially social anxiety, are more likely to develop an addiction to technology (Weinstein et al., 2015). Adults who suffer from anxiety are more likely to use technology as a way of coping with stress, situational problems, and difficult life events such as the death of a loved one (Young, 1998). Young people with low self-esteem are likely to take more selfies and overuse social media for validation and likability, often easing their fears by spending more time retreating to an inner virtual world (Barry, Doucette, Loflin, Rivera-Hudson, & Herrington, 2017). Technology also enables youth who suffer from social anxiety and low self-esteem to hide behind their computer screens given the anonymous nature of electronic communication so that they can find comfort, acceptance, belonging, and companionship without the same face-to-face complications of relationship rejection, disapproval, and failure. Children were not able to overcome their social insecurities and fears when they can comfortably engage in online activities behind their screens that keep them from physically seeing other people.

Beyond the psychological concerns, there are physical risks that result from too much screen time. Think of a child who slumps over a tablet and devices all day. Early studies found that users who spent more time on computers were more likely to have suffered from back pain, eyestrain, carpel tunnel syndrome, and a number of repetitive injury disorders (e.g., Young, 1998). As technology is more portable and mobile, access is ubiquitous and young people are more sedentary in front of their screens instead of getting outside and playing. The more sedentary the lifestyle, the more children were likely to engage in irregular eating and poor sleeping patterns, and the lack of physical activity resulted in a higher occurrence of obesity (Li, Deng, Ren, Guo, & He, 2014).

Overuse of technology limits a child's physical development due to lack of movement during use (Rosen et al., 2014). Movement enhances learning ability as well as the ability to focus and pay attention; therefore, the lack of movement would have a negative impact on literacy and academic development (Barrense-Dias, Berchtold, Akre, & Surís, 2015). Not only did the lack of physical activity due to screen time result in a higher incidence of obesity, but studies also found that the use of technology in children younger than 12 years was harmful to their future development. The lack of movement can cause children to become obese, contributing to major health problems and putting them at a higher risk of early stroke, heart disease, and other serious health issues.

Screen Addiction and Social Behavior

Screens allow all of us to connect through texts, e-mails, and social media. This allows those who suffer from social phobias and anxieties, Asperger's syndrome, and autism to find a safe place to retreat (Weinstein et al., 2015). Young people with social problems and fears are most at risk of developing technology addictions because the Internet can provide social support in a non–face-to-face setting. Adults as well as adolescents with social problems feel more relaxed and engaged online, and in serious cases, the use of technology replaces all social relationships.

Suffering from screen addiction can result in problems while socializing with other children. As children retreat into technology, electronic communication isolates them from others and there is a lack of face-to-face social interaction. In young children, the lack of social interaction may impair their ability to develop effective social skills, which hinders the ability to develop and maintain healthy relationships in adolescence and beyond. We may see children who do not know how to make friends, talk to the opposite sex, or just *hang out* and enjoy people's company. The social awkwardness created by the isolationism of screens feeds the addiction, as the child is likely to retreat back to the online world where relationships are easier and already waiting for the child. Too much screen time can result in other social problems, such as conduct disorder and worse overall psychosocial adjustments. Children who fight to protect their screen time are likely to argue with their parents over screen use, disobey time limits, and react with aggression and even violence.

MEDIA USE SCREENING

When conducting a formal evaluation of a child, most often screen and Internet addiction is the not the primary presenting problem. Children and adolescents may be brought into therapy for other behavioral or psychiatric problems. Given the areas that co-occur with screen addictions such as anxiety and depression, it is important for therapists who treat children and adolescents to develop a media use screening tool to measure and profile their media use (e.g., reach, time spent) across all relevant forms of media including television, radio, and online. Screening helps to identify those who are at risk for development addiction problems, and identifying the addiction helps with treatment planning of the associated co-occurring conditions. Screening media use among children and adolescents can also help to measure behavior and attitudes of parents and caregivers in relation to their children's media consumption.

Unfortunately, there is not one standard tool identified that effectively screens media use among children and adolescents and its impact. As a general guideline, therapists should consider asking questions related to all media types and ask how much time is spent on each of the following:

- Internet and computers
- TV and movies
- Video games
- Mobile media
- Music
- Reading and print media
- Social media

Therapists, school counselors, and teachers can gain an incredible amount of information about media use by going through this list and the responses give a good idea of the child's level of risk for media-related problems. It is also helpful to engage parents and caregivers about media use at home and gauge their attitudes to the suitability of content on key media. For instance, do parents restrict TV programs that are unsuitable or restrict TV use in general? Do they react to challenging or inappropriate content that a child sees online? Do they know who their children talk with online or what kinds of mobile apps they use or what sites they visit? Do they have safeguards in place such as time limits or restricted places where a child uses devices?

Signs of Addiction

For many families, use of technology and digital devices happens early in a child's life. It could be school-based use in preschool or a toddler who plays with a parent's tablet. The therapist should evaluate media use in general and, among those children who seem to be heavy users of devices, screens, and technology, should evaluate signs of problem use of screens and digital devices. According to the Center for Internet Addiction, the following are the most common signs of screen and technology addiction where the term "technology" means any Internet activity completed on a computer, laptop, tablet, gaming console, or any other digital device:

- The child spends vast amounts of time engaged with technology.
- The child is constantly preoccupied by technology.
- The child withdraws from social situations, preferring to use digital devices.
- The child is tired and irritable because of inadequate sleep, and because of the overuse of technology.

The child announces that he or she is *bored* when he or she is not using digital devices.

The child withdraws from activities that he or she previously enjoyed, to pursue activities only on digital devices.

The child's school performance is compromised because he or she is focused on technology.

The child has lied or hidden the extent of technology use.

The child has become angry or disobedient when you set time limits on technology use.

These signs in combination with screening for media use should give the therapist a clear sense of how technology and devices are used at home and in school. Broadly, these signs focus on behavioral symptoms where a child's online usage interferes with his or her normal everyday activities such as getting ready for school, joining the family for meals, or attending sports practice. Other behavioral signs include: A child sacrifices needed hours of sleep to spend time online, a child disobeys time limits that have been set for Internet usage, a child has lost any interest in activities that were enjoyable before he or she had online access, and a child prefers to spend time using online applications rather than being with friends or family. When using this framework as an additional screening tool, three or more signs indicate addiction and further testing.

Media Use and the Parent–Child Internet Addiction Test

The younger a child is developmentally, the more his or her parents become a rich source of information. Just as parents are the first ones to suspect that their child is abusing alcohol or using drugs, they are the first to suspect that their child may have a problem related to their screen use. Parents usually notice some changes in their children and are in the best position to monitor their daily consumption of devices and technology. The Parent–Child Internet Addiction Test (PCIAT) assists in clinical evaluation of children suspected to suffer from Internet addiction (Young, 2016).

Based on the Internet Addiction Test (Young, 2016), a widely used screening measure used in clinical assessment, the PCIAT was developed to assess a child's online use from a parent's perspective (Figure 8.1). The PCIAT uses behavioral indicators of addiction to the Internet and technology along a five-point Likert scale (0 = not applicable, 1 = rarely, 2 = occasionally, 3 = frequently, 4 – often, 5 = always) where the parent selects the response that best represents the frequency of the behavior described in the following 20-item questionnaire.

After all the questions have been answered, the numbers for each response are added to obtain a final score. The higher the score, the greater the level of

---

FIGURE 8.1 Parent–Child Internet Addiction Test (PCIAT)

___ 1. How often does your child disobey time limits you set for online use?
___ 2. How often does your child neglect household chores to spend more time online?
___ 3. How often does your child prefer to spend time online rather than with the rest of your family?
___ 4. How often does your child form new relationships with fellow online users?
___ 5. How often do you complain about the amount of time your child spends online?
___ 6. How often do your child's grades suffer because of the amount of time he or she spends online?
___ 7. How often does your child check his or her e-mail before doing something else?
___ 8. How often does your child seem withdrawn from others since discovering the Internet?
___ 9. How often does your child become defensive or secretive when asked what he or she does online?
___ 10. How often have you caught your child sneaking online against your wishes?
___ 11. How often does your child spend time alone in his or her room playing on the computer?
___ 12. How often does your child receive strange phone calls from new "online" friends?
___ 13. How often does your child snap, yell, or act annoyed if bothered while online?
___ 14. How often does your child seem more tired and fatigued than he or she did before the Internet came along?
___ 15. How often does your child seem preoccupied with being back online when offline?
___ 16. How often does your child throw tantrums with your interference about how long he or she spends online?
___ 17. How often does your child choose to spend time online rather than doing once enjoyed hobbies and/or outside interests?
___ 18. How often does your child become angry or belligerent when you place time limits on how much time he or she is allowed to spend online?
___ 19. How often does your child choose to spend more time online than going out with friends?
___ 20. How often does your child feel depressed, moody, or nervous when offline, which seems to go away once back online?

Note: 0 = not applicable, 1 = rarely, 2 = occasionally, 3 = frequently, 4 = often, 5 = always.
Source: Young (2016).

---

addiction and potential for problems resulting from such Internet usage. The severity impairment index is as follows:

NONE: 0 to 30 points

MILD: 31 to 49 points: The child is an average online and screen user. He or she may surf the Internet a bit too long at times, but seems to have control of screen usage.

MODERATE: 50 to 79 points: The child seems to be experiencing occasional to frequent problems because of the Internet and screen use. Therapists should further evaluate the full impact of technology on the child's life and the impact on the family.

SEVERE: 80 to 100 points: Internet usage and screen time are causing significant problems in the child's life, and most likely with the family and at school. Therapists should address the underlying problems and explore family dynamics, parental monitoring of screen use, and school issues.

INTERVIEWING ISSUES

The assessment of a child or adolescent today should include at the very least some media use screening tools or questions about media use. It is important to understand how children are using technology and devices in general. With a thorough media screening assessment and testing, a therapist has a clear sense of behavioral and functional analysis of technology use at home, school, and work for a child. For toddlers and very young children, therapists should also learn about their current media diets and watch for risky technology behaviors using the Problematic and Risky Media Use in Children Checklist (Figure 8.2).

Answers to the Problematic and Risky Media Use in Children Checklist should assess all screen use such as tablets, computers, laptops, TVs, smart

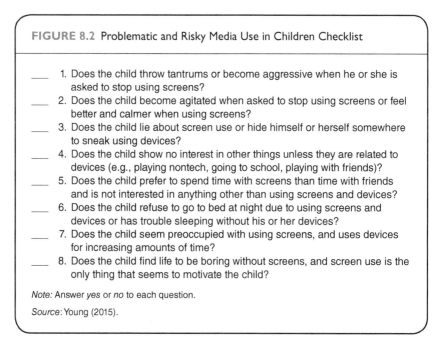

FIGURE 8.2 Problematic and Risky Media Use in Children Checklist

____ 1. Does the child throw tantrums or become aggressive when he or she is asked to stop using screens?
____ 2. Does the child become agitated when asked to stop using screens or feel better and calmer when using screens?
____ 3. Does the child lie about screen use or hide himself or herself somewhere to sneak using devices?
____ 4. Does the child show no interest in other things unless they are related to devices (e.g., playing nontech, going to school, playing with friends)?
____ 5. Does the child prefer to spend time with screens than time with friends and is not interested in anything other than using screens and devices?
____ 6. Does the child refuse to go to bed at night due to using screens and devices or has trouble sleeping without his or her devices?
____ 7. Does the child seem preoccupied with using screens, and uses devices for increasing amounts of time?
____ 8. Does the child find life to be boring without screens, and screen use is the only thing that seems to motivate the child?

Note: Answer yes or no to each question.

Source: Young (2015).

phones, and any portable digital devices. Answering *yes* to at least three of these behaviors in children aged 3 years to 11 years indicates that they are exhibiting risky or problematic behaviors associated with excessive screen and device use.

Rapport Building Among Internet-Addicted Children

As Internet-addicted children often suffer from social anxiety, depression, and shyness, the ability to establish rapport with them in a clinical interview is very important. The place of the interview should be a neutral place, quiet and secure, and there should not be too many toys in the room, and definitely no computers, tablets, or devices, as this distracts the child. It is useful to keep the paper and crayons handy. Sit in such a way as to allow eye-level contact with the child. If a small child is sitting on the floor, sit on the floor as well. Do not talk sitting behind a desk or a table; it is better to sit at the table with the child, sitting close but not too close. Do not enter "the child's territory," as it might be too endangering for him or her. It is also important to consider general techniques for interviewing this type of child, such as:

- Use phrases containing only one question or one thought, simple words, simple tenses and short sentences, and do not use double negatives.
- Avoid the use of "if/then" statements and "yes/no" questions with young children.
- Be specific in your questions—young children are very literal.
- Always ask the child to explain the words or expressions that you do not understand, especially any media or technology terms with which you are unfamiliar.
- Adjust the pace of the interview according to the child's abilities to open up.
- Control your emotions, the tone of your voice, and your mimics; do not show curiosity or shock, regardless of what the child says about his or her media and screen use.
- Move from general questions to more specific ones regarding a child's media and screen use to encourage more honest communication and less defensiveness.
- Have a list of questions prepared (either in your head or on paper) to encourage more informal conversation with the child.

Family Factors to Consider

Studies have shown that family factors also influence a child's media and screen use. For instance, being from a divorced family was a strong predictor for adolescent Internet addiction (J.-Y. Yen, Yen, Chen, Chen, & Ko, 2007). In a divorced family, either the mother or the father needs to support the whole family alone. The parent may work longer hours to support the family and the children are alone at home with their devices. Adolescents from divorced families may access the Internet to connect with friends as a means to relieve the insecurity developed in a single-parent family environment. In one case, Susie, a 13-year-old who lived with her mother after her father left them for another woman, said, "I was so sad after my dad left. My mom was never home that I relied solely on my friends and social media to get through my life."

In other circumstances, overuse of the Internet for social interaction may stem from family conflict and poor family relationships (Kabasakal, 2015). In families with high conflict or dysfunction such as poor relationships or poor parent mental health perhaps due to depression or addiction (Lam, 2015), the family system breaks down resulting in inadequate parental monitoring over technology use. This increases the likelihood of problem behavior because of the lack of family interactions and communication, leaving children unsupervised and alone.

It is important to assess the presence of family conflict and poor family bonding, and specifically investigate the level of supervision or monitoring by a child's parents. Severe family dysfunction implies inadequate familial resources, fewer shared decision-making and nurturing responsibilities, leaving it possible for parents to ignore their children and to ignore their device and screen use throughout the day. Children, in turn, feel a lack of support and guidance, and to compensate for possible psychological deficiencies, they connect more through the virtual world to build up relationships and gain a temporary sense of affection, inclusion, and belonging.

In addition to assessing the family dynamics associated with children and adolescents who spend too much time using screens and devices, it is important to understand how parents use their own screens and devices. Are parents modeling this type of compulsive use of screens? Do they frequently check their e-mail, Facebook, or Twitter accounts while watching their children? Do they use their screens constantly in front of their children? Or are parents very strict and have rules about Internet use? Where should therapists draw the line is fuzzy at best.

Some studies have found that there needs to be a balance between setting rules about Internet and screen use. For instance, van den Eijnden, Spijkerman, Vermulst, van Rooij, and Engels (2009) found that excessive parental control over the time of Internet use promotes the development of adolescent Internet addiction. When adolescents start growing up, they want more autonomy and independence, especially with technology, devices, and screens, and the parents who do the best job are those who serve as mentors to their children about technology, teaching them to avoid using screens as a way of coping with daily stressful life events and to balance screen use with their nonscreen lives.

Survey What Is Happening at School

Today, nearly all children use computers at school on a regular basis, but the amount varies considerably. Variables may include grade level, how high-tech the school is or wants to be, and how much the curriculum depends on classroom technology and mobile applications. Furthermore, with the growing population of school-aged children owning a mobile phone, the debate surrounding the role a phone plays within a classroom continues to cause controversy.

In 2007, New York City Mayor Michael Bloomberg implemented a state-wide cell phone ban in classrooms, which affected more than one million school children; the ban was not popular (Monahan & Chapman, 2011). Bloomberg heard complaints from numerous disgruntled parents and students, while others took him to court over the policy. Despite the outrage, the Department of Education defended the ban (until recently), insisting that cell phones led students to cheat in class, participate in drug deals, and share inappropriate pictures.

Although many teachers say cell phones provide too much of an enticing distraction for students, others argue that cell phones can be useful in the classroom—for taking notes or doing research—but use needs to be monitored. Despite the controversy, schools continue to rely on technology in the classroom. It is therefore important to assess school-related screen time. Questions to ask include:

- How much interactive screen time does the child receive at school on a daily basis?
- How unregulated is the child's screen time at school?
- How much do teachers use technology and mobile applications for the students?
- How much technology-related homework does the child get?
- How possible (or how complicated) would it be to remove or eliminate technology use and still achieve good grades in school?

For grade-school children, it might be worth observing the classroom to see how much screen time occurs in a typical day. It would also be important to assess whether the teacher uses video games and computer time as a reward for students. Often, classrooms rely on technology for teaching methods but with a little investigation, this evaluation may uncover that the student does not need technology to learn the class material, do homework, and pass the class. When developing a treatment plan, it would be helpful to talk with the teachers about strategies to reduce or remove screen time for doing homework and learning for the child or the teen. This is part of putting together screen-time goals to reduce use and, once the teachers understand, they work with the therapist to develop a time-management plan that still allows the child to participate in class.

"3–6–9–12" PREVENTION
FOR SCREEN ADDICTION

What can parents do to help? Young children have far more access to media technology now than they did even just a few years ago. Technology is changing the nature of childhood. Parents need to be proactive in stopping and controlling how much screen time kids have on devices today. Children now rely on technology for the majority of their play, grossly limiting challenges to their creativity and imagination, as well as limiting necessary challenges to their bodies to achieve optimal sensory and motor development. Worse yet, when parents try to stop or control screen time, children react with defiance, disobedience, and even violence. It is important that children have different rules at different developmental ages. The 3–6–9–12 prevention for screen addiction outlines steps parents can take at each developmental age (Young, 2016).

Birth to 3 Years Rules: Never/Nowhere

No technology; this includes smartphones, computers, and TVs. The American Psychiatric Association (APA) states no screen use at this age bracket. It is vital that parents stay committed to this. Any screen time impairs social communication, development, and a child's attachment to the parent or other family members. If children are completely disconnected from technology, they have time to develop relationships with others, and can develop other needed sensory–motor skills by playing with physical toys, reading, and building relationships with other children.

3 to 6 Years Rules: 1 Hour a Day

At this age, children should be introduced to technology under careful parental supervision. Parents too often give a child a tablet or smartphone as a "babysitter" or a reward for good behavior. This is a crucial time in childhood development for learning prosocial behavior and social behavior. Keep children involved in activities away from the computer and avoid multiplatform portable devices (e.g., phones, tablets, laptops). If children are exposed to too much screen time at this age, aggressive behavior and impulsivity result. Allow use only in public areas of the home and block video games and pornography.

6 to 9 Years Rules: Supervised Use

Children need to balance technology with social and physical behaviors. We have a major obesity crisis in America partly because of kids sitting and using their technology devices and not getting exercise. Now that children have passed the physical milestones of mastery of running and kicking, and bending over without falling, screen use may include games that the entire family can play on gaming consoles. It is important that this screen time is a family bonding experience. Some of the best all-ages games are Just Dance Kids and Epic Mickey. If parents are not sure about a game's content, the Entertainment Software Rating Board app (it is free) will help parents judge the game's appropriateness. Parents still need to control use and avoid multiplatform portable devices as these are hard to monitor; if used, children can be allotted 2 hours of screen time per day under close parental supervision with blocked access to video games and pornography. At this age, children need to be mentally and physically stimulated through reading, taking nature walks, riding bikes, getting involved in school and sport activities, making friends at school, and spending time with family. Parents need to create sacred family time with no technology.

9 to 12 Years Rules: Integration

At age 9 to 12 years, as children cognitively develop, it is important that they understand that not all media are educational. Their lessons can be either accurate and healthful, or misleading and harmful. This is a time for parents to help their children be mindful about the videos they watch, the sites they visit, and the games they play, by talking about the messages portrayed and what it means to them and why. At this age, teach tweens to hone their media literacy skills by thinking critically about the TV shows, movies, and advertisements they see.

12 to 18 Years Rules: Independence

As children enter the teenage years, they want independence. Rules of the house usually change as children can now stay out later, or meet friends at parties, or by the age of 16 years start to drive. These are all signs of independence and screen use is no different. At this age, teenagers desire their own social media accounts and demand privacy and unsupervised online time.

Digital diet and *digital nutrition* are important at this age. If parents grant unrestricted use, have the child maintain a digital log. This is so important and can provide parents with updates on their child's time online. A digital log helps teenagers keep track of their own media use as well. Too much time online, like too much food, can result in harmful habits. A digital log helps track a child's balanced digital diet without hovering over their daily online use.

Regarding digital nutrition, this is a time to help children make better choices about their activities online. Do they play video games all day or are they doing homework? Are they using social media or are they researching a paper for school? Like food addiction, online use is about making healthy choices. Instead of the candy bar or bag of chips, it's better to snack on vegetables. Good digital nutrition can be the difference between a young person gaming for hours or learning through educational apps and websites. It means that as an independent teenager the technology is used responsibly.

CONCLUSION

The latest study by Common Sense Media, a nonprofit organization that tracks children and their use of technology, surveyed more than 2,600 teenagers (aged 13–18 years) and tweens (aged 8–12 years). Their findings showed that tweens spend almost 6 hours a day on *entertainment media* and teenagers spend almost 9 hours per day. The study suggested that kids spend more time with media and technology than with their parents, at school, or on anything else. Further studies on screen addiction show that children and adolescents who sit in front of screens are more at risk to develop problems in attention, psychological and physical health, and social behavior.

At young ages, children are more likely to suffer from problems with attention deficit disorders due to the point-and-click mentality of screens. They also show problems with depression and social anxiety because of overuse of screens and hide behind screens as a way of coping with their feelings, or use online friends to find friendship, comfort, and support. Children who overuse screens suffer from physical inactivity caused by the sedentary lifestyle associated with screen use and the lack of motor play because of sitting in front of screens. This may ultimately lead to obesity in children. Children who overuse screens are more likely to be isolated from socialization with other children and friends; they also suffer from obedience problems, conduct disorder, Asperger's syndrome, and other social issues in peer group relationships.

Remedies to deal with these issues include limiting TV exposure (especially background TV) before the age of 2 years, which is well advised. When we think about parenting issues, contextual factors such as maternal depression, trauma, work/life stress, and social economic status should be assessed as part of the family dynamics. It is also important to assess children characteristics such as attention deficit risk, family history, genetic background, temperament, self-regulation, motor coordination, and opportunities to engage in the community and with friends should be assessed. Issues within the family such as family attachment, sibling attachment, parental stress index, and parenting style should be assessed. As part of the prevention, identifying children at greatest risk for addiction is also important. Children with preexisting psychosocial morbidities may be at greatest risk, and their

Internet and technology usage should be more explicitly monitored and regulated by guardians and protectors.

Finally, at the earliest possible age, parents should be mindful of the impact of their own media use, including smartphones and tablets, on their interactions with their infants and toddlers. Parents should be encouraged to interact with toddlers and touchscreen devices (including e-books) in much the same way they are encouraged to use and interact with children while reading traditional books. Media diets should be rich in educational content, but heavy screen media use should be discouraged, especially when children are beginning to learn to read.

REFERENCES

American Academy of Pediatricians. (2015). Retrieved from https://www.aap.org/en-us/advocacy-and-policy/aap-health-initiatives/pages/media-and-children.aspx

Barrense-Dias, Y., Berchtold, A., Akre, C., & Surís, J. C. (2015). The relation between internet use and overweight among adolescents: A longitudinal study in Switzerland. *International Journal of Obesity, 37*, 54–60.

Barry, C. T., Doucette, H., Loflin, D. C., Rivera-Hudson, N., & Herrington, L. L. (2017). "Let me take a selfie": Associations between self-photography, narcissism, and self-esteem. *Psychology of Popular Media Culture, 6*(1), 48–60.

Brand, M., Young, K. S., & Laier, C. (2014). Prefrontal control and internet addiction: A theoretical model and review of neuropsychological and neuroimaging findings. *Frontiers in Human Neuroscience, 8*, 375.

Chou, W.-J., Liu, T.-L., Yang, P., Yen, C.-F., & Hu, H.-F. (2015). Multi-dimensional correlates of Internet addiction symptoms in adolescents with attention-deficit/hyperactivity disorder. *Psychiatry Research, 225*(1–2), 122–128.

Dong, G., Devito, E. E., Du, X., & Cui, Z. (2012). Impaired inhibitory control in "internet addiction disorder": A functional magnetic resonance imaging study. *Psychiatry Research, 203*(2–3), 153–158.

Dong, G., Hu, Y., & Lin, X. (2013). Reward/punishment sensitivities among internet addicts: Implications for their addictive behaviors. *Progress in Neuro-psychopharmacology & Biological Psychiatry, 46*, 139–145.

Gentile, D. (2009). Pathological video-game use among youth ages 8 to 18: A national study. *Psychological Science, 20*(5), 594–602.

Ha, J. H., Yoo, H. J., Cho, I. H., Chin, B., Shin, D., & Kim, J. H. (2006). Psychiatric comorbidity assessed in Korean children and adolescents who screen positive for Internet addiction. *Journal of Clinical Psychiatry, 67*(5), 821–826.

Han, D. H., Lee, Y. S., Yang, K. C., Kim, E. Y., Lyoo, I. K., & Renshaw, P. F. (2007). Dopamine genes and reward dependence in adolescents with excessive internet video game play. *Journal of Addiction Medicine, 1*(3), 133–138.

Kabali, H. K., Irigoyen, M. M., Nunez-Davis, R., Budacki, J. G., Mohanty, S. H., Leister, K. P., & Bonner, R. L., Jr. (2015). Exposure and use of mobile media devices by young children. *Pediatrics, 136*, 1044–1050. doi:10.1542/peds.2015-2151

Kabasakal, Z. (2015). Life satisfaction and family functions as predictors of problematic Internet use in university students. *Computers in Human Behavior, 53*, 294–304.

Lam, L. T. (2015). Parental mental health and Internet addiction in adolescents. *Addictive Behaviors, 42*, 20–23.

Li, M., Deng, Y., Ren, Y., Guo, S., & He, X. (2014). Obesity status of middle school students in Xiangtan and its relationship with Internet addiction. *Obesity (Silver Spring, Md.), 22*(2), 482–487.

Liu, M., & Luo, J. (2015). Relationship between peripheral blood dopamine level and internet addiction disorder in adolescents: A pilot study. *International Journal of Clinical and Experimental Medicine, 8*(6), 9943–9948.

Monahan, R., & Chapman, B. (2011, July 16). Mayor Bloomberg insists on school cell phone bans while parents demand ban lift for communication. *The Daily News*. Retrieved from http://www.nydailynews.com/new-york/mayor-bloomberg-insists-school -cell-phone-bans-parents-demand-ban-lift-communication-article-1.161049

Park, S., Hong, K.-E. M., Park, E. J., Ha, K. S., & Yoo, H. J. (2013). The association between problematic internet use and depression, suicidal ideation and bipolar disorder symptoms in Korean adolescents. *The Australian and New Zealand Journal of Psychiatry, 47*(2), 153–159.

Rosen, L. D., Lim, A. F., Felt, J., Carrier, L. M., Cheever, N. A., Lara-Ruiz, J. M., … Rokkum, J. (2014). Media and technology use predicts ill-being among children, preteens and teenagers independent of the negative health impacts of exercise and eating habits. *Computers in Human Behavior, 35*, 364–375.

Sharma, K. N. (2014). Technology and the future brain. *Annals of the National Academy of Medical Sciences* (India), *49*(1 & 2), 48–54.

van den Eijnden, R. J., Spijkerman, R., Vermulst, A. A., van Rooij, T. J., & Engels, R. C. (2010). Compulsive Internet use among adolescents: Bidirectional parent-child relationships. *Journal of Abnormal Child Psychology, 38*(1), 77–89.

Weinstein, A., Dorani, D., Elhadif, R., Bukovza, Y., Yarmulnik, A., & Dannon, P. (2015). Internet addiction is associated with social anxiety in young adults. *Annals of Clinical Psychiatry: Official Journal of the American Academy of Clinical Psychiatrists, 27*(1), 4–9.

Yen, C.-F., Chou, W.-J., Liu, T.-L., Yang, P., & Hu, H.-F. (2014). The association of Internet addiction symptoms with anxiety, depression and self-esteem among adolescents with attention-deficit/hyperactivity disorder. *Comprehensive Psychiatry, 55*(7), 1601–1608.

Yen, J.-Y., Ko, C.-H., Yen, C.-F., Wu, H.-Y., & Yang, M.-J. (2007). The comorbid psychiatric symptoms of Internet addiction: Attention deficit and hyperactivity disorder (ADHD), depression, social phobia, and hostility. *The Journal of Adolescent Health: Official Publication of the Society for Adolescent Medicine, 41*(1), 93–98.

Yen, J.-Y., Yen, C.-F., Chen, C.-C., Chen, S.-H., & Ko, C.-H. (2007). Family factors of internet addiction and substance use experience in Taiwanese adolescents. *CyberPsychology & Behavior: The Impact of the Internet, Multimedia and Virtual Reality on Behavior and Society, 10*(3), 323–329.

Yoo, H. J., Cho, S. C., Ha, J., Yune, S. K., Kim, S. J., Hwang, J., … Lyoo, I. K. (2004). Attention deficit hyperactivity symptoms and internet addiction. *Psychiatry and Clinical Neurosciences, 58*(5), 487–494.

Young, K. S. (1998). Internet addiction: The emergence of a new clinical disorder. *CyberPsychology & Behavior, 1*(3), 237–244.

Young, K. S. (2015). The 3-6-9-12 Parenting guidelines for technology use at home. Retrieved from http://netaddiction.com/wp-content/uploads/2015/07/Screen-Smart-Guidelines.pdf

Young, K. S. (2016). Parent-Child Internet Addiction Test. Retrieved from https://www.healthyplace.com/addictions/center-for-internet-addiction-recovery/parent-child-internet-addiction-test

Young, K. S., & Rodgers, R. C. (1998). The relationship between depression and Internet addiction. *CyberPsychology & Behavior, 1*(1), 25–28.

Yuan, K., Chenwang, J., Ping, C., Xuejuan, Y., Tao, D., Yanzhi, B., ... Jie, T. (2013). Amplitude of low frequency fluctuation abnormalities in adolescents with online gaming addiction. *PLOS ONE, 8*(11), e78708. doi:10.1371/journal.pone.0078708

9 RESILIENCE AND PREVENTIVE PARENTING

Evelyn Eisenstein, Tito De Morais, and Emmalie Ting

How early is really considered early for children and adolescents to use technological devices and Internet social networks is still a very controversial theme for many families and also for health and other professionals. It involves ethical, safety, and educational considerations, as well as all the behavioral repercussions that have positive or negative health consequences later in life. There are not enough longitudinal research studies as yet, although evidence and reports have started appearing and are being published in scientific and general literature. It remains a worrisome point for many specialists and even for some parents who are concerned with the limits and criteria of the definition of a simple distraction during playtime versus a precocious Internet addiction and hope to find ways to recognize the signs and symptoms of Internet addiction during childhood and adolescence (Carr, 2011).

Some examples of new parental complaints in a pediatric office are the case of a 3-year-old girl who is so engrossed playing with her tablet during mealtime that her spoonful of food does not reach her mouth correctly; or a 7-year-old boy who is shouting "Kill, kill!" while moving his thumbs quickly in front of his video-game equipment; or an 11-year-old preteen boy who has been having sleeping problems and learning difficulties, as he stays up late talking to his friends and sharing music, movies, and playing games on his smartphone! Parents or grandparents have been startled by the way children and teenagers nowadays are becoming experts with these technologies. Many schools now have computers as part of the new curricula but many teachers were not trained on how to use this equipment to build safer relationships. Even at many homes of diverse social and contextual backgrounds, parents are underresponsive to their children's and adolescents' technological questions and demands, and many complaints are now part of the medical or psychological evaluations, deserving more attention in terms of intervention and prevention, and also public policies (Young & Abreu, 2010). What would be the best measures for resilience and community protection for some of the social determinants of digital diseases in the future are presented in this chapter for further discussion with families, school workers, and allied health professionals.

PROBLEMS WITH DIGITAL CHILDREN

Since the 1990s, when computers got cheaper and simpler and the World Wide Web made it possible for everyone to share content and information through the Internet, it became a growing method of communication for people all over the globe. More and more websites were linking people and places, and by 1996 the Internet was connecting more than 150 countries, including Brazil, Korea, China, Japan, the United Kingdom, and the United States. Soon afterward, smartphones, tablets, notebooks, laptops, Bluetooth, blogs, multiplayers, YouTube, Google, software, websites, video games, apps, Wi-Fi, and so many more new words and appliances became part of any family's vocabulary, infiltrating routines and changing habits.

Children are discovering the world and the way to survive the difficulties of socialization each day, through curiosity and learning. All parents wish their best for their offspring, with protection and responsibility duties being shared with the schools, next door neighbors, and local communities. Nowadays, everyone is busy looking at their new devices, talking to each other through texting and messages, viewing images, sounds, music, colorful movements at their screens, even when walking on the streets with their children. Meanwhile, the significance of the presence or absence of someone who is nearby to hold you or to love you became harder to feel or even to be perceived and measured, through social or scientific indicators. Human interaction seems to be facing serious competition against technology. Science is still coming up with ways to measure the effect of technology over people, especially those still in their growth and developmental phases.

New social codes and behaviors have emerged thanks to social media. Children of all ages are now surrounded by all kinds of gadgets that their grandparents would have never imagined to exist in their lifetime. Kids and teens are online more than any earlier generation, but the ability to use these appliances and devices does not correlate with the ability to understand how the technology should be used safely. Technology is changing very quickly and the biggest reason our kids and teens get into trouble online is not because they are malicious or taken over by aliens, but because they are kids, still developing and not quite grasping the greater world around them with all the consequences (O'Keefe, 2011).

"To be connected" got to be the new world's order and tune. No leisure moment to rest, or play outside in the garden, or with your toys around your room during rainy days. Parents are busy working late hours and all their friends are also connected around chats and social networks even in their own work spaces. Therefore, just click, link, use a nickname or a password and the world is entirely at your fingertips. So easy and the world is yours and available 24 hours a day, 7 days a week, all year long. No more solitude, no more boredom, no more worries for parents on how to safely raise their children, as they can access many sites with all the information on what to do next, how to cook the best meal, how to enjoy life, how to smile at the camera, how to take selfies and send them to friends and foes. It seems to be getting harder and harder to resist the charms of technology and keep it from driving us away from real social interaction. Online security is more than a state of mind but protecting and empowering kids in the digital world continues to be a challenge of resilience for every family.

New health conditions are nowadays more frequent during childhood and the teenage years, and have being associated with the growing amount of hours spent in front of televisions, computers, tablets, and other devices. These are the times when children and teens should not be inactive or passive or close to it—they could and should be profiting from outdoor activities (Sharif & Sargent, 2006).

Some medical complaints are sleeping disorders, headaches, loss of concentration with attention deficit disorder, obesity and sedentary habits, postural disorders, carpal tunnel syndrome, repetitive strain injuries, with numbness and tingling of the hands, hearing and noise-induced hearing loss or buzzing in their ears with the use of headphones that are louder than 70 dB (maximum recommended for children), and also, refraction deficits, retinal phototoxicity because of blue LED light ("Blue Light Has a Dark Side," 2015), dry eyes, and computer vision syndrome (Rosenfield, 2011), as children simply forget to blink their eyes while playing video games and shed no tears while their heroes are being sacrificed on a battlefield (Abreu, Eisenstein, & Estefenon, 2013; Estefenon & Eisenstein, 2008). A review study done with 11,931 teenagers with an average age of 14.89 ± 0.87 years, all students at different schools in 11 European countries, demonstrated 89% of multiple risky behaviors associated with prolonged use of the Internet, including bad sleeping and eating habits, sedentary habits, use of nicotine, and mental health problems (Durkee et al., 2016).

RESILIENCE: INTERNAL AND EXTERNAL FACTORS

The word "resilience," originally used in physics, means the level of resistance that any material can suffer pressure and the material's capability of returning to its original state without the occurrence of any rupture, damage, or injury. Psychology also uses this word and created the term "psychological resilience" to describe how people deal with daily frustrations at all levels and their ability for emotional recovery. Another way of putting it: The more resilient a person is, the stronger he or she is to deal with all adversities in life (Abreu, 2017).

Resilience also refers to an individual's capability to employ a collection of protective factors to successfully adapt and cope following any traumatic event, disadvantage, or adversity. It is the strength to persist, bounce back to reality and routine activities, and even thrive in the face of stressful circumstances.

There are some controversies about the indicators for a good resilience pattern, and it is not well understood whether it would be a personality or a character trait. The best definition for this term would be that it is the result of a lifelong learning process (Abreu, 2017).

It involves the ability, when faced with stress or adversity, to actively employ individual traits (internal factors) and wider social, community, and environmental supports (external factors) to return to or maintain a positive state of mental health and functioning. Internal resilience factors include personal strengths and factors such as self-efficacy and problem-solving skills, which can be nurtured by stimulating a person's self-control and thinking skills, confidence, positive outlook, and sense of responsibility and participation.

For example, parents who actively protect their children from obstacles or daily troubles, as many parents do to save their children further sufferings, do not help their offspring build their resilience skills. Therefore, once they grow, these individuals do not have the necessary skills to confront their problems and lose the opportunities to solve their life crises constructively. The lack of mental skills makes them react excessively and increases the size of adversities, as demonstrated by aggressive behavior or acting-out by children. At the opposite end, some respond passively or with a depressive mood, and they stay almost shocked facing their dilemmas and consequently perpetuating their troubles for life.

For instance, parents can help their children strengthen their resilience skills by asking the children to talk about their daily difficulties, or to write about them, if they are older, such as what happened during the school day or what were the most meaningful experiences for the last week. Parents can learn to listen to their children, to understand how they react and how would they prefer to have reacted to daily-life situations. When one deals with problems with such a perspective, one also learns how to safely deal with different options or alternatives for solutions. It is a good exercise for children to learn to cope or to develop other possibilities for new attitudes. Therefore, parents can help them by serving as guides or role models, by giving examples for their children to find an answer to their daily emotional troubles, by practicing dialogues, and by keeping a door open for problem solving (Abreu, 2017).

Parents play a critical role in the socialization and regulation of emotions and behaviors in children, and children also shape and contribute to their parents' own behavior and regulatory functioning. Indeed, families have their own capacities for self-regulation and set clear limits that may provide protective effects against the emergence of addictive behavior. Most probably, some of these rules also apply to other addictive habits, especially for children who have mental or behavioral problems and who may become screen addicted more often.

High levels of family resilience may prevent the development of mental health problems in adolescents, even problems such as Internet addiction. Resilience is strengthened when caring and supportive relationships have been developed within and outside the family, through love and trust, providing positive role models, and offering encouragement and reassurance during daily activities.

External resilience factors include caring relationships, positive role models, and values in families and communities, meaningful schooling and educational background, and other resources, such as cultural and social participation and prosocial peers (Dray et al., 2014).

Resilience in the context of adolescence and mental health is defined as a process by which risks are encountered, and assets or resources (internal and external resilience factors) are used to avoid a negative outcome, such as mental health problems. Previous research in this area is limited; however, it suggests that high levels of resilience may prevent the development of mental health problems, like depression, stress, anxiety and obsessive-compulsive symptoms, supporting the suggestion that fostering resilience may prevent the development of mental health problems in adolescents. Not all young people who experience disadvantage or adversity experience negative mental health outcomes. The concept of resilience provides one possible explanation for the ability of some individuals to maintain positive mental health in the face of adverse life circumstances or complex social situations (Dray et al., 2015).

Another important component for resilience is the capability of children or adolescents to understand better what and how they feel. This may seem easy and simple, but it is not for the digital generation, as they are hyper-stimulated with the constant and uninterrupted use of technology as almost a new type of anesthesia to block their negative humor status. Therefore, when children and teens connect to hide from their daily contextual problems, they also lose the ability for self-perception and to confront their difficulties in a more direct and positive way. This gets to be a vicious cycle of screen addiction and emotional deviance. This process opens possibilities for youngsters to be connected and distracted from the negative events around them, and makes the "digital life" an alternative route for dysphoric humor state and further screen addiction.

A simple therapeutic way that could be practiced more frequently is the use of a diary, where youngsters can record their daily tasks and add their feelings, so that they can even revisit their assumptions and compare it with their negative or aggressive humor state. This could be an option for further dialogue and as an ice-breaking method between parents and children. This could even be a future model for more adaptive behavior and for resilience building (Abreu, 2017).

The capabilities that underlie resilience can be strengthened at any age. Age-appropriate activities that have widespread health benefits can also improve resilience. For example, regular physical exercise, outdoor leisure activities, and stress-reducing practices, such as music or meditation, as well as family or community programs that actively build executive function and self-regulatory skills, can improve the abilities of children and adults to cope with, adapt to, and even prevent adversities in their lives. Adults who strengthen these skills in themselves can model positive behaviors for their children, thereby improving the resilience of the next generation.

It is of utmost importance to provide supportive and nurturing experiences for young children in the earliest years, when brain development is most rapid. The brain and other biological systems are most adaptable early in life, and the development that occurs in the earliest years lays the foundation for a wide range of resilient behaviors. However, resilience is shaped throughout life by accumulation of experiences, both good and bad, and the continuing development of adaptive coping skills connected to those experiences. What happens early in life may matter most, but it is never too late to build resilience. From a policy perspective, it is in society's best interest to strengthen the foundations of healthy brain architecture in all young children to maximize the return on investments in education, health, and workforce development (Dauncey & Pell, 1998; Skuse, 1998).

There are several theoretical models for building a resilient family, but what is most important is to learn how to deal with children and adolescents, using these same models but adapted to a highly technological and digital era. These models include:

- Social emotional learning: emotional self-regulation, communication, relationships
- Cognitive behavioral: causal links among thoughts, feelings, and actions
- Positive psychology: activities and processes that seek to boost positive emotions
- Mindfulness: meditation, contemplation, and silent moments to reduce stress
- Stable, responsible relationships: Security, close and friendly attachments
- Skills in communication and problem solving

CASE REPORT

Felipe is a 14-year-old, an only son brought to consultation by his mother, Vanessa, who has been worried about his weight. She noticed that he looked very thin the past few months.

Vanessa starts talking very anxiously about her fears of him not developing well, or getting sick because of his poor eating habits.

Felipe has always been a bright student, not very fond of sports or any other kind of physical activities. He studies in the morning and spends most of his afternoons at home, by himself. He says his favorite activity lately has been playing a particular game on the computer. He is surprised at first, when asked to count how many hours of screen time he spends per day (around 10 hours a day). However, he shrugs his shoulders as a sign of contempt.

His physical examination reveals moderate scoliosis and kyphosis. His body mass index (BMI) is 15 kg/m^2, which puts him slightly over the third percentile of BMI for his age. His BMI chart shows that he used to follow the 10th percentile and his actual Tanner Stage of Sexual Maturation is 2, beginning of puberty. He also complains of worsening eyesight, blurring, and occasional headaches.

Felipe's father abandoned him and Vanessa when Felipe was 2 years old. Vanessa works full time as a nurse, leaving home every day at 6 a.m. and returning by 7 p.m.; she spends 3 hours in traffic every day. She uses the weekends to clean the house, do the grocery shopping, and cook meals for the week ahead. She leaves Felipe's meals in the refrigerator defrosting every day but complains that she often comes home to find them untouched. This has been happening more frequently over the past few months.

Felipe turns his face away and says sometimes he just doesn't feel hungry and she shouldn't force him to eat. He says he doesn't mind being thin and doesn't care about his growth. He is passively negative, and looks a bit depressive.

It is prescribed that he starts on some physical activity and improve his eating habits. He is very reluctant to accept most of our suggestions. Finally, he agrees to go on walks with Vanessa every other day when she arrives home from work, and on the weekends to play soccer outside with friends.

Two months later, the pair returns to consultation. He says he did not notice any difference but mentioned that at least now his mother would listen to him during the walks, as she does not bring her phone with her.

Felipe had gained nearly 1.5 pounds on that consultation, and said that he would agree to start swimming, because he started being friends with a girl from school, and wanted to gain some muscles and improve his looks.

Vanessa says that it was hard at first raising energy to go on the walks, but on the third week she started feeling more energetic and was delighted to realize that she fit into some old clothes she was about to give away.

DISCUSSION

This case report points out how important it is to build up resilience skills through the development of caring and supportive relationships within and outside the family.

Had Vanessa insisted that Felipe pursue other interests, such as sports, martial arts, dancing, or a musical instrument, or had started walking with him earlier in life, to overcome together some of the trauma of separation and the absence of the father during the childhood period, Felipe might have been less prone to overusing the Internet.

Luckily, in their case, Felipe and Vanessa were able to quickly find, after a short mediated conversation, a shared activity that they both agreed on, and that allowed them to spend some quality time together on a regular basis. This might seem like a small intervention, but it's a first step to strengthening one important bond that can lead Felipe back to a healthy and more balanced life as a happier teen and off the screen. It is also an example of how resilience can be applied within a family routine by the establishment of mother–son positive constructive dialogue and affection bond, despite a traumatic past event of separation and father´s abandonment.

FOUR-PRONGED PREVENTIVE APPROACH

Using different equipment and technologies has been one of the first alerts for parents and educators that a child may be overusing the Internet, and many booklets, guides, instructions, and information have been developed and are already available, in many languages; the Internet itself can be used as a helpline (CGI—Comite Gestor da Internet no Brasil, 2014; Safernet-Brasil, 2016; Insafe, 2016).

Morais (2015) suggested a four-pronged approach to prevent the excessive use of and the problems associated with the Internet. It includes regulatory, parental, educational, and technological approaches.

Regulatory Level

At the regulatory level, many places such as theaters, museums, hospitals, and other publicly accessible venues usually place restrictions on the use of computers, tablets, cell phones, smartphones, and digital cameras. Some public and school libraries, information and communications technology centers, and other venues that provide Internet access sometimes also impose time limits and network access restrictions for Internet use by their patrons. The same also applies to schools that impose restrictions, either within the premises in general or just in some classrooms. In some countries, despite the fact that it is illegal to use cell phones and smartphones while driving, people—young and not so young—still do it, giving rise to numerous awareness-raising campaigns to prevent accidents.

Parental Level

At the parental level, parents and educators can also impose or negotiate with their children a set of rules within the home that address time limits for using the devices mentioned earlier, be it by session, day, week, or month. These rules may include chores a child has to perform before being allowed to use the computer, tablet, smartphone, or video-game console, or a reward system that can take the form of extra digital time in exchange for good school grades, good behavior, chores well performed, and so forth. Nurturing family conversations and building a culture where asking questions, discussing perspectives, and working together are the true foundations for technology success with your children and teens. When rules and boundaries are met with dialogue and understanding, then families see the best results.

Therefore, as important as establishing some ground rules for the use of technology, is engaging our children in other activities that do not involve screens. These can be collective and outdoor activities such as sports, or individual activities such arts and crafts, but also indoor family activities at home, such as playing board games, or just having a fun family conversation, and so forth. Doing house chores with children from an early age also helps them in the future by turning them into autonomous and independent citizens. Teaching kids how to make their own beds, folding and storing their clothes, helping with housekeeping and gardening, and washing the car are activities that are fun and can be learned by children. Better teach them sooner than later, because as time progresses, learning these activities at a later stage is met with fierce resistance.

Families need to organize and manage their time to allow quality time with their children on the kids' terms. This can also be helpful for adults who might find themselves buying a bike to ride along with their kids. If parents and educators don't find attractive and engaging activities for parents and for their children, kids use the time they have on their hands with what they have within easy reach, and screens are appealing and usually the preferred choice. However, parents need to implement this when their children are at a very young age, almost from the cradle. And it is not just the parents' job; it needs to involve the whole family and even the surrounding community. Realizing this, for instance, some public libraries and even bookstores are helping out by creating library spaces for babies with special baby books, pillows, and other accessories that make those spaces comfortable for very young children. They are fostering the development of their future adult patrons.

Educational Level

At the educational level, teaching time management is also essential. It can be done at home, by the family, but it is something that should also be taught at school. For this purpose, a good resource for both parents and teachers is a section dedicated to time management on the PBS Kids website. It includes information such as "have-to's," "want-to's," and "goals"; how to make a budget; choose priorities; make a daily schedule; make a weekly planner; monthly calendars; tips from mentors; tips on chores and duties, schoolwork, sports and activities; and a list of top time wasters.

Technology Level

Many parents approach the excessive use of technology as a technology problem, thus usually looking for solutions at the technology level, forgetting that technology can only be helpful in the enforcement of the rules and time limits, defined by a regulatory or parental approach. Technology should not be used as a pacifier or a nanny and cannot replace the role of parents and educators, but it doesn't need to be complicated. Any kitchen clock can be used to control screen time. Nevertheless, most devices and operating systems now include parental control tools that can help setting and controlling time limits. Parents should make the effort to learn about these tools and the way to use them when they are away from home at work.

It should also be noted that specialized software, which allows setting of time limits and controls, exists and can be installed on devices and operating systems that don't include that functionality. There are also online platforms that allow these controls to work across a range of devices (desktops, laptops, smartphones, game consoles, and smart TVs) even with different operating systems. Better yet, there is free software to complement these controls, forcing users to take breaks or perform body and vision exercises, aiming to minimize the potential harm resulting from being in front of a screen for too long. They can even be useful for those who spend too much time at work, sitting at a desk, or lying in bed at night staring at a computer or a smartphone screen.

BUILDING RESILIENCE IN FAMILIES

There are strategies for parents to keep building the idea of resiliency at home. It is very important that parents spend their free time with their children and adolescents without any appliances, performing outdoor activities; arranging family reunions; visiting interesting places such as museums, parks, and zoos; vacationing together; enjoying nature landscapes; or just watching a nice sunset or a full moon through a window or from a balcony, and being there, hugging each other, talking to each other, expressing concerns or sharing thoughts or inspirations. Children need to feel they are loved, and there are way to express emotions and feelings other than by just using emoticons and emojis.

Ubiquitous connectivity with the Internet is also observed among adults, who habitually arrive in public places, such as restaurants and hotels, or even private places, like a friend's home, and request a password to access the Internet to stay plugged and watch all messages through their smartphones uninterruptedly. Such behavior is also giving a silent message that the child is *not* important, or is just taken for granted. This elicits a negative reaction from the child simply to gain the positive attention that he or she deserves.

Obviously, mealtime is a family time to be reunited and to share not only meals but also to renew affection, and any kind of tablets or smartphones should be off the table, all the time, so that no one gets interrupted while eating or talking. This is a simple and important rule that has to be part of the routine for every member of the family. This rule should also apply to restaurants, parties, or friend's houses during the weekends, as sharing one's time is a consideration of respect for each other, and provides opportunities to build up positive resilience internal factors. Children and teens/ young people also like to help with preparing their meals and sharing their preferred recipes and expertise in cooking, although everyone seems to disappear afterward for table clearing or dish washing.

For some parents, displaying their children on the Internet can be very appealing. After all, every moment has its charm: each age, all the child's discoveries; and each event can be photographed, shared, commented, and liked. For this reason, it is necessary to reflect on the limits of such behavior and the inherent risks, for both parents and children. By overexposing their children on the Internet, parents can expose them to risks (Von Zuben, 2015) such as:

- Unwanted digital legacies: Many parents create profiles on behalf of their children and post on them. Some even do it in the first person, interacting as if the children were actually doing it.

- Public embarrassment: To what extent parents have the right to display the lives (or complaints) of their children and at what age are children entitled to their own privacy are controversial themes. Things that are private, typical of the relationship between parents and children, do not need to be posted on public profiles.

- Attaching too much importance to social approval: Children are in the process of forming their personalities and may lack emotional maturity or not know how to deal with the opinions, disapproval, or even scorn of others. Photos that are shared can generate in children mixed feelings and paradoxical expectations of how they will be received.

- Misuse of photos by third parties: Pictures of naked or partly naked children or teens wearing bikinis and playing on a beach may be innocent for parents or nice to share with distant relatives, but the same pictures can be viewed with another connotation by others not related to the family or strangers.

- Violence: Exposing children's routines, with information about where they study, or places they attend, or any other photos with details could put them at risk.

- Digital kidnapping: Virtual kidnapping is a new type of identity theft that has been happening on the Internet, where photos of children posted by their parents are being misused, for different and criminal reasons.

Therefore, we need to apply to the Internet the same care and precautions that we do in our day-to-day lives. The Internet is a public venue, in which the degree of control imposed on the dissemination of published information is very low. Once the information is posted, anyone in your network of contacts can disseminate it, and it is very difficult to erase later. The difference between the real world and virtual world is not subtle, it is nil, nonexistent, nowadays.

It is important to highlight again that the construction of a positive relationship between mother or father or any member of the family with a growing child/tween/teen/young adult is based on their interaction with each other about their feelings, emotions, bonding, and attachments. For this reason these words have been automatically spread in the vacuum of technologies and the Internet—words such as stay connected, like, dislike, share, save, network, selfie, and so on—and multiplied by the use of emojis and emoticons, exactly because of the difficulties people have in expressing their own emotions and also their ambivalent feelings. The Internet is not a psychological couch or a medical office to treat diseases, so let's prevent them, especially during childhood and adolescence, before all the negative repercussions happen later in the adult life. Parents themselves have to learn how to be resilient. Technological devices are not electronic babysitters, like TVs used to be, and there is a huge gap between what we consider a distraction or entertainment to be used for a few moments (although these are available 24 hours × 7 days, all year long) and excessive use or addiction. Many adolescents get addicted or just never stop using their devices, and this could be evaluated and diagnosed simply as parental deprivation and social isolation, or even mental health disturbances caused by Internet addiction. The best advice for parents is to learn to disconnect more often. The message has been the same message for generations: Be with your children on a daily basis, constructing a real bond, a real attachment, a positive and healthy relationship, and a functional family (Bowlby, 1965, 1969).

Finally, when building resiliency in the family to prevent Internet and screen addictions, it is important for parents to encourage open communication at home. Talking about the problem can bring emotional relief, and it is the first step to understand what is happening and to reach a suitable solution if a child feels bothered by online risks. Parents can help and show children from an early age how to use online proactive coping strategies such as to delete messages, block intruders or strange contacts, and report any strange messages or videos, taking into account developmental factors such as interest in sexuality or other issues. Children who know how to adopt one such strategy and social network privacy configurations easily adopt other similar ones.

Parents also need to help their children tackle their psychological problems and build self-confidence. Special attention to children with low self-efficacy and psychological difficulties such as peer, conduct, or emotional problems is crucial. Experiencing difficulties and problems offline is a good indicator of being more at risk of negative experiences online. This relationship between resilience to offline and online adversities indicates the so-called double jeopardy effect: Children who are more vulnerable offline also tend to be less resilient online. Also, parents should be careful with restricting children's Internet usage because this does not prevent children from having a negative experience after risk exposure. Depending on the type of risk, a monitoring or mediating approach seems to be more beneficial for children's online resilience as does helping them maintain time limits when using technology.

In building a resiliency strategy, it is also important for parents to talk to their children about appropriate websites and games appropriate for their development and maturation, and help them to learn about risks and privacy configurations. At early ages, it is helpful to start children off right by teaching them which information or videos can and cannot be shared through the Internet, and by establishing some clear limits and rules, especially disconnecting around mealtimes, and for rest and sleep at night. Ultimately, parents can be a positive reference model in managing their own technology use at home and can help to develop family quality time without any devices, computers, notebooks, or smartphones, and enjoy the experience of sharing time together.

CONCLUSION

Schools, families, and parents now have to deal with technological intruders—not just from outside spaces, but even in their homes and classrooms with invasion of their privacy—in building their relationship with their children and adolescents. For some families, depending on many cultural and socioeconomic issues, online and offline routines are well established, but for many others, there is an increasing gap of communication and risks that have to be acknowledged and managed.

The road toward the construction of the next generation of healthy digital citizens is long, as is protecting them not only from so many health hazards while using their devices but also while on the Internet and social networks. We need to reflect cautiously on the appropriateness of the Internet during the important life phases of childhood and adolescence. Parents have to learn how to act as mediators in the social adequacy process for new technologies. Some of the developmental risk and protective factors for children and adolescents from the Internet are described with some recommendations to be implemented by all parents and educators.

To construct resilient and preventive parenting and protection for all children and adolescents, society at large has to provide tools for education and recommendations online and also during the school's prevention and health education proactive activities. Protection and prevention has to start as early as today in all families that have young children and new technological devices at home, not only to establish an open dialogue of affection and respect for the other members of the family, but also to play an important role in screen addiction, nowadays and in the future.

ACKNOWLEDGMENTS

The authors acknowledge Comitê Gestor da Internet-Brasil, CGI.br, and CETIC.br teams of researchers, especially Dr. Alexandre F. Barbosa and Dr. Miriam von Zuben for their collaboration and review of this chapter, and Dr. Cristiano Nabuco de Abreu for his psychological insight and professional expertise and friendship all these years. Also, we appreciate many parents, educators, and professional specialists who shared their experiences with us, through our work and presentations at Miudos Seguros na Net (www.miudossegurosna.net) and the network ESSE Mundo Digital (www.essemundodigital.com.br).

REFERENCES

Abreu, C. N. de (2017). *Psicología do cotidiano* [Psychology of daily life]. Porto Alegre, Brazil: Artmed.

Abreu, C. N. de, Eisenstein, E., & Estefenon, S. G. B. (Org.). (2013). *Vivendo esse mundo digital, impactos na saúde, na educação e nos comportamentos sociais* [Living in this digital world: Impacts on health, education and social behavior]. Porto Alegre, Brazil: Artmed.

Blue light has a dark side. (2015). *Harvard Health Letter*. Boston, MA: Harvard Health Publications. Retrieved from http://www.health.harvard.edu/staying-healthy/blue-light-has-a-dark-side

Bowlby, J. (1965). *Child care and the growth of love*. London, UK: Penguin Books.

Bowlby, J. (1969). *Attachment and separation. Vols. I and II, Attachment and loss*. New York, NY: Basic Books.

Carr, N. (2011). *The shallows: What the Internet is doing to our brains*. New York, NY: W. W. Norton.

Comitê Gestor da Internet no Brasil. (2014). TIC Kids Online Brasil. São Paulo, Brazil: Author. Retrieved from http://cetic.br/media/pdfs/apresentacoes/tic_kids_online_brasil_2014_hangout_imprensa.pdf

Dauncey, M. J., & Pell, J. M. (1998). Genetic regulation of growth-promoting factors by nutrition. In S. J. Ulijaszek, F. E. Johnston, & M. A. Preece (Eds.), *The Cambridge encyclopedia of human growth and development* (Pt. 3.4, pp. 142–144). Cambridge, UK: Cambridge University Press.

Dray, J., Bowman, J., Freund, M., Campbell, E., Wolfenden, L., Hodder, R. K., & Wiggers, J. (2014). Improving adolescent mental health and resilience through a resilience-based intervention in schools: Study protocol for a randomised controlled trial. *Trials, 15*, 289. Retrieved from http://www.trialsjournal.com/content/15/1/289

Dray, J., Bowman, J., Wolfenden, L., Campbell, E., Freund, M., Hodder, R., & Wiggers, J. (2015). Systematic review of universal resilience interventions targeting child and adolescent mental health in the school setting: Review protocol. *Systematic Reviews, 4*(1), 186. doi:10.1186/s13643-015-0172-6

Durkee, T., Carli, V., Floderus, B., Wasserman, C., Sarchiapone, M., Apter, A., . . . Wasserman, D. (2016). Pathological internet use and risk-behaviors among European adolescents. *International Journal of Environmental Research and Public Health, 13*(3), pii: E294. doi:10.3390/ijerph13030294

Estefenon, S. G. B., & Eisenstein, E. (Org.). (2008). *Geração digital: Riscos e benefícios das novas tecnologias para crianças e adolescentes* [Digital generation: Risks and benefits of new technologies for children and adolescents]. Rio de Janeiro, Brazil: Vieira & Lent.

Insafe. (2016, April 10). Brussels: European schoolnet. Retrieved from http://www.safer internet.org

Morais, T. (2015, May 5). O uso excessivo da internet & a cadeira de 4 pernas [Excessive use of the internet & the 4-leg chair]. Retrieved from https://www.youtube.com/ watch?v=HzsKoQ8ombU&feature=youtu.be

O'Keefe, G. S. (2011). *Cybersafe: Protecting and empowering kids in the digital world of texting, gaming and social media.* Elk Grove Village, IL: American Academy of Pediatrics.

Rosenfield, W. (2011). Computer vision syndrome: A review of ocular causes and potential treatments. *Ophthalmic Physiology, 31*(5), 502–515. doi:10.1111/j.1475-1313.2011.00834. xEpub2011

Safernet-Brasil. (2016, April 10). Retrieved from http://www.safernet.org.br

Sharif, I., & Sargent, J. D. (2006). Association between television, movie and video game exposure on school performance. *Pediatrics, 118*(4), e1061–e1070. doi:10.1542/peds .2005-2854

Skuse, D. H. (1998). Growth and psychosocial stress. In S. J. Ulijaszek, F. E. Johnston, & M. A. Preece (Eds.), *The Cambridge encyclopedia of human growth and development* (Pt. 9.4, pp. 341–342). Cambridge, UK: Cambridge University Press.

Von Zuben, M. (2015). Internet users of ages 5 to 8: Challenges and recommendations for parents and educators. In Comitê Gestor da Internet no Brasil, *TIC Kids Online Brazil Survey* (pp. 111–120). São Paulo, Brazil: Comitê Gestor da Internet no Brasil.

Young, K. S., & Abreu, C. N. de (Eds.). (2010). *Internet addiction: A handbook and guide to evaluation and treatment.* New York, NY: Wiley.

10 TEEN DRIVERS AND DEADLY DIGITAL DISTRACTIONS: PREVENTION AND POLICIES

David Strayer

One teen fatality on our highways is unacceptable;
six fatalities every day is an outrage.

At about 9 p.m. on January 14, 2012, Taylor Sauer, an 18-year-old college student was driving from Utah State University, where she was an elementary education major, to her parent's house in Caldwell, Idaho, some 4 hours away on Interstate I-84. Taylor's future was bright. She had recently graduated from Marsing High School, where she was class salutatorian and a National Merit Scholar. She had aspirations to "go even further and take on the world." While driving, she was using her cell phone to send text messages and to post on Facebook every 90 seconds or so, to pass the time. Many of her posts were about her favorite football team, the Denver Broncos. Seconds after posting "I can't discuss this now. Driving and Facebooking is not safe! Haha," her vehicle slammed into a slow-moving tanker truck traveling in the right-hand lane. At the moment of impact, her car was going at 80 mph, and there was no evidence that she had applied the brakes or taken any evasive action before the impact. After the initial impact, her vehicle was struck from behind by another semi tractor-trailer. Taylor was pronounced dead at the scene of the crash. In an interview after the crash, her mother stated that Taylor was a "typical teen who got caught up in the modern-day multitasking world."

Tragic stories like Taylor's unfold every day on our highways. What is particularly noteworthy in this case is that immediately before the crash Taylor acknowledged that she was engaging in an unsafe behavior (e.g., "Driving and Facebooking is not safe!"). Therefore, this crash cannot be attributed to a lack of awareness about the risks of texting/Facebooking and driving, rather there was a disconnect between the declarative knowledge of the risks and her actual behavior while operating a motor vehicle. This chapter discusses some of the known risks of the different forms of digital distraction and then considers how to use that information to change the behavior of teen drivers.

In fact, vehicle crashes are the number one source of accidental death for teens in the United States (National Safety Council [NSC], 2012). The Centers for Disease Control and Prevention (CDC) estimates that six teens are killed in motor vehicle crashes every day (CDC, 2016). Figure 10.1 presents the fatal crash rate for different ages normalized by million miles driven. The U-shaped function depicted in Figure 10.1 shows that drivers younger than 30 years or older than 65 years are more likely to be involved in fatal crashes. Younger drivers have less experience, take greater risks, are more likely to multitask, and have a higher likelihood of being intoxicated from drugs and alcohol as compared to drivers aged 30 years to 65 years. On the other hand, drivers older than 65 years tend to have more experience, take fewer risks, are less likely to drive at night, are more likely to use seat belts, and they have the lowest proportion of intoxication of all adults.

The combination of novice drivers and potentially addictive sources of digital distraction is all too often a deadly mix. In 2015, a naturalistic study of

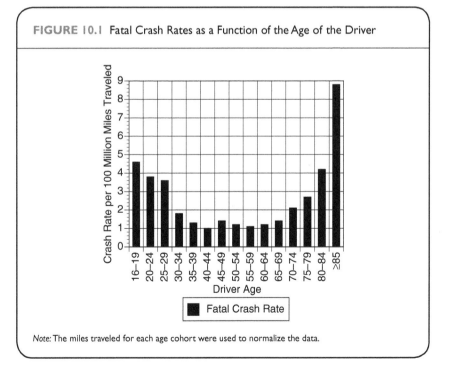

FIGURE 10.1 Fatal Crash Rates as a Function of the Age of the Driver

Note: The miles traveled for each age cohort were used to normalize the data.

1,691 teen crashes (Carney, McGehee, Harland, Weiss, & Raby, 2015) found that distractions of one sort or another were observed in 66% of the cases in the 6 seconds preceding the crash. This study used an in-vehicle recording system to collect video, audio, and accelerometer data that were triggered by a hard braking event, or caused by an impact that exceeded 1 g of lateral or longitudinal force. Participants in the study were teens between the ages of 16 and 19 years who had taken part in a teen-driving program that used the DriveCam video recording system. Some of the most common sources of distraction were:

- 15% were interacting with one or more passengers
- 12% were using a cell phone
- 10% were looking at something in the vehicle
- 9% were looking at something outside the vehicle
- 8% were singing/dancing to music
- 6% were grooming
- 6% were reaching for an object

It is clear from the Carney study that teen drivers get into trouble when they divert attention from the primary task of operating the vehicle (see also Regan & Strayer, 2014). Interacting with other passengers,[1] using a cell phone, or looking at or reaching for something in the vehicle were significant sources of distraction for teen drivers. Moreover, the Carney study found that cell phone use was more likely to lead to road-departure crashes than any of the other crash types. Roadway departure crashes are frequently severe and account for the majority of highway fatalities. In fact, in 2013, roadway departure crashes accounted for 56% of the traffic fatalities in the United States (Federal Highway Administration [FHWA], 2015).

THE SCIENCE OF DRIVER DISTRACTION

A motorist's awareness of the driving environment, often referred to as their situational awareness, is a mental state that is dependent on several cognitive processes (e.g., Endsley, 1995, 2015). These include visual *scanning* of the driving environment for indications of threats, *predicting* and anticipating where potential threats might materialize if they are not visible, *identifying* threats and objects in the driving environment when they are in the field of view, *deciding* whether an action is necessary and what action is necessary, and *executing* appropriate *responses*—SPIDER for short (Strayer & Fisher, 2016).

When drivers engage in secondary-task activities that are unrelated to the safe operation of the vehicle, attention is often diverted from driving, impairing performance on these SPIDER-related processes (Regan & Strayer,

2014). Consequently, activities that divert attention from the task of driving degrade the driver's situational awareness and compromise the ability of the driver to safely operate his or her vehicle.

Driver distraction can also arise from visual/manual interference; for example, when a driver takes his or her eyes off the road to look at or manually interact with a device (this is often referred to as *structural interference*—e.g., your eyes cannot focus on two disparate locations at the same time). Naturalistic studies of driving (e.g., Olson, Hanowski, Hickman, & Bocanegra, 2009) have found that the average text message takes a driver's eyes off the road for a duration of 4.6 seconds. At 80 mph, every time that Taylor Sauer used her cell phone to send text messages or post on Facebook, she traveled more than the length of a football field (actually an average of 525 ft.) in an effectively blindfolded state! In fact, texting while driving is associated with an eightfold increase in the risk of crashing (Drews, Yazdani, Godfrey, Cooper, & Strayer, 2009).

THE BRAIN: SELF-REGULATION, REWARD, AND DISTRACTION

The fact that Taylor Sauer acknowledged the risks associated with using digital media while driving and, nevertheless, continued to repeatedly send text messages and post on Facebook indicates that awareness of the risk, by itself, is not sufficient to curb the unsafe behavior. Indeed, smartphones are proving to be a game-changing technology with regard to driver distraction (Strayer, 2015). Not only can teens use their smartphone to talk and text, but the wireless technology also allows them to navigate with Global Positioning System (GPS), stream music, search the Internet, engage using social media, and interact with other *infotainment* systems. In many instances, an incoming text or a Facebook post is a rewarding social stimulus that is likely to stimulate the dopaminergic reward circuits in the brain.

As illustrated in Figure 10.2, modern neuroscience has helped to localize the neural pathways for reward. In particular, the dopaminergic mesolimbic system, comprised primarily of the ventral tegmental area (VTA), the amygdala, and the nucleus accumbens (NAc), plays a key role in an individual's response to rewarding stimuli such as food, sex, gambling, and social interactions (Banich, 2004). The VTA is a primitive brain structure that synthesizes dopamine and plays an important role in determining if an environmental stimulus is rewarding or aversive. The amygdala is important in the processing of emotional stimuli. The NAc helps to mediate the rewarding effects of the stimulus. Activation of the mesolimbic system helps the organism repeat what it just did to get a reward and to pay attention to the features of the rewarding experience, so that it can be repeated.

The reward circuit is regulated by the prefrontal brain regions, including the ventromedial prefrontal cortex, dorsolateral prefrontal cortex, and

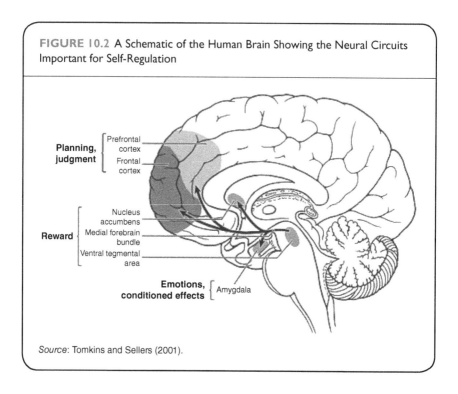

FIGURE 10.2 A Schematic of the Human Brain Showing the Neural Circuits Important for Self-Regulation

Source: Tomkins and Sellers (2001).

orbitofrontal prefrontal cortex, which together provide executive control over choices made in the environment (Watson, Miller, Lambert, & Strayer, 2011). These prefrontal regions provide "top-down" control of the sub-cortical regions involved in reward and emotion regulation (Heatherton & Wagner, 2011). Self-regulatory failure occurs if the balance is tipped in favor of subcortical regions, either because of the strength of an incoming stimulus (e.g., a rewarding text message) or because of a failure to engage top-down control (e.g., because of fatigue associated with excessive multitasking).

Importantly, the prefrontal cortical brain regions are not fully developed until individuals reach their mid-20s (e.g., Watson et al., 2011). It is noteworthy that the U-shaped function relating fatal crash rate across the life span (Figure 10.1) is a mirror image of the inverted U-shaped function describing prefrontal cortical function across the life span (Watson et al., 2011). Compared to the adult brain, a teen's brain is less able to regulate (using top-down control) the response to rewarding social stimuli such as an incoming text messages.

The developmental neuroscience of self-regulation and cognitive control helps to explain why public service campaigns and other messages that may be effective in influencing adult drivers are often ineffective for teen drivers. Teens are less capable of suppressing rewarding behaviors such as interacting with social media, because the prefrontal regions of their brain are not fully developed. Consequently, teen drivers are more likely to act impulsively and engage in sensation seeking (Sanbonmatsu, Strayer, Biondi, Behrends, & Moore, 2013).

Teen drivers like Taylor Sauer can become so connected to their smartphones that they cannot put them down even if they know that using them is risky. Whether smartphone use rises to the level of a behavioral addiction using the *Diagnostic and Statistical Manual for Mental Disorders*, Fifth Edition (*DSM-5*; American Psychiatric Association, 2013) criteria, or it is *merely* a compulsive behavior continues to be hotly debated (e.g., Griffiths, 2013; Roberts, 2015), and is beyond the scope of this chapter. However, I have developed a simple quiz based on the estimated crash risk associated with several multitasking activities (e.g., Strayer, 2015). To take the quiz, give yourself the assigned points, noted in the parentheses, if you have engaged in the listed behavior while driving during the last week.[2]

- Accepting phone call while driving (1 point)
- Placing a call (including dialing) while driving (2 points)
- Reading a textual message while stopped at a traffic light (1 point)
- Sending a textual message while stopped at a traffic light (1 point)
- Reading a textual message while driving (2 points)
- Sending a textual message while driving (2 points)

The sum total obtained from the quiz provides an estimate of the risk associated with distracted driving over the preceding week. Safety advocates from the National Transportation Safety Board (NTSB, 2011) and the NSC (2012) suggest that driving is compromised if the obtained score is greater than 0.[3] In fact, both the NTSB and the NSC have called for a total ban on smartphone use while operating a vehicle (*for drivers of all ages*). I consider a rating between 1 and 3 to be a moderate level of risk, a rating between 4 and 6 would be considered a high level of risk, and a rating greater than 6 would be an extreme level of risk. Griffith (2005) suggests that the distinction between healthy enthusiasm and addiction is that the former adds to life and the latter takes away from life. In the case of using a smartphone to text and Facebook while driving, it is difficult to argue that Taylor Sauer's behavior wasn't an example of the latter category.

Teen drivers may attempt to self-regulate their nondriving activities to periods where they perceive the risks to be lower. Strayer and Cooper (2015) suggested that there are two forms of self-regulation in driving: *proactive* and *reactive*. An example of proactive self-regulation is when a driver chooses to send a text when stopped at traffic lights. In contrast, reactive self-regulation refers to situations where a driver moderates his or her usage in *real-time* based on the driving difficulty or the perception of driving errors. An example of reactive self-regulation is when a driver terminates his or her call when the demands of driving increase (e.g., when they enter a school zone).

Reactive self-regulation depends on the driver being aware of his or her driving errors and adjusting his or her behavior accordingly. Sanbonmatsu, Strayer, Biondi, Behrends, and Moore (2016) found that a driver's ability to reactively self-regulate his or her multitasking behavior is limited. In this study, a positive correlation was found between self-awareness of driving errors and actual driving errors when young adult drivers were not talking on cell phones. By contrast, a negative correlation was found between self-awareness of driving errors and actual driving errors when these drivers were talking on cell phones. Alarmingly, the cell phone drivers who made the most errors were blithely unaware of their driving impairments. Hence, any reactive self-regulatory behavior on the part of a driver using a smartphone would appear to be minimal.

Another alarming statistic is that the drivers least capable at multitasking are the ones most likely to use a smartphone while driving (Sanbonmatsu et al., 2013). Multitasking activity was found to be negatively correlated with *actual* ability and positively correlated with *perceived* ability (i.e., frequent users exhibited a pattern of overconfidence in their multitasking ability). In fact, the frequency of smartphone use while driving was positively correlated with high levels of impulsivity and sensation seeking, and negatively correlated with measures of executive control.

PREVENTION AND POLICIES

In this final section, some guidance for parents, schools, and policy makers is provided to help teens make good decisions when driving. It is clear that the digital sources of distraction are a temptation for all drivers. This problem is particularly acute for teens because they are just learning to drive and the self-regulatory control circuits in the prefrontal cortex are not fully developed; hence, they are more likely to use these new sources of distraction. Providing scaffolding to help them make good decisions is an important first step. Although there is no single solution to the problem, a concerted effort from all the stakeholders holds promise.

For Parents

There are direct measures a parent can take to influence driving behavior. Teen drivers learn how to drive, in part, by watching how their parents drive. The teen driver emulates many of the behaviors in which parents engage. If parents want their son or daughter to avoid using a cell phone to talk, text, or interact with social media, and so forth while driving, then they should not engage in these activities behind the wheel of a moving vehicle.

The "do as I say, not as I do" approach does not work with teens. Moreover, parents should discuss with their son or daughter the risks that come with driving, well before they begin driving. Establishing clear-cut guidelines and expectations in advance helps the teens make good decisions behind the wheel (e.g., don't drink and drive; always wear a seat belt; don't use your smartphone while driving).

There are also technological solutions that a parent can adopt to decrease teen distractions in the vehicle. One approach is to install a video recording system in the vehicle, such as the one used by Carney et al. (2015), that is triggered by a hard braking event or caused by an impact that exceeded 1 g of lateral or longitudinal force. Notifications can be sent in real time to the parents (e.g., in e-mail messages) and can be used to help cull unsafe driving behavior. In fact, some insurance companies provide these in-vehicle camera systems free of charge to their clients and other insurers offer a reduction in the insurance rates for teen drivers (the options vary with the insurance provider and are likely to change over time).[4]

For Drivers

Other methods can lockout smartphone functions when the vehicle is in motion. For example, Apple's CarPlay® system uses onboard sensors to determine when a user is driving. If he or she is, the ability to manually enter textual messages (texting, Facebook, etc.) is locked out. Google has developed a similar system, Android Auto®, which also supports a restricted set of smartphone interactions: Manual interaction is locked out and all commands are voice based. However, research from my lab has found that these voice-based interactions to send texts, perform GPS navigation, and to activate infotainment features can lead to surprisingly high levels of driver distraction (Strayer, Turrill, et al., 2015). Without doubt, the safest strategy for novice drivers is to avoid using the smartphone altogether.

For Schools

Zero Teen Fatalities (2016; with the Twitter hashtag #stayingundead) is a national program that is funded by the Departments of Public Safety and Transportation to provide information on how to make teen drivers safer drivers. State-of-the-art information is available for helping teens learning to drive, to assist parents in teaching their teens how to drive safely, and to help administrators with school-wide programs to advance driving safety. In many respects, the laudable goals of this program are the hardest to accomplish. Consider the fact that Taylor Sauer was well aware of the risks, yet it did not change her multitasking behavior. Many safety advocates suggest that risky multitasking behaviors need to be stigmatized to change the norm of driving distracted. Drunk driving became stigmatized with a concerted public awareness campaign promoted in large part by the Mothers Against Drunk Driving (madd.org). This may also prove to be an effective approach to change teen's driving behavior.

For Policy Makers

In 2015, the American Automobile Association (AAA) released a set of primary-enforcement[5] policy recommendations to limit the sources of distractions for novice drivers. These included (a) having no more than 1 non-family passenger younger than 20 years in the vehicle for at least the first 6 months of licensure and (b) prohibiting texting and handheld cell phone use while driving for persons younger than 18 years. As of 2015, only 17 states and Washington, DC, met AAA's recommendations for limiting nonfamily members in the vehicle and only 29 states and Washington, DC, met AAA's recommendations for prohibiting texting or handheld cell phone use while driving. One clear way to address teen-driver crash risk would be for all states to adopt the policy recommendations by AAA and for these primary-enforcement regulations to be enforced. In fact, the National Highway Traffic Safety Administration's (NHTSA) high-visibility enforcement programs in Hartford, Connecticut, and Syracuse, New York, were found to significantly reduce the number of drivers using handheld devices while driving (Chaudhary, Casanova-Powell, Cosgrove, Reagan, & Williams, 2012).

CONCLUSION

Taylor Sauer was a "typical teen who got caught up in the modern-day multitasking world." When she died, she was performing an activity that is the leading cause of accidental death for her age cohort—texting while driving an automobile. Despite her stated awareness of the risks, Taylor repeatedly engaged in sending and receiving textual messages, an activity that is known to significantly increase the risk of a crash. The lure of an incoming text message can be difficult for adult drivers to ignore and the immature prefrontal inhibitory circuits in the teen's brain make ignoring these digital distractions even more difficult. Putting a smartphone at the fingertips of a novice driver is a recipe for disaster. Adding scaffolding to the driving environment (e.g., installing video recording equipment in the vehicle and/ or disabling the smartphone when the vehicle is in motion) may help the teen to keep their eyes on the road and their mind on the drive. Parents play a key role in providing that scaffolding for their children when they learn to drive.

Sources of digital distraction in the vehicle are growing at an alarming rate. After decades of slowly declining traffic fatalities, researchers are now seeing a sharp uptick in fatalities (Ziv, 2016), some of which have been linked to smartphone use in the vehicle. As exemplified by Taylor Sauer, teens lack the top-down inhibitory control to regulate their smartphone usage to nondriving periods of their life. Teens are also novice drivers, so their skills as motorists have yet to be refined. Moreover, the rapid growth of in-vehicle information systems that come as standard equipment in new vehicles and provide access to a motorist's social network are sources of temptation that teens may not be able to resist. The combination of these influences may create the perfect storm of driver distraction. In their purchase decision, I suggest that parents consider features that lockout social media interactions when the vehicle is in motion—if these in-vehicle information systems are operational when the vehicle is in motion, then teens are tempted to use them while driving. Without a concerted effort from all stakeholders to address this issue, the problem is poised to become more acute.

NOTES

1. The distraction from passengers is not observed in the epidemiological data from adult drivers, where there is a slight safety advantage for having another adult passenger in the vehicle (Rueda-Domingo et al., 2004; Vollrath, Meilinger, & Krüger, 2002). Drews, Pasupathi, and Strayer (2008) found that adult passengers are often actively engaged in supporting the driver by pointing out hazards, helping to navigate, and reminding the driver of the task (i.e., exiting at the rest stop). In other cases, the conversation is temporally halted during a difficult section of driving and then resumed when driving becomes easier. In effect, the passenger acts as another set of eyes that help the driver control the vehicle, and this sort of activity is not afforded by cell phone conversations.

2. The points were derived from estimates of the crash risk for each behavior. Talking on a cell phone is associated with a fourfold increase in the crash risk (e.g., McEvoy et al., 2005; Redelmeier & Tibshirani, 1997). Typing textual messages or dialing is associated with an eightfold increase in crash risk (e.g., Drews et al., 2009; Olson et al., 2009). Finally, the distraction effects of texting linger for up to 27 seconds (Strayer, Cooper, Turrill, Coleman, & Hopman, 2015).

3. Activities such as listening to music are less risky than using a smartphone to talk or text (e.g., Strayer, Turrill, et al., 2015). However, given the naturalistic study by Carney et al. (2015), drivers may want to minimize singing and dancing while driving.

4. The implication of the reduced rate offered by insurance companies when in-vehicle cameras are installed in the car suggests that the Carney et al. (2015) study provides a *best case* estimate of the prevalence of teen distraction in crashes. Even so, 66% of the teen crashes involved some sort of distraction in the 6 seconds before the crash. One can only speculate on the sources of distraction for teens when there is no video system installed in the vehicle.

5. Under primary enforcement, a driver can be pulled over and cited based on an activity by itself.

REFERENCES

American Psychiatric Association. (2013). *Diagnostic and statistical manual of mental disorders* (5th ed.). Arlington, VA: American Psychiatric Publishing.

Banich, M. (2004). *Cognitive neuroscience and neuropsychology* (2nd ed.). Boston, MA: Houghton Mifflin.

Carney, C., McGehee, D., Harland, K., Weiss, M., & Raby, M. (2015). *Using naturalistic driving data to assess the prevalence of environmental factors and driver behaviors in teen driver crashes.* Washington, DC: American Automobile Association Foundation for Traffic Safety.

Centers for Disease Control and Prevention. (2016). Teen drivers: Get the facts. Retrieved from http://www.cdc.gov/motorvehiclesafety/teen_drivers/teendrivers_factsheet.html

Chaudhary, N. K., Casanova-Powell, T. D., Cosgrove, L., Reagan, I., & Williams, A. (2012, August). *Evaluation of NHTSA distracted driving demonstration projects in Connecticut and New York* (Report No. DOT HS 811 635). Washington, DC: National Highway Traffic Safety Administration.

Drews, F. A., Pasupathi, M., & Strayer, D. L. (2008). Passenger and cell-phone conversation during simulated driving. *Journal of Experimental Psychology: Applied, 14,* 392–400.

Drews, F. A., Yazdani, H., Godfrey, C. N., Cooper, J. M., & Strayer, D. L. (2009). Text messaging during simulated driving. *Human Factors, 51*(5), 762–770.

Endsley, M. R. (1995). Towards a theory of situation awareness in dynamic systems. *Human Factors, 37*(1), 32–64.

Endsley, M. R. (2015). Situation awareness misconceptions and misunderstandings. *Journal of Cognitive Engineering and Decision Making, 9,* 4–32.

Federal Highway Administration. (2015). Roadway departure safety—A publication of the U.S. Department of Transportation Federal Highway Administration. Retrieved from http://safety.fhwa.dot.gov/roadway_dept

Griffiths, M. D. (2005). A "components" model of addiction within a biopsychosocial framework. *Journal of Substance Use, 10,* 191–197.

Griffiths, M. D. (2013). Adolescent mobile phone addiction: A cause for concern? *Education and Health, 31,* 76–78.

Heatherton, T. F., & Wagner, D. D. (2011). Cognitive neuroscience of self-regulation failure. *Trends in Cognitive Sciences, 15*(3), 132–139.

McEvoy, S. P., Stevenson, M. R., McCartt, A. T., Woodward, M., Haworth, C., Palamara, P., & Cercarelli, R. (2005). Role of mobile phones in motor vehicle crashes resulting in hospital attendance: A case-crossover study. *British Medical Journal, 331* (7514), 428.

National Safety Council. (2012). Understanding the distracted brain: Why driving while using hands-free cell phones is risky behavior. Retrieved from http://www.nsc.org/DistractedDrivingDocuments/Cognitive-Distraction-White-Paper.pdf

National Transportation Safety Board. (2011). No call, no text, no update behind the wheel: NTSB calls for nationwide ban on PEDs while driving. Retrieved from http://www.ntsb.gov/news/press-releases/Pages/No_call_no_text_no_update_behind_the_wheel_NTSB_calls_for_nationwide_ban_on_PEDs_while_driving.aspx

Olson, R. L., Hanowski, R. J., Hickman, J. S., & Bocanegra, J. (2009). Driver distraction in commercial vehicle operations. DOT F 1700.7 (8–72). Retrieved from https://www.fmcsa.dot.gov/sites/fmcsa.dot.gov/files/docs/DriverDistractionStudy.pdf

Redelmeier, D. A., & Tibshirani, R. J. (1997). Association between cellular-telephone calls and motor vehicle collisions. *The New England Journal of Medicine, 336*(7), 453–458.

Regan, M. A., & Strayer, D. L. (2014). Towards an understanding of driver inattention: Taxonomy and theory. *Annals of Advances in Automotive Medicine, 58*, 5–14.

Roberts, J. A. (2016). *Too much of a good thing: Are you addicted to your smartphone?* Austin, TX: Sentia Publishing Company.

Rueda-Domingo, T., Lardelli-Claret, P., Luna-del-Castillo, J. d. e. D., Jiménez-Moleón, J. J., García-Martín, M., & Bueno-Cavanillas, A. (2004). The influence of passengers on the risk of the driver causing a car collision in Spain. Analysis of collisions from 1990 to 1999. *Accident; Analysis and Prevention, 36*(3), 481–489.

Sanbonmatsu, D. M., Strayer, D. L., Biondi, F., Behrends, A. A., & Moore, S. M. (2016). Cell-phone use diminishes self-awareness of impaired driving. *Psychonomic Bulletin & Review, 23*(2), 617–623.

Sanbonmatsu, D. M., Strayer, D. L., Medeiros-Ward, N., & Watson, J. M. (2013). Who multitasks and why? Multi-tasking ability, perceived multi-tasking ability, impulsivity, and sensation seeking. *PLOS ONE, 8*(1), e54402. doi:10.1371/journal.pone

Strayer, D. L. (2015). Is the technology in your car driving you to distraction? *Policy Insights From Behavioral and Brain Sciences, 2*, 156–165.

Strayer, D. L., & Cooper, J. M. (2015). Driven to distraction. *Human Factors, 57*(8), 1343–1347.

Strayer, D. L., Cooper, J. M., Turrill, J. M., Coleman, J. R., & Hopman, R. J. (2015). *The smartphone and the driver's cognitive workload: A comparison of Apple, Google, and Microsoft's intelligent personal assistants.* Washington, DC: American Automobile Association Foundation for Traffic Safety.

Strayer, D. L., & Fisher, D. L. (2016). SPIDER: A framework for understanding driver distraction. *Human Factors, 58*(1), 5–12.

Strayer, D. L., Turrill, J., Cooper, J. M., Coleman, J. R., Medeiros-Ward, N., & Biondi, F. (2015). Assessing cognitive distraction in the automobile. *Human Factors, 57*(8), 1300–1324.

Tomkins, D. M., & Sellers, E. M. (2001). Addiction and the brain: The role of neurotransmitters in the cause and treatment of drug dependence. *Canadian Medical Journal, 164*(6), 817–821.This work is protected by copyright and the making of this copy was with the permission of Access Copyright. Any alteration of its content or further copying in any form whatsoever is strictly prohibited unless otherwise permitted by law.

Vollrath, M., Meilinger, T., & Krüger, H. P. (2002). How the presence of passengers influences the risk of a collision with another vehicle. *Accident; Analysis and Prevention, 34*(5), 649–654.

Watson, J. M., Miller, A. E., Lambert, A., & Strayer, D. L. (2011). The magical letters P, F, C, and sometimes U: The rise and fall of executive attention with the development of prefrontal cortex. In K. L. Fingerman, C. A. Berg, J. Smith, & T. C. Antonucci (Eds.), *Handbook of life-span development* (pp. 407–436). New York, NY: Springer Publishing.

Zero Teen Fatalities. (2016). Be a zero. Retrieved from http://zeroteenfatalities.com

Ziv, S. (2016, February 17). 2015 brought biggest percent increase in U.S. traffic deaths in 50 years. *Newsweek.* Retrieved from http://www.newsweek.com/2015-brought-biggest-us-traffic-death-increase-50-years-427759

THE IMPROVE TOOL: A RESOURCE TO ASSIST FAMILIES AND CLINICIANS

Philip Tam

Over the past two decades or so, many positive strides have been made in the broad field of Internet and computer-related psychology and psychopathology, following the first clinical descriptions of Internet addiction disorder (IAD) in the mid-1990s (Young, 1996), and the subsequent emergence of research and clinical interest in this complex and ever-evolving domain. There are now a number of internationally recognized, peer-reviewed journals dedicated to the study of the broad field of *Internet psychology*, and many large, powerful, and significant studies have been published in the domain. One important domain that is less well studied is that of the role of parenting factors in the evolution of IAD, and how adolescents and more importantly children situate within the parenting and family environment. This chapter aims to highlight the key relevance of family and social context in IAD subjects, through the development of a novel, holistic framework for assessment, the IMPROVE tool.

CLINICAL ASSESSMENT OF INTERNET ADDICTION IN CHILDREN AND TEENAGERS

The field of Internet psychology and of Internet addiction research is now well established, despite ongoing debates about terminology, phenomenology, and the diagnostic status of IAD as a legitimate mental health condition. In particular, important findings have been made—and will continue to be made—in the domains of neuroimaging and neuropsychological changes in IAD (Han, Kim, Bae, Renshaw, & Anderson, 2015; Tam, 2017), and in the exploration of comorbidity of IAD with other mental disorders such as depression, anxiety, autistic disorders, attention deficit hyperactivity disorder (ADHD), and bipolar disorder (Gundogar, Bakim, Ozer, &

Karamustafalioglu, 2012; Mazurek, Shattuck, Wagner, & Cooper, 2012; Park, Hong, & Park, 2012; Wei, Chen, Huang, & Bai, 2012; Ybarra, Alexander, & Mitchell, 2005; Young & Rodgers, 1998). A recent major global stimulus to research and to clinical recognition of this complex and novel disorder was the inclusion of a specific form of Internet addiction, termed *Internet gaming disorder* (IGD), in the latest edition of the *Diagnostic and Statistical Manual of Mental Disorders*, Fifth Edition (*DSM-5*; American Psychiatric Association [APA], 2013). It was not accorded the status of a full mental health disorder, but was placed in the "condition for further study" section, with a set of international consensus criteria on its diagnosis subsequently appearing (Petry et al., 2013), including translated versions into numerous languages other than English to promote valid cross-cultural work.

A domain within the broad field of Internet psychology and mental health, which appears to attract a relative paucity of research interest, compared to many other areas, is that of the role of family and parenting factors in the evolution, perpetuation, or protection against Internet- and gaming-related disorders, as they relate to children (defined here as between 2 and 12 years old) and adolescents (those aged 13–18 years). This domain is highly important, as it is well recognized that intrafamilial and parenting factors can often play a major role in the development of a wide range of mental health and psychological disturbances (Rutter et al., 2010). Furthermore, children and often toddlers are now using technology for longer and longer periods, and from a younger age (Common Sense Media, 2013), with mobile media use rates in the 0- to 8-year group nearly doubling from 38% to 72% in the period studied. It is also notable that many mental disorders and illnesses first manifest themselves in childhood, adolescence, and young adulthood—or at least some "early warning signs" of an emerging illness are present in these age ranges (Rutter et al., 2010)—and these are the times when the client is likely to be still living with parents or caregivers, who will thus play a significant role in the client's psychosocial and emotional development. In this regard, the development of effective family-based interventions (e.g., Han, Kim, Lee, & Renshaw, 2012) is highly important and to be welcomed. Furthermore, parents and family members will often be the first to notice any such warning signs of an illness, such as depression, anxiety, eating disorders, drug misuse, and indeed Internet addiction. Thus, in the practice of child and adolescent mental health, obtaining some level of "family history and observation" as part of the assessment process is of key importance.

There is likely to be a range of potential reasons for this relative lack of research. It may be a result of the logistical difficulties and the complexity of performing quality, large-scale or longitudinal studies involving not just the affected *subjects* (or the control group), but also the parents or carers in the household and family unit. Matching data sets of the clients to the relevant data sets of the parents will also be highly problematic, if not impossible, given the de-identified and anonymous nature of most studies that are done within a school, college, or clinic setting. Studies that involve more than just the subject of interest will cost much more, and potentially require more researchers involved in the project and a greater data-gathering capacity. Another well-recognized difficulty in mental health research in children and adolescents is ethical and consent-related complexities, particularly in studies that involve an active intervention such as a medication or other active therapy.

Another potential reason for this relative lack of research focus is that many validated, robust assessment tools and surveys exist, but they focus on young adults (e.g., Beard, 2005; Byun et al., 2009; Kuss & Griffiths, 2012). Many of the key assumptions and phenomenological features within those tools derive from gambling, impulse control problems, and substance dependence problems, and thus may not be readily, or validly, transposable to children who lack the higher order cognitive capacity, executive control, and overall self-reflective capacity of adults. Thus, few *tailored* approaches to appraising children and families are readily available.

However, given the awareness that many mental disorders do arise in childhood and adolescence, other mental health disorders have had specific appraisal tools developed to elucidate and quantify the role of intrafamilial and parenting factors in the *shaping* of the condition, such as the Family Accommodation Scale (FAS) for obsessive-compulsive disorder (OCD; Calcovoressi et al., 1999) in the study of OCD and the role of family context in the disorder's evolution, and the Accommodation and Enabling Scale for Eating Disorders, or AESED (Sepuvelda et al., 2009), which explores similar family factors in the context of anorexia nervosa and other eating disorders. As the present chapter argues and demonstrates, it is likely that similar factors in the parenting and broader household environment are of key importance in the development and evolution of IAD in clients still living at home; any holistic and informed appraisal of a young IAD case will thus need to take these factors strongly into account.

IAD IN CLINICAL PRACTICE: AN ILLUSTRATIVE CASE

Jayden H. (a pseudonym) is a 13-year-old schoolboy who lives with his mother Michaela and 7-year-old sister in a single-parent household in an inner-city area. Jayden has shown concerning behaviors over the past 6 months both at home and at school, with increasing oppositionality, mostly around rules and expectations, and at bedtimes. He has covertly been using his mother's smartphone in the evenings to access app-based games, and has accrued an $800 bill over 6 weeks for *in-app* purchases.

He has always been allowed 45 minutes of computer time on the laptop once his homework and chores are complete, but in recent weeks has refused to get off the computer game when his allocation has finished, leading to tensions and arguments. Jayden's school counselor (SC) was made aware of issues from his teachers, who have noted that his grades have dropped significantly in the past term, he is sometimes distracted in class, and on one occasion fell asleep on his school desk. Though he has not been aggressive, Jayden has shown disregard for many of the school rules in class, and in the playground. He has not been diagnosed with any mental health disorder in the past, and is healthy apart from mild asthma. His mother, at the suggestion of the SC considered utilizing the IMPROVE tool to help explore the situation in more depth, and to assist in deciding on the optimum treatment path. Having looked at a printed copy of IMPROVE with the SC, it was fully completed over a 2-week period. A detailed account of Jayden's usage of the IMPROVE tool, followed by the treatment decisions and pathways resulting from the findings, is given subsequently, following the outline of each item in IMPROVE.

DEVELOPMENT OF THE IMPROVE TOOL

It is with these previously mentioned considerations in mind that the IMPROVE tool was conceived and developed, to assist families in the appraisal and assessment of a young family member suspected of having some form of Internet-overuse problem. It highlights the key importance of parenting styles and attitudes, and broader family environment by exploring them in a semistructured fashion. However, IMPROVE it is not devised as a *rating scale* as such, and does not yield a *score* or quantified set of variables as is the case with the FAS and AESED, and of the commonly used Internet addiction rating scales. It can readily be utilized in conjunction with those rating scales, notwithstanding the validity concerns they may pose, as already noted.

Parenting and intrafamilial styles can affect mental disorder development in a range of ways, and it is recognized that no single *right* way of raising a child exists. The IMPROVE tool makes no suppositions or judgments as to the quality of the subject's attachment and parenting experience, but seeks to collect objective, observable, and easily documented data about the subject's well-being and overall parenting and family experience.

The IMPROVE tool contains elements of the some of the mechanisms investigated in the FAS and AESED scales, through which parenting factors may *shape* the development of an Internet-overuse problem, though not in a quantitative fashion.

As with any such client-centered tool, designed to be used without the requirement of specialist input, it would need to utilize nontechnical language and concepts, and be not too complex or onerous to complete. As with all surveys and questionnaires, finding the right number of *items* within the format is vital: Too few items, and not enough depth and breadth of data will be obtained; too many items, and there is a risk that the tool would not end up getting completed in its entirety, or that the tool as whole is only superficially addressed. With this in mind, a total of seven individual *aspects* of Internet usage within a family context was chosen. An easy-to-remember—and positive sounding—acronym was chosen, which again could optimize the family's engaged usage of the tool. Once fully completed, it may then assist the family in, firstly, judging the severity of the IAD condition and in being aware of many of the associated factors, and, secondly, in indicating the optimal method of actively addressing and ameliorating the problem situation.

IMPROVE may also be of use to a treating clinician or counselor, involved in any subsequent care pathway for the client. Many of the items within the tool can be utilized in the clinician's gathering and documenting the psychosocial history of the client and his or her family, and in the subsequent development of the *psychological formulation*. The IMPROVE tool could thus be a useful addition to the many well-recognized questionnaires and surveys that routinely form part of the assessment process of mental health clients, while also optimizing valuable and expensive face-to-face clinical time. It could also be used to assess and monitor treatment progress and success, by repeating the IMPROVE process after a 6- or 12-month period and observing any significant changes across the relevant items. Each item will now be described in full, with a background on its underlying principles and clinical utility.

THE IMPROVE TOOL: EACH ITEM IN DETAIL

I—Internet Inventory

The first step when utilizing the IMPROVE tool is to prepare a detailed *inventory* of how the client spends his or her time online and across all computer-based devices, including the use of gaming consoles that may not necessarily be linked to the web. It is important to map out in as much detail as possible the *landscape* of screen-based activity as this will inform the subsequent, and more complex, items in the tool. A thorough inventory will also provide guidance for any ongoing treatment and therapy plan. Computer gaming, in particular the playing of massively multiplayer online role-playing games (MMORG), is the activity most commonly associated with Internet overuse and addiction (Berle & Starcevic, 2015), but it is clear that other aspects of Internet and web use, such as social media and networking, video-viewing, online shopping, or pornography consumption, can equally provide a highly compelling, even *addictive* experience for the user. Indeed, many young Internet users may classify themselves as *nongamers* or occasional gamers, so it is wise to not focus on this activity exclusively. Thus, all online and console-related activities that are engaged in should be tabulated, including the time spent on each one. Screen-based time that is directly related to schoolwork or school assignments, or to employment requirements, such as resume preparation or researching jobs, should not be included.

It is recognized, however, that the lines between *education* and *entertainment* elements over which Internet and computer technology (ICT) is used are becoming increasingly blurred: A judgment by the appraising family will need to be made on where to draw that line. The period over which ICT usage is tabulated should not be too lengthy, and should be decided prior to commencing: A 2-week period is suggested, which would include two weekends, alongside a representative number of school days.

As well as the *total number* of hours spent through the day on the various activities, the time of this usage must be noted—for example, does it encroach on mealtimes, on periods when clients should be asleep, doing homework assignments, or even at school. A simple method of tabulating this activity through the day would be having sections for morning, afternoon, evening and, if relevant, nighttime. Similarly, an inventory should be taken for school day usage patterns, and for patterns on the weekend. A notable feature of the ICT landscape in the past decade has been the emergence of a range of various devices through which the web can be accessed. Although desktop and laptop computers have been in use for many decades, most young people now routinely use smartphones, tablets, and *wearable tech* devices (Common Sense Media, 2015).

It is due to this multitasking, multimedium nature of ICT usage that the phenomenon of *continuous partial attention* was described (Stone, 1998). Given that multiple devices are often live and online at the same time, it is not inconceivable that the total hours spent across each medium within one day, could actually exceed 24 hours! As noted previously, the inventory should, where possible, note and record usage patterns across *all* devices.

Another type of game and gaming platform to consider observing and documenting are the *active games consoles*: This is explored in detail in the Real-World Activities section later. The inventory may be gathered in a number of ways, dependent on the situation within the family and the perceived severity of the behaviors. A self-report *diary* may be of use in less severe cases, but this would require a commitment on the part of the client to regularly complete it, as well as a level of honesty and openness. Another method of gathering data may be through a diary completed by an external observer, such as a parent or carer. This method may lessen the potential for usage underreporting or even avoidance; a potential negative aspect with this method is that the external observer could be seen as intrusive, even annoying, to the client. Furthermore, being made aware of being monitored and observed through the day could impact on the very behaviors being examined—for example, time spent on gameplay could be reduced by the subject in order to present as *less affected* by the IA problem. It is also, in the current era of very high smartphone usage, unfeasible for this method to be used throughout the day given the mobility of many ICT devices. An objective, and potentially much more accurate and representative, method would involve the installation of a web- and computer-use monitoring software package or app. There are many such software programs commercially available, which can often be tailored to the individual's or family's needs—for example, taking into account the age of the subject, or adjusting how often a *printout* of ICT usage is required. Of note, it is not recommended that such a software package be installed *covertly*, without the subject's knowledge and consent, even at a young age. This could be seen as unfair and a breach of trust, and thus undermine the whole collaborative and empathic nature of a treatment program.

M—Monitor Over Time

Although the initial inventory will provide a detailed outline of ICT usage within a small window of time, for example, 1 or 2 weeks, it is also necessary to make an appraisal of how these habits may change over a longer period of time, such as at 3 months or at 6 months after the initial observations. This is because usage could alter quite significantly at these later times. For example, extremely avid gameplay of a newly acquired game could drop off significantly once the initial *rush of excitement* wears off and interest wanes. On the other hand, more entrenched gaming play with the same game—such as game time consistently interfering with healthy sleep patterns—could be an indicator of a serious problem developing. The computer games industry is always developing and releasing new titles, or updated versions of an established *franchise*, so again it is important to look at how patterns of new game acquisition form over time, or if gameplay is limited to just a few titles.

As already noted, gaming forms one domain of a rich online and computerized environment; tracking how other online activities vary in their usage pattern at the different times should be noted. As highlighted previously, there are numerous commercially available software programs that can track, and then display, how the various usage patterns alter over time. The key feature of *persistence over time* is a generally accepted criterion in the formal diagnosis of a many mental illnesses (APA, 2013).

In other words, the presence of, for example, depressive or anxiety symptoms need to be maintained at a follow-up time (usually at 3 or 6 months) for a formal diagnosis to be made. Internet use disorders can be expected to follow a broadly similar time course; as noted previously, it is important to distinguish between a time-limited *passing phase*, and a deeper, more prolonged obsession or addiction. Of note, one large, longitudinal study of pathological video gaming in schoolchildren (Gentile et al., 2011), demonstrated that a significant majority (84%) of young pathological gamers at the study commencement, had persistent problems at the 2-year follow-up, indicating that the condition is likely to be long term and entrenched.

P—Parenting Factors

It is well established that parenting styles, attitudes, and behaviors can influence the development of child and adolescent mental health disorders. Conversely, the presence of stable, nurturing, supportive, and empowering family environments are known to be of key importance in healthy psychosocial development (Rutter et al., 2010). In recent years, a small number of IA studies were published looking at parenting styles as a possible causative factor in young people developing IAD (e.g., Yang, Sato, Yamawaki, & Miyata, 2013), with a distant, controlling, and unempathic style being associated more strongly with the condition than a close, empathic relationship. Given the limited number of studies, it is probably too early to draw robust conclusions about how differing styles may impact on the condition. As noted, such studies often contrast an authoritative, controlling, or distant parenting style to one being more nurturing, empathic, and supportive. These two styles are in many ways situated at the opposite ends of a *parenting spectrum*, but there are numerous other styles to note, such as permissive, enmeshed, dysfunctional, overprotective, and conflictual. A study of 1,289 adolescents in Taiwan (Lin, Lin, & Wu, 2009) demonstrated that a high level of parental monitoring of Internet and gaming usage in the subject was protective against later development of IAD.

Another parenting phenomenon well recognized within the substance-use research is that of the *enabler parent* where messages and instructions, both explicit and implied, given to the child indicate one thing, but actions and behaviors then carried out convey a conflicting or contradictory meaning (Bernstein, 2014). The phenomenon of parental enabling is also a key factor measured in the AESED scale in eating-disordered teenagers. Enabling parenting behavior could thus play a key part in the emergence of IAD in a child or teenager; examples would be the repeated *telling off* of a child to reduce their online activities, but then allowing the child to game all night without consequence, or the parent purchasing more games as a *reward* for good behavior. In more extreme cases, aggression or violence (e.g., by breaking a computer or device), is implicitly *rewarded* by the parent purchasing a replacement item and not enforcing consequences of the behavior. Overall, prolonged enabling parenting can lead to frustration and confusion in the subject—and a worsening of the problem behavior. Any examples of enabling parenting behaviors should be noted, including specific, objective details where possible.

It is also clear that parenting environments and styles can alter over time—in response to external events and stressors, for example—and that one child within the family unit could experience a differing style to another child. If these alterations or differences have been observed, they should be noted. Another aspect of the parenting style is the online usage pattern in *the parents or carers themselves.* This is relevant, particularly for younger children, because of the possibility of *modeling* behavior in the child. This potential association was recently studied in a group of Hong Kong parent–child dyads (Lam, 2016), which did demonstrate a significant association between parental and child Internet-overuse patterns. Furthermore, a mediating model of the data gathered in this study indicated that parental mental health (most commonly depression) was a key factor in the development of IAD in the parent. Thus, in this section of the IMPROVE tool, some comment on the Internet (over) use patterns in the parents, as well as where relevant any mental health condition in the parents, is important to note. It is recognized that many parents or caregivers completing this section of the IMPROVE tool may find it difficult, even confronting, to complete this section, but optimal outcomes in a range of family-based interventions are often achieved when there is robust and honest *self-reflection* about one's own behaviors and attitudes, rather than an avoidance of family issues and an *externalization of blame* for the problem onto the child being studied. This open perspective is a prerequisite of all successful family therapy approaches, and is likely to also be important in addressing IAD in a family member. However, it is important to remember that *positive* and *nurturing aspects* of the parenting experience should also be noted (particularly if they apply to address ICT usage), and not just the *negative* perceived aspects.

R—Real-World Activities

One of the main concerns over IAD issues, from both a psychological and physical perspective, is that time spent on screen-based activities can have a significantly negative impact on *real-world* activities, interests, and hobbies. There can also be negative impacts on a client's daily routines such as sleep patterns, regular meal times, and bathing/washing. Having a clear structure and set of routines through the day, supported and monitored by the caregivers, can play an important role in optimizing mental well-being as well as having positive impacts on healthy sleep patterns, cardiometabolic health, and a healthy body weight (Tiberio et al., 2014). Conversely, the impact of IAD in young people has been shown to significantly affect their quality of sleep (Cain & Gradisar, 2010; Hysing et al., 2015), and also their body weight and physical health (Rosen et al., 2014). There have also been concerns raised about worsening myopia (short-sightedness) rates following heavy ICT usage from a young age, with the importance of *outdoors time* through the school day potentially reducing those rates (Wu, Tsai, Wu, Yang, & Kuo, 2013).

It is well recognized that the pro-social aspects of playing sports and other group-based activities are vital in teaching social skills and empathy in the developing individual, and more broadly in passing on the norms and values of the cultural group in which the individual is growing up (Huizinga, 1938). Though there are undoubtedly some social and cooperative aspects to many computer games—most notably in team-based multiuser games where live chat and broader social interaction are now common features—there have been strong concerns raised that the often-anonymous nature of gameplay, where face-to-face contact, expressions, nonverbal communications and so on, are minimized and a game can just be *switched off* at will, are not an adequate substitute for real-life socializing and friendship formation where much more deep, engaged responsibility and commitment is a key aspect (Greenfield, 2015; Turkle, 2015). In the Lin et al. (2009) study noted previously, the promotion of family and outdoors activities was shown to be protective against the development of IAD. Thus, an inventory of the full range of activities and daily routines should be taken, over the same time period that the ICT use is being recorded. This inventory should include both the *routine* daily activities such as eating, sleeping, and self-care patterns, and external hobbies, interests, and sporting pursuits. Where possible, the *actual amount of time* spent on each of these activities should be noted. This will facilitate a direct, day-to-day comparison of time spent on online activities and on *real-world* activities. This information could also be usefully compared to the real-world activities and behaviors *prior* to when the IAD problem began to arise; again, this will provide some useful information about the development of the IAD problem, and how it may have impacted on the subject's broader environment.

Another interesting aspect to the link between gaming and physical activity concerns the potential role of *active console games*, which require the bodily movement of a handheld controller to effect gameplay (most notably in sports games such as tennis and baseball simulations). Indeed, such consoles have been actively marketed as a *healthy alternative* to the more passive types of standard games, as well as having the potential to bring families together in a fun, active activity. Active games have attracted much research interest, as these could offer *positive* health benefits, such as weight loss or improved cardiometabolic health (with indirect benefits on mental well-being). A recent systematic review of 51 studies in this domain (LeBlanc et al., 2013) showed that, overall, such anticipated improvements were minimal or minor in long-term or *real-world* settings, although in controlled or supported conditions in special populations, a positive health benefit was often demonstrated. Thus, if active console gameplay is a regular or significant aspect of the subject's total game playing, this should be documented, particularly if play is in a family or other social setting. If relevant to a teenaged subject, it will be appropriate to note any addiction or dependence problem to non-Internet and gaming activities, such as alcohol, drugs, or specific food types, such as sugar. Though the association of IAD with other addictions has not been extensively researched to date, it has been postulated that there may be links (Griffiths, 1999), and as noted previously, there are many plausible factors in common with the development of both, such as the *enabling* parenting environment, social marginalization, and other psychosocial stressors. There are at least two specific subgroups of subjects where exploring and tabulating real-world activities are of key importance. These are clients with anxiety and avoidance issues, and clients with an established or a suspected autistic disorder. In both conditions, there are commonly pervasive patterns of social avoidance, a reduced sphere of interests and activities, and a resistance to new, challenging environments and experiences. There may also be overlap between the conditions of autism and anxiety. The world of the Internet and gaming can thus present a comparatively safe, predictable, yet still rewarding and empowering setting for clients with anxiety or with autistic disorders (Shane & Albert, 2008). The timeline of changes in real-life activities should thus be explored in some detail here, to delineate if the social avoidance came first, with heavy computer usage then *filling in the gap* of these lost interests, as this will yield important insights into addressing the difficulties.

O—Other Mental Health Conditions

As noted in the opening sections of this chapter, one of the most important domains of IA research in recent years has been the exploration of associated mental health disorders that may occur in a client with IAD. This area of inquiry is necessary in many ways: Firstly, preexisting mental disorders may play a *causative* role in the emergence of Internet addiction. In turn, IAD, if prolonged and severe, may *precipitate* a mental disorder or dysfunction such as anxiety, clinical depression, or severe family dysfunction and conflict. There could also be a common underlying cause of both IA and another mental disorder—such as prolonged socioeconomic deprivation or a history of abuse suffered by the subject. The presence of a mental disorder other than IA in a subject is important to document, as treating that disorder as well as the IA itself is likely to result in much better long-term improvements.

All established mental health conditions—whether they have been professionally treated or not—should thus be included. Suspected mental health disorders or *early warning signs* of these could also be noted, though of course the family completing the IMPROVE tool is not expected to be professionally qualified to make a formal diagnosis in this domain. If specific interventions have occurred in the past, such as medication and psychotherapy, these should be noted along with the relevant chronology and the success or the failure of that intervention.

V—Vulnerability Factors

As well as existing mental health conditions, other factors may be relevant in causing, contributing to, or worsening any IAD problem. These can be called *vulnerability factors*, and are known to be highly relevant in a range of mental illness that arises in the childhood and young-adult years (Brown & Harris, 1979; Caspi et al., 2003). Life stresses have also been demonstrated to be positively associated with the development of IAD (Leung, 2007). Vulnerability factors generally fall into two types: ongoing and recurrent factors, and time-limited, or acute, factors or events. An example of the first type could be growing up in a socioeconomically deprived locale or household, or having one or both parents suffering from a major mental illness or substance use problem. Examples of the latter would be an episode of bullying or physical abuse suffered at school, a major *life event* such as a robbery at the family home or the death of a parent. Another term to describe these events would be *stress factors*. Both types of such factors can affect the mental health and well-being of a client, sometimes in subtly different ways. There may also be some overlap of factors recorded in this section and those in the Parenting Aspects section mentioned previously. It is acceptable for such factors or events to be tabulated in both. Another form of vulnerability concerns factors *within* the subject—personality traits, temperament, and so on. These are often called *intrapsychic* factors or variables, and these also have been shown to be of importance in the development of mental health disorders. Such factors may be predisposing in the development of IAD, such as having low self-esteem, poor motivation and procrastination, and poor problem-solving capacity (Young & Abreu, 2010). On the other hand, personality variables quite different to these types may equally play a role in predisposition to IAD, such as need for excitement and novelty, high *reward dependence*, and inability to sustain concentration on a single task. Such personality traits are already well established as being important in the development of substance-use disorders (Terracciano, Lockenhoff, Crum, Joseph Bienvenu, & Costa, 2008), and are often colloquially dubbed the *addictive personality*. In the longitudinal study noted previously, the presence of impulsivity was found to be of key importance in the persistence of the pathological gaming over the time examined. Conversely, the effect of gaming and the *gaming experience* upon personality itself has also attracted much interest. In an innovative study utilizing a popular fantasy-based, role-playing game, Yee and Bailenson (2007) demonstrated that external manipulation by a researcher of the gameplayer's *avatar* (the online, tailored physical representation of the character) could affect their behavior, confidence, and success within the game. They have dubbed the effect of altering characteristics such as height, perceived attractiveness, and strength the *Proteus effect*, and have speculated whether these *virtual* behaviors could be transposed into the *real* world. A similar theory, dubbed the *e-personality effect*, relates more to the world of social networking and media (Aboujaoude, 2011). The theory describes vulnerable clients who show an overinflated self-image, narcissism, grandiosity, and, ultimately, a closer and potentially pathological identification in subjects' *false online image* of themselves than in their *real self*. If such effects on the personality of the subject over time have been observed, this should be carefully noted.

For this section of the IMPROVE tool, all such known—or even suspected—vulnerability factors should be listed, including whether they are of the ongoing or single-episode type, and also noting the timing/chronology of them if possible. Stressful life events that occurred some years back are likely to be of lesser importance than those that may have occurred a short time earlier. If *protective* factors are observed, such as known high resilience, ability to cope with sudden change or challenge, or strong collaborative problem-solving capacity within the subject or within the family unit, these could also be usefully included.

E—Is Extra Help or Assistance Needed?

By this point in the IMPROVE appraisal process, it is likely to have become clear to the participants how severe any IAD problem is—both from the individual's perspective and from broader ecological considerations such as family dynamics, education engagement, and social contact. Internet addiction—in keeping with most other psychological disorders—follows a *spectrum of severity* from mild to moderate to severe. Based on where the client may lie on this spectrum, a decision could be made about enlisting specialist professional help. If the problems as revealed through IMPROVE indicate that the condition is not too severe or advanced, it may be decided to manage the issues *in house* without any external help—for example, by addressing negative parenting factors or major real-world activity impacts.

Regarding children and teenagers, a first point of contact for an evolving ICT overuse case is often the SC—indeed, it may be the counselor who first alerts the family to emerging concerns that are initially observed in the school environment. SCs can then play a very important role in the "extra help needed" domain, by acting as a referrer to a specialist for any ongoing, targeted therapy. Such health professionals would generally be a child psychologist or child psychiatrist, and less commonly a pediatrician. Most SCs have a network of competent psychologists and child psychiatrists to whom they refer clients, including ones who are skilled in IAD appraisal and treatment. This referral decision should of course be made in collaboration with the client and the family.

APPRAISAL PROCESS FOR FAMILIES: SUBSEQUENT STEPS

Successfully completing the IMPROVE tool in an engaged and robust manner could be of benefit to the subject and to the family in a variety of important ways. It may be that, prior to the diligent collation of the Internet Inventory, the presence or severity of IAD was not fully appreciated by the subject or by the family; for example, just how much time was spent on ICT, and what daily activities were negatively impacted. Similarly, a consideration of possible parental factors in the precipitating or maintenance of an IAD problem may not have been done prior to the IMPROVE tool: Some degree of denial or active avoidance of these discussions may have existed. In this sense, IMPROVE could be an important *first step* in the family providing a more empathic, supportive, and structured environment for the subject, irrespective of his or her age.

As is illustrated in the case description, the SC or an equivalent professional can play a key role in the appraisal and treatment path from the outset. They are very much located at the *coal face* of IAD and their presentations in school-aged children: They are placed at the nexus of interactions with the student and the family. A recent survey of 120 SCs' experience of IAD in a large, inner city area of Sydney, Australia (Tam, 2012), demonstrated that IAD was almost always ranked in the top four of commonly presenting psychological disorders in schools. Furthermore, it was rated as *hard, or very hard, to treat* by 80% of respondents, and a notable minority of counselors, just more than 5%, had seen 50 or more separate cases of IAD in their recent practice.

In common with all mental disorders, IAD follows a *spectrum of severity*, ranging from early/mild, to moderate, and then severe levels of impairment. It is important, when embarking on a treatment pathway, to have a clear idea of how advanced the IAD may be in a particular child, as differing levels of severity (as well as any comorbidity) will require different strategies. This concept is also of key relevance in the appraisal and management of physical ailments, such as cancer, dementia, diabetes, and bone fractures.

THE IMPROVE TOOL:
IMPLICATIONS FOR THERAPISTS

The tool may also be of use at the start of, or during, any structured treatment path. Given the broad reach of domains explored in all of the items, it could be a useful and time-saving part of the background history-taking/assessment process that is necessary in many complex mental health disorders in a family setting, and of particular relevance with IAD. The successful completion of the Internet Inventory over a 2-week period or so, would be of great benefit when assessing the severity level of the condition, deciding on optimal treatment paths, and indicating where particular focus should lie; for example, on disrupted sleep–wake cycles, or on impaired schoolwork. IMPROVE also can form part of the process to gauge the success, or lack of success, of treatment after a period of time. Again, as it is the family that performs this task in the home, the often-pressured times in the clinic are used more efficiently.

CASE REPORT OF JAYDEN (CONTINUED):
USING THE IMPROVE TOOL IN A FAMILY SETTING

Internet Inventory

As the household owned only one laptop computer and one smartphone, it was not too difficult for Michaela to monitor reasonably accurately Jayden's usage throughout the week and the weekend, by observing his computer time and recording it. Given the aforementioned concerns, she ensured her smartphone was passcode-locked and that he could not use it; he was unhappy with this situation but eventually accepted it. She attempted to continue to enforce the *45-minute* rule of laptop/gaming in weekday evenings, but tensions continued each evening. Five days after commencement of IMPROVE, following a *5-minute warning* to wind up his game and then the mother coming to log off his usage, he became angry and aggressive, refusing to turn off the computer and then, when mother insisted, he got up violently, pushed her, then threw objects on the table at the wall, causing extensive damage.

Jayden and his sister were generally allowed *free access* to the computer as long as it was shared and they had completed home chores and homework. The Inventory revealed that Jayden was using the laptop for about 5 hours each weekend day, much more than his sister, who totaled only 90 minutes. His sister noted that he would regularly stay on playing despite her wishing some time online, saying it *was really important*. His usage was equally divided between video watching and playing a popular three-dimensional construction game. His mother also discovered that every Saturday morning, when he went to his best friend's home where she understood they played ball in the garden, they were in fact playing a popular multiplayer *First Person Shooter* game that was classified for play by 15-year-olds and older. That boy's mother was aware of this usage but had no specific rules in her home about computer game playing and was allowing this. At nighttime, both Jayden and his sister had no access to electronic devices or phones, and generally slept well through the night on most nights. They were trusted to settle themselves to bed in the evenings.

Monitor Over Time

As the Internet-use issues had only recently come to light, the priority was to complete the first IMPROVE tool for Jayden, before considering repeating it in a few months. It was likely that any intervention had to commence promptly, without the need for any monitoring over time, at that stage. However, one aspect of this monitoring pertained to his *real-world activities* and their changes up to the present time—these are expanded in the relevant section, mentioned subsequently.

Parenting Factors

The key factor noted here was that Michaela was a single mother, having separated from Jayden's father 4 years ago. The separation went smoothly and the father's work took him to another state, meaning that the children saw their father only every 6 weeks or so, and would stay for 3 or 4 days with him and his new partner. Michaela always tried to support her children while still adhering to rules around the home—such as overusage of computers. She tried to be consistent with both children, and to be equitable. Prior to the incident over computer use noted earlier, there had been no significant aggressive episodes with Jayden.

She did not feel that the separation of the parents had significantly affected the children, and they appeared to have coped well. In this section of IMPROVE, Michaela asked about Jayden's experience at his father's home when he stayed there. He informed her that he spent much of the days playing computer games unsupervised, while his father was either working or watching TV himself. Jayden said that he enjoyed not having "unfair rules" imposed on him like at home, so he could play his construction game uninterrupted. He admitted to often playing late into the night, being left to settle himself. He proudly demonstrated his complex constructions from his stays with his father to her, having saved them on the family laptop.

Real-World Activities

Jayden has always been an active boy who enjoyed a range of sports and activities, both within the school times and in his free time. He also had local friends with whom he would play in the park. He had no difficulties maintaining friendships and was a popular and outgoing boy. However, as the

Inventory noted, the 2 to 3 hours of playing ball that Michaela thought had been occurring on a Saturday, has been replaced by 2 to 3 hours of unbroken computer gaming at his friend's home. This situation, according to Jayden, had been occurring for about 6 months. He continued to play soccer about two times a week with his school team, and enjoyed this. Jayden, up to the age of 11 years, used to enjoy playing the violin, including playing in the school orchestra. He had started playing at the age of 6 years. However, he told his mother, without warning, that he was *quitting* violin as he no longer enjoyed it and found it *boring*. Though a bit upset by this decision, she was unable to convince Jayden to continue his violin.

He has always been a good sleeper, with healthy sleep hygiene and patterns. However, on three occasions during IMPROVE's completion, she noticed in the morning that the computer was strangely left on, with Jayden's own log-in in the memory; however, all recent Internet history had been deleted. Michaela then recalled that this had happened on a number of occasions in the past 12 months, but she had thought it not significant, and had not pursued it. She confronted him, however, at the end of this 2-week IMPROVE period, and the outcome is discussed subsequently.

Jayden has always been a healthy eater, enjoying a range of foods that mother would prepare for the family. On one occasion, it was noted that Jayden declined to cease his gaming at home due to "working on a very important construction with friends." She allowed him to eat while at the computer, while she and his sister ate in the dining room. He is of normal weight and in good physical shape.

Other Mental Health Issues

Jayden has never been diagnosed with a child psychiatric disorder, and has not been on psychotropic medication. Michaela noted that, when Jayden was 6 years old he visited a developmental pediatrician for assessment of his mild asthma and it was noted then that he had been restless and occasionally overly active in first grade. The pediatrician felt that the problems were not overly serious and assured them that Jayden "would grow out of it." In retrospect, Michaela recalls that Jayden did continue to be occasionally inattentive in class, particularly with subjects he did not like, but she did not pursue these concerns further with any professional.

Vulnerabilities

As noted in the parenting section, Jayden and his sister experienced the separation of the parents 4 years ago, which also led to the father moving interstate. Michaela had considered that Jayden adjusted well to this. On specific questioning for completion of this item, he noted that he had been quite upset and sometimes angry at both parents for the major life changes, but had not wanted to mention it to them. This period of feeling upset had lasted about 2 years. Furthermore, he revealed that he had been extensively teased at school by a group of two or three classmates about this separation, which had distressed him at the time. He had never revealed this to anyone else. Michaela realized that he had also quit the violin around this time.

Otherwise, Jayden was noted to be an easygoing, popular boy. He suffered no major anxiety and was confident socially and in class, but the drop in school grades was noted. Jayden's own explanation for this was that he "didn't find class very interesting."

Extra Help Needed

As the IMPROVE process was concluding, it was clear to Michaela that his problems with Internet and gaming issues were more serious that she had previously realized. For example, he had been covertly using the computer during the night, had recently been aggressive toward his mother when told to cease gaming, and had misled her over his gaming when at a friend's home. Furthermore, his school grades had dropped this year. One explanation for this could be his distractedness, and possible negative sleep impacts, due to the problem gaming; another could be the teasing he had suffered at school. She was determined to work closely with the SC and his teachers to address the situation and get him "back on track," and to seek professional mental health assistance also. The family doctor informed Michaela that he knew of a good clinical psychologist who was experienced in treating similar cases, and also was happy to make a referral to the local university clinic's child psychiatrist, for an assessment of any underlying mental health disorder.

Jayden's Subsequent Treatment Path

The day after IMPROVE was completed, Michaela booked an appointment for her and Jayden with the SC. The findings were discussed in detail, and Michaela got Jayden to complete and sign an "Internet and computer use contract," which set reasonable limits on computer use both at home and at school. Jayden was happy to sign the contract. He accepted that covertly logging-on to the family laptop in the night had to cease, and that his laptop usage would now be strictly limited during weekdays and weekends: an initial limit of 30 minutes during the week, and 90 minutes on Saturday and Sunday. He was also confronted about his covert nighttime usage. Jayden did admit to going onto the laptop when he knew that the others were asleep, but it was just to "check on his and his friend's [who lived overseas] construction," and he could not recall how long he actually had spent online. He may have deleted his Internet history after logging on, but this was "only by accident." He did accept that this behavior had to cease completely, and that he had fallen asleep in class due to tiredness. Jayden agreed to cease playing the often violent shooting games at his friend's, and to go outside and play ball instead. Regarding his heavy usage at his father's home, Jayden gave permission for Michaela to contact Jayden's father to discuss a higher level of supervision through the day and evening, and a limitation on his computer gaming.

It was still felt appropriate to organize a referral to the child psychologist to consolidate Jayden's undertakings, and to address any deep-seated distress following the parental separation, and the subsequent teasing at school. That psychologist was highly experienced in the usage of a specially designed structured therapy model for IAD, cognitive behavioral therapy for Internet addiction (CBT-IA; Young, 2011), and Jayden agreed to work with this mode of therapy.

It was also recommended that Jayden be assessed by the child psychiatrist at the university clinic, to explore the possibility of a previously undiagnosed ADHD, which could necessitate the use of psychotropic medication. Both Michaela and Jayden agreed for this referral to be made. In terms of the *severity level*, he could reasonably be placed at Level 2 on this system, with the possibility of upgrading this to Level 3, dependent on the mental health findings that were to be formally explored.

CONCLUSION

The IMPROVE tool was developed to assist primarily concerned families in their appraisal and addressing of what is often a frustrating, challenging condition. It is designed to be easy to complete, practical, yet still comprehensive in its scope and coverage. There are many validated assessment tools and surveys in regular use globally, translated into numerous languages, but they are best suited to young adult, or older teenage, subjects and do not take into account the subtle and often powerful influences that family, social, and outdoor-activity experiences can play in the evolution of IAD. It can also be of key assistance to SCs, who are in the privileged position of being able to work directly with the clients, their families, and the school teachers, and also in any future treatment path with a child psychologist or psychiatrist, if such a professional is brought into the management plan. IMPROVE may also be of utility in structured, formal research involving young subjects and their families, an area where there is a relative lack of knowledge in comparison to other domains of IAD. Treatment studies, when examining for changes in Internet usage and improvements in overall functioning, could use the Inventory and the real-world activities items in particular (possibly using a more structured format of data collation), to assess such changes over time. Parenting and family–environment factors relevant to IAD development could also be studied and delineated, as well as the role of vulnerability factors associated with IAD. Another domain of potential use could be at a global level, to assist transcultural research into relevant factors across different nationalities and ethnic groups. Given the simple and nontechnical language and concepts employed in IMPROVE, it will lend itself to translation to other languages.

A number of robust, valid, and clinically acceptable assessment tools and questionnaires now exist to assist clinicians and researchers in this challenging, and ever-evolving, domain. All of these, in conjunction with an empathic and holistic assessment, can mean that, for the young users of the Internet today and beyond, we can as a society look forward to that complex future not with trepidation or anxiety, but with optimism and confidence.

Parents and families can play a key role in the development, and severity, of an emerging IAD problem in an adolescent and in a child. They can also have an important potentially protective or moderating role in this condition. Possible mechanisms include simple modeling of behavior, the use or lack of boundaries and limits on computing and device use, family stress, dysfunction or conflict, and the failure to promote and support real-world activities and interests.

The role of the family is an area that is understudied in IAD, both from the assessment and the treatment perspective. The IMPROVE tool was specifically developed to assist families, possibly in conjunction with education and health professionals, in the appraisal and treatment decisions of a young client with suspected or actual IAD.

The IMPROVE tool may be made widely available to schools, parenting groups, and specialists such as clinical psychologists. The IMPROVE tool could be translated into other major languages. This will be of particular importance in multicultural families, where English might not be the primary language of a parent.

The engaged, evidence-based training of interested health professionals (clinical psychologists, youth workers, child psychiatrists) in the appraisal and management of complex Internet addiction clients and their families, including the utilization of evidence-based protocols such as CBT-IA, is necessary as computing and technology use increases in all segments of the population.

With younger children regularly now accessing the Internet, and for longer periods, the promotion of a *healthy digital diet* from an early age, through evidence-based awareness programs, parenting guidance and support in the purchasing and usage of computer technologies, and promotion of balanced, positive usage in schools and at home, is strongly indicated.

REFERENCES

Aboujaoude, E. (2011). *Virtually you: The dangerous powers of the e-personality*. New York, NY: W. W. Norton.

American Psychiatric Association. (2013). Conditions for further study: Internet gaming disorder. In *Diagnostic and statistical manual of mental disorders* (5th ed., pp. 795–798). Arlington, VA: American Psychiatric Publishing.

Beard, K. W. (2005). Internet addiction: A review of current assessment techniques and potential assessment questions. *CyberPsychology and Behaviour, 8*, 7–14.

Berle, D., & Starcevic, V. (2015). Are some video games associated with more life interference and psychopathology than others? Comparing massively multiplayer online role-playing games with other forms of video game. *Australian Journal of Psychology, 67*, 105–114.

Bernstein, J. (2014, November 25). Stop enabling your addicted adult child. *Psychology Today*. Retrieved from https://www.psychologytoday.com/blog/liking-the-child-you-love/201411/stop-enabling-your-addicted-adult-child

Brown, G. W., & Harris, T. (1979). *Social origins of depression: A study of psychiatric disorders in women*. London, UK: Tavistock Press.

Byun, S., Ruffini, C., Mills, J. E., Douglas, A. C., Niang, M., Stepchenkova, S., & Blanton, M. (2009). Internet addiction: Metasynthesis of 1996-2006 quantitative research. *CyberPsychology and Behaviour, 12*(2), 203–207.

Cain, N., & Gradisar, M. (2010). *Electronic media use and sleep in school-aged children and adolescents: A review*. Adelaide, SA, Australia: Flinders University, School of Psychology. doi:10.1016/j.sleep.2010.02.006

Calcovoressi, L., Mazure, C. M., Kasl, S. V., Skolnick, J., Fish, D., Vegso, S. J., . . . Price L. H. (1999). Family accommodation of obsessive-compulsive symptoms: Instrument development and assessment of family behavior. *The Journal of Nervous and Mental Diseases, 187*(10), 636–642.

Caspi, A., Sugden, K., Moffitt, T. E., Taylor, A., Craig, I. W., Harrington, H., . . . Poulton, R. (2003). Influence of life stresses on depression: Moderation by polymorphism in the 5-HTT gene. *Science, 301*(5631), 386–389.

Common Sense Media. (2013). *Zero to eight: Children's media use in America*. San Francisco, CA: Author.

Gentile, D. A., Choo, H. K., Liau, A., Sim, T., Li, D. D., Fung, D., & Khoo, A. (2011). Pathological video game use among youths: A two-year longitudinal study. *Pediatrics, 127*(2), 319–329.

Greenfield, S. (2015). *Mind change: How digital technologies are leaving their mark on our brains*. London, UK: Random House.

Griffiths, M. D. (1999). Internet addiction fuels other addictions. *Student BMJ, 7*, 428–429.

Gundogar, A., Bakim, B., Ozer, O., & Karamustafalioglu, O. (2012). The association between Internet addiction, depression and ADHD among high school students. *European Psychiatry, 27*(1), 1–8.

Han, D. H., Kim, S. M., Bae, S. J., Renshaw, P., & Anderson, J. (2015). Brain connectivity and psychiatric co-morbidity with Internet gaming disorder. *Addiction Biology*. doi:10.1111/adb.12347

Han, D. H., Kim, S. M., Lee, Y. S., & Renshaw, P. F. (2012). The effect of family therapy on the changes in the severity of on-line game play and brain activity in adolescents with on-line game addiction. *Psychiatry Research: Neuroimaging, 202*, 126–131.

Huizinga, J. (1938). *Homo Ludens: A study of the play-element in culture*. Boston, MA: Beacon Press.

Hysing, M., Pallesen, S., Stormark, K. M., Jakobsen, R., Lundervold, A. J., & Sivertsen, B. (2015). Sleep and use of electronic devices in adolescence: Results from a large population-based study. *BMJ Open, 5*(1), 1–7. doi:10.1136/bmjopen-2014-006748

Kuss, D. K., & Griffiths, M. D. (2012). Internet gaming addiction: A systematic review of empirical research. *International Journal of Mental Health and Addiction, 10*(2), 278–296.

Lam, L. T. (2016). Parental Internet addictive behavior and Internet addiction in adolescents: A mediating model through parental mental health. *Austin Addiction Sciences, 1*(1), 1–5. id1001.

LeBlanc, A. G., Chaput, J.-P., McFarlane, A., McFarlane, A., Colley, R. C., Thivel, D., . . . Tremblay, M. (2013). Active video games and health indicators in children and youth: A systematic review. *PLOS ONE, 8*(6), e65351. doi:10.1371/journal.pone.0065351

Leung, L. (2007). Stressful life events, motives for Internet use and social support among digital kids. *Cyberpsychology and Behaviour, 10*(2), 204–214.

Lin, C.-H., Lin, S.-L., & Wu, C.-P. (2009). The effects of parental monitoring and leisure boredom on adolescents' internet addiction. *Adolescence, 44*, 993–1004.

Mazurek, M. O., Shattuck, P. T., Wagner, M., & Cooper, B. P. (2012). Prevalence and correlates of screen-based media use among youths with autism spectrum disorders. *Journal of Autism and Developmental Disorders, 42*(8), 1757–1767.

Park, S., Hong, K.-E., & Park, E.-J. (2012). The association between problematic Internet use, depression, suicidal ideation and bipolar disorder symptoms in Korean adolescents. *Australian & New Zealand Journal of Psychiatry, 47*(1), 153–159.

Petry, N., Rehbein, F., Gentile, D. A., Lemmens, J. S., Rumpf, H.-J., Mossle, T., . . . O'Brien, C. (2013). An international consensus for assessing Internet gaming disorder using the new *DSM-5* approach. *Addiction, 109*(9), 1399–1406.

Rosen, L., Lim, A. F., Felt, J., Carrier, L. M., Cheever, N. A., Lara-Ruiz, J. M., . . . Rokkum, J. (2014). Media and technology use predicts ill-being among children, preteens and teenagers independent of the negative health impacts of exercise and eating habits. *Computers in Human Behavior, 35*, 364–375.

Rutter, M., Bishop, D., Pine, D., Scott, S., Stevenson, J., Taylor E., & Thapar A. (2010). *Rutter's child and adolescent psychiatry* (5th ed.). New York, NY: Wiley–Blackwell Press.

Sepuvelda, A. R., Kyriacou, O., & Treasure, J. (2009). Development and validation of the Accommodation and Enabling Scale in Eating Disorders (AESED) for caregivers in eating disorders. *BMC Health Services Research, 9*, 171. doi:10.1186/1472-6963-9-171

Shane, H., & Albert, P. D. (2008). Electronic screen media for persons with autism spectrum disorders: Results of a survey. *Journal of Autism and Developmental Disorders, 38*, 1495–1508.

Stone, L. (1998). What is continuous partial attention? Retrieved from www.lindastone.net/qa/continuous-partial-attention

Tam, P. (2012). [A survey of 120 school counselors' experience and attitudes towards problematic Internet use in high school students]. Unpublished data; available on request.

Tam, P. (2017). Invited review on "white matter connectivity and Internet gaming disorder," and broader considerations in the field. *Addiction Biology, 22*(1), 44–46.

Terracciano, A., Lockenhoff, C., Crum, R., Joseph Bienvenu, O., & Costa, P., Jr. (2008). Five-factor model of personality profiles of drug users. *BMC Psychiatry, 8*, 22. doi:10.1186/1471-244X-8-22

The Common Sense Census: Media use by tweens and teens. (2015). San Francisco, CA: Common Sense Media.

Tiberio, S., Kerr, D., Capaldi, D., Pears, K., Kim, H., & Nowicka, P. (2014). Parental monitoring of children's media consumption: The long-term influences on body mass index in children. *JAMA Pediatrics, 168*(5), 414–421.

Turkle, S. (2015). *Reclaiming conversation: The power of talk in a digital age.* New York, NY: Penguin Press.

Wei, H. T., Chen, M. H., Huang, P. C., & Bai, Y. M. (2012). The association between online gaming, social phobia, and depression: An Internet survey. *BMC Psychiatry, 12*(92), 1–7.

Wu, P. C., Tsai, C. L., Wu, H. L., Yang, Y. H., & Kuo, H. K. (2013). Outdoor activity during class recess reduces myopia onset and progression in school children. *Ophthalmology, 120*(5), 1080–1085.

Yang, C. Y., Sato, T., Yamawaki, N., & Miyata, M. (2013). Prevalence and risk factors of problematic Internet use: A cross-national comparison of Japanese and Chinese university students. *Transcultural Psychiatry, 50*(2), 263–279.

Ybarra, M. L., Alexander, C., & Mitchell, K. J. (2005). Depression, youth Internet use and online interactions: A national survey. *Journal of Adolescent Health, 36*(1), 9–18.

Yee, N., & Bailenson, J. (2007). The Proteus effect: The effect of transformed self-representation on behaviour. *Human Communication Research, 33*, 271–290.

Young, K. (1996). Internet addiction: The emergence of a new clinical disorder. *CyberPsychology and Behavior, 1*(3), 237–244.

Young, K. (2011). CBT-IA: The first treatment model for Internet addiction. *Journal of Cognitive Psychotherapy, 25*(4), 304–312.

Young, K. S., & Abreu, C. N. de (Eds.). (2010). *Internet addiction: A handbook and guide to evaluation and treatment* (p. 228). New York, NY: Wiley.

Young, K. S., & Rodgers, R. C. (1998). The relationship between depression and Internet addiction. *CyberPsychology and Behavior, 1*, 25–28.

ELECTRONIC SCREEN SYNDROME: PREVENTION AND TREATMENT

Victoria L. Dunckley

In many ways, interactive screen time behaves like a stimulant, not unlike caffeine, cocaine, or amphetamines. As such, like all stimulants, symptoms or *side effects* from daily screen time can be produced well before the user is addicted. Indeed, because electronic media stimulates the nervous system in an intense and unnatural manner, regular exposure can easily overwhelm and detune various processes in the brain and body. This detuned state—essentially a form of chronic hyperarousal—can mimic or worsen a wide variety of psychiatric, learning, or behavioral issues. Unfortunately, symptoms produced by screen time are often wrongly attributed to other disorders, resulting in ineffective treatment, overuse of medication, and misuse of health and education resources. Meanwhile, children suffering from these effects often remain *stuck* because the root problem is not being addressed.

These overstimulation effects, collectively termed *electronic screen syndrome* or ESS, are common—including in children whose electronics use falls within the recommended guidelines. This only makes the problem harder to recognize. Yet ESS is highly treatable, and addressing it can provide dramatic benefits to a child in terms of mood, focus, sleep, and behavior—regardless of any underlying diagnoses the child may have.

This chapter describes how interactive screen time impacts nervous system physiology and how these effects translate into symptoms that have become commonplace in today's youths. The chapter also provides an overview of an intervention that has been used successfully in hundreds of patients to reverse such changes: the Reset Program. The protocol, which can be implemented by families on their own or with clinical support as needed, consists of a strict, extended electronic "fast" followed by individualized screen management. It is virtually cost free, safe, and effective, and its principles can be applied to the full spectrum of screen-related disorders, from ESS to more overt cases of technology addiction.

ELECTRONIC SCREEN SYNDROME

ESS is essentially a disorder of *dysregulation*. *Dysregulation* can be defined as an inability to modulate one's mood, attention, or arousal level in a manner appropriate to one's environment. Each time a child views and interacts with a screen, the nervous system shifts into fight-or-flight, leading to disruption and disorganization of various biological systems. The mechanisms of screen-induced stress reactions are varied and numerous, and are reviewed in a subsequent section. Notably, most of them occur *irrespective of content*, which means that, from a functional perspective, even *educational* screen time can (and does) contribute to overstimulation. This disruptive chain of events occurs in all of us, but the process occurs more readily and acutely in still-developing children—particularly in those with underlying vulnerabilities.

Indeed, several emerging trends concerning children point to the existence of a new environmental culprit. Over the past couple of decades, there has been a marked increase in diagnoses of childhood psychiatric disorders including bipolar disorder, attention deficit hyperactivity disorder (ADHD), tics, and autism (Atladóttir et al., 2007; Lefever, Arcona, & Antonuccio, 2003; Moreno et al., 2007), as well as increases in obesity and other stress-linked medical conditions that were previously rare in children, such as metabolic syndrome (e.g., Mark & Janssen, 2008; Pervanidou & Chrousos, 2011). During this same period, there has also been a sharp rise in psychotropic medication use in children, particularly antipsychotics, stimulants, and antidepressants (Lefever et al., 2003; Moreno et al., 2007; Olfson, Marcus, Weissman, & Jensen, 2002). Perhaps the most telling sign, though, is the recent addition of a new childhood disorder in the latest *Diagnostic and Statistical Manual of Mental Disorders*, Fifth Edition (*DSM-5*; American Psychiatric Association [APA], 2013) with the word *dysregulation* in its name, a syndrome characterized by irritability, age-inappropriate tantrums, and disruptive, oppositional-defiant behavior—disruptive mood dysregulation disorder or DMDD (APA, 2013). The reason for the addition? Aside from evidence that the presentation of children displaying such symptoms was becoming increasingly common, there was legitimate concern that these children were being misdiagnosed and prescribed antipsychotic medication (Grohol, 2012). The descriptions of DMDD and ESS are strikingly similar; it is this author's belief that DMDD actually represents screen-induced hyperarousal: ESS.

Like DMDD, the concept of ESS was developed to describe a common cluster of symptoms in children that could closely imitate other disorders. Defining a syndrome helps avoid misdiagnosis and overuse of medication.

An additional purpose of naming ESS, however, is to underscore that there is a root cause—which in turn points to appropriate treatment. Finally, because hyperarousal, and thus ESS, can present in a myriad of forms—from rages to anxiety to poor focus—an umbrella term helps conceptualize the collective phenomena.

CHARACTERISTICS OF ESS IN CHILDREN

Although varied, many of the effects of ESS can be grouped into symptoms related to mood, cognition, and behavior. The root of these symptoms appears to be linked to repeated stress on the nervous system, making self-regulation and stress management less efficient. ESS can occur in the absence of a psychiatric disorder and mimic it, or it can occur in the face of an underlying disorder, exacerbating it. Similarly, ESS can worsen most learning disorders and some neurological conditions as well.

Children with ESS exhibit symptoms due to chronic hyperarousal that cause significant dysfunction in school, at home, or with peers. Presentations closely mirror the variety seen in children suffering from chronic or post-traumatic stress, and reflect malfunction of the brain's frontal lobe. Typical signs and symptoms include emotional dysregulation, poor executive functioning, and disruptive or maladaptive behavior. Insomnia or nonrestorative sleep is common. Parents commonly report that the child is highly irritable, has *meltdowns*, tantrums, or even rages over minor frustrations, and has trouble focusing, staying organized, following directions, and keeping up with schoolwork. The child tends to display immature or defiant behavior, and is often described by parents and teachers as *stressed out* or *revved up*. Family members often remark that they "have to walk on eggshells" around the child.

Symptoms markedly improve or resolve with an electronic fast; that is, the strict removal of interactive electronic screen media for several weeks. To have a lasting impact, a 3-week fast is necessary, but may not be sufficient in some cases, particularly in older teens and young adults with high amounts of daily screen use. Symptoms of ESS often recur with the reintroduction of electronic media following a fast, particularly if screen-time exposure returns to previous levels. After a fast, some children with ESS can tolerate small amounts of screen time with strict moderation, while others seem to relapse immediately on re-exposure. Frequently, the child will be intensely drawn to screen devices and will have difficulty pulling away. However, children with ESS are not always addicted per se to technology, and children with vulnerabilities can experience symptoms even when daily screen time is well below recommended guidelines. In comparison to technology addiction, these caveats make the syndrome easy to miss unless one knows what to look for.

Certain factors increase risk for ESS, many of which echo those seen in technology addiction. Children with underlying psychiatric, learning, emotional, or neurodevelopmental issues are at higher risk, as are children experiencing psychological stress. At particularly high risk are children with ADHD, autism, sensory issues, or a history of trauma or neglect—that is, children who are already prone to trouble regulating arousal levels.

To help parents recognize whether a child's struggles might be related to ESS, a questionnaire is given. The question list can also serve to help clinicians and teachers learn to identify signs that, especially when occurring together, suggest ESS should be ruled out. The following is a sampling of the approximately 20 questions:

- Does your child seem revved up a lot of the time, or have meltdowns over minor frustrations?
- Has your child become increasingly oppositional, defiant, or disorganized?
- Does your child become irritable when told it is time to stop playing video games or to get off the computer?
- Would you describe your child as being attracted to screens "like a moth to a flame?"
- Do you ever feel your child is not as happy as he or she should be, or that your child is not enjoying activities like he or she used to?
- Does your child have trouble making or keeping friends due to immature behavior?
- Are your child's grades falling, or is he or she not performing academically up to his or her potential and no one is certain why?
- Does your child seem lazy, low energy, and have poor attention to detail?
- Would you describe your child as being stressed, despite few or no stressors you can clearly point to?

These questions all represent scenarios—related to symptoms, functioning, or treatment effectiveness—that occur when an overstimulated child starts operating from a more primitive part of the brain. During this state, two things tend to happen: (a) symptoms and overall functioning worsen and (b) interventions do not work very well. Parents of children with ESS are typically frustrated and sense that something's being missed, and will feel these questions strike a familiar chord. Resonating with what the family may be experiencing can also open the door to helping them consider a new explanation for the child's difficulties.

PHYSIOLOGICAL MECHANISMS OF ESS

Contrary to popular belief, it does not take much electronic stimulation to throw a sensitive and still-developing brain off track. Further, many parents mistakenly believe that *interactive* screen time—Internet or social media use, texting, e-mailing, and gaming—is not harmful, especially compared to passive screen time like watching television. But, in fact, both immediately and over time, interactive screen time is *more likely* to cause sleep, mood, and cognitive issues (Dworak, Schierl, Bruns, & Strüder, 2007; Gradisar et al., 2013; Kondo et al., 2012), most likely because it is more stimulating, more engaging, and more likely to trigger compulsive use.

Because the eyes are actually part of the central nervous system (CNS)—in fact the eyes are the *only* part of the CNS exposed to the outside world—the eyes provide a particularly potent route for electronic screen media influence. Screen devices interface with the brain through visual pathways, nonvisual pathways, eye muscle movement, and the vestibular system, which in turn affect sensorimotor integration, arousal, and attentional processes (Kohyama, 2011; Rowan, 2010). Screen media also impacts the user via direct influences on brain activity and whole-body physiology, and can exploit psychological and social needs.

Many of the mechanisms contribute to hyperarousal and likely act synergistically; in turn, higher arousal increases risk for both addiction and aggression (Ivory & Kalyanaraman, 2007). The following are some of the physiological mechanisms that may explain electronics' tendency to produce disturbance in mood, cognition, sleep, and behavior.

Desynchronization of the Body Clock

Light emitted by screens is bright and rich in blue and white tones. Because this light mimics the sky, it signals to the brain that it is daytime—time to be alert. This signaling, which occurs via nonvisual pathways from the eyes to clock cells in the brain, increases arousal and suppresses melatonin, a sleep hormone naturally released by darkness. Numerous studies show that screen stimulation in the evening can delay melatonin release by several hours and desynchronize the body clock, and that higher amounts of overall screen time throughout the day negatively impact sleep (e.g., Cain & Gradisar, 2010; Cajochen et al., 2011; Van den Bulck, 2004). Screen exposure delays sleep onset, suppresses REM sleep, and prevents core body temperature from dropping to levels supportive of deep sleep (Higuchi, Motohashi, Liu, Ahara, & Kaneko, 2003). Meanwhile, aside from poor sleep, low melatonin is linked to depression, brain inflammation, and alterations in hormone function, including reproductive hormones, cortisol, and growth hormone (Figueiro & Rea, 2010; Kasuya, Kushibiki, Yayou, Hodate, & Sutoh, 2008; Luboshitzky & Lavie, 1999; Wetterberg et al., 1992). Moreover, research on *light-at-night* from electronics use reveals associations with poor memory, irritability, depression, suicidality, and impaired academic performance (Oshima et al., 2012; Polos et al., 2010; Van den Bulck, 2007). Restful sleep with proper *architecture* is how we recover from the day's assaults.

Desynchronization may also blunt serotonin levels (Kohyama, 2011); serotonin is a brain chemical important for mood regulation and sense of well-being. Healthy levels require exposure to morning light, physical activity, and adequate melatonin levels—the same factors that synchronize the clock. In contrast, serotonin activity tends to be low in states of depression, aggression, and suicidality.

Overactivation of Reward Pathways

Intense activation of reward pathways and subsequent release of dopamine, a brain chemical associated with reward and seeking behaviors, are key mechanisms in virtually all addiction processes. Imaging studies suggest gaming releases copious amounts of dopamine in the prefrontal cortex (Koepp et al., 1998). But when reward pathways are intensely stimulated too often, they become desensitized, and more and more stimulation is needed to experience pleasure and to maintain interest (Niehaus, Cruz-Bermúdez, & Kauer, 2009). Moreover, imaging studies on Internet addiction show reduced dopamine transporters and reduced receptors (Hou et al., 2012; Kim et al., 2011).

Because dopamine is critical for focus and motivation, even small changes in dopamine functioning can wreak havoc on how well a child feels and functions. Meanwhile, the addiction process itself creates a *hair trigger* response to stress, reinforcing use as an escape (Koob & Kreek, 2007). Additionally, hijacked reward pathways may prevent natural reward circuitry from being paved, while priming the brain for other types of addiction (Niehaus et al., 2009; Ream, Elliott, & Dunlap, 2011). All of these dynamics create and perpetuate vicious cycles.

Finally, clinical observation and a small body of research suggest screen stimulation can induce or worsen dopamine-sensitive phenomena, including psychosis, obsessive-compulsiveness, and tics (Association for Comprehensive Neurotherapy [ACN], 2004; Dunckley, 2012; Ha et al., 2007; Nitzan, Shoshan, Lev-Ran, & Fennig, 2011). These symptoms mirror the array of side effects seen with chemical stimulants, and also suggest that screen time triggers dopamine release in motor as well as other brain areas.

Acute and Chronic Stress Reactions

Interactive screen time presents the nervous system with an evolutionary "mismatch" of sorts: fight-or-flight reactions unaccompanied by a discharge of physical energy. When fight-or-flight occurs too often, especially if the energy is not released, the brain and body have trouble regulating themselves to a calm state, leading to a state of chronic stress. Numerous studies have demonstrated a relationship between interactive screen time and physiological stress markers, both for acute stress, such as elevated blood pressure and heart rate, reduced heart rate variability, and increased food intake (Chaput et al., 2011; Ivarsson, Anderson, Åkerstedt, & Lindblad, 2009; Wang & Perry, 2006) and chronic stress, such as cortisol dysregulation, increased blood pressure, high cholesterol and blood sugar, weight gain, metabolic syndrome, and cardiovascular changes (Figueiro & Rea, 2010; Gopinath et al., 2011; Mark & Janssen, 2008; Wallenius, 2010). Interestingly, the link between screen time and obesity or metabolic syndrome holds true regardless of physical activity level, supporting the notion that screen time itself disturbs metabolism (Mark & Janssen, 2008).

But how does electronic stress translate to ESS symptoms? During acute and chronic stress states, blood flow is shunted *away* from the frontal lobe and toward deeper, more primitive brain areas. Stress impairs emotional and executive functioning in the near term and alters frontal lobe brain structure in the long term (Arnsten, 2009). Chronic stress can also lead to memory impairment from damage to the hippocampus (Maras et al., 2014). Meanwhile, high cortisol—the hormone that becomes elevated and/or desynchronized with chronic stress—increases risk for anxiety and depression, increases brain inflammation, and impairs regulation of other hormones and brain chemistry (Pervanidou & Chrousos, 2012). Thus, both hyperarousal and addiction processes impair brain and body functioning via stress.

Electrical Excitability

Because the eyes are an extension of the central nervous system, intense visual stimulation can sometimes trigger excitation or *firing* of neurons, particularly in vulnerable individuals. Research and observation suggest some people experience screen-induced seizures, tics, or migraine headaches (ACN, 2004; Funatsuka, Fujita, Shirakawa, Oguni, & Osawa, 2001; Montagni, Guichard, Carpenet, Tzourio, & Kurth, 2015). Some screen-induced seizure activity may actually present as behavioral issues (Solodar, 2014). Manic episodes may also be due (in part) to overfiring or aberrant firing of neurons, which may be why seizure medications are often an effective means to treat them. It is likely that there is a spectrum of electrical excitation manifestations, from the more tangible seizure or tic on one end, to more generalized *irritation* of the nervous system on the other.

Sensory Overload

Screen brightness, rapid movement, supersaturated colors, fantastical events, vividness, interactivity, and a high ratio of screen size to visual field all contribute to visual overload and hyperarousal (Fortin & Dholakia, 2005; Funatsuka et al., 2001; Ivory & Kalyanaraman, 2007; Lillard & Peterson, 2011; Reeves, Lang, Kim, & Tatar, 1999). When excessive stimulation overwhelms the sensory system, it may effectively shut down other parts of the brain in order to compensate. After such intense exposure, the brain experiences a relative sensory deprivation, which, along with a drop in dopamine, may explain why children are irritable and struggle to self-regulate after using a screen device. From a developmental perspective, repeated exposure to intense sensory stimuli leads to an overactive visual system: the child attempts to pay attention to everything around him or her, making it difficult to focus and causing other sensory integration issues (Rowan, 2010).

Depletion of Mental Reserves

According to *attention restoration theory*, what is often behind explosive or aggressive behavior is poor focus (Kaplan, 1995). When attention suffers, so does the ability to process one's internal and external environment, so little demands become big ones. By depleting mental energy with high visual and cognitive input, screen time contributes to low reserves via multitasking, information and sensory overload, increased decision making, frequent interruptions, and processing of pixelated images (DeStefano & LeFevre, 2007; Mangen, Walgermo, & Brønnick, 2013; Ophir, Nass, & Wagner, 2009; Wästlund, Reinikka, Norlander, & Archer, 2005). The *high load* produced by screens is also evidenced by research demonstrating that compared to paper, screens slow reading, hinder deep learning, and produce inferior exam performance—in children *and* adults (e.g., Mangen et al., 2013; Yamamoto, 2007). Depletion of mental reserves is particularly relevant for children with vulnerabilities, who have reduced reserves—or inefficient use of reserves— to begin with.

Electromagnetic Fields

A growing body of evidence suggests that radiation from manmade electromagnetic fields (EMFs) produced by wireless communications, such as the kind used by mobile phones and Wi-Fi, may cause harm, particularly in still-developing children (Kheifets, Repacholi, Saunders, & van Deventer, 2005). Numerous studies have demonstrated that EMFs can cause adverse effects such as cellular inflammation, DNA damage, melatonin suppression, cellular and systemic stress reactions, and reproductive harm (Blank & Goodman, 2009; Gye & Park, 2012; Jarupat, Kawabata, Tokura, & Borkiewicz, 2003; Pall, 2013). At particular risk are children with autism, who are inherently prone to having low melatonin, hyperarousal, electrical excitability, a compromised blood–brain barrier, and brain inflammation (Herbert & Sage, 2013).

Indirect Mechanisms

Along with the direct effects mentioned previously, there are also a host of indirect effects resulting from less time spent engaged in activities known to support mental health and nervous system integration. These factors include eye contact, face-to-face contact, touch, bonding with caregivers, active and imaginary play, varied levels of natural stimulation, creative expression, and exposure to the outdoors, sunshine, and greenery.

Thus, time spent with electronics reduces exposure to natural mood, sleep, and cognition enhancers—factors that are also known to support brain development. Each minute spent on a screen represents a trade-off.

IMAGING STUDIES ON GAMING AND INTERNET ADDICTION

ESS and technology addiction can both be considered arousal disorders, and likely represent parts of the same spectrum. In fact, imaging research findings on gaming/Internet addiction dovetail nicely with the symptoms and dysfunction seen in children with ESS. As one researcher noted, "Taken together, the research shows that Internet addiction is associated with structural and functional changes in brain regions involving emotional processing, executive attention, decision making, and cognitive control" (F. Lin et al., 2012). Thus, the presence of ESS may be an early warning of technology addiction, at least in some children. In others it may simply mean the child is not tolerating their current level of electronics exposure. Indeed, addiction aside, a much broader concern is the risk that *screen time is creating subtle damage even in children with "regular" exposure*—especially considering the substantial amounts of time the average child or teen clocks in on screens every day.

Brain imaging studies on Internet and gaming addiction have found abnormalities in both brain structure and function similar to damage caused by alcohol and substance abuse. Research on adolescents and young adults with Internet/gaming addiction demonstrates gray matter atrophy (loss of volume) in the frontal lobe and abnormalities in the striatum, an area involved in reward and suppression of socially unacceptable impulses (Weng et al., 2013; Yuan, Qin, Liu, & Tian, 2011; Zhou et al., 2011). Another concerning finding is atrophy and other changes in the insular region (Weng et al., 2013; Zhou et al., 2011). The insula has a role in empathy development, integrating bodily sensations with emotion, and emotional components of addiction (Naqvi & Bechara, 2010). Other research has shown patchy white matter, representing reduced connectivity within and between brain areas (Hong, Zalesky, et al., 2013; F. Lin et al., 2012; Weng et al., 2013), and thinning of the cortex (Hong, Kim, et al., 2013; Yuan, Cheng, et al., 2013). Finally, imaging studies looking at function have found impaired information processing, reduced impulse control, and aberrant spontaneous brain activity (Dong, Devito, Du, & Cui, 2012; Dong, Hu, & Lin, 2013; Yuan, Jin, et al., 2013).

The Reset Program

The Reset Program is designed to reverse hyperarousal, realign nervous system physiology, and release the hold of electronics on the child and family. To overview, the *resetting* portion of the program consists of up to 1 week of planning and a minimum of 3 weeks for the electronic fast. Following the fast and thereafter, decisions are made based on rules of thumb, algorithms, and risk factors. Ultimately, above all else, screen management decisions following the fast are based on *tolerability*—what the individual can handle without becoming dysregulated or symptomatic, without exhibiting signs of addictive behavior or use, and without any deterioration of functioning compared to being screen free.

For the fast to be effective, the goal is to eliminate all *interactive* screen time, which is any screen activity where the user is interfacing with a device, be that via a screen, keyboard, or controller. Interactive screen time includes video gaming, Internet use, social media use, texting, e-mailing, Skyping/video chatting, using a digital device or tablet, using an e-reader, and so on. It includes *educational* and *creative* games and apps. Passive screen time, on the other hand, consists of viewing TV programs or movies on a regular TV set from across the room. For the Reset, patients are allowed a modest amount of passive screen time—5 hours or less per week—provided the content is slow-paced, nonviolent, and not too visually stimulating. In addition, certain Reset TV rules are applied; for example, if sleep issues persist, passive screen time should be cut back further—particularly in the evenings—or eliminated altogether. Importantly, watching TV shows, movies, or videos on a device (e.g., on a tablet or laptop) *counts* as interactive screen time and is therefore not allowed.

Through trial and error with hundreds of patients, it has become clear that even *a little* interactive screen time (such as gaming on the weekends or 15 minutes of device play after school) will often render the Reset useless, while *a little* passive screen time typically does not. This will seem counterintuitive to many parents, but it is consistent with certain research already mentioned. This is not to say that reducing or *moderating* screen time does not have benefits; in fact research suggests that parental efforts to cut back screen time produce significant positive changes in mental and physical health (Gentile, Reimer, Nathanson, Walsh, & Eisenmann, 2014). Rather, it may be that once the child's nervous system has reached a certain *tipping point* and becomes dysregulated, it is simply *not enough* to merely cut back.

Once parents understand the nature of ESS and have agreed to implement the Reset, preparation for the fast begins. Proper planning significantly impacts results by strengthening commitment, forming a unified front among the adults involved, establishing joint goals, and sealing the inevitable *cracks* that tend to creep in. Families who do not anticipate and prepare often wind up missing something crucial that undermines success, like forgetting about a device the child rarely uses, failing to provide adequate replacement activities, or not making sure other caregivers, like the babysitter, know the rules.

Reset planning consists of 10 steps, which include defining problem areas and setting goals, getting one's spouse and other caregivers on board, deciding on how to replace screen devices and activities, structuring the 3-week calendar with activities and breaks for each parent, performing a thorough *screen sweep*, and informing the child and other family members of the plan. For many of the steps, idea lists and case examples are provided, and a final checklist is given to underscore the most crucial action items. Following are notes regarding particular steps and caveats.

Tracking Problem Areas

Parents are asked to define and track two to three problem areas, using lists of categories including emotional, behavioral, school-related, social, and physical problems areas from which to pick. As much as possible, problem areas are quantified, for example, by rating severity or counting frequency of meltdowns in a week, calculating the proportion of completed homework assignments, documenting time spent outdoors, or tracking what time the child falls asleep. For these and other exercises, clinicians should encourage the parents to do the exercises in a handwritten journal to document their journey.

Scheduling Play, Activities, and Bonding

Although children and even teens will naturally return to more creative and physical play in the absence of electronics if left on their own, parents today are likely to become anxious when imagining their child working through boredom. Thus, filling in the calendar and brainstorming ideas for screen-free activities and toys (including for solitary, sibling, friend, and family play) helps parents better envision how the fast will go. In addition, scheduling one-on-one "dates" with each parent as well as family time lets the child know he or she is valued and loved, and that the solution involves the entire family. Bonding further boosts resetting of the brain through increased eye contact, conversation, and nurturing touch—factors known to lower the stress response, improve self-regulation, and optimize brain growth (Siegel, 2006). Interestingly, bonding and addiction circuits share common pathways (Insel, 2003), which may explain why healthy attachment and family time seem to buffer against addiction of all kinds, including screen addiction (C.-H. Lin, Lin, & Wu, 2009; Pressman, Owens, Evans, & Nemon, 2014; Richards, McGee, Williams, Welch, & Hancox, 2010).

Getting Both Parents on Board

Not uncommonly, one parent will be ready to do the Reset, but the other resists. The lead parent will sometimes presume it is a foregone conclusion that their spouse would not agree to the plan or will refuse to read educational materials, and so would not make much of an effort to talk about it. This becomes a self-fulfilling prophecy. Regarding parenting and fathers' involvement, both human and animal research shows that fathers tend to step up caregiving when they feel needed (and vice versa when unneeded), and that while mothers are somewhat more likely to set boundaries, fathers are more likely to *enforce* boundaries (Farrell, 2001). Research also suggests that fathers' style of play—which tends to be more rough-and-tumble and to involve more risk-taking and competition—helps build empathy, emotional resilience, sensorimotor skills, and frustration tolerance (Farrell, 2001). Thus, for screen management (and in general), bringing Dad into the fold and valuing his contributions can have a positive impact on outcome while providing Mom with much-needed breaks.

Inevitably, some parents will resist the electronic fast if they enjoy gaming with the children, or if they feel their own gaming, Internet, or social media use is being criticized. Others may resist if they feel the fast will mean more work for them, that they will be even *more* stressed in losing the *electronic babysitter*, or if they predict that their efforts will be undermined by others. For many, the realization that screen time may be causing harm produces anxiety or deep-seated guilt about past or ongoing screen allowances, so parents may minimize, rationalize, or deny the problem rather than face these uncomfortable feelings. Intimacy issues or conflicts that have been avoided may also come to the surface.

Taken together, resistance issues affect many if not most families, but can be worked around. Whatever the case, clinicians should attempt to uncover the reasons *behind* the resistance, validate the feelings surrounding it, and discuss the scientific rationale behind ESS and the Reset as it applies *specifically to that child.* Finally, hearing from other parents who have benefited from the Reset can be highly persuasive and reassuring. Thus, having families mentor each other or having a group of families do the Reset together can help parents overcome resistance and receive extra support at the same time.

School–Based Screen Time

The amount of school-related screen time children receive varies widely. Often the electronic fast will still be successful if all interactive screen time outside of school is eliminated, as long as certain rules related to homework are followed, such as scheduling computer-related work as early in the afternoon or evening as possible, requiring that the child use a stationary computer in a common area where he or she can be seen, and strictly banning media multitasking. However, even if these guidelines are followed, there will be some children for whom the elimination of school screen time will be necessary for the fast to be effective. In fact, for some children with ESS, school *is* the primary source of screen time, and thus addressing it becomes necessary. In other cases, the child is simply too dysregulated—or too sensitive—to leave school-based screen exposure in the mix.

If the decision is made to eliminate school screen time (either preemptively or as part of troubleshooting the Reset), this can often be accomplished by having a health provider write a letter to give to the teacher. The letter should include the rationale and a clear order:

> Because interactive screen time can put the nervous system into a state of hyperarousal (fight-or-flight) and thereby impair attention, mood regulation, sleep, and the ability to complete tasks, Johnny is to be off of all electronic screen media, including computer use for class work and homework, for 4 weeks.

Having a physician sign or cosign the letter, presenting it as a *doctor's note,* and having two or more clinicians from different disciplines sign the letter may carry more weight while framing the request as a medical necessity—which indeed it is. The note can refer to nonspecific symptoms (such as trouble sleeping) or to the child's actual diagnosis or disability should there be one (such as ADHD or a reading disorder).

In any case, proposing the electronic fast as an experiment and as a potential win–win to assist the child getting back on track can facilitate compliance. Particularly in cases where a child is disruptive and utilizing a lot of resources, the administration may agree to remove screens in the name of *trying everything*. Requests may need to be repeated; offering specific recommendations, providing measurable data, and brainstorming alternatives are all helpful. Longer term accommodation requests can include such recommendations as elimination of screen-based homework, opting out of tablet- or laptop-based programs, selecting teachers who do not use whiteboards or document cameras on a daily basis, or requesting a Wi-Fi free classroom. It is also helpful to put together a list of citations relating specifically to the child's struggles; for example, regarding screen time's impact on attention, aggression, technology addiction, autism, impulsivity, tics, and so on. An abundance of peer-reviewed research linking screen time to particular symptoms, disorders, and learning challenges can be found in the endnotes of Chapters 2, 3, and 11 of *Reset Your Child's Brain* (Dunckley, 2015).

As an aside, for children of all ages, it is worth finding out if teachers use electronics as rewards and if they allow their use during recess or other breaks. These practices have become exceedingly common even in special education classrooms. Parents should request *in writing* that these practices be stopped when it comes to their child. They should also follow up periodically to make sure the request is being honored.

Cell Phone Usage

With the recent proliferation of cell phones into young hands, cell or smartphone use has become a common source of noncompliance with the fast. Many parents have difficulty with this step, but leaving a smartphone in place defeats the purpose of the fast. The simplest (and most effective) solution is to simply have the child survive the fast without having a phone, period. If communication is the main concern, remind parents that even if their child does not have a phone, others around him or her will. If parents insist that the child must carry a phone, swap out any type of smartphone for a bare-bones flip-phone that the child turns in as soon as they walk in the door. No texting is best, limited texting (to parents only) is next best, and this use still needs to be monitored. Remind parents that studies show the mere *presence* of a phone is distracting (Thornton, Faires, Robbins, & Rollins, 2014), that checking social media *just once* while studying has been linked to lower grades (Rosen, Mark Carrier, & Cheever, 2013), and that *any* texting or phone use after bedtime can impair mood and cognitive performance (Polos et al., 2010; Van den Bulck, 2007).

Informing the Child

One of the steps that cause parents much angst is informing the child that a strict electronic fast will indeed take place. Some will need help with phrasing—for which age-appropriate scripts and suggestions are given—and some will need help managing their child's (or their own) reactions. Parents are coached about traps to avoid, such as engaging in a debate or allowing guilt feelings to weaken resolve. For many parents, it is helpful to role-play the conversation with the clinician, taking turns as child and parent. In general, parents should aim to be compassionate but matter-of-fact and convey that the intention of the fast is not to punish but to help, and to help not just the child but the whole family. At the same time, parents should share how they will help the child through it, and should try to be honest about their own usage, too. If the child begins to employ arguing or negotiating tactics, the parent should disengage and end the conversation. Clinicians can also reassure parents that the child will be reacting to whatever he or she *imagines* is going to happen—which is far worse than what the reality will be—and that removing screens reduces risk for the very things parents are afraid of triggering, such as depression, loneliness, and aggression.

Children's reactions to hearing the news vary. Children, teens, and young adults demonstrate a range of reactions, including panic, crying, anger, agitation, relief, emotional withdrawal, or any combination thereof. Not surprisingly, parents of teens are more likely to be acutely fearful of their child's reaction, whether they are predicting the child will collapse into despair, threaten to hurt themselves, or fly into a rage. If parents are concerned about handling rage, threats, or depressive states, a safety plan is in order, discussed briefly subsequently. It is also important to explore what's *behind* a parent's fears: Is the parent afraid of being attacked? Does the parent fear he or she will lose the child's love? And so on. Aside from being a roadblock to healthy screen management, these fears often point to other unhealthy parent–child dynamics that need to be worked through.

Safety Plans

Threats and destructive behavior tend to occur in children who are severely dysregulated, whether from ESS, addiction processes, or mental illness. Often, the dysregulation itself turns the hierarchy of power upside down as the parent attempts to appease the child in order to avoid a meltdown. Meanwhile, the child's difficult disposition may cause the parent to avoid spending time with the child, and the disconnect grows further still. In any case, safety plans can shift a parent from being paralyzed and helpless to being mobilized and in charge.

Safety plans range from simply preparing mentally for how a parent will handle a situation to verbal discussions between parents and the clinician to formalizing a plan in writing signed by everyone, including the child. Parents are given the basic elements for developing a safety plan as well as case examples.

For danger-to-others situations, the safety focus is on high-risk moments or periods in which the child is likely to become explosive, such as when the parent(s) inform the child and when devices are removed from the child's room or taken out of the home. For many families, this concern may be handled by simply having at least one other adult present during these times, preferably someone the child knows and respects. Safety plans for an aggressive child should include specific coping strategies to lower the child's arousal levels, either through redirecting energy or by giving the child time and space to calm down. It should also include the kinds of behaviors that are and are not acceptable (e.g., yelling is okay, throwing objects is not), and a specific action to be taken if the child cannot calm down or continues to be out of control. For children with a history of assaultiveness, the final step of the safety plan should include calling 911, particularly if the child can physically overpower the parents. Though adding this step may alarm parents, the message to both child and parent is that the purpose is to contain the situation and keep everyone safe *no matter what*. Truly, when a child feels out of control, the child will seek containment, and pushes boundaries in an attempt to feel more safe.

For concerns about depression or a child hurting himself or herself in relation to the Reset, the safety plan's main focus is to ensure there is no time during which the child is left unmonitored until the child is feeling better as well as safe. Worsening depression and intense anxiety are most likely to occur on separation from devices, and at night if the child is accustomed to the *company* of a device, so focusing on the period between informing the child and the end of the week of the first fast is most crucial. One mother embarking on the Reset shared that she slept in her 13-year-old girl daughter's room the first four nights. The mother reported: "She was furious with me but I could tell she liked me being there." Indeed, the fear of being isolated and alone is part of what prompts a child's despair, so close monitoring and "being there" during this period can help provide a sense of grounding and connectedness—even if the child acts as though he or she does not want the parent there.

For safety plans and the Reset in general, it goes without saying that the initial adjustment period is a particularly critical time for parents to stay off their own devices.

The Electronic Fast

These 3 (or more) weeks allow a child's brain the chance to rejuvenate by obtaining the deep rest needed to reset out-of-balance systems, and to redirect energy, blood flow, and nutrients to the brain's frontal lobe. Parents are given descriptions and lists about "what to expect" as well as exercises to do for each of the three fast weeks. During the first week, the child may or may not be in the throes of a true withdrawal syndrome. With school-aged children, for the first few days the child might mope around, complain, and not know what to do with himself or herself, but they quickly adapt—often faster than parents expect. Younger children and tweens also tend to *forget* about playing video games or using the computer sooner than older children do. However, even for teens and young adults, unless the individual is severely physically addicted, most will start to show signs of improvement and become more engaged in real life by the second week.

Physiologically, the removal of electronic screen devices immediately sets into motion a healthy chain of events. Removing bright screens helps initiate a resynchronization of circadian rhythms, allowing melatonin to be secreted earlier in the evening and in larger amounts. In addition to being a sleep aid, melatonin is a powerful antioxidant and regulator of the nervous system: It fights inflammation, protects DNA, supports production of serotonin, lowers stress, and regulates other hormones.

Thus, brain chemistry and hormones enjoy an immediate shift toward normalization once melatonin is no longer suppressed. Likewise, the lack of screen stimulation means dopamine is no longer forced into a *surge and deplete* pattern, which serves to improve mood and attention span. Overstimulated networks are quieted, make stress levels lower, and mental reserves are restored. On the removal of unnatural and intense sensory and psychological stimulation, the brain is free to seek more balanced stimulation through physical interaction with the environment. Instead of being in a survival state of reacting and defending, the brain begins to self-organize and self-regulate. These dynamics create a positive synergy, magnified by continued deep sleep and the activities that naturally take place in lieu of screens.

Although the timing and specific nature of results vary from child to child, many parents report strikingly similar changes during the fast in terms of mood, attitude, focus, ability to follow directions, curiosity, motivation, level of engagement, and kindness. This holds true regardless of underlying diagnoses, and indicates that an extended fast fosters right brain, whole-brain, and frontal lobe function, thereby improving emotional regulation, executive functioning, impulse control, creative expression, and capacity for empathy and intimacy.

Within the first week ("Unplug in Order to Reset"), most parents can expect to see the child beginning to return to healthier, more imaginative, and more physical forms of play. They also typically report improved mood, less-extreme or less frequent meltdown, improved compliance with following direction, and reduced oppositional–defiant behavior. For nearly all families, the first week is the hardest. By the second week ("Allow Your Child's Brain Deep Rest"), the child's brain chemistry and biorhythms should be significantly closer to normalizing. Fight-or-flight symptoms or reactions may still be present, but should continue to ebb. On the other hand, underlying factors such as concurrent psychiatric or neurological disorders, or ongoing psychosocial stressors, may continue to play a role, and their severity may affect how long it takes the brain and body to return to calmness. Many parents report at this stage that the child goes to bed earlier and has more energy, that there is less arguing and negotiating about returning devices, and that the child is more organized; for example, when getting ready for school or with keeping track of belongings.

By the end of the third week ("Healing and Reclaiming the Brain"), parents and sometimes teachers may notice the child seems more respectful or kind and displays better manners. With several weeks of deep sleep, hormones previously affected by high cortisol and low melatonin should start to rebalance. If the child is anxious, there may be reduced nail biting, nightmares, headaches, or stomachaches. Meanwhile, as the child moves further and further away from chronic stress, the brain's energy is freed up for learning new concepts and processing emotions. The child is more curious, retains more of what has been learned, and may start reading more. In fact, at this point many parents will see a measurable rise in their child's grades or homework scores. In contrast to the survival state—which is inherently selfish, impulsive, and one-track minded—the child is now on his or her way to becoming healthier in mood, thought, behavior, and relationships.

Toward the end of 3 weeks, parents take some time to assess how things went, analyze their data, and document positive changes. At this point they will need to consider next steps; children who have improved but still demonstrate significant ESS symptoms may need a longer fast. Indeed, extending the fast builds and maintains benefits, so the more vulnerabilities the child has, the more consideration this option should be given.

Studies implementing screen fasts and/or screen-time restriction have shown similar findings in terms of improving cognition, social competency, attachment and emotional regulation (Gentile et al., 2014; Robinson, Wilde, Navracruz, Haydel, & Varady, 2001; Uhls et al., 2014). Longitudinal research on problematic gamers has shown that those who reduce or give up gaming become less depressed and more socially competent (Gentile et al., 2011), and the Learning Habit study determined that children with the least amount of daily screen time tended to have the highest grade point averages (GPAs), better social and emotional health, and healthier family relationships (Pressman et al., 2014).

Elimination Versus Moderation: A Game Plan Going Forward

Immediately following a Reset, there are essentially three choices: extend the fast for a longer period, eliminate interactive screen time indefinitely, or try reintroducing limited amounts. In the short term, parents should be cautious and conservative and proceed gradually. Over the long term, moderation needs may ebb and flow, and parents will need to periodically assess whether to continue the status quo, relax or tighten restrictions, or regroup by embarking on another fast. Parents will need to manage screen time for as long as the child is dependent on them; they will need to be both mindful of risks and flexible as circumstances change. As children grow older, as their brains develop, as life happens, and as technology evolves, the child's needs and vulnerabilities will change, and so will their relationship with screens. Parents may need to repeat the Reset multiple times over the years, and each fast may result in new rules or realizations for how screen time can be best managed going forward.

Generally speaking, following the fast parents tend to allow too much too soon, and symptoms return. As parents feel relief, they may "forget" the severity of screen-related problems and become more lax with rules. They may also start to doubt screen-symptom connections, or indulge in wishful thinking: *Maybe my son can tolerate a little bit of gaming . . . it breaks my heart when I have to tell him "no" all the time.* As parents become complacent and as new devices are introduced in the home, sudden or more gradual return of the problematic behaviors often resume, along with the realization that screen time will need to be restricted a lot more than anticipated. Indeed, most families wind up experiencing a "learning curve" as they figure out how much—if any—screen time their child can tolerate.

The best defense against this is simply to be aware of this tendency, and to document what's happening. For clinical documentation, it is powerful to be able to show families—even years later—a chart note that specifically outlines improvements, such as better grades or less frequent meltdowns, as well as parental descriptions of the child during times of fasting or strict management. It is also effective to document timelines of "before" and "after" periods surrounding acquisition of a new device, even if dysfunction takes months to emerge, and to use parents' and the child's own words when documenting.

The Post–Reset Decision Tree

The course of action to take immediately following the electronic fast is guided by a decision tree (Figure 12.1), with the first question being whether the Reset was effective or helpful. If parents and the clinician feel the fast was not successful and the child is still dysregulated, the next step is to troubleshoot. Common troubleshooting issues include overlooked devices and opportunities, insufficient fast length, relaxation of the rules, lack of support, and school-based screen time. If something is uncovered that may have undermined the fast, parents should attempt to fix the issue and continue fasting or try the fast again.

If the fast has produced obvious benefits, the next decision is whether to keep the restrictions in place, thereby maintaining and even building the benefits, or to allow modest amounts of screen time and see if benefits are

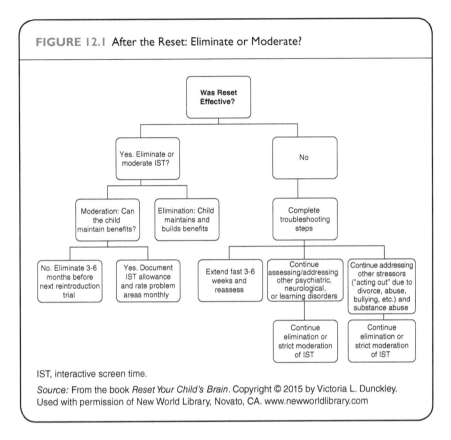

FIGURE 12.1 After the Reset: Eliminate or Moderate?

IST, interactive screen time.

Source: From the book *Reset Your Child's Brain.* Copyright © 2015 by Victoria L. Dunckley. Used with permission of New World Library, Novato, CA. www.newworldlibrary.com

maintained. If parents decide to reintroduce screen time, they proceed very cautiously, using "Start Low and Go Slow" guidelines. These should be considered *trials,* and any allowances also require that the child be physically active, completing homework and chores, respectful, and compliant (without arguing) with allotted amounts. It is recommended that children begin with just 15 minutes (teens can have 30) for *one weekend-day only.* If problems promptly return, the child may need to fast again for a period of several months before attempting another reintroduction trial. Conversely, if screens are reintroduced and problems do not return, then the family maintains the new screen allowances for *3 months* while monitoring problem areas before adjusting screen time any further.

It is important to remind parents that even if the child can tolerate a moderate amount of screen time after the Reset, this may change over time; new devices can upset the balance, and it is always possible for the effects to "build up," hit a tipping point and become intolerable—which means another fast is in order. In addition, it is recommended that violent gaming and online role-playing games not be allowed, period. Also, for many cases, because social media poses special risk, it may need more permanent restrictions too. Particularly for parents of teens, it is helpful to hear from other parents who have navigated these challenges successfully.

Mindful Screen Management

Aside from the post-Reset decision tree, guidelines for screen management following the fast are augmented by consideration of the child's underlying vulnerabilities, following *house rules* on a daily basis, using rules-of-thumb to individualize limits and make adjustments, and implementing protective practices to counteract dysregulation. House rules apply to everyone—including parents, though they may have their own rules—and include banning screens in bedrooms, establishing screen-free zones, times, and activities, and enacting mutual accountability measures (such as paying a "tax" when rules are violated or commitments are broken). Other house rules include creating a family work station and matching screen time with exercise or outdoor time. Rules-of-thumb include edicts such as "the more symptoms or risk factors your child has, the stricter you'll need to be," and "if dysregulation returns, before making other treatment decisions—especially medication-related or expensive ones—try another fast first."

Regarding risk factors, some conditions have more severe and life-altering consequences from ongoing screen-time exposure than others. For example, in the presence of autism, psychosis, reactive attachment disorder, or suicidal depression, it is *strongly recommended that interactive screen time be permanently eliminated altogether.* (Even so, parents will be more open to this idea if they do the fast first.) Clinicians should emphasize that by controlling the child's environment, parents will have considerable influence over the child's prognosis. Other vulnerabilities, such as sensory dysfunction, severe ADHD, or academic failure also warrant consideration for ongoing elimination.

Protective Practices

In contrast to screen limits, protective practices are countermeasures against screen-induced dysregulation. These evidence-based practices foster whole-brain integration, strengthen natural biorhythms, reduce hyperarousal, and promote healthy family dynamics. For example, adjustments that optimize the child's environment include turning down brightness controls on devices, avoiding screen time after sundown, and using warm, incandescent light in the bedrooms (Kozaki et al., 2005). Activities that promote brain integration and self-regulation include exposure to greenery, outdoors, and sunlight (Kaplan & Talbot, 1983; Loge & Charles, 2012; N. M. Wells, 2000), robust exercise, movement, and free play (Ratey & Hagerman, 2013; S. L. Wells, 2012), and mindfulness (Flook et al., 2010; Kang et al., 2013). These activities have been shown not only to improve functioning but actually make the brain bigger and more robust—the polar opposite effect of screen time.

CONCLUSION

In the short term, children with ESS tend to display impairment of functions governed by the frontal lobe, including emotional regulation, executive functioning, impulse control, empathy, and creativity. Over the long term, screen time and ESS effectively create drag on cognitive, social, and psychological development, resulting in an immature, reactive, and unmotivated child.

The overarching theme of ESS and the Reset Program is that screen management should be based on *functional* status—in other words, how an individual child is feeling, behaving, thinking, and functioning at home, school, and with friends. In this way, electronics management becomes both precise and self-adjusting: The child's health and behavior dictate tolerability—and thus screen limits—not how much the child *should* be able to handle based on blanket guidelines, cultural norms, or school requirements. The functional perspective also takes into account not just children who are addicted to technology, but those at risk for addiction—*and* those who are simply not tolerating their current usage. By examining how screen-induced hyperarousal occurs and the variety of ways it can present in youths, we can see how efficient it is to address screen time aggressively and methodically, not just for the child affected but for society as a whole.

We also need to be cognizant of the impact of misdiagnosis, overmedication, and misuse of health and education resources, including secondary impacts such as that the use of antipsychotics contributes to obesity and metabolic syndrome. There are also the costs of young adults with ESS and technology addiction becoming unemployed, disabled, or criminalized. The *true* cost of not recognizing technology-related illness is exorbitant.

Regarding school policy, technology can still be learned, but it needs to be introduced *much* more slowly, paced according to developmental and individual needs, and driven by nonbiased research. Private and public charter schools that wait to introduce technology until age 12 are growing in popularity, tend to produce high-achieving students, and have long waiting lists. Ironically, the best way to optimize screen tolerance and healthy use as the child grows older is to protect the frontal lobe—the part of the brain that not only determines life success but also capacity for self-discipline—by limiting screens as much as possible for as long as possible. Additionally, for children who display signs of ESS or technology addiction or who have other brain-based vulnerabilities, schools need to make technology-related accommodations readily available. To accomplish this, the Department of Education needs to explicitly state its support for implementing such measures so that schools do not feel doing so puts them at risk of losing federal funding. Currently—whether valid or not—the belief that providing screen-free accommodations will violate Common Core or other federal standards has created a major barrier to obtaining technology-based accommodations. This attitude hurts everyone, because accommodations could potentially prevent or mitigate a large number of academic, mental health, and social issues.

In closing, while chronic illness produced by complex interactions between the environment and our brains and bodies continues to grow, the solution remains strikingly simple. Perhaps Dr. Mark Hyman, world-renowned functional medicine expert, puts it best: "All medicine comes down to this: Find out what's bugging you; get rid of it. Find out what you need; get it. The body does the rest."

REFERENCES

American Psychiatric Association. (2013). *Diagnostic and statistical manual of mental disorders* (5th ed.). Arlington, VA: American Psychiatric Publishing.

Arnsten, A. F. T. (2009). Stress signaling pathways that impair prefrontal cortex structure and function. *Nature Reviews. Neuroscience, 10*(6), 410–422. doi:10.1038/nrn2648

Association for Comprehensive Neurotherapy. (2004). ACN survey on tic triggers. From S. Rogers DeMare. *Natural treatments for tics and Tourette's* (p. 62). Berkeley, CA: North Atlantic Books.

Atladóttir, H. O., Parner, E. T., Schendel, D., Dalsgaard, S., Thomsen, P. H., & Thorsen, P. (2007). Time trends in reported diagnoses of childhood neuropsychiatric disorders: A Danish cohort study. *Archives of Pediatrics & Adolescent Medicine, 161*(2), 193–198. doi:10.1001/archpedi.161.2.193

Blank, M., & Goodman, R. (2009). Electromagnetic fields stress living cells. *Pathophysiology: The Official Journal of the International Society for Pathophysiology/ISP, 16*(2–3), 71–78. doi:10.1016/j.pathophys.2009.01.006

Cain, N., & Gradisar, M. (2010). Electronic media use and sleep in school-aged children and adolescents: A review. *Sleep Medicine, 11*(8), 735–742.

Cajochen, C., Frey, S., Anders, D., Späti, J., Bues, M., Pross, A., . . . Stefani, O. (2011). Evening exposure to a light-emitting diodes (LED)-backlit computer screen affects circadian physiology and cognitive performance. *Journal of Applied Physiology (Bethesda, MD: 1985), 110*(5), 1432–1438. doi:10.1152/japplphysiol.00165.2011

Chaput, J.-P., Visby, T., Nyby, S., Klingenberg, L., Gregersen, N. T., Tremblay, A., . . . Sjödin, A. (2011). Video game playing increases food intake in adolescents: A randomized crossover study. *The American Journal of Clinical Nutrition, 93*(6), 1196–1203. doi:10.3945/ajcn.110.008680

DeStefano, D., & LeFevre, J.-A. (2007). Cognitive load in hypertext reading: A review. *Computers in Human Behavior, 23*(3), 1616–1641. doi:10.1016/j.chb.2005.08.012

Dong, G., Devito, E. E., Du, X., & Cui, Z. (2012). Impaired inhibitory control in "Internet addiction disorder": A functional magnetic resonance imaging study. *Psychiatry Research, 203*(2–3), 153–158. doi:10.1016/j.pscychresns.2012.02.001

Dong, G., Hu, Y., & Lin, X. (2013). Reward/punishment sensitivities among Internet addicts: Implications for their addictive behaviors. *Progress in Neuro-Psychopharmacology & Biological Psychiatry, 46*, 139–145. doi:10.1016/j.pnpbp.2013.07.007

Dunckley, V. (2012, June 30). Computer, video games & psychosis: Cause for concern [*Psychology Today*]. Retrieved from http://www.psychologytoday.com/blog/mental -wealth/201206/computer-video-games-psychosis-cause-concern

Dunckley, V. (2015). *Reset your child's brain: A four-week plan to end meltdowns, raise grades, and boost social skills by reversing the effects of electronic screen-time.* Novato, CA: New World Library.

Dworak, M., Schierl, T., Bruns, T., & Strüder, H. K. (2007). Impact of singular excessive computer game and television exposure on sleep patterns and memory performance of school-aged children. *Pediatrics, 120*(5), 978–985. doi:10.1542/peds.2007-0476

Farrell, W. (2001). *Father and child reunion: How to bring the dads we need to the children we love* (pp. 29–31, 55–64). New York, NY: Tarcher.

Figueiro, M. G., & Rea, M. S. (2010). The effects of red and blue lights on circadian variations in cortisol, alpha amylase, and melatonin. *International Journal of Endocrinology, 2010*, 1–9. doi:10.1155/2010/829351

Flook, L., Smalley, S. L., Kitil, M. J., Galla, B. M., Kaiser-Greenland, S., Locke, J., . . . Kasari, C. (2010). Effects of mindful awareness practices on executive functions in elementary school children. *Journal of Applied School Psychology, 26*(1), 70–95. doi:10.1080/15377900903379125

Fortin, D. R., & Dholakia, R. R. (2005). Interactivity and vividness effects on social presence and involvement with a web-based advertisement. *Journal of Business Research, 58*(3), 387–396. doi:10.1016/S0148-2963(03)00106-1

Funatsuka, M., Fujita, M., Shirakawa, S., Oguni, H., & Osawa, M. (2001). Study on photo-pattern sensitivity in patients with electronic screen game-induced seizures (ESGS): Effects of spatial resolution, brightness, and pattern movement. *Epilepsia, 42*(9), 1185–1197.

Gentile, D. A., Choo, H., Liau, A., Sim, T., Li, D., Fung, D., & Khoo, A. (2011). Pathological video game use among youths: A two-year longitudinal study. *Pediatrics, 127*(2), e319–e329. doi:10.1542/peds.2010-1353

Gentile, D. A., Reimer, R. A., Nathanson, A. I., Walsh, D. A., & Eisenmann, J. C. (2014). Protective effects of parental monitoring of children's media use: A prospective study. *JAMA Pediatrics, 168*(5), 479–484. doi:10.1001/jamapediatrics.2014.146

Gopinath, B., Baur, L. A., Wang, J. J., Hardy, L. L., Teber, E., Kifley, A., . . . Mitchell, P. (2011). Influence of physical activity and screen time on the retinal microvasculature in young children. *Arteriosclerosis, Thrombosis, and Vascular Biology, 31*(5), 1233–1239. doi:10.1161/ATVBAHA.110.219451

Gradisar, M., Wolfson, A. R., Harvey, A. G., Hale, L., Rosenberg, R., & Czeisler, C. A. (2013). The sleep and technology use of Americans: Findings from the National Sleep

Foundation's 2011 Sleep in America poll. *Journal of Clinical Sleep Medicine: Official Publication of the American Academy of Sleep Medicine, 9*(12), 1291–1299. doi:10.5664/jcsm.3272

Grohol, J. M. (2012, May 16). What is disruptive mood dysregulation disorder? *World of Psychology* [Psych Central]. Retrieved from http://psychcentral.com/blog/archives/2012/05/16/what-is-disruptive-mood-dysregulation-disorder

Gye, M. C., & Park, C. J. (2012). Effect of electromagnetic field exposure on the reproductive system. *Clinical and Experimental Reproductive Medicine, 39*(1), 1. doi:10.5653/cerm.2012.39.1.1

Ha, J. H., Kim, S. Y., Bae, S. C., Bae, S., Kim, H., Sim, M., . . . Cho, S. C. (2007). Depression and Internet addiction in adolescents. *Psychopathology, 40*(6), 424–430. doi:10.1159/000107426

Herbert, M. R., & Sage, C. (2013). Autism and EMF? Plausibility of a pathophysiological link—Part I. *Pathophysiology: The Official Journal of the International Society for Pathophysiology/ISP, 20*(3), 191–209. doi:10.1016/j.pathophys.2013.08.001

Higuchi, S., Motohashi, Y., Liu, Y., Ahara, M., & Kaneko, Y. (2003). Effects of VDT tasks with a bright display at night on melatonin, core temperature, heart rate, and sleepiness. *Journal of Applied Physiology (Bethesda, MD: 1985), 94*(5), 1773–1776. doi:10.1152/japplphysiol.00616.2002

Hong, S.-B., Kim, J.-W., Choi, E.-J., Kim, H.-H., Suh, J.-E., Kim, C.-D., . . . Yi, S.-H. (2013). Reduced orbitofrontal cortical thickness in male adolescents with internet addiction. *Behavioral and Brain Functions, 9*(1), 11. doi:10.1186/1744-9081-9-11

Hong, S.-B., Zalesky, A., Cocchi, L., Fornito, A., Choi, E.-J., Kim, H.-H., . . . Yi, S.-H. (2013). Decreased functional brain connectivity in adolescents with Internet addiction. *PLOS ONE, 8*(2), e57831. doi:10.1371/journal.pone.0057831

Hou, H., Jia, S., Hu, S., Fan, R., Sun, W., Sun, T., & Zhang, H. (2012). Reduced striatal dopamine transporters in people with Internet addiction disorder. *Journal of Biomedicine & Biotechnology, 2012*, 854524. doi:10.1155/2012/854524

Insel, T. R. (2003). Is social attachment an addictive disorder? *Physiology & Behavior, 79*(3), 351–357. doi:10.1016/S0031-9384(03)00148-3

Ivarsson, M., Anderson, M., Åkerstedt, T., & Lindblad, F. (2009). Playing a violent television game affects heart rate variability. *Acta Paediatrica, 98*(1), 166–172. doi:10.1111/j.1651-2227.2008.01096.x

Ivory, J. D., & Kalyanaraman, S. (2007). The effects of technological advancement and violent content in video games on players' feelings of presence, involvement, physiological arousal, and aggression. *Journal of Communication, 57*(3), 532–555. doi:10.1111/j.1460-2466.2007.00356.x

Jarupat, S., Kawabata, A., Tokura, H., & Borkiewicz, A. (2003). Effects of the 1900MHz electromagnetic field emitted from cellular phone on nocturnal melatonin secretion. *Journal of Physiological Anthropology and Applied Human Science, 22*(1), 61–63.

Kang, D.-H., Jo, H. J., Jung, W. H., Kim, S. H., Jung, Y.-H., Choi, C.-H., . . . Kwon, J. S. (2013). The effect of meditation on brain structure: Cortical thickness mapping and diffusion tensor imaging. *Social Cognitive and Affective Neuroscience, 8*(1), 27–33. doi:10.1093/scan/nss056

Kaplan, S. (1995). The restorative benefits of nature: Toward an integrative framework. *Journal of Environmental Psychology, 15*(3), 169–182.

Kaplan, S., & Talbot, J. (1983). Psychological benefits of a wilderness experience. In I. Altman & J. Wohlwill (Eds.), *Behavior and the natural environment* (Vol. 6, pp. 163–203). New York, NY: Springer. doi:10.1007/978-1-4613-3539-9_6

Kasuya, E., Kushibiki, S., Yayou, K., Hodate, K., & Sutoh, M. (2008). Light exposure during night suppresses nocturnal increase in growth hormone secretion in Holstein steers. *Journal of Animal Science, 86*(8), 1799–1807. doi:10.2527/jas.2008-0877

Kheifets, L., Repacholi, M., Saunders, R., & van Deventer, E. (2005). The sensitivity of children to electromagnetic fields. *Pediatrics, 116*(2), e303–e313. doi:10.1542/peds.2004-2541

Kim, S. H., Baik, S.-H., Park, C. S., Kim, S. J., Choi, S. W., & Kim, S. E. (2011). Reduced striatal dopamine D2 receptors in people with Internet addiction. *Neuroreport, 22*(8), 407–411. doi:10.1097/WNR.0b013e328346e16e

Koepp, M. J., Gunn, R. N., Lawrence, A. D., Cunningham, V. J., Dagher, A., Jones, T., . . . Grasby, P. M. (1998). Evidence for striatal dopamine release during a video game. *Nature, 393*(6682), 266–268.

Kohyama, J. (2011). Neurochemical and neuropharmacological aspects of circadian disruptions: An introduction to asynchronization. *Current Neuropharmacology, 9*(2), 330.

Kondo, Y., Tanabe, T., Kobayashi-Miura, M., Amano, H., Yamaguchi, N., Kamura, M., & Fujita, Y. (2012). Association between feeling upon awakening and use of information technology devices in Japanese children. *Journal of Epidemiology/Japan Epidemiological Association, 22*(1), 12–20.

Koob, G., & Kreek, M. J. (2007). Stress, dysregulation of drug reward pathways, and the transition to drug dependence. *American Journal of Psychiatry, 164*(8), 1149. doi:10.1176/appi.ajp.2007.05030503

Kozaki, T., Kitamura, S., Higashihara, Y., Ishibashi, K., Noguchi, H., & Yasukouchi, A. (2005). Effect of color temperature of light sources on slow-wave sleep. *Journal of Physiological Anthropology and Applied Human Science, 24*(2), 183–186.

Lefever, G., Arcona, A., & Antonuccio, D. (2003). ADHD among American schoolchildren: Evidence of overdiagnosis and overuse of medication. *Scientific Review of Mental Health Practice, 2*, 49–60.

Lillard, A. S., & Peterson, J. (2011). The immediate impact of different types of television on young children's executive function. *Pediatrics.* doi:10.1542/peds.2010-1919

Lin, C.-H., Lin, S.-L., & Wu, C.-P. (2009). The effects of parental monitoring and leisure boredom on adolescents' Internet addiction. *Adolescence, 44*(176), 993–1004.

Lin, F., Zhou, Y., Du, Y., Qin, L., Zhao, Z., Xu, J., & Lei, H. (2012). Abnormal white matter integrity in adolescents with Internet addiction disorder: A tract-based spatial statistics study. *PLOS ONE, 7*(1), e30253. doi:10.1371/journal.pone.0030253

Loge, A. S., & Charles, C. (2012). *Children's contact with the outdoors and nature: A focus on educators and educational settings.* Children and Nature Network. Retrieved from https://www.education.ne.gov/21stcclc/Afterschool/Programming/Children%27sContactOutdoorsNature.pdf

Luboshitzky, R., & Lavie, P. (1999). Melatonin and sex hormone interrelationships—A review. *Journal of Pediatric Endocrinology & Metabolism, 12*(3), 355–362.

Mangen, A., Walgermo, B. R., & Brønnick, K. (2013). Reading linear texts on paper versus computer screen: Effects on reading comprehension. *International Journal of Educational Research, 58,* 61–68. doi:10.1016/j.ijer.2012.12.002

Maras, P. M., Molet, J., Chen, Y., Rice, C., Ji, S. G., Solodkin, A., & Baram, T. Z. (2014). Preferential loss of dorsal-hippocampus synapses underlies memory impairments provoked by short, multimodal stress. *Molecular Psychiatry, 19*(7), 811–822.

Mark, A. E., & Janssen, I. (2008). Relationship between screen time and metabolic syndrome in adolescents. *Journal of Public Health, 30*(2), 153–160. doi:10.1093/pubmed/fdn022

Montagni, I., Guichard, E., Carpenet, C., Tzourio, C., & Kurth, T. (2015). Screen time exposure and reporting of headaches in young adults: A cross-sectional study. *Cephalalgia: An International Journal of Headache.* doi:10.1177/0333102415620286

Moreno, C., Laje, G., Blanco, C., Jiang, H., Schmidt, A. B., & Olfson, M. (2007). National trends in the outpatient diagnosis and treatment of bipolar disorder in youth. *Archives of General Psychiatry, 64*(9), 1032–1039. doi:10.1001/archpsyc.64.9.1032

Naqvi, N. H., & Bechara, A. (2010). The insula and drug addiction: An interoceptive view of pleasure, urges, and decision-making. *Brain Structure & Function, 214*(5–6), 435–450. doi:10.1007/s00429-010-0268-7

Niehaus, J. L., Cruz-Bermúdez, N. D., & Kauer, J. A. (2009). Plasticity of addiction: A mesolimbic dopamine short-circuit? *The American Journal on Addictions/American Academy of Psychiatrists in Alcoholism and Addictions, 18*(4), 259–271. doi:10.1080/10550490902925946

Nitzan, U., Shoshan, E., Lev-Ran, S., & Fennig, S. (2011). Internet-related psychosis—A sign of the times? *The Israel Journal of Psychiatry and Related Sciences, 48*(3), 207–211.

Olfson, M., Marcus, S. C., Weissman, M. M., & Jensen, P. S. (2002). National trends in the use of psychotropic medications by children. *Journal of the American Academy of Child and Adolescent Psychiatry, 41*(5), 514–521. doi:10.1097/00004583-200205000-00008

Ophir, E., Nass, C., & Wagner, A. D. (2009). Cognitive control in media multitaskers. *Proceedings of the National Academy of Sciences, 106*(37), 15583–15587. doi:10.1073/pnas.0903620106

Oshima, N., Nishida, A., Shimodera, S., Tochigi, M., Ando, S., Yamasaki, S., . . . Sasaki, T. (2012). The suicidal feelings, self-injury, and mobile phone use after lights out in adolescents. *Journal of Pediatric Psychology, 37*(9), 1023–1030. doi:10.1093/jpepsy/jss072

Pall, M. L. (2013). Electromagnetic fields act via activation of voltage-gated calcium channels to produce beneficial or adverse effects. *Journal of Cellular and Molecular Medicine, 17*(8), 958–965. doi:10.1111/jcmm.12088

Pervanidou, P., & Chrousos, G. P. (2011). Stress and obesity/metabolic syndrome in childhood and adolescence. *International Journal of Pediatric Obesity: An Official Journal of the International Association for the Study of Obesity, 6*(Suppl. 1), 21–28. doi:10.3109/17477166.2011.615996

Pervanidou, P., & Chrousos, G. P. (2012). Metabolic consequences of stress during childhood and adolescence. *Metabolism: Clinical and Experimental, 61*(5), 611–619. doi:10.1016/j.metabol.2011.10.005

Polos, P. G., Bhat, S., Smith, I., Kabak, B., Neiman, E., Sillari, J., . . . Seyffert, M. (2010). The effect of sleep time related information and communication technology (STRICT) on sleep patterns and daytime functioning in children and young adults: A pilot study. *CHEST Journal, 138*(4_MeetingAbstracts), 911A. doi:10.1378/chest.9771

Pressman, R. M., Owens, J. A., Evans, A. S., & Nemon, M. L. (2014). Examining the interface of family and personal traits, media, and academic imperatives using the learning habit study. *The American Journal of Family Therapy, 42*(5), 347–363. doi:10.1080/01926187.2014.935684

Ratey, J. J., & Hagerman, E. (2013). *Spark: The revolutionary new science of exercise and the brain.* New York, NY: Little, Brown.

Ream, G. L., Elliott, L. C., & Dunlap, E. (2011). Playing video games while using or feeling the effects of substances: Associations with substance use problems. *International Journal of Environmental Research and Public Health, 8*(12), 3979–3998. doi:10.3390/ijerph8103979

Reeves, B., Lang, A., Kim, E. Y., & Tatar, D. (1999). The effects of screen size and message content on attention and arousal. *Media Psychology, 1*(1), 49–67. doi:10.1207/s1532785xmep0101_4

Richards, R., McGee, R., Williams, S. M., Welch, D., & Hancox, R. J. (2010). Adolescent screen time and attachment to parents and peers. *Archives of Pediatrics & Adolescent Medicine, 164*(3), 258–262. doi:10.1001/archpediatrics.2009.280

Robinson, T. N., Wilde, M. L., Navracruz, L. C., Haydel, K. F., & Varady, A. (2001). Effects of reducing children's television and video game use on aggressive behavior: A randomized controlled trial. *Archives of Pediatrics & Adolescent Medicine, 155*(1), 17–23.

Rosen, L. D., Mark Carrier, L., & Cheever, N. A. (2013). Facebook and texting made me do it: Media-induced task-switching while studying. *Computers in Human Behavior, 29*(3), 948–958. doi:10.1016/j.chb.2012.12.001

Rowan, C. (2010). Unplug—Don't drug: A critical look at the influence of technology on child behavior with an alternative way of responding other than evaluation and drugging. *Ethical Human Psychology and Psychiatry, 12*(1), 60–68. doi:10.1891/1559-4343.12.1.60

Siegel, D. J. (2006). An interpersonal neurobiology approach to psychotherapy. *Psychiatric Annals, 36*(4).

Solodar, J. (2014). Commentary: ILAE definition of epilepsy. *Epilepsia, 55*(4), 491. doi:10.1111/epi.12594

Thornton, B., Faires, A., Robbins, M., & Rollins, E. (2014). The mere presence of a cell phone may be distracting. *Social Psychology, 45*(6), 479–488. doi:10.1027/1864-9335/a000216

Uhls, Y. T., Michikyan, M., Morris, J., Garcia, D., Small, G. W., Zgourou, E., & Greenfield, P. M. (2014). Five days at outdoor education camp without screens improves preteen skills with nonverbal emotion cues. *Computers in Human Behavior, 39,* 387–392. doi: 10.1016/j.chb.2014.05.036

Van den Bulck, J. (2004). Television viewing, computer game playing, and Internet use and self-reported time to bed and time out of bed in secondary-school children. *Sleep, 27*(1), 101–104.

Van den Bulck, J. (2007). Adolescent use of mobile phones for calling and for sending text messages after lights out: Results from a prospective cohort study with a one-year follow-up. *Sleep, 30*(9), 1220–1223.

Wallenius, M. (2010). Salivary cortisol in relation to the use of information and communication technology (ICT) in school-aged children. *Psychology, 1*(2), 88–95. doi:10.4236/psych.2010.12012

Wang, X., & Perry, A. C. (2006). Metabolic and physiologic responses to video game play in 7- to 10-year-old boys. *Archives of Pediatrics & Adolescent Medicine, 160*(4), 411–415. doi: 10.1001/archpedi.160.4.411

Wästlund, E., Reinikka, H., Norlander, T., & Archer, T. (2005). Effects of VDT and paper presentation on consumption and production of information: Psychological and physiological factors. *Computers in Human Behavior, 21*(2), 377–394. doi:10.1016/j.chb.2004.02.007

Wells, N. M. (2000). At home with nature: Effects of "greenness" on children's cognitive functioning. *Environment and Behavior, 32*(6), 775–795. doi:10.1177/00139160021972793

Wells, S. L. (2012). Moving through the curriculum: The effect of movement on student learning, behavior, and attitude. *Rising Tide, 5,* 1–17.

Weng, C.-B., Qian, R.-B., Fu, X.-M., Lin, B., Han, X.-P., Niu, C.-S., & Wang, Y.-H. (2013). Gray matter and white matter abnormalities in online game addiction. *European Journal of Radiology, 82*(8), 1308–1312. doi:10.1016/j.ejrad.2013.01.031

Wetterberg, L., Aperia, B., Gorelick, D. A., Gwirtzman, H. E., McGuire, M. T., Serafetinides, E. A., & Yuwiler, A. (1992). Age, alcoholism and depression are associated with low levels of urinary melatonin. *Journal of Psychiatry & Neuroscience, 17*(5), 215–224.

Yamamoto, K. (2007). Banning laptops in the classroom: Is it worth the hassles. *Journal of Legal Education, 57,* 477.

Yuan, K., Cheng, P., Dong, T., Bi, Y., Xing, L., Yu, D., . . . Tian, J. (2013). Cortical thickness abnormalities in late adolescence with online gaming addiction. *PLOS ONE, 8*(1), e53055. doi:10.1371/journal.pone.0053055

Yuan, K., Jin, C., Cheng, P., Yang, X., Dong, T., Bi, Y., . . . Tian, J. (2013). Amplitude of low frequency fluctuation abnormalities in adolescents with online gaming addiction. *PLOS ONE, 8*(11), e78708. doi:10.1371/journal.pone.0078708

Yuan, K., Qin, W., Liu, Y., & Tian, J. (2011). Internet addiction: Neuroimaging findings. *Communicative & Integrative Biology, 4*(6), 637–639.

Zhou, Y., Lin, F.-C., Du, Y.-S., Qin, L., Zhao, Z.-M., Xu, J.-R., & Lei, H. (2011). Gray matter abnormalities in Internet addiction: A voxel-based morphometry study. *European Journal of Radiology, 79*(1), 92–95. doi:10.1016/j.ejrad.2009.10.025

FAMILY THERAPY FOR ADOLESCENT AND CHILDHOOD INTERNET GAMING ADDICTION

Kimberly S. Young

Internet Gaming Disorder is now listed in Section III in the *Diagnostic and Statistical Manual of Mental Disorders*, Fifth Edition (*DSM-5*; American Psychiatric Association [APA], 2013) as a condition for further study. This inclusion was spawned by a growing number of statistics showing children younger than 18 years are addicted to online video games, and studies from China, Taiwan, and Korea that showed Internet gaming addiction is considered an epidemic and serious public health crisis. This chapter reviews the evolution of Internet gaming addiction and how it has impacted adolescents and children. Looking at the research, the chapter outlines how online gaming provides a medium for youth to indulge in gaming as a form of mental escape. This chapter also describes signs of Internet gaming addiction, reasons that gaming is especially addictive, and how to apply brief strategic family therapy (BSFT) to treat adolescents and children addicted to games.

INTERNET GAMING ADDICTION

Although it is not yet officially recognized as a diagnosable disorder by the APA, Internet Gaming Disorder is included in Section III for further study in the *DSM-5* (APA, 2013). This is important as there is increasing evidence that people of all ages, especially teens and preteens, are facing very real, sometimes severe, consequences associated with compulsive use of video games.

Video games are becoming increasingly complex, detailed, and compelling to a growing international audience of players. With better graphics, more realistic characters, and greater strategic challenges, it is not surprising that some teens would rather play the latest video game than hang out with friends, play sports, or even watch television.

Of course, all gamers are not addicts—many teens can play video games a few hours a week, successfully balancing school activities, grades, friends, and family obligations. But for some, gaming has become an uncontrollable compulsion. Studies estimate that 10% to 15% of gamers exhibit signs that meet the World Health Organization's criteria for addiction (Kuss, 2014) and based on a national poll that surveyed a randomly selected sample of 1,178 American youth ages 8 to 18 years, about 8% of video-game players in this sample exhibited pathological patterns of play (Gentile, 2009). The study also found that pathological gamers spent twice as much time playing as nonpathological gamers and received poorer grades in school; pathological gaming also showed comorbidity with attention problems. Pathological status also significantly predicted poorer school performance even after controlling for sex, age, and weekly amount of video-game play.

Many people like to spend at least part of their free time playing video games. However, what starts out as innocent recreation can become an addiction for some. Soon, friends, family, school, and even personal hygiene are neglected as nearly every spare moment is spent playing the game. As this is a relatively new problem, this chapter reviews the diagnostic and treatment considerations associated with Internet gaming addiction among children and adolescents.

DSM-5: A NEW CONDITION

The Internet is now an integral, even inescapable, part of many people's daily lives; they turn to it to send messages, read news, conduct business, and much more. But recent scientific reports have begun to focus on the preoccupation some people develop with certain aspects of the Internet, particularly online games. As part of the diagnosis, gamers play compulsively, to the exclusion of other interests, and their persistent and recurrent online activity results in clinically significant impairment or distress. People with this condition endanger their academic or job functioning because of the amount of time they spend playing. They experience symptoms of withdrawal when pulled away from gaming.

Much of this literature stems from evidence from Asian countries and centers on young males (e.g., Blaszczynski, 2014; Montag et al., 2014). The studies suggest that when these individuals are engrossed in Internet games, certain pathways in their brains are triggered in the same direct and intense way that a drug addict's brain is affected by a particular substance (Brand, Young, & Laier, 2014). The gaming prompts a neurological response predominantly in the prefrontal cortex that influences feelings of pleasure and reward, and the result, in the extreme, is manifested as addictive behavior.

Further research will determine if the same patterns of excessive online gaming are detected using the proposed criteria. At this time, the criteria for this condition are limited to Internet gaming and do not include general use of the Internet, online gambling, or social media (APA, 2013). By listing Internet Gaming Disorder in *DSM-5* Section III, the APA hopes to encourage research to determine whether the condition should be added as a disorder. The criteria include persistent and consistent use of the Internet to engage in games, often with other players, leading to clinically significant impairment or distress. *DSM-5* signs include a preoccupation with Internet games; withdrawal symptoms when Internet gaming is taken away, such as depression, anxiety, or sadness; the need to spend increasing amounts of time engaged in Internet games; unsuccessful attempts to control the participation in Internet games; loss of interest in previous hobbies and entertainment as a result of, and with the exception of, Internet games; continued excessive use of Internet games despite knowledge of psychological problems; lying about use; use of Internet games to escape or relieve a negative mood; and jeopardizing a significant relationship, job, or educational or career opportunity because of participation in Internet games.

WHAT MAKES GAMES ADDICTIVE?

Are there certain characteristics that make some games more addictive than others? As with any addiction, video-game or *gaming* addiction is usually a multifaceted issue. To begin with, video games are designed to be addictive, not in the clinical sense of the word, but game designers are always looking for ways to make their games more interesting and to increase the amount of time people will spend playing them.

Consequently, games are designed to be just difficult enough to be truly challenging allowing players to achieve small accomplishments that compel them to keep playing. In that respect, the design of video games is similar to the design of gambling casinos, which will allow players to have small *wins* that keep them playing. There are several *hooks* that are built into games with the intent of making them addictive such as having a high score, one of the most easily recognizable hooks, as players try to beat the high score, or in online role-playing games, players try to *level up* to achieve higher status, power, and recognition, creating an emotional attachment to their game characters.

As online gaming evolved, so have the forms that characters can take, so that players can select more detailed representations for their characters. For instance, for human characters, players can select skin color, hair color, height, weight, and gender. They also can decide on a character's profession, ranging from a banker, lawyer, dancer, engineer, thief, bounty hunter, elf, or gnome, depending on the game. Each player must choose a name for the character. Some take great care and pride in determining just the right name.

In fact, in some strange way, a character's name seeps into the player over time. They spend hours living as this *other person* and begin to identify with a character that feels more real and less fictional the longer they play.

Many adolescents have trouble with social relationships and feel lonely as if they have never truly belonged. Adolescents can develop a sense of belonging in the game. In some cases, the game provides the only friends they interact with. Gamers can become hooked on the social aspect of the game. Gamers can join guilds that provide a great sense of community and accomplishment when they take out those big monsters or strategize about their next online session. Through these quests or nightly turns playing the game, gamers can form close bonds and friendships with fellow players that replace the social contact missing in their lives.

The problem arises when players rely on these new online personas and the distinction between what is real and what is a fantasy role-play game becomes blurred. In some extreme cases, addicted gamers become violent toward those trying to stop or control how much they play. In one tragic story, a 14-year-old boy stabbed his 77-year-old great-grandmother to death when she had taken away his video game (Turner, 2011).

SIGNS AND RISK FACTORS

The addiction process begins with a preoccupation with online gaming. Gamers think about the game when offline and often fantasize about playing the game when they should be concentrating on other things such as homework for school or visiting friends; instead, they miss deadlines, and neglect work or social activities as playing the game becomes their main priority.

Some gamers do not eat, sleep, or take a shower because of the game. They lie to family and friends about what they are really doing on the computer. As the addiction progresses, gamers become less interested in hobbies or activities that they used to enjoy and become more fascinated with living inside the game. As one mother explained,

> My son loved baseball and played varsity team in high school until he discovered [live gaming]. His grades plummeted after he discovered the game, but it wasn't until he quit the baseball team that I knew that something [was] seriously wrong. He loved baseball too much. He won a baseball scholarship for college and dreamed about playing professionally. Now, nothing else matters to him except the game.

Some gamers experience personality changes the more addicted they become. A normally happy son or daughter becomes withdrawn only to prefer making friends in the game as the people who were once important in real lives become less important. Especially at young ages, their minds become so fixated on the game that they can experience a psychological withdrawal and may act out toward parents who make them stop playing. All that they can think about is getting back to the game and they become angry and even violent at anyone who threatens taking it away.

Pathological or *hard-core* players often suffer from other emotional problems or low self-worth and esteem (Gentile, 2009). This research suggests that adolescents who suffer emotional problems gravitate toward interactive role-playing games as way to experiment with parts of their personality, where they can be more vocal, try out leadership roles, and establish new identities that are soothing.

Adolescents also use games as a psychological escape and as a means to cope with life's problems. "For me, gaming was a way of coping with my parent's divorce," said Matt, 16 years old and a regular player of online games. "I met lots of gamers who had family problems too and I didn't have to think about going to live with my father and his new girlfriend."

Like other addicted players, Matt had struggled with finding time to study while spending nearly 11 hours a day on the game. As children and teens go through various situational stresses or family problems, gaming becomes a convenient way to escape negative or harmful feelings. Young children especially are focused on their home environment. They need that stability in their family life and, without it, gaming and the ability to create an online persona allow them to escape parental arguments or stress at home, so that the child becomes dependent on the need to escape to deal with his or her feelings of abandonment by a parent.

Gaming also appeals to highly intelligent and imaginative adolescents, especially among adolescents who are academically bright and who feel understimulated in school. They turn to games for adventure and intellectual stimulation. Such games also lure players with complex systems of goals and achievements. Drawn to goal-oriented games, some children and teen players engage in activities to develop their characters from one level to the next and compete to find valuable in-game elements such as armor and weapons. Players can find themselves wrapped up in the game for hours as they struggle to gain one more skill or weapon.

FAMILY-BASED MENTAL HEALTH

In individual treatment, cognitive behavioral approaches have been found to be effective in treating Internet addiction (e.g., Young, 2011, 2013). In cases of working with adolescents and children, family therapy and involving the parents have been shown to be more effective to deal with the developmental issues associated with this population (e.g., Blumer, Hertlein, Smith, &

Allen, 2014). With this in mind, family-based therapy is often used for childhood and adolescent Internet gaming addiction. Internet gaming addiction continues to be a major issue in our society as teen abuse is growing at an alarmingly high rate. Adolescence alone, regardless of the involvement in the Internet, is an extremely challenging and complex transition. Exploring and attempting to discover one's identity as an adolescent can be an overwhelming stage in life. In the event that an adolescent is using online games, it may be that family dynamics play an important role in how children use these games to cope with life's problems.

Peer pressure and environmental distresses are chief influences for an adolescent becoming involved with gaming. Friends are often gamers, and, as discussed, family dynamics can play a role in the development of online gaming addiction. Furthermore, children of substance abusing parents are shown to have an increased risk of using gaming as a means to cope with problems such as developmental issues, school problems, health problems, delinquency, sexual problems, mental health issues, and family problems.

It is much harder for a teen to recover from gaming addiction, especially when computers and technology are a necessary component of their home and school environments. Effective treatment requires that the dynamics of the family should be assessed and that family members must also be helped to achieve health or a relapse is much more likely.

Using family-based approaches helps an adolescent navigate the normal developmental tasks of identity formation that are often neglected while using gaming as a means of coping with life's problems. Many gamers lack a strong sense of self, using gaming as means to form their identities, as already explained. However, self-esteem in real life is fragile or nonexistent. Family-based approaches focus on ways to build or rebuild gamers' identities within a nongaming environment.

Gamers often minimize the extent they game and avoid dealing with family issues that may be driving their desire to game. It is important to consider an adolescent's individual family situation when treating his or her addiction. Family-based approaches help comprehend the teen's or the child's immediate environment, in most cases enhancing the understanding of why the addiction is taking place. It is necessary to look at family dynamics such as family history of addiction, background, communication dynamics, or conflict to understand how these factors may be impacting the child's developmental stages, emotional well-being, and self-esteem.

Family-based approaches are also used to educate the family on ways in which they can help the child to manage his or her online behavior. This may include counseling for family members, education on problem/compulsive gaming for the family, strategies on how to cope with anger and loss of trust from the addicted loved one, and education on the emotional costs of Internet gaming addiction.

BRIEF STRATEGIC FAMILY THERAPY

Family-based approaches to treating adolescent and childhood gaming addiction highlight the need to engage the family in therapy, including parents and siblings, and sometimes peers, in the adolescent's treatment. Involving the family can be particularly important, as the adolescent often lives with at least one parent and is subject to the parent's controls, rules, and/or supports. Using family-based approaches generally addresses a wide array of problems in addition to the young person's online problems, including family communication and conflict; other co-occurring behavioral, mental health, and learning disorders; problems with school or work attendance; and peer networks. New studies show that family-based approaches are highly efficacious, especially when working with younger children with drug abuse problems (Lindstrøm, Filges, & Jørgensen, 2015; Murray, Labuschagne, & Le Grange, 2014). In particular, BSFT has been frequently found effective when treating adolescents with interpersonal problems (e.g., Park, Kim, & Lee, 2014), substance abuse (e.g., Hernandez, Rodriguez, & Spirito, 2015), and gaming addiction (Young, 2015).

BSFT is a short-term, problem-focused therapeutic intervention, targeting children and adolescents 6 to 17 years old, which improves youth behavior by eliminating or reducing maladaptive Internet use and its associated behavior problems and changes the family members' behaviors that are linked to both risk and protective factors related to online use. This model can also be applied to Internet gaming addiction among adolescents and children. Minuchin (1974) describes three therapeutic techniques:

- Joining—forming a therapeutic alliance with all family members

- Diagnosis—identifying interactional patterns that allow or encourage the youth's problematic behavior

- Restructuring—the process of changing the family interactions that are directly related to the problem

Joining

BSFT assumes that each family has its own unique characteristics and properties that emerge and are apparent only when family members interact. This family *system* influences all members of the family. Thus, the family must be viewed as a whole organism rather than merely as the composite sum of the individuals or groups that compose it (Minuchin, 1974). In BSFT, this view of the family system assumes that the family is a system with interdependent/interrelated parts. The behavior of one family member can only be understood by examining the context (i.e., family) in which it occurs. Interventions must be implemented at the family level and must take into account the complex relationships within the family system.

Individuals from families that include youth with behavior problems are very difficult to engage in treatment, which may lead to family resistance and a lack of participation in treatment. Engagement or joining begins from the very first contact with the family. Resistance can be understood in the same way as any other pattern of family interaction (Minuchin, 1974). In BSFT, joining occurs at two levels. First, at the individual level, joining involves establishing a relationship with each participating family member. Second, at the level of the family, the therapist joins with the family system to create a new therapeutic system. Joining thus requires both sensitivity and an ability to respond to the unique characteristics of individuals and quickly discern the family's governing process. A number of specific techniques can be used to join the family, including maintenance (e.g., supporting the family's structure and entering the system by accepting their rules that regulate behavior), tracking (e.g., using what the family talks about [content] and how their interactions unfold [process] to enter the family system), and mimesis (e.g., matching the tempo, mood, and style of family member interactions).

Diagnosis

In BSFT, diagnosis refers to identifying interactional patterns (structure) that allow or encourage problematic youth behavior. In other words, diagnosis determines how the nature and characteristics of family interactions (how family members behave with one another) contribute to the family's failure to meet its objective of eliminating youth problems. Addictive gaming behavior, especially among youth, may be a symptom of a dysfunction within a family. In this model, problematic behaviors serve a purpose for the family. Poor communication, aggressive parenting styles, a family's inability to operate productively, or symptomatic patterns handed down across generations may serve as a root cause of addictive gaming among adolescents.

Gamers immerse themselves into captivating virtual worlds that seem more exciting and interesting than their real lives. This often serves to reinforce the addictive behavior and can be used as a coping mechanism to deal with missing or unfulfilled needs. In this way, gaming can allow the gamer to forget his or her problems. In the short term, gaming may be a useful way to cope with the stress of a hard situation; however, addictive behaviors used to escape or run away from unpleasant situations in the long run only end up making the problem worse. For the gaming addict, situations such as a death of a loved one, a divorce, or problems at school may trigger using the game as a mental distraction that temporarily makes such problems fade into the background. Because the escape is only temporary, players return to gaming as a means of making themselves feel better without dealing with and resolving the underlying problems in their lives.

In this way, the game produces a type of drug *high* that provides an emotional escape or an altered state of reality or mental rush. That is, online gaming, the excitement of becoming someone new in a role-playing game, the challenge of winning a new weapon or potion, or the ability to make new friends through the game, provides an immediate mental escape from their problems and serves to reward future behavior.

Diagnosis not only investigates gaming behavior and its abstinence but it must assess the way the family functions and engages in treatment activities. Therapists should evaluate how the family externalizes problem behaviors, the level of pro-social activities the family engages in, family communication styles, and the overall level of family functioning. Patterns to look for are watching for signs that family members are critical about and negative toward the adolescent gaming addict. The addicted gamer may be using the virtual world to escape the pressure and stress from being seen as a failure to feel good about themselves in the game. Another family system pattern to examine is the level of denial or avoidance of family conflict. Does the family jump from conflict to conflict without achieving any real depth of one particular issue? This may be a symptom of poor conflict resolution among the family or diffusion of problems that are sustaining the addictive behavior. An adolescent may be compensating for family problems that are not being discussed openly at home. Fearing rejection, an adolescent may use the game as a safe place to share feelings and confront conflicts with other players. Other patterns in family therapy to observe are enmeshment, triangulation, or disengagement (Minuchin, 1974), which may be creating pressure on the adolescent to turn to the game as a means of escape.

Restructuring

As therapists identify what a family's patterns of interaction are and how these fit with the adolescent's addictive behavior, therapists develop specific plans for changing the family interactions and individual and social factors that are directly related to the child's behavior. The ultimate goal of treatment in BSFT is to change those family interactions that maintain the problems to more effective and adaptive interactions that eliminate the problems. Adolescence is known to be a period of exploratory self-analysis and self-evaluation culminating in the establishment of a cohesive and integrative sense of self or identity. Adolescent gaming addicts can use the game to explore and test alternative ideas, beliefs, and behaviors, marking this period as one of both dramatic change and uncertainty. Restructuring means understanding how the child may use the game to form identity (through personas and virtual worlds) and encourage healthy family interactions by working in the present, reframing, and working with boundaries and alliances.

Working in the present not only involves creating positive lifestyle changes that take clients away from the computer but that improve their emotional and family well-being (Young, 2011). This varies depending on the client's family situation. Within BSFT, family enactments are a critical feature of working in the present. Enactments encourage, help, and/or allow family members to behave or interact as they would if the therapist were not present. Very frequently, family members will spontaneously behave in their typical way when they fight, interrupt, or criticize one another. Therefore, when families become rigidly focused on speaking to the therapist, the therapist should systematically redirect communication to encourage interactions between session participants. Encouraging enactments help the therapist observe problematic interactions directly rather than relying on stories about what happens when the therapist is not present. The family may blame the gamer for the problem, deny the problem, or triangulate the gamer into a marital problem—this root cause will vary among families. Enactment will enable the therapist to see clearly how these relationships have been maintained and give them the tools necessary to restructure the family system in a healthy manner.

Perhaps one of the most interesting, useful, subtle, and powerful techniques in BSFT is reframing (Minuchin & Fishman, 1981). Reframing creates a different sense of reality; it gives family members the opportunity to perceive their interactions or situation from a different perspective. Reframing is a restructuring technique that typically does not cause the therapist to lose his or her rapport with the family. For this reason, reframing should be used liberally in the treatment process, especially at the beginning of treatment when the therapist needs to bring about changes but is still in the process of building a working relationship with the family.

Adolescent gamers may be using the Internet and the game as a form of mental escape from stress and tension in the family. Poor family alliances or parent–child relationships may cause the adolescent to turn to the game as a safe place to vent about problems going on at home. The child may be the family scapegoat and suffer from poor relationships with others only to use the game as a safe place to make friends and socialize. Instead of turning to the game, therapists must reframe an adolescent's negative distortions, enabling the family to develop new ways of communicating and relating without hostility, anger, or blame. The therapist must reframe situations of family tension so that the gamer does not see the game as the only safe place to express feelings. The family will learn new ways of communicating, allowing the adolescent gaming addict to share more openly and honestly with family members instead of online friends.

One major goal of therapy is to create the opportunity for the family to behave in constructive new ways (Minuchin, Lee, & Simon, 2006). Working with alliances and boundaries, the therapist is able to examine the social *walls* that exist around family members who are allied with one another and who stand between individuals and others who are not allied with one another. A common situation of a youth addicted to online games is a strong alliance with only one parent. This alliance may cross generational lines. For example, there may be a strong bond between a youth and his or her mother (or mother figure). Whenever the youth is punished by the father (or father figure) for inappropriate behavior, the youth may solicit sympathy and support from the *mother* to undermine the *father's* authority and remove the sanction. In a single-parent family, it may be the grandmother who overprotects the youth and undermines the parent's attempts at discipline.

Shifting boundaries to create equality in parenting involves creating a more solid bond between the parents so that they make executive decisions together. Removing the inappropriate parent–child alliance and replacing it with an appropriate alliance between either parents or parent figures will meet the youth's need for support and nurturance (decreasing the need to find it through the game). Understanding the alliances the youth has formed inside the game will also help the youth rely less on the game for desired attention not being met in real life. Questions to ask the gamer may be: How much time do you spend customizing your character during character creation? How important is it to you that your character is unique or looks different from other characters? Does your character have many friends? Do you try out new roles and personalities with your characters? Do you enjoy making up stories and histories for your characters? Do you role-play with your character? What do you like about your character? The answers will reveal the virtual world the gamer has created including alliances, friendships, and quality of those relationships. Therapists can begin to merge the outside family system with the inside game support system, once understanding the kind of alliances the gamer seeks.

Therapy involves a parallel form of intervention among adolescents. First, family dynamics, interactions, and communications impact addictive gaming behavior. Second, the virtual world inside the game impacts addictive gaming behavior. If the game provides a more appealing, exciting, and supportive environment than does the family, the adolescent will continue to gravitate to the game to meet unmet needs. Once the family system can be realigned to provide these needs, the game becomes less important and less irresistible, allowing the gamer to form his or her identity within the context of a normal childhood development scheme.

CONCLUSION

Family therapy is based on the idea that a family is a system of different parts. A change in any part of the system will trigger changes in all the other parts. This means that when one member of a family is affected by a behavioral health disorder such as mental illness or addiction, everyone is affected. As a result, family dynamics can change in unhealthy ways. Lies and secrets can build up in the family. Some family members may take on too much responsibility, other family members may act out, and some may just shut down. Sometimes conditions at home are already unhappy before a family member's mental illness or addiction emerges. That person's changing behaviors can throw the family into even greater turmoil. Often a family remains stuck in unhealthy patterns even after the family member with the behavioral health disorder moves into recovery. Even in the best circumstances, families can find it hard to adjust to the person in their midst who is recovering, who is behaving differently than before, and who needs support. Family therapy can help the family as a whole recover and heal. It can help all members of the family make specific, positive changes as the person in recovery changes. These changes can help all family members heal from the trauma of mental illness or addiction.

Gaming addicts have such problems as:

- Significant interference with school, work, or relationships
- Often avoiding other commitments in order to keep playing
- Frequently turning down social invitations in favor of gaming
- Using most or all free time for gaming
- Regularly playing late into the night, which results in poor sleep habits
- Loss of interest in previously enjoyed activities

Family therapy can help the identified patient—the gaming addict—and his or her family to understand the process of technology addiction and specifically help the gaming addict reduce these symptoms. Involving parents and family can help gamers set a regular schedule for gaming that is reasonable, perhaps making gaming only a weekend activity, or limiting *screen time* to an hour a night. Involving parents and family can also help gamers stay active in hobbies they always enjoyed, or try a new sport, volunteer activity, or extracurricular pursuit. This type of involvement can also help gamers make real-life relationships a priority. Even though the virtual fantasy world can be enticing, parents can encourage children to schedule time with friends, family, and loved ones regularly. Family therapy can also help with overall dynamics of the family. It can help a family learn new problem-solving skills, improve the coping skills of all family members, and teach parenting skills and new ways of managing child behavior.

REFERENCES

American Psychiatric Association. (2013). *Diagnostic and statistical manual of mental disorders* (5th ed.). Arlington, VA: American Psychiatric Publishing.

Blaszczynski, A. (2014). Youth and internet addiction in China. *International Gambling Studies*, 14(1), 181–182.

Blumer, M. L., Hertlein, K. M., Smith, J. M., & Allen, H. (2014). How many bytes does it take? A content analysis of cyber issues in couple and family therapy journals. *Journal of Marital and Family Therapy, 40*(1), 34–48.

Brand, M., Young, K. S., & Laier, C. (2014). Prefrontal control and Internet addiction: A theoretical model and review of neuropsychological and neuroimaging findings. *Frontiers in Human Neuroscience, 8*, 375–398. doi:10.3389/fnhum.2014.00375

Gentile, D. (2009). Pathological video-game use among youth ages 8 to 18: A national study. *Psychological Science, 20*(5), 594–602.

Hernandez, L., Rodriguez, A. M., & Spirito, A. (2015). Brief family-based intervention for substance abusing adolescents. *Child and Adolescent Psychiatric Clinics of North America, 24*(3), 585–599.

Kuss, D. J. (2014). Internet gaming addiction: Current perspectives. *Psychological Research Behavioral Management, 6*, 125–137.

Lindstrøm, M., Filges, T., & Jørgensen, A. M. K. (2015). Brief strategic family therapy for young people in treatment for drug use. *Research on Social Work Practice, 25*(1), 61–80.

Minuchin, S. (1974). *Families and family therapy*. Cambridge, MA: Harvard University Press.

Minuchin, S., & Fishman, H. C. (1981). *Techniques of family therapy*. Cambridge, MA: Harvard University Press.

Minuchin, S., Lee, W. Y., & Simon, G. M. (2006). *Mastering family therapy: Journeys of growth and transformation*. New York, NY: Wiley.

Montag, C., Bey, K., Sha, P., Li, M., Chen, Y. F., Liu, W. Y., & Reuter, M. (2014). Is it meaningful to distinguish between generalized and specific Internet addiction? Evidence from a cross-cultural study from Germany, Sweden, Taiwan and China. *Asia-Pacific Psychiatry, 7*(1), 20–26. doi:10.1111/appy.12122

Murray, S. B., Labuschagne, Z., & Le Grange, D. (2014). Family and couples therapy for eating disorders, substance use disorders, and addictions. In T. D. Brewerton & A. Baker Dennis (Eds.), *Eating disorders, addictions and substance use disorders: Research, clinical and treatment perspectives* (pp. 563–586). New York, NY: Springer.

Park, T. Y., Kim, S., & Lee, J. (2014). Family therapy for an Internet-addicted young adult with interpersonal problems. *Journal of Family Therapy, 36*(4), 394–419.

Turner, E. (2011). Teen stabs grandmother, goes to school covered in blood. *NBC News.* Retrieved from http://www.nbc33tv.com/news/teen-stabs-grandmother-go

Young, K. S. (2011). CBT-IA: The first treatment model to address Internet addiction. *Journal of Cognitive Therapy, 25*(4), 304–312.

Young, K. S. (2013). Treatment outcomes using CBT-IA with Internet-addicted patients. *Journal of Behavioral Addictions, 2*(4), 209–215.

Young, K. S. (2015). Video games: Recreation or addiction? *Psychiatric Times, 32*(4), 27–31.

14 | THE FITSC-IA MODEL: A COMMUNITY-BASED APPROACH

Tracy Markle

The opposite of addiction is not sobriety. The opposite of addiction is connection.

—Johann Hari (2015)

Family, social, and community environments influence the dynamics of adolescents' thoughts, behaviors, and beliefs about themselves and the situations in which they are involved. The Family, Integrated Treatment, Social Connection–Internet Addiction (FITSC-IA™) approach is an intensive, community-based, integrated approach to the treatment of adolescent Internet addiction. Adolescents with Internet addiction and their families benefit from this approach because it emphasizes treating the whole person by addressing physical, mental, emotional, relationship, and social elements. FITSC-IA assesses and treats adolescents in the context of their functioning within their families and social systems in order to implement real-time intervention and treatment approaches to stabilize the addictive behaviors and common co-occurring diagnoses, such as social anxiety and depression. Using the FITSC-IA, a collaborative team of professionals works together to develop and provide treatment to the adolescent and the family based on the development of one integrated treatment plan. This approach supports effective continuity of care and communication among team members and between the adolescent and the family. The expected outcomes of implementing FITSC-IA while treating the adolescent in the community are improved family functioning, social functioning, and academic performance.

It is commonplace today for young and old people alike to refer to their own and others' use of digital media as an "addiction" due to the level of distress and conflict they experience. In some respects, they may

be correct; in most cases, however, it is not an addiction by clinical definition. Researchers estimate that 4% of adolescents in the United States meet
the criteria for Internet addiction (Liu, Desai, Krishnan-Sarin, Cavallo, &
Potenza, 2011). The number is much higher in Hong Kong, where 17% to
26.8% of adolescents meet the criteria for addiction (Shek & Yu, 2016); only
up to 1.5% meet the criteria in Greece (Kormas, Critselis, Janikian, Kafetzis,
& Tsitsika, 2011).

The proposed criteria for Internet addiction includes: (a) functional
impairments (reduced social, academic, working ability) that result in loss
of a significant relationship, a job, an education or a career opportunity;
(b) preoccupation with the Internet; (c) experiences of withdrawal and tolerance; (d) inability to control use; (e) loss of interest in hobbies; and (f) use
of the Internet to escape or relieve dysphoric mood (Tao et al., 2010). The
term Internet addiction generally encompasses five types of problematic
Internet applications, which include video games, social networks, information overload (e.g., compulsive surfing, TV/Netflix "binges"), cybersex and cyber-relationships, and Internet compulsions (e.g., shopping,
gambling).

Despite adolescents having a lower Internet addiction rate than most
other age groups, adolescents are one of the most vulnerable groups for
developing an addiction to the Internet due to their lower cognitive control and tendency to engage in impulsive and high-risk behaviors. Excessive
Internet use over time is found to interfere in healthy development during
adolescence in the areas of cognitive, physical, psychological, and behavioral
development. The specific areas that may be impacted are: (a) development
of healthy, executive function cognitions, including emotional and self-regulation; (b) development of physical health problems, such as becoming overweight, experiencing vision loss, or developing back problems; (c) identity
formation and individuation; (d) independence and responsibility; (e) prior-
itization of social and peer interactions; and (f) engagement in exploratory
behavior (Dong, Shen, Huang, & Du, 2013).

A Kaiser Family Foundation Study (Rideout, Foehr, & Roberts, 2010)
found that children ages 8 to 18 years spend an average of 7 hours and 38
minutes a day using media; children who send texts, send an average of 118
text messages each day; and the "typical 8- to 18-year olds' home contains an
average of 3.8 televisions, 2.8 DVD or VCR players, 1 digital video recorder,
2.2 CD players, 2.5 radios, 2 computers, and 2.3 console video game players" (p. 9). The study also found that 21% of all 8- to 18-year olds are heavy
media users who consume more than 16 hours of media in a typical day;
47% of these heavy users had fair or poor grades (Cs or lower). This study
highlights the importance of parents developing limits for media use in and
out of the home. In turn, teenagers will be more likely to regulate their media
use once limits are set.

CLINICAL ASSESSMENT

A qualified clinician who is familiar with the symptoms and treatment of Internet addiction and its common co-occurring disorders is necessary in order to provide a thorough clinical assessment. In most cases, it is necessary to use a collaborative team of clinicians who can provide effective intervention and treatment to enable the family system to make necessary changes. The assessment stage of treatment is critical in identifying the presence of Internet addiction, co-occurring disorders, and determining the course of treatment and recommendations.

According to an editorial in the *American Journal of Psychiatry* (Block, 2008), an estimated 86% of Internet addiction cases have some other diagnosis present. In the United States, clients generally present only for the co-occurring condition(s). If a clinician is not assessing for digital media overuse issues, Internet addiction is often not detected. It is important to note that with increasing awareness, parents are more apt to identify their child's use of the Internet as a presenting problem when seeking professional help.

Several researchers have suggested a co-occurring relationship between Internet addiction and several psychiatric issues, which include depression (Yen et al., 2008), aggressive behavior (Ko, Yen, Liu, Huang, & Yen, 2009), impulsivity (De Berardis et al., 2009), substance abuse disorders (Bai, Lin, & Chen, 2001), anxiety disorders (Bernardi & Pallanti, 2009), and attention deficit hyperactivity disorders (Bernardi & Pallanti, 2009).

In order to assess for probable co-occurring disorders, it is important that the clinician interviews the parents, reviews available educational and psychological testing, and speaks with current or former treatment providers to determine a history of diagnosis, treatment approaches, and areas of success. If the clinician determines there is not a previous history of treatment or if information is limited, the clinician must complete a thorough biopsychosocial interview, which may include recommendations for psychological and educational testing in order to differentiate diagnoses.

In cases of Internet addiction where the teen is experiencing unstable mental health issues, the teen may need to be referred to a residential treatment program. Reasons for this may include being a danger to oneself or to others. A thorough safety and threat assessment is essential as one of the initial steps in the assessment process.

Adolescents with Internet addiction have higher risks of suicidal ideation and attempts than those without, and online gaming is associated with an increased risk of suicidal ideation and attempt (Lin et al., 2014). Over time, the virtual world, a novel way to escape real-life stressors for many teens, may lead teens to disconnect from others and the activities they once enjoyed. As a result, their susceptibility to depression increases due to a lack of face-to-face communication, social supports, and loneliness (Shaw & Gant, 2002). During the assessment phase of treatment it is common to hear from teens and their parents that bullying occurred at some point in their lives. Teens are often not accepted by peers due to factors that include physical and developmental disabilities, presenting as awkward to others, and racial or cultural differences. When teens are not accepted in their peer group, they often experience loneliness and low self-esteem, which, along with being bullied, increase their level of depression. Frequent exposure to bullying is significantly correlated to higher risks of depression, suicidal ideation, and suicide attempts in teenagers (Klomek, Marrocco, Kleinman, Schonfeld, & Gould, 2007). Teens who experience bullying may have personality traits and exhibit behaviors that increase the likelihood of being targeted by their peers.

Specific personality and temperament styles have been linked as causal factors of Internet addiction. The personality traits most commonly associated with Internet addiction include anxiety, aggression, hostility, and sensation seeking. Behavioral inhibition is a temperament that has been connected to the development of social anxiety disorder (SAD), a co-occurring diagnosis often found alongside Internet addiction. Affected young people experience distress and tend to withdraw from unfamiliar situations, people, or environments. It is a personality style that has been studied and linked to the development of anxiety disorders in adulthood, particularly social anxiety (Muris, van Brakel, Arntz, & Schouten, 2010). Adolescents who continue to be inhibited as they move into middle school are at risk of Internet overuse due to being socially withdrawn, uncomfortable or distressed in new situations, and anxious about making friends. The virtual world offers them a reprieve from face-to-face contact with others, in particular those who victimize them. They report feeling a sense of confidence, achievement, social connection while in the game, and connection with others through social media or chat rooms.

A study by Watson, Fischer, Andreas, and Smith (2004) found that children who experienced more peer victimization also reported engaging in aggressive fantasies more frequently, which was then associated with greater aggression levels. Adolescent boys in particular may express depression differently than their female counterparts. Although it is typical for boys with depression to recede into isolation, it is also typical for them to show persistent signs of anger expressed through violent acts, such as being aggressive toward peers at school and toward family members, engaging in verbal warfare, and threatening others online. It is a commonplace for depressed, lonely adolescent males in particular to exert their need for power and control while online or playing a video game. Pew Research Center (Lenhart et al., 2008) found that "nearly two-thirds (63%) of teens who play games report seeing or hearing 'people being mean and overly aggressive while playing,' and 49% report seeing or hearing 'people being hateful, racist, or sexist' while playing" (p. 5).

Teens can aggressively act out when parents intervene and attempt to limit or eliminate their online and/or video-game use without ample notice. This quick reaction from the parents is often due to concern about how the child's online behavior is impacting academic success and mental health. As a result of parents intervening in the teen's screen use, aggressive behaviors have been reported, such as breaking closet doors off their hinges, physically assaulting the parents, and breaking into locked rooms, cars, or safes where electronics are being hidden.

In situations where there is an extensive history of ongoing threats, acts of aggression toward others, or self-harming behavior, seeking consultation and a recommendation for out-of-home placement may be a necessary intervention to ensure the safety of the teen and others around him or her.

PARENTING STYLE

Once the clinician establishes that the teen's mental health is stable, and the teen, as well as the family, demonstrate a willingness to engage in outpatient treatment, family therapy is a necessary approach in order to support recovery with the teen and family system.

It is important to evaluate parenting style before starting family therapy, because parenting style is considered to be a significant contributor to the development of a teen's ongoing emotion regulation and ability to modulate emotions (Thompson, 1994). Adolescents who struggle with emotional regulation are at higher risk of engaging in addictive behaviors in an attempt to escape and find relief from distressing feelings and thoughts. As studies have identified that adolescent substance abuse problems are linked with poor emotional regulation (Wills, Pokhrel, Morehouse, & Fenster, 2011), several studies have found the same to be true for Internet addiction. Adolescents seek to escape a conflictual relationship with parents and the resulting emotional distress; therefore, if a teen cannot establish a healthy intimate relationship with his or her parents, there is a strong developmental need to find such a relationship elsewhere.

Teens who experience strict parenting seek out the Internet as a way to escape and relieve pressure (China Internet Network Information Center [CNNIC], 2010). Social networking sites, chat rooms, and video games are common Internet applications to escape into in an attempt to develop supportive connections. Teens who experience stricter discipline are at higher risk to be addicted to the Internet.

Families with higher conflict have been found to have lower levels of parent–child involvement, which may result in inadequate parental monitoring and may be a causal factor for the development of adolescent Internet addiction. In addition, adolescents with higher conflict with parents are more likely to refuse to conform to their parent's supervision, including rules set for digital media and Internet use. Unfortunately, heavy Internet use by adolescents usually results in further conflict with their parents, which may make the problem of adolescent Internet addiction more difficult to resolve (Ary et al., 1999).

INTEGRATED TREATMENT APPROACH

As noted earlier, adolescents with Internet addiction are commonly found to have one or more co-occurring disorders. The type of treatment approach will have long-lasting implications for the adolescent's recovery. There are generally three types of treatment for people with co-occurring disorders: (a) sequential treatment: services are delivered one at a time; (b) parallel treatment: services are provided in the same time period, but by different agencies or systems who have different assessments and treatment plans; and (c) integrated treatment: both mental health and Internet addiction services are provided by one team in the same program, using one individualized, integrated treatment plan. The integrated treatment approach provides treatment to the client that is seamless with a cohesive philosophy, set of goals, and recommendations. It may offer different therapy models, medications if necessary, and the appropriate tools to best treat co-occurring disorders without compromising one or the other.

Key elements of evidence-based integrated treatment for addiction and co-occurring mental health diagnoses include:

- Staged interventions: Forming a therapeutic alliance and helping motivated clients acquire skills and attain goals, and promoting remission and relapse prevention
- Assertive outreach: Effective programs engage clients and their families through intensive case management, at times in the clients' homes, to receive support and maintain a consistent treatment program
- Motivational interventions: Using motivational interviewing approach and stages of change
- Active treatment: Effective programs use cognitive behavioral or evidence-based treatments
- Social support interventions: Programs provide support to help improve the client's social environment; therefore, recovery is promoted
- Long-term perspective: Effective programs have a long-term, community-based focus

- Comprehensiveness: Programs integrate the treatment addiction and co-occurring disorders into all levels of the program
- Cultural sensitivity and competence: Effective programs provide services to meet their specific client population

Better outcomes in treatment are usually associated with these strategies, while absence of these strategies is associated with poorer outcomes (Drake et al., 2001).

FAMILY SYSTEMS TREATMENT

Therapy that includes the family is an essential part of treatment for adolescents struggling with addiction and co-occurring disorders. Family relationships and parenting style can positively or negatively impact the development of the adolescent, just as the behavior of the adolescent can influence the overall health of the family. The integrated treatment approach prioritizes parent and family involvement as it recognizes how influential each member of the family is on the health of the whole family unit. Although family therapy is a time-intensive requirement, it produces positive outcomes when compared to treating the adolescent on an individual basis. Adolescents whose families engage in family therapy are found to have a higher rate of engagement in treatment and stabilization of behavior. Family-based treatments have been found to be more effective than individual therapy and peer group therapy (Stanton & Shadish, 1997).

Because Internet addiction is not a recognized mental health disorder, parents often have not found the appropriate guidance and direction they are seeking from others, such as other parents, school personnel, pediatricians, and mental health clinicians. Parents are fatigued and overwhelmed due to the duration and intensity of their child's addiction and the impact on home environment. Because of this dynamic, parents often feel alone in their couple relationship, are polarized on how to intervene in their child's addiction, and have engaged in the Karpman Drama Triangle (Karpman, n.d.), either in the role of the rescuer, persecutor, and, at times, the victim. The child's addiction to the Internet holds the family emotionally hostage.

THE FAMILY AGREEMENT: THE FOUNDATION OF FITSC-IA

A key step toward intervening in and stabilizing the teen's addictive behaviors and conflictual family relationship is the development of the family agreement. This process is most successful when facilitated and directed by a trained family therapist and a co-therapist who also works with the adolescent individually. The family therapist is not required to ascribe to a specific family systems theory. However, in order to support the development of an effective family agreement, the therapist must have an ability to: (a) be directive; (b) join with the family as an effective leader, which occurs through an ability to listen; (c) be empathetic while maintaining an objective point of view; and (d) be genuinely interested in the clients.

Key Components of the Family Agreement

Setting Expectations

The family agreement sets five to seven well-defined, concrete, and measurable expectations with correlating consequences. The expectations and consequences must be developmentally appropriate and achievable by the teen.

The family therapist works closely with the parents to develop their version of the family agreement, which includes expectations that are negotiable and nonnegotiable. It is important that the teen has the opportunity to negotiate in order to feel included, make decisions, and empowered in the family recovery process. Nonnegotiable expectations are typically those that will maintain safety and stability in the home.

The clinician challenges and clarifies the parents' stated expectations and consequences to ensure they have the resources and ability to follow through. It is critical that the therapist educates the parents on the importance of providing the teen with ample notice of when the expectations and consequences will begin to occur. Providing teens with advance notice of expectations and consequences allows them to more effectively prepare, plan, and successfully follow through (Benson, Galbraith, & Espeland, 1998).

The teen works with his or her assigned clinician to develop his or her own version of the agreement with guidance and direction from the clinician to ensure the final product is both realistic and relevant. The clinician problem solves different ideas with the teen and helps the teen to consider what parents may expect. During this process, the teen often experiences many difficult emotions as he or she is asked to step into a more responsible role than in the past. A clinician who is well informed in the areas of adolescent developmental needs, addiction treatment, and motivational interviewing is able to support the teen to overcome the need for unhealthy control and willful behavior and to begin to move toward an agreeable stance on change.

It is important to note that areas, such as the adolescent's cognitive and developmental abilities, length of problematic behavior, age, level of insight, and desire for change will influence the amount of time the clinician will spend working with the teen to develop and finalize his or her version of the agreement. In some cases where a teen has a developmental disability, such as autism spectrum disorder, or the teen is emotionally immature, the teen may not be able to be an active participant in the development of the agreement. It is still critical that the teen works with a clinician to be prepared for the family agreement meeting.

Negotiation Meeting

Once the clinicians feel confident that their clients have created a well-prepared agreement, the family agreement negotiation meeting occurs. The family therapist is in the role of facilitator, which includes stating what the structure of the meeting will be. All parties involved attend and are supported to share their ideas and expectations. The adolescent is supported to have a voice and to use the negotiation skills taught by his or her therapist.

Agreement Active Period

Once finalized after the negotiation meeting, the family agreement occurs for a period of 30 days. Toward the end of each 30-day period, a family session, co-facilitated by the clinicians, takes place in order to reevaluate and make necessary changes. It is important that the clinicians check in frequently with their clients, typically weekly in the early stages of treatment, to ensure they are following through with the agreement and if not, to provide support and accountability to do so.

The family agreement is typically developed over a period of 3 to 6 weeks. The length of time to develop the agreement is dependent on several factors. First and foremost, the family must demonstrate a level of motivation, willingness, and the resources necessary for change. Important areas relating to the problem behaviors are evaluated and worked on during the process of developing the family agreement. The clinician will evaluate the following areas and provide education and engage the clients in a therapeutic process: (a) communication style; (b) the parents' digital media use and attitudes; (c) parenting style and current approach to the teen's problematic Internet behaviors, family values; and (d) level of parental fatigue. Parental fatigue is an important area to evaluate, as it will dictate the ability of the parents to endure the expected power struggle by the adolescent once the adolescent is held accountable to change the behavior as well as maintain a consistent ability to follow the family agreement. In extreme cases, out of home placement may be recommended for the teen, while the parents recover and work on rebuilding their resilience and develop tools to parent effectively once the teen returns home.

HARM REDUCTION AND ABSTINENCE APPROACHES

Harm reduction and abstinence approach are applicable in the treatment of Internet addiction. These approaches are often used simultaneously when treating adolescents with Internet-addicted behaviors.

Harm reduction, originally developed for adults with substance abuse problems, has recently been explored as an effective approach for the prevention and intervention of adolescent Internet-related addictions (Young, 2011). Harm reduction interventions focus on moderating the harmful consequences of the problematic behavior rather than eliminating the Internet use altogether.

Harm reduction interventions that may be used to prevent and treat adolescent Internet addiction include: (a) limiting or eliminating access to certain applications, such as pornography, video games, and social networking sites; (b) installation of software monitoring programs and parental controls; and (c) prevention and education programs provided to parents and adolescents about the risks and rewards of the Internet. The goal is to provide accurate and credible information to promote responsible use of the Internet. American Academy of Pediatrics (Strasburger et al., 2013) guidelines for digital media use recommend that parents not allow TV and Internet-connected devices in the teen's bedroom and enforce curfew for media devices at mealtimes and bedtimes.

Many clinicians and treatment providers who work with addictions view abstinence as the only way to recovery based on the definition of addiction and the idea that the user has lost control. The abstinence model follows the science behind addiction. Science has shown that some people are genetically predisposed to addiction and are more likely to get hooked to substances or behaviors. It is estimated that 40% to 60% of a person's predisposition to addiction is genetic (National Institute on Drug Abuse, 2014).

In many cases, it is required that the teen abstains only from the problematic application(s) (e.g., video games, pornography, YouTube) while still using all other digital media in a moderate, supervised manner. In more serious cases, Internet-addicted adolescents may not be viable candidates for the harm reduction approach and require abstinence from technology, which, if it cannot occur in the outpatient setting, can successfully occur in a residential treatment program that specializes in adolescent Internet addiction. A period of abstinence is the recommended treatment approach when the teen's Internet use has reached the extreme end of the continuum and the behavior is negatively impacting the teen in the areas of mental health, relationships, and academics.

Based on the severity of the Internet addiction, co-occurring mental health factors, and family health and support, it may be possible for the teen to fully abstain from all screens and digital media while living in the home in order to stabilize co-occurring mental health issues, reduce stress, and increase opportunity for social interaction. This is referred to as a "digital detox."

When the adolescent is able to engage in community-based treatment, the digital detox approach allows for the teen to remain at home while working on individual and family issues. Extended academic breaks, such as the winter holiday and summer months, provide the best opportunity for a digital detox. It is difficult to successfully guide a teen toward an abstinence plan due to academic requirements, which often involves the use of digital media in order to complete assignments, participate in classroom requirements, and obtain important academic information. Due to this, treating adolescents with Internet addiction in the outpatient setting is often more difficult and the recovery process can be delayed, particularly during the academic year. Conversely, treating adolescent Internet addiction in the outpatient setting by using FITSC-IA and its core components, allows the adolescent and the family to experience real, long-lasting change. Incorporating the harm-reduction approach, which includes using motivational interviewing, provides the teen with the opportunity to engage in recovery from the problematic applications by abstaining from them, while learning how to moderate other applications and using technology as a tool to enhance the academic experience.

As mentioned earlier, engaging the family in the development of the family agreement will clarify Internet use expectations for the teen, including which application(s) are no longer supported by the parents. Once the family agreement, the foundation of FITSC-IA, is completed, a plan for abstinence from the problematic application(s) is developed among the treatment team, client, and parents.

SOCIAL RECOVERY

Consistent, regular face-to-face social connection with others is a protective factor and a remedy when it comes to preventing and effectively treating Internet addiction and common co-occurring diagnoses, such as depression. Feeling connected to others may be the best medicine when it comes to successful recovery. Portugal designed a program specifically to recreate connection between the addicted person and his or her community (Drug Policy Alliance, 2015). By providing structure and support to obtain employment and develop social connections, a 50% drop in substance addiction was reported.

One reason social connection and engaging in meaningful activities, such as volunteer work or employment, empower recovery is due to what neuroscience calls "limbic resonance." Limbic resonance is the release of neurochemicals in the limbic region of the brain that occurs when two or more people are interacting in a face-to-face caring and safe relationship. Limbic resonance is necessary for full emotional and physical health. Without this process occurring, adolescents who are socially isolated have an increased risk for depressive symptoms, suicide attempts, and low self-esteem (Hall-Lande, Eisenberg, Christenson, & Neumark-Sztainer, 2007).

Because one of the strongest indicators of psychological health in adolescents is a sense of meaningful connection with peers, it is critical for those who are addicted to the Internet to receive the guidance, support, and accountability to engage in an integrated treatment program, such as what FITSC-IA offers, in order to reduce social anxiety and depressive symptoms and to begin developing the confidence and skills to connect with others. A study of sixth graders found that parental and peer support was associated with decreased loneliness and social anxiety across early adolescence (Cavanaugh & Buehler, 2016). Prevention measures, such as healthy peer relationships, promoting and supporting family connectedness, and school-based support, are critical.

A large percentage of adolescents who experience the symptoms of Internet addiction experience significant social anxiety. SAD is one of the most common anxiety disorders in children and adults (Hudson & Dodd, 2011), and affects up to 8.6% of teenagers ages 13 to 18 years in the United States (Burstein et al., 2011). SAD is indicated uniquely by an extreme, irrational, and impairing fear of social situations, such as being criticized or negatively evaluated by other people. The teen may suffer significant distress or impairment that interferes with ordinary routine in social situations, at work or school, or during other everyday activities (American Psychiatric Association, 2013). Social anxiety is linked to major depression, academic, underachievement, and substance abuse.

A review of the literature finds that adolescents who are shy, lack social skills, and are socially anxious are more likely to form online friendships and prefer to communicate with strangers online rather than face to face. It is important for the clinician to remember while engaged in the assessment phase of treatment, that the adolescent may possess adequate social skills, but his or her ability to focus on social interactions and use these skills is hindered by anxiety. This suggests that social anxiety is associated with a performance deficit, not a skill deficit (Hopko, McNeil, Zvolensky, & Eifert, 2001). If this is the case, it can be assumed that by eliminating the social anxiety, the appropriate social skills will emerge.

SAD during adolescence is an important predictor of subsequent depressive disorders. If the teen's social anxiety is not treated effectively with treatment modalities, the likelihood of other emerging disorders will increase, which will impact successful treatment outcomes. In addition, social anxiety may also impact the teen's willingness and ability to begin to engage in social activities and groups with peers, as well as perpetuate the addiction to the Internet. To enhance the mental health level of addicted teens, adequate social support should be provided to address their feelings of isolation, loneliness, and exclusion. Results of a study by Alfano et al. (2009) suggest that improvements in social anxiety and overall functioning are predicted by decreases in loneliness and improvements in social skill irrespective of child's age and depressive symptoms.

EFFECTIVE TREATMENT APPROACHES

Because it has been determined through practical experience and clinical trials that SAD (Bernardi & Pallanti, 2009) and depressive disorders (Yen et al., 2008) commonly co-occur with Internet addiction, it is important to include treatment approaches found to be successful at treating these disorders.

Cognitive behavioral therapy (CBT) has been shown to be efficacious for the treatment of anxiety and depressive disorders in adolescents. Clinical trials indicate that approximately 66% of children and adolescents treated with CBT will be free of their primary diagnosis at post treatment (Seligman & Ollendick, 2011).

Initially the focus of the CBT approach is to understand the roots of the presenting problem in order to provide the clinician with an understanding on how to intervene in the "here and now" and help change maladaptive behaviors and thought patterns. It is important for the clinician to address the factors that maintain the teen's symptoms in order to develop new approaches, rather than spend time coming to an understanding about why the disorder developed.

Successful treatment outcomes will increase when the teen is treated simultaneously for Internet addiction either through the harm reduction approach and/or abstinence approach, as well as incorporating the other key components of FITSC-IA. Otherwise, if interventions do not occur and the teen's use of the Internet remains unchanged, the teen will continue to seek escape from anxiety-provoking situations by way of the Internet, which will make it difficult to successfully treat both issues.

CBT is a skill-building approach and the clinician is often directive and didactic when working with the client and the parents. In many cases with adolescents, their parents and even their siblings are introduced to new skills in order to support the desired change outside of treatment sessions. As we typically find in family therapy, parents are often asked to change their behavior and approach to the teen's anxiety in order to support the teen's ability to incorporate new skills and engage less, if not eliminate entirely, in identified escapist behaviors, such as the Internet. The family agreement may include an expectation about attending treatment meetings and groups as scheduled, using the skills being taught, and doing the assigned homework in between sessions. This structure and accountability will support the teen and the parents to prioritize these areas and follow through.

When working with teens who struggle with Internet addiction and social anxiety, it is recommended to incorporate the following tenets of CBT. These include: (a) a comprehensive assessment; (b) development of a therapeutic relationship and working alliance; (c) cognitive restructuring; (d) repeated imaginal and/or in vivo exposure; and (e) coping and social skills training (Hazlett-Stevens & Craske, 2002).

Because the treatment for anxiety in adolescents is distressing, continued involvement in treatment depends on the clinician's strong relationship with the parents and the teen, as well as an agreement on what the tasks and goals of treatment are (Hayes, Hope, VanDyke, & Heimberg, 2007). In addition to empathic listening skills, warmth, genuineness, and unconditional positive regard being the primary means of establishing the therapeutic relationship, a collaborative relationship inherent in CBT between the clinician(s) and the teen will empower the teen to experience the clinician as someone who can help.

Cognitive behavioral therapy for Internet addiction (CBT-IA), developed by Kimberly Young (2011), is the first evidence-based digital detoxification recovery program. When treating adolescents with Internet overuse and addiction, it is recommended that the clinician address cognitive restructuring from this perspective. Maladaptive cognitions that are commonly associated with addictive Internet use, such as overgeneralization, magnification, all-or-nothing thinking, and magical thinking, will need to be identified by the client in order to help the client identify and dispute his or her distorted negative thoughts about the real world, as well as distorted positive thoughts about the virtual world. Helping the teen recognize his or her "self-talk" and then understand the links between self-talk and symptoms of anxiety is a critical step in creating awareness. This tenet of CBT-IA will support the teen to begin to develop awareness and understanding that the teen is using the Internet to avoid situations and feelings.

Exposure therapy used in conjunction with CBT has considerable efficacy for social anxiety, as well as many other types of anxiety disorders (Acarturk, Cuijpers, Van Straten, & De Graaf, 2009). Exposure therapy to the feared stimuli is the central component in most CBT treatment approaches for adolescent anxiety. There are four phases of exposure-based treatments: (a) instruction, (b) hierarchy development, (c) exposure proper, and (d) generalization and maintenance (Seligman & Ollendick, 2011).

When treating adolescents with Internet addiction by using FITSC-IA, exposure therapy is a core tenet of the treatment plan for those adolescents with significant social anxiety issues, and SAD, which is often a problem with which most, if not all, teens with Internet addiction are dealing. In many cases, the teen entering treatment has been struggling for a number of years with anxiety, escapist behaviors, and lack of peer connection and support. Many times parents reach out to the treatment provider identifying academic problems as the primary concern. As the teen enters middle school and high school, the academic expectations and pressures increase, as do the peer expectations and pressures. The teen may have had a successful experience in elementary school and felt supported by teachers and often by peers; however, many teens are unprepared for the stressors of middle school and high school. This tends to be when they first enter treatment. Preparing the teen for and integrating exposure therapy, provides the teen an opportunity to begin to develop coping skills, change distorted thought patterns, decrease anxiety, feel more confident when interacting with peers, and ultimately be less interested in escaping into the virtual world of the Internet.

The steps to exposure therapy must be graded and well thought out by the treatment team, while assessing the adolescent's level of functioning and mental health stability in individual and family sessions. In most cases, in vivo exposure, the direct confrontation of feared objects, activities, or situations, is generally preferred and more effective than imaginal exposure. When circumstances do not allow, imaginal exposure is used as an alternative. The client is asked to vividly imagine and describe the feared stimuli, usually using present tense language and including details about internal (thoughts, emotions) and external (sights, sounds) cues. When the adolescent is engaged in treatment in a residential treatment center, the use of imaginal exposure may be more relevant to that setting; however, when using FITSC-IA, engaging the client in in vivo exposure when the client is prepared will produce more benefits and more lasting change.

The instruction phase of exposure treatment includes providing parents and the teen with basic information on the understanding of fear and anxiety. Education is provided about the nature of anxiety and the prediction that it will peak and then decrease with prolonged exposure as long as escapist behaviors (e.g., Internet, screens) have been limited and are monitored closely by the parent, or are eliminated by applying the abstinence approach to technology and screens.

Once the clinician feels confident the teen and the parents understand the rationale for exposure therapy, the first step in successful exposure therapy is the development of an exposure hierarchy. A graded hierarchy is developed of feared situations that will be used for exposure sessions. The teen with the support of the clinician brainstorms as many feared stimuli and internal stimuli as possible and then rates them in order of difficulty. The use of Subjective Units of Distress Scale (SUDS) is recommended to provide the clinician and teen with a tool to consistently grade the feared situations each session. This tool is a scale of 0 to 100 for measuring the subjective intensity of distress experienced by the teen. The SUDS is used as a benchmark for the individual clinician, group leader, treatment team, and parents to evaluate the progress of treatment. Data from a study on the validity of SUDS supports this scale as a global measure of both physical and emotional discomfort (Tanner, 2012).

The clinician uses this tool to measure distress as they integrate exposure experiences in a gradual and systematic manner. Once the teen's anxiety decreases significantly and in most cases dissipates on a lower ranked item, higher ranked items will be attempted in an organized manner. It is important that the clinician set clear expectations regarding what is allowed during the exposure process in order to prevent "safety behaviors" (e.g., cell phone) from being available to the teen. Teens with social anxiety often engage the use of their cell phone to help them feel more comfortable in distressing, feared situations.

Exposure proper, the third phase of exposure therapy, involves the teen being exposed to each of the situations in the hierarchy until the anxiety dissipates. The clinician will model behaviors by engaging in the anxiety-provoking task while allowing the teen to observe. For example, the teen has identified talking to a cashier as a moderately ranked item in their hierarchy. The clinician and the client may go to a coffee shop to get a drink. The teen will accompany the clinician to the counter to put the order in and observe the step-by-step process. Thereafter, a discussion occurs about what the teen observed, feelings of fear are scaled and physiological arousal is explored to determine the next steps in the exposure process, which may lead to the teen being willing to engage in the task with the clinician observing.

The last phase of exposure therapy is generalization and maintenance. In order to generalize treatment gains across situations, the teen is given homework assignments to repeat exposures outside of the time he or she is with the clinician either in the office or in the community. To increase accountability and follow through, the clinician also shares the homework assignments with the parents so they understand how to support their child to follow through. It is important that the clinician and parents support the teen to engage in this homework, as it will help to solidify the skills learned in session and ensure that the child does not see the company of the clinician as necessary for the control of the anxiety.

Group Treatment and Support

Within the Digital Media Treatment and Education Center's (D-TEC) adolescent program, the opportunity for in vivo exposure experiences is provided in all levels of the program. Individual and family therapy is a critical component of successful exposure therapy, as well as group therapy, support groups, and unstructured social experiences within the program. Clinicians work with their individual client to prepare for and engage in group and social situations in the program as one of the first graduated steps in the exposure therapy process. By engaging the teen in a supportive environment that promotes and values group norms and safety, the teen is able to speak about his or her Internet addiction and related behaviors, feelings, and everyday adolescent struggles, often for the first time with others in the teen's age group. Each member of the treatment team is aware of the exposure hierarchy the teen is working on, which allows the team to support the teen to continue working on his or her homework assignments outside of the individual therapy sessions.

Generalization treatment by repeating exposures in the structured group and social settings is a successful way to bridge the gap between the one-to-one work with the clinician and engaging in assigned tasks at home, school, and in the community. For many teens with long-term screen exposure, high social anxiety, limited resiliency, and lack of social skills and/or practice, engagement in structured group treatment increases the teen's willingness to engage in these steps, and provides parents with a sense of peace and confidence.

The FITSC-IA approach incorporates weekly group therapy facilitated by two clinicians. In group therapy, self-exposure and practice are combined with group education and discussion of experiences that clients have during exposure to feared situations, while also discussing their Internet-related behaviors. Incorporating unstructured peer generalization activities, which allow for social interaction, is a critical component of the group treatment. Several social activities during the week are scheduled, which allow for the teen to engage in social interaction with peers. These activities are typically set up to meet the interests of the teens, as well as to encourage practice of important tools and skills. Teens with Internet addiction issues often are interested in activities that allow for engagement in the fantasy world, role-playing, intellectual discussions and debates, and board games. These are the factors that often compel teens to immerse into the virtual worlds of video games; however, it is not the program's intent to eliminate these interest areas. The clinical team recognizes the importance of providing opportunities that are interesting to teens, yet encourage social face-to-face contact versus behaviors (e.g., Internet, video games) that will continue to perpetuate their social anxiety symptoms by allowing them to avoid and escape fearful and distressing social situations. Each social activity provided by the D-TEC includes a clinician who provides accountability, support, and encouragement. It is this clinician's responsibility to report updates to the adolescent's individual and family clinicians about how teens performed and engaged in the groups.

Examples of social activities, which integrate interest areas and increase the teen's willingness to participate, follow:

- *Book club* is a group that, with the support of the clinician, identifies a book of interest to read. The group gathers weekly to discuss their thoughts and impressions as well as engage in lively debates. It is important to note that "real" books are required, often a novel experience for the teens.

- *Film and philosophy night* is a group that incorporates a TV screen, which is meant to model appropriate use of screens in healthy social situations, as well as provide a platform to engage in watching a film with the group and then discuss it in a lively, philosophical manner.

- *Board game night* incorporates board games that take between 1 to 2 hours to finish. It is important to note that time-intensive board games resemble the immersive and escapist quality of video games; therefore, choosing games with shorter timeframes is recommended to help the teen create balance. This social group incorporates the teen's interest in fantasy, strategy, and, for some, competition while engaging with peers face to face.
- *Breakfast club* is an opportunity for teens to meet in the community at a restaurant. This is a time for them to engage in tasks that are typically part of their hierarchy, such as ordering food from a stranger, demonstrating appropriate social skills while eating, eating in front of others, and engaging in conversation.

Generally, teens who have a history of Internet addiction issues are not as interested in physical outlets, such as team sports, hiking, or biking. Because it is critical to teens' overall well-being to engage in outdoor physical outlets on a regular basis, incorporating these activities are important. Research examining the relationships between green space and children's quality of life reports positive impacts in the areas of health and well-being, and social and community value for children. Dr. Stephen Kellert of Yale University studies nature and childhood development. Kellert (2012) states, "Play in nature, particularly during the critical period of middle childhood, appears to be an especially important time for developing the capacities for creativity, problem-solving, and emotional and intellectual development" (p. 83).

Martial arts are recognized as an activity that teens with Internet-overuse issues have engaged in in the past or have an interest in engaging. D-TEC incorporates a weekly Tai Chi group, which is led by a trained instructor who is also part of the clinical team. Tai Chi Chuan is an ancient martial art that uses moving mindfulness to teach soft relaxation and balance in order to support strong roots, healthy bones and organs, vitality, and dignity of oneself (Nathan Torti, personal communication, March 1, 2016). In addition to this weekly group, FITSC-IA places importance in scheduling bimonthly or monthly physical activities, such as hiking, fly fishing, Frisbee golf, and miniature golf, for the teens to engage in as a group. When clinically indicated, the teen's individual clinician will attend the activity in order to support the teen to work on distressing feelings and thoughts as part of the exposure therapy process.

Community-Based Support Groups

It is important as a clinician to consider the benefits of support groups for adolescents with Internet addiction. These groups can support the teen to meet others who understand what they are going through, create an opportunity to develop relationships and friendships, and increase the likelihood of long-term recovery. The experience of a support group can normalize the problem behavior and decrease feelings of shame and guilt. Supporting the teen to engage in support groups in the community provides a support system that the teen can continue to engage in once they have completed treatment.

The team at the D-TEC recognizes the benefits of support groups for those in recovery from substance addictions and other process addictions, such as Gamblers Anonymous and Sex and Love Addicts Anonymous; however, support groups specific to Internet overuse and addiction are still rare.

Dr. Lee Ann Kuskutas, a senior scientist at the Alcohol Research Group, states that Alcoholics Anonymous (AA) support groups show between a 10% to 20% advantage when it comes to total days abstinence over more standard treatment like CBT. Kuskutas stated, "People who self-select to attend AA, end up having people in their social network who are supportive of their abstinence" (as cited in Singal, 2015). Research shows that the social networks, and the norms contained within the group, are powerful drivers of recovery-focused behavior. Young adults identified cohesiveness, belonging, and instillation of hope as the most helpful aspects of attending 12-step groups (Labbe, Slaymaker, & Kelly, 2014).

It is important to establish support groups that focus on problematic Internet use if they are not available, as it is difficult for clients to find a sense of belonging and validation with support groups such as AA and Narcotics Anonymous. However, when the client is also dealing with a co-occurring substance abuse issue, they find value in groups such as AA.

Dr. Hilarie Cash, CEO and founding member of reSTART, developed a 12-step support group for Internet and technology addiction, called Internet and Technology Addiction Anonymous (ITAA) 12-Step Support Group. In collaboration with Dr. Cash and her team, the ITAA 12-step support group in Boulder, Colorado, was offered. Because no young people were in recovery from Internet and technology addiction at the time, a facilitator was assigned to be in the role of educator and moderator in order to support a new group of recovering addicts to develop norms and experience the group as helpful.

The team at D-TEC developed a support group called Problematic Internet-Technology Facilitated (PITF) support group for teenagers and young adults. This support group is structured by themes, which are accompanied by objectives to achieve by each group and occur over a 12-week period. The facilitator's role is to support group norms and provide group moderation and education. Themes include social connection, moderation versus abstinence of Internet applications, escapism, coping, as well as several other areas. The PITF group provides a platform for young people deterred by the philosophy of 12-step groups to have the opportunity to meet and receive support from others struggling with similar issues and challenges.

Motivational Interviewing

Motivational interviewing (MI) is a widely used approach for addressing adolescent substance use. MI has met the American Psychological Association's criteria for promising treatment of adolescent substance use (Macgowan & Engle, 2010). The clinician emphasizes the importance of being in a partnership instead of an expert role with the client, respecting the adolescent's need for autonomy and freedom of choice, and understanding the consequences regarding behavior. MI emphasizes exploring and reinforcing the client's intrinsic motivation toward healthy behaviors while supporting his or her autonomy. Because adolescents have a developmental need to be independent and make decisions for themselves, MI can be a successful approach in the treatment of substance abuse. The MI model is adaptable to adolescent Internet abuse and addiction due to the adolescent experiencing the same developmental processes and need for independence and making their own decisions. Using MI while treating adolescents in the outpatient setting is important due to the teen's level of ambivalence about recognizing that there may be a problem with his or her Internet behaviors.

Although MI is a more time-intensive approach, the awareness and motivation to change that MI elicits come from the teen and are not being imposed on him or her. Adolescents do not respond to being persuaded to make changes and their level of resistance increases and the probability of change decreases when they are approached in this manner. It is not unusual for the adolescent to enter treatment for Internet addiction feeling willful and disinterested in engaging openly in the process. Incorporating MI during and throughout the phases of integrated treatment will support the adolescent to begin to develop intrinsic motivation toward healthy behaviors, which is essential for long-lasting change.

Transition

For those adolescents returning from a residential treatment program for Internet addiction issues, it is important to develop a transition plan from the residential program to an aftercare, community-based program, such as the D-TEC, which provides treatment to the teen and family during the teen's reintegration period, as well as providing guidance, education, and support when it is time to reintroduce screens and Internet-based technology. A factor that will inhibit the teen and family from transferring the knowledge and skills to the home environment is the lack of preparing and planning for the transition home. The residential treatment program encompasses very important information that needs to be shared with the aftercare program before the adolescent leaves the program, as well as connecting the client and parents to the aftercare treatment provider in order to begin preparing for the transition to the aftercare program.

The team at D-TEC sees increased success when the clinician has the opportunity to meet the parents before the teen's arrival home and to support them to prepare the home environment to be an environment conducive to the child's early stages of recovery from Internet addiction. Important areas in the home to assess and make recommendations about are:

- Ensure the environment will allow for a 30-day period of abstinence from Internet-based technology, which includes mobile devices and computers. If there is a computer accessible by the teen, parents are instructed to password protect the computer. If the teen is returning to school in this time period, parents will be guided by the clinician to set up a computer in an easily supervised common area for the teen to use when he or she is required to use the computer for schoolwork.

- Provide the teen with a phone that does not have Internet access. Cell phone companies continue to provide "flip phones." Although flip phones are capable of being connected to the Internet, the parent can turn off this feature and secure the phone by requiring a password to enable the wireless capability. Receiving a "dumb phone" on return from treatment, the teen will have the opportunity to connect with others and will take the first steps toward the reintroduction of technology.

- Create a Technology Reintroduction Plan (TRP).

Technology Reintroduction Plan

A TRP is an accountability tool to support the teen and family to prepare to reintegrate technology. Internet-based technology is required in most K–12 schools, university campuses, and places of employment. Because of this, it is critical that the teen is supported to learn how to use computers, mobile devices, and other screens with Internet capability in a moderate manner while abstaining from the problematic applications (e.g., video games, pornography, video streaming). Public schools in the United States now provide at least one computer for every five students. In many schools, students are given district-owned devices or allowed to bring their own devices from home. The White House website highlights the ConnectED Initiative, a federal government-led program to connect 99% of America's students to the digital age through next generation broadband and high-speed wireless in schools and libraries by 2018 ("ConnectED Initiative," n.d.).

The TRP includes:

- An overview of what type of technology will be used on returning home from the treatment program (e.g., cell phone without Internet, computer for academics)

- Core structure requirements that are set up must be met for a minimum of 30 days before Internet-based technology is integrated. Examples of core requirements include: attending all scheduled treatment meetings and groups, including support groups; participating regularly in healthy outlets, such as engaging in physical activity and stress-reducing activities (e.g., Tai Chi, meditation, yoga); and attending school and staying in good standing

- The teen being honest and transparent with the team about triggers and using behaviors if and when they occur

- Obtaining and maintaining a recommended number of hours of employment or volunteer work each week

- Teen and parent agreement to the installation of monitoring software on all devices as they are reintroduced. D-TEC uses and recommends Covenant Eyes (CE)

The clinical team, teen, and the parents meet every 30 days to reevaluate the TRP and areas of progress and areas in need of improvement. It is a team decision when it is time to integrate technology. This approach provides support to the parents to increase the likelihood of consistency and not to impulsively allow their child to obtain a device before it is time. The plan is updated accordingly.

The team provides support to the parents and teen to install a software-monitoring program such as CE, an Internet accountability and filtering program that monitors websites visited, search terms used, and videos watched, and lists them in an easy to read report that is designed to start a conversation about online habits. A clinician trained to install CE receives direction from the teen's clinician regarding what limits to set up. The clinician sits down with each family and walks them through the process, which includes setting time limits, blocking certain websites and applications, as well as determining what sensitivity levels are appropriate (e.g., everyone, youth, teen, mature teen). These settings will determine which websites the teen can visit. Only the clinician knows the password, which is needed to change the settings. Installing CE or other monitoring software allows for reintegration to occur in a timely manner while the client and the clinician receive accountability reports daily. CE sends reports to the client and clinician's e-mails. The reports include: areas of concern, notifications anytime a client installs CE or generates an uninstall code, websites visited, and how many times visited. These accountability reports, which can be set up to be received daily, weekly, or monthly, allow the client and the clinician to gain awareness of the Internet use each day, as well as provide the opportunity for real-time feedback. Information from the accountability reports is shared with parents by the teen to support transparency and accountability.

Lastly, the TRP highlights the importance of using technology as an important tool for academics and employment, as well as Internet-based applications that are not supported. These applications include streaming videos, video games, pornography, YouTube, chat rooms, as well as any other problematic application the client and/or parents identify. The use of these Internet applications are discouraged during the integration of technology. During the duration of the client's treatment, the client's team promotes abstinence from video games, both online and offline.

CONCLUSION

A call to action is occurring for clinicians, educators, and pediatricians to be a source of reference for our young people and their parents as it relates to the complicated nature of digital media use. For mental health clinicians working with young people and their families, it is evident that having the knowledge and understanding about how to identify and treat Internet addiction in adolescents is critical due to prevalence rates reaching 30% in some areas of the world. In the United States, approximately 4% of adolescents meet the criteria for Internet addiction (Liu et al., 2011), and in 2015 ChildStats. gov reported there were almost 23 million 12- to 17-year-olds in the United States (ChildStats.gov, 2015). This translates to roughly 920,000 adolescents who may be addicted to the Internet.

The field of Internet addiction study is producing valuable research findings and efficacious and innovative assessment and treatment approaches for clinicians to use with the adolescents and families for whom they are providing services. Internet and screen addictions and mental health problems experienced by young people who still rely on their parents for emotional and financial guidance and support must be treated from an integrated treatment approach. Prioritizing the inclusion of the family system and social connection support as core components in the treatment for adolescent Internet addiction has proven to be invaluable when it comes to the teen and his or her family having a successful recovery process. The FITSC-IA is a community-based approach to the treatment of adolescent Internet addiction. It is a relevant treatment approach that can be used in residential treatment programs, as many of the components are also recommended for the treatment of adolescent Internet addiction in general. Integrated treatment approaches, such as FITSC-IA, will provide the adolescent and the family with skilled, knowledgeable treatment providers, interventions, and the possibility for the best outcome.

REFERENCES

Acarturk, C., Cuijpers, P., Van Straten, A., & De Graaf, R. (2009). Psychological treatment of social anxiety disorder: A meta-analysis. *Psychological Medicine, 39*(2), 241–254.

Alfano, C. A., Pina, A. A., Villalta, I. K., Beidel, D. C., Ammerman, R. T., & Crosby, L. E. (2009). Mediators and moderators of outcome in the behavioral treatment of childhood social phobia. *Journal of the American Academy of Child & Adolescent Psychiatry, 48*(9), 945–953.

American Psychiatric Association. (2013). *Desk reference to the diagnostic criteria from DSM-5.* Arlington, VA: American Psychiatric Publishing.

Ary, D. V., Duncan, T. E., Biglan, A., Metzler, C. W., Noell, J. W., & Smolkowski, K. (1999). Development of adolescent problem behavior. *Journal of Abnormal Child Psychology, 27*(2), 141–150.

Bai, Y. M., Lin, C. C., & Chen, J. Y. (2001). Internet addiction disorder among clients of a virtual clinic. *Psychiatric Services, 52*(10), 1397.

Benson, P. L., Galbraith, J., & Espeland, P. (1998). *What teens need to succeed: Proven, practical ways to shape your own future.* Minneapolis, MN: Free Spirit.

Bernardi, S., & Pallanti, S. (2009). Internet addiction: A descriptive clinical study focusing on comorbidities and dissociative symptoms. *Comprehensive Psychiatry, 50*(6), 510–516.

Block J. J. (2008). Issues for *DSM-V*: Internet addiction. *American Journal of Psychiatry, 165*(3), 306–307.

Burstein, M., He, J.P., Kattan, G., Albano, A.M., Avenevoli, S., & Merikangas, K. R. (2011). Social phobia and subtypes in the National Comorbidity Survey-Adolescent Supplement: Prevalence, correlates, and comorbidity. *Journal of the American Academy of Child and Adolescent Psychiatry, 50*(9), 870–880.

Cavanaugh, A. M., & Buehler, C. (2016). Adolescent loneliness and social anxiety: The role of multiple sources of support. *Journal of Social and Personal Relationships, 33*(2), 149–170.

ChildStats.gov. (2015). America's children: Key national indicators of well-being [XLS Spreadsheet]. Retrieved from http://www.childstats.gov/americaschildren/tables.asp

China Internet Network Information Center. (2010). *Statistical survey report on Internet development in China.* Beijing, China: Author.

ConnectED Initiative. (n.d.). What is ConnectED? Retrieved from https://obama whitehouse.archives.gov/blog/2013/06/06/what-connected

De Berardis, D., D'Albenzio, A., Gambi, F., Sepede, G., Valchera, A., Conti, C. M.,... & Serroni, N. (2009). Alexithymia and its relationships with dissociative experiences and Internet addiction in a nonclinical sample. *CyberPsychology & Behavior, 12*(1), 67–69.

Dong, G., Shen, Y., Huang, J., & Du, X. (2013). Impaired error-monitoring function in people with Internet addiction disorder: An event-related fMRI study. *European Addiction Research, 19,* 269–275.

Drake, R. E., Essock, S. M., Shaner, A., Carey, K. B., Minkoff, K., Kola, L.,... & Rickards, L. (2001). Implementing dual diagnosis services for clients with severe mental illness. *Psychiatric Services, 52*(4), 469–476.

Drug Policy Alliance. (2015, February 5). *Drug decriminalization in Portugal: A health-centered approach* [PDF document]. Retrieved from http://www.drugpolicy.org/resource/drug-decriminalization-portugal-health-centered-approach

Hall-Lande, J. A., Eisenberg, M. E., Christenson, S. L., & Neumark-Sztainer, D. (2007). Social isolation, psychological health, and protective factors in adolescence. *Adolescence, 42*(166), 265.

Hari, J. (2015). Everything you think you know about addiction is wrong. Retrieved from https://www.ted.com/talks/johann_hari_everything_you_think_you_know_about_addiction_is_wrong

Hayes, S. A., Hope, D. A., VanDyke, M. M., & Heimberg, R. G. (2007). Working alliance for clients with social anxiety disorder: Relationship with session helpfulness and within-session habituation. *Cognitive Behaviour Therapy, 36*(1), 34–42.

Hazlett-Stevens, H., & Craske, M. G. (2002). Brief cognitive-behavioral therapy: Definition and scientific foundations. In F. W. Bond & W. Dryden (Eds.), *Handbook of brief cognitive behaviour therapy* (pp. 1–20). New York, NY: Wiley.

Hopko, D. R., McNeil, D. W., Zvolensky, M. J., & Eifert, G. H. (2001). The relation between anxiety and skill in performance-based anxiety disorders: A behavioral formulation of social phobia. *Behavior Therapy, 32*(1), 185–207.

Hudson, J., & Dodd, H. (2011). Introduction to special issue on social phobia in children. *Journal of Experimental Psychotherapy, 2,* 449–453.

Karpman, S. (n.d.). The original drama triangle article reprint and selected transactional analysis articles. Retrieved from https://www.karpmandramatriangle.com

Kellert, S. R. (2012). *Building for life: Designing and understanding the human-nature connection.* Covelo, CA: Island Press.

Klomek, A. B., Marrocco, F., Kleinman, M., Schonfeld, I. S., & Gould, M. S. (2007). Bullying, depression, and suicidality in adolescents. *Journal of the American Academy of Child & Adolescent Psychiatry, 46*(1), 40–49.

Ko, C.-H., Yen, J.-Y., Liu, S.-C., Huang, C.-F., & Yen, C.-F. (2009). The associations between aggressive behaviors and Internet addiction and online activities in adolescents. *Journal of Adolescent Health, 44*(6), 598–605.

Kormas, G., Critselis, E., Janikian, M., Kafetzis, D., & Tsitsika, A. (2011). Risk factors and psychosocial characteristics of potential problematic and problematic internet use among adolescents: A cross-sectional study. *BMC Public Health, 11*(1), 1.

Labbe, A. K., Slaymaker, V., & Kelly, J. F. (2014). Toward enhancing 12-step facilitation among young people: A systematic qualitative investigation of young adults' 12-step experiences. *Substance Abuse, 35*(4), 399–407.

Lenhart, A., Kahne, J., Middaugh, E., Macgill, A., Evans, C., & Vitak, J. (2008). Teens, video games and civics. Pew Internet & American Life Project. Retrieved from http://www.pewinternet.org/2008/09/16/teens-video-games-and-civics

Lin, I.-H., Ko, C.-H., Chang, Y.-P., Liu, T.-L., Wang, P.-W., Lin, H.-C., . . . & Yen, C.-F. (2014). The association between suicidality and Internet addiction and activities in Taiwanese adolescents. *Comprehensive Psychiatry, 55*(3), 504–510.

Liu, T. C., Desai, R. A., Krishnan-Sarin, S., Cavallo, D. A., & Potenza, M. N. (2011). Problematic Internet use and health in adolescents: Data from a high school survey in Connecticut. *The Journal of Clinical Psychiatry, 72*(6), 836–845.

Macgowan, M. J., & Engle, B. (2010). Evidence for optimism: Behavior therapies and motivational interviewing in adolescent substance abuse treatment. *Child and Adolescent Psychiatric Clinics of North America, 19*(3), 527–545.

Muris, P., van Brakel, A. M., Arntz, A., & Schouten, E. (2010). Behavioral inhibition as a risk factor for the development of childhood anxiety disorders: A longitudinal study. *Journal of Child and Family Studies, 20*(2), 157–170.

National Institute on Drug Abuse (2014, July). Drugs, brains, and behavior: The science of addiction [PDF document]. Retrieved from https://www.drugabuse.gov/publications/drugs-brains-behavior-science-addiction

Rideout, V. J., Foehr, U. G., & Roberts, D. F. (2010). *Generation M²: Media in the lives of 8- to 18-year-olds.* Menlo Park, CA: Henry J. Kaiser Family Foundation.

Seligman, L. D., & Ollendick, T. H. (2011). Cognitive-behavioral therapy for anxiety disorders in youth. *Child and Adolescent Psychiatric Clinics of North America, 20*(2), 217–238.

Shaw, L. H., & Gant, L. M. (2002). In defense of the Internet: The relationship between Internet communication and depression, loneliness, self-esteem, and perceived social support. *CyberPsychology & Behavior, 5*(2), 157–171.

Shek, D. T., & Yu, L. (2016). Adolescent Internet addiction in Hong Kong: Prevalence, change, and correlates. *Journal of Pediatric and Adolescent Gynecology, 29*(1), S22–S30.

Singal, J. (2015, March 17). Why Alcoholics Anonymous works. *New York Magazine.* Retrieved from http://nymag.com/scienceofus/2015/03/why-alcoholics-anonymous-works.html

Stanton, M. D., & Shadish, W. R. (1997). Outcome, attrition, and family–couples treatment for drug abuse: A meta-analysis and review of the controlled, comparative studies. *Psychological Bulletin, 122*(2), 170–191.

Strasburger, V. C., Hogan, M. J., Mulligan, D. A., Ameenuddin, N., Christakis, D. A., Cross, C., ... & Moreno, M. A. (2013). Children, adolescents, and the media. *Pediatrics, 132*(5), 958–961.

Tanner, B. A. (2012). Validity of global physical and emotional SUDS. *Applied Psychophysiology and Biofeedback, 37*(1), 31–34.

Tao, R., Huang, X., Wang, J., Zhang, H., Zhang, Y., & Li, M. (2010). Proposed diagnostic criteria for internet addiction. *Addiction, 105*(3), 556–564.

Thompson, R. A. (1994). Emotion regulation: A theme in search of definition. *Monographs of the Society for Research in Child Development, 59*(2–3), 25–52.

Watson, M., Fischer, K., Andreas, J. B., & Smith, K. (2004). Pathways to aggression in children and adolescents. *Harvard Educational Review, 74*(4), 404–430.

Wills, T. A., Pokhrel, P., Morehouse, E., & Fenster, B. (2011). Behavioral and emotional regulation and adolescent substance use problems: A test of moderation effects in a dual-process model. *Psychology of Addictive Behaviors, 25*(2), 279.

Yen, J.-Y., Ko, C.-H., Yen, C.-F., Chen, S.-H., Chung, W.-L., & Chen, C.-C. (2008). Psychiatric symptoms in adolescents with Internet addiction: Comparison with substance use. *Psychiatry and Clinical Neurosciences, 62*(1), 9–16.

Young, K. S. (2011). CBT-IA: The first treatment model for Internet addiction. *Journal of Cognitive Psychotherapy, 25*(4), 304–312.

15 SCREEN SMART SCHOOLS: INITIATIVES, POLICIES, AND METHODS FOR MAINTAINING STUDENT CYBERHEALTH

Marsali Hancock

Digital technology has quickly revolutionized the way we live, including how we consume information, communicate with others, spend our free time, and more. Although adults have been quite aware of this shift, children are learning and growing alongside technology. This shapes both their experience and their relationship with technology in unique and unprecedented ways. The field of Internet safety has followed a path determined by the most immediate and apparent needs of children. Although attention has initially been targeted at direct risks to physical safety, other forms of danger to the health and well-being of users have gradually become apparent.

The integration of technology into educational institutions has the potential to provide a plethora of benefits to both students and educators. Technology has become ubiquitous in most work fields, allowing tasks and duties to be simplified and expedited. Thus, teaching proper use of digital devices and systems as a part of the learning process provides students with a competitive advantage. According to an article published by Edutopia (2008), a nonprofit organization focused on educational innovation, the incorporation of technology into schools aids students in developing the skills needed "to survive in a complex, highly technological knowledge-based economy."

Just as digital technology has the potential to benefit students, it also has been shown to enhance student–teacher rapport. The use of digital tools and computer programs allows teachers to reach students with different learning styles, and be more interactive and engaged with students throughout the learning experience. Additionally, technology has facilitated the assessment and tracking of student progress and advancement. Thus, the use of technology in the classroom has lead to a new brand of teaching, one in which education can be more specialized to students' individual needs.

Although introducing digital devices and Internet access into educational programs can be advantageous, there still exist concerns and potential negative effects resulting from improper use of technology. The integration of programs, systems, and devices brings a different dimension to teaching. Teachers must take on the new responsibility of ensuring that students use technology appropriately and maintain proper balance. In fact, there are many ways in which communication and media consumption can fail to be consistent with a healthy lifestyle. iKeepSafe™ defines *cyberhealth* as the maintenance of a healthy relationship with digital technology. Favorable and effectual cyberhealth is characterized by the maintenance of appropriate exposures to digital content, healthy communication and relationships with others online, and technology usage that does not adversely interfere with other aspects of life (iKeepSafe, n.d.). Similarly, iKeepSafe defines *cyberbalance* as the healthy balance of technology use with other activities in life. Cyberbalance is a subset of overall cyberhealth (iKeepSafe, n.d.). Issues pertaining to cyberhealth intersect with the world of education, creating unique problems and imperatives for all involved stakeholders. In order for educators and their communities to foster thriving relationships with technology, they must understand cyberhealth and implement strategies that align with psychological and health research in the field. This chapter seeks to contextualize the concept of cyberhealth within the field of Internet safety, as well as illustrate its implications for educational culture and practice. An actionable academic framework for addressing these issues in school settings must be applied in order to implement solutions in a comprehensive and holistic fashion. Therefore, the benefits resulting from technology in the classroom are largely conditional on the way in which it is integrated into the curriculum. If digital developments and technologies are not properly incorporated into school programs, potential results include: (a) complications in educators' teaching plans; (b) unhealthy cyberbalance among students; and (c) improper use of programs and devices. Thus, proper integration is essential in order to maximize the benefits and minimize the potential risks of using technology scholastically.

This chapter begins with a discussion of the many benefits that can result from the presence of technology in educational systems. Next, the concept of cyberhealth is further described with a focus on the importance of maintaining proper balance with technology use. The issue of "problematic interactive media use" is also defined and explained in order to convey the serious concerns related to excessive and improper use of technological devices. This exploration leads into a discussion of the importance of proper integration of technology into the classroom, including recommended strategies based on relevant research in the field. The chapter concludes with a summary of the concerns related to digital device use, and an outline of the recommended steps and models for teachers and administrators aimed at maintaining good cyberhealth and proper cyberbalance among students and in classrooms.

BENEFITS OF TECHNOLOGY IN EDUCATION

Digital devices and computer programs, in combination with Internet access, have led to revolutionary advancements in education. They have opened up a whole new dimension of learning, one in which students have the opportunity to explore, interact, and learn using different techniques. One such development is the creation of computer programs, which has made possible computer modeling and thus advanced fields such as economics, mathematics, and epidemiology. The ability to graph equations, model the spread of diseases, and illustrate financial trends has enabled students to visualize abstract concepts, and thus better recall and understand them. Additionally, the incorporation of images into the process of learning allows students to comprehend concepts using another sense, deepening their understanding and their ability to apply the information. Similar innovations, including coding programs and editing software, have led to advancements in the fields of video production and digital design and have proven beneficial for both students and educators. Videos and images have provided teachers with a variety of teaching methods, allowing them to reach students with different styles of learning. For example, many videos have been created explaining chemical and biological processes. The videos frequently use color coding and distinct shapes allowing students to visualize processes, making them more real and comprehensible. However, although some students best retain information through visual means (e.g., videos or pictures), others learn best through auditory means (e.g., music), and others learn through activity and hands-on projects. As there exist technological tools that benefit visual learners, there are also resources, activities, and programs targeted at students with other learning preferences. Thus, when educators incorporate varied resources and a wide range of teaching techniques they are able to teach more effectively and benefit students with all different learning inclinations.

In addition to facilitating teaching students with different learning styles, technological innovations have led to the creation of new areas of study. Digital design and computer science are two fields that are products of technological advancements. In fact, due to the revolutionary emergence of technology, both fields have been "indemand" with large job markets and many opportunities for competitive salaries and high-level occupations. Digital design has combined computer graphics, image manipulation, and modeling with artistic design, changing and advancing the fields of advertising and film production. Similarly, computer science has allowed advancements in various industries and fields of study, such as national security, gaming, science, economics, mathematics, and business. This development and progression of new fields of study provide students with more opportunities for employment and a greater likelihood of finding an occupation that matches their interests.

Not only have educators and students benefited individually, but technology in the classroom has also been shown to enhance student–teacher relations, and keep students more engaged throughout class. Since the establishment of the Internet, the resources available on the web have continued to grow exponentially. This growth and expansion has benefited students as the Internet provides countless learning materials from the most updated sources, and makes them available in a variety of ways. Therefore, students can seek out sources that most interest them and also connect with academically reputable resources for research on almost any topic imaginable. Students have most of the world's information right at their fingertips, accessible in multiple forms, allowing them to tailor their research to their preferred learning style. Whether they would like to learn through watching a video, listening to a podcast, using online flashcards, or by reading, the option is available. In the same vein, educators can use different mediums to engage their students and build a good relationship with them. According to Edutopia (2008), when technology is properly integrated into the classroom, teacher–student relationships are generally enhanced as teachers "grow into roles of adviser, content expert, and coach." Teachers become more engaged with students and assist them with a method of learning in which they are more interested. Due to this heightened level of interest, and also familiarity, technology has also been shown to help students stay engaged and focused and less distracted in the classroom. Although technological advancements have contributed to countless benefits in the educational system, it is essential to remember that such success was in part due to how such technology was used and incorporated into the classroom. Therefore, in order to maximize the advantages, it is imperative that cyberhealth remains a part of the discussion and a top priority.

THE EMERGENCE OF CYBERHEALTH

Within the history of Internet safety, cyberhealth follows a fairly distinct narrative, illustrating the needs to which society has paid the most attention over time. A focus on cyberhealth has not emerged in one moment, but rather in a gradual and fragmented way. The primary areas of focus within this progression that have implications for understanding cyberhealth include physical safety, cyberbalance, and digital content exposure. It has only been in recent years that cyberbalance has become a prime area of concern.

When the Internet became widely consumed by the public, the rise of chat rooms and other forms of online communication greatly opened up the potential for sexual predation and child abduction. Internet predators began to thrive in an anonymous environment, as most Internet sexual offenders disguise their true identity online (Dowdell, Burgess, & Flores, 2011). Scholars such as David Finkelhor (2011) acknowledged that the Internet was not a creator, but an *amplifier* of these types of risks for children. Internet safety policy and discourse began to focus widely on the physical safety of children, attempting to prevent them from either giving away personal information that could put them at risk, or arranging meetings with strangers with potentially hazardous intentions.

Soon after these risks became recognized, cyberbullying and online harassment came to the forefront of public attention. Scholars and policymakers began to lift the veil of digital communication, which had maintained a dangerous reservoir of both anonymous and identifiable users. Instant messaging tools (such as AIM) had become havens for digital bullying. In fact, instant messaging forums are acknowledged as the most likely digital environment where one will be harassed (Huang & Chou, 2010). Although harassment is neither a new phenomenon, nor a creation of digital communication, online communication platforms have created many new ways in which harassment can surface. For example, it is likely that individuals who are aggressive in offline contexts begin extending this type of behavior into the online world (Dempsey, Sulkowski, & Storch, 2010). However, anonymous online settings have also made it easier for users to act more inappropriately in online settings than offline ones. Like many aspects of digital culture, cyberbullying has acted both as an extension of our lives from the physical world into the digital world, with elements of an entirely new terrain.

The importance of less immediate needs, such as a healthy balance of online and offline activities, was eventually recognized as another priority pertaining to proper Internet use. Because technology has applications for so many elements of our lives, such as communication, entertainment, work, and education, it also has the potential to consume too much of our time. Even more important, some users have become *addicted* to technology and the Internet or use it so frequently that it has negative implications for their health or well-being. Recently, iKeepSafe conducted extensive research, titled *Cyberbalance in a Digital Culture*, which demonstrated that a substantial number of teenagers and preteens struggle with balanced media usage. Specifically, 23% of 8- to 10-year-olds report having *cyberbalance challenges*, of which 73% describe the problem as media distracting them from daily activities and tasks. Twenty percent note that their media usage interferes with their relationships. Teenagers appear to struggle even more with their media usage: 36% of teens say they struggle with cyberbalance, 44% say they are unable to get enough sleep due to media usage, and 40% note not completing their homework as a result. Although only 28% of 8- to 10-year-olds report not getting enough sleep due to digital device usage, this is a significant number for such a young age, emphasizing the need for intervention and proper attention from the academic community, physicians, educators, and so on (iKeepSafe, n.d.).

CYBERHEALTH IN EDUCATION

Online safety issues have quickly carried themselves into the classroom, particularly with the emerging use of technology in schools. Each of these issues impacts and intersects with education in a unique way. Because children live a substantial portion of their lives online, these emergent phenomena regarding safety concerns can have significant implications for the mental and physical health, interpersonal relationships, and academic performance of students everywhere.

If a child experiences an unhealthy digital life, it can negatively shape his or her educational experience. Consider a student being bullied at school. Harassment that may once have ended on the student's return home, will now follow him or her. In fact, about 40% of youths have been the victim of cyberbullying at least once in their lifetime (Tokunaga, 2010). Consider another possible scenario, a student with attention deficit disorder (ADD) attending a school that has a bring your own device (BYOD) policy. The student struggles to complete homework with the competing allure of social media and other digital entertainment just a click away. School life and digital life are not two entirely distinct entities; they intertwine at many points. Although the overlap may have beneficial aspects, it also comes with many risks.

Educational agencies have not been able to keep their policies, procedures, and initiatives up to pace with emerging technology. Specifically within the last decade, technology has changed the narrative of daily life; an adaption that educators and schools could not have predicted, and now struggle to understand. Policy has not kept up with the technological revolution as very few laws and regulations have been implemented across the country in order to comprehensively address cyberhealth. However, educational agencies have an ethical imperative to employ the most effective and scientifically sound methods available to address concerns related to cyberhealth. Educational administrators need to learn about the complexity of digital issues and help students develop safe and healthy habits that will not only assist them in school but will also follow them outside the classroom. Although policy and regulations surrounding cyberhealth and balance have lagged behind technological advancement, due to an unprecedented rate of production, it would be unfair to not acknowledge successes at both the political and educational level. There are in fact several laws and organizations that address concerns and issues related to cyberhealth. For example, the Children's Internet Protection Act (CIPA), a policy enforced by the Federal Communications Commission (FCC), has requirements for education surrounding cyberbullying and Internet safety, particularly on social media. Additionally, nonprofit organizations such as Common Sense Media provide a great deal of resources supporting healthy media usage. Although policies and organizations such as CIPA, the FCC, and Common Sense Media seek to promote safe Internet usage, many of the requirements put forth are vague and one dimensional, neglecting the concern with cyberbalance (FCC, 2015). iKeepSafe is one of the first Internet safety organizations to track and follow the impact that technology has on mental and physical health. iKeepSafe recognizes the importance of promoting and ensuring not only a healthy relationship with the Internet, but also with all digital devices and forms of technology (iKeepSafe, n.d.). As the potential benefits that can result from the integration of technology into educational curriculum are countless, it is essential to have policies put into place that support proper incorporation of technology and cyberbalance.

CURRICULAR INTEGRATION OF TECHNOLOGY

When taken on its own, media is neutral; it has the potential to both benefit or disadvantage students' educational experience. In order to achieve the advantages of scholastic technology usage, there must be policies in place that promote cyberhealth, ensure balanced integration, and support early detection of unhealthy behaviors among students. Parents of students have been shown to notice their child's unhealthy media usage late in the process and seek help when the issue is already severe. Many times the child's academics have already been negatively affected, and he or she is less interactive with family and friends (Rich, 2016). In fact, according to iKeepSafe research, approximately 31% of teens have no rules regarding digital device usage (iKeepSafe, n.d.). Based on this lack of supervision and regulation, recognition and detection of unhealthy behaviors becomes an important responsibility for educators.

Contrary to what many may believe, integrating technology into the classroom is not as easy as having a computer class and teaching software programs. Rather, proper media incorporation should span across the curriculum and be carefully implemented to ensure balance and efficacy (Edutopia Team, 2008). Technology should be woven into lesson plans and classroom activities as a supplement to traditional teaching methods, expanding and strengthening students' educational experience.

According to Edutopia, effective technology incorporation can be achieved by supporting particular components of learning. Specifically, integrated digital tools should support (a) active engagement, (b) participation in groups, (c) frequent interaction and feedback, and (d) connection to real-world experts (Edutopia Team, 2008). In this way technology can support students' learning experience and help educators achieve curricular objectives.

A CYBERHEALTH FRAMEWORK FOR EDUCATION

When it comes to cyberhealth and online safety, leaders in education need to shift the overall cultural paradigm from being *reactive* to *proactive*. Reliance solely on risk management and incident response techniques merely addresses the individual symptoms of an underlying cultural problem. Creating a positive digital culture depends not only on how we respond to digital incidents, but on the social norms we establish to prevent these issues from occurring. In order to comprehensively conceptualize what is needed to achieve this goal, education stakeholders including educators, policymakers, parents, law enforcement, and more, need to consider the four points of access: location, network, device, and application. Each of these considerations needs to be addressed in order to have a broad and complete grasp on digital safety issues affecting youth. *Location* concerns where the device and user are located physically (and socially), while *network* concerns how and under what circumstances a device is connected to others. *Device* refers to what type of device is being used, and *application* refers to what digital software or applications are being used (including how they are intended to be used).

Under this lens, iKeepSafe has sought to develop a coherent intellectual framework for understanding and addressing cyberhealth and online safety for youth and students. Our group summarized the current issues surrounding cyberhealth into a few key principles, an essential resource to increase awareness and understanding. These principles, in conjunction with the most up-to-date scientific research, can best inform a school's policies, programs, and initiatives with respect to cyberhealth.

We began by documenting all known digital offenses by gathering credible, academic research from cyber security professionals, media and digital literacy experts, media psychologists, law enforcement officers, and public health professionals. This included research conducted by the Rochester Institute of Technology, which identified the offenses from wireless and Internet-connected devices experienced by 40,000 New York students in grades K–12 (iKeepSafe Team, n.d.). Life-disrupting experiences, both legal and health related, were closely examined. After verifying the known list of risks and offenses, iKeepSafe worked with Harvard University's Center on Media and Child Health (2016) and the School of Public Health to translate the known risks into a framework of positive concepts. These concepts include: balance, ethics, privacy, reputation, relationships, and online security (BEaPRO™):

> **Balance**: Maintaining a healthy balance between online activities and offline activities

Ethics: Making ethical decisions, being considerate of others, and understanding consequences of online behavior

Privacy: Protecting personal information and that of others

Reputation: Building a positive online presence that will contribute to future success

Relationships: Engaging in safe and healthy online connections

Online Security: Using good habits for securing hardware and software

It is important to note that these principles are not intended to be considered exhaustive—they constitute a list of necessary, albeit not sufficient, conditions for a safe and healthy digital experience. Although each of these core areas plays a role in determining an individual's cyberhealth, *balance* specifically refers to issues surrounding Internet addiction and maintaining healthy screen time (iKeepSafe Team, n.d.).

Employing interventions in schools aimed at helping students successfully develop essential skills and competencies can strengthen each of the aforementioned areas of cyberhealth in children's lives. Educational programs that help students develop these habits will foster a positive, prepared, and healthy digital culture in schools. In order for students to properly balance technology with the development of strong bodies and healthy minds, students should understand how and when to be digitally connected, and how to set healthy boundaries for themselves. As the use of technology affects children in different age groups differently, parents must be able to recognize what kind and level of technology use is developmentally appropriate for their child.

Each of the six principles of cyberhealth and online safety has the potential to be weakened by unhealthy behavior. For example, a student's cyberhealth can be damaged if he or she shares too much personal information with unknown commercial entities or anonymous users. By jeopardizing his or her privacy, this student may face a number of consequences. The student may become a victim of harassment, have intellectual property stolen, or have information sold to and used by commercial vendors. An example of the ways in which such privacy breaches could occur include: sharing one's password, putting one's personal information into online scams, or including one private information publicly on social media forums. Therefore, *privacy* along with the other five principles, each overlapping to a certain extent, are the key areas that should be protected and focused on in order to promote and maintain good cyberhealth.

One of the most effective ways parents and educators can foster positive behaviors in children and students is through educational games. iKeepSafe has worked with David Bickham in the development and study of mobile video gaming as a method to teach children safe and healthy digital behaviors. The program *Cyberhero Mobile Safety* contains games that focus on six core areas of cybersafety: reputation, relationships, multitasking, domains of use (cyberbalance), responsibility, and maximizing the positive (constructive use promotion). In addition, the programs *Tech Zombies* and *Brain Drain* focus specifically on cyberhealth (Hswen, Rubenzahl, & Bickham, 2014). *Tech Zombies* focuses on the management of online and offline relationships; for example, the game portrays characters that turn into zombies if they use technology or mobile devices when talking to others. In order to advance to the next level, players must address these issues; the goal is to learn that there are contexts in which device use is inappropriate. *Brain Drain* addresses the problems associated with multitasking by teaching users to engage in only one activity at a time. The game incorporates distractions to demonstrate how one's personal performance on tasks decreases as they succumb to multiple tasks simultaneously (Hswen et al., 2014). Each of these games was indicated to resonate well with the users. A self-report measure was used based on three factors: likability, applicability, and perceived message effectiveness. Each game received favorable scoring in each of the three categories. According to the study, "videogame usability criteria were achieved on 82.7 percent of the students' gameplays," in which mean ratings indicated efficacy. On a scale ranging from 1 (low) to 5 (high), mean ratings were 3.54 for acceptability, 4.09 for likability, and 4.16 for perceived message usefulness. Though these data cannot be considered completely conclusive, they certainly reinforce the notion that educational gaming can be an engaging technique to teach children about maintaining their cyberhealth (Hswen et al., 2014).

In addition, iKeepSafe provides children with an overall online safety narrative through another interactive and engaging program. iKeepSafe's initial module, *Faux Paw's Adventures in the Internet*, focuses primarily on the physical safety of children, teaching them how to safely navigate interactions with strangers online. The second course, *Faux Paw Meets the First Lady: How to Handle Cyberbullying*, focuses on cyberbullying and online harassment. The third, *Faux Paw Goes to the Games*, focuses on cyberbalance and the physical effects resulting from overuse of technology and mobile devices (iKeepSafe Educators, n.d.). Each of these animated episodes incorporates an entertaining video for children, accompanied by a curriculum for educators to ensure they are asking the right questions and that the children are comprehending the lessons of each video.

RECOMMENDED STEPS FOR SCHOOLS

Foremost, schools and educational agencies must remember that as the lives of children are directly extending into the digital environment, cyberhealth and safety must be made top priorities. Students' online health and safety must be considered as important as the protection of physical safety. In fact, the two realms often interact as discussed earlier with reference to multiple studies and research.

However, even in cases where technology does not directly affect physical health, weak cyberhealth can be just as damaging to a student's personal growth and academic performance as poor physical health. Students who suffer from Internet addiction are much more likely to have poor mental health, and subsequently engage in self-injury (Lam, Peng, Mai, & Jing, 2009). Lonely individuals are at a particularly great risk of mental and physical instability; they are more likely to engage in behaviors that indicate poor cyberbalance, leading to negative life outcomes, such as poor performance at work, school, or even in personal relationships (Kim, LaRose, & Peng, 2009). In most nondigital contexts, these concerns are taken very seriously; however, they are many times neglected or ignored when related to media use. As student safety is a top priority, it is important to also take into account the digital causes of such risks posed to students' mental and physical health.

iKeepSafe has used this information to inform and develop a variety of programs that can help educators achieve their goals in cyberhealth and balance. For example, iKeepSafe developed the *Wise Tech Choices* program in partnership with Boy Scouts of America. It is a set of activities and information for scout leaders or parents to help their scouts or children develop habits necessary for maintaining a positive cyberhealth. The program addresses the technology challenges that emerged from iKeepSafe's *Cyberbalance in a Digital Culture* research and the framework provided by leading experts in digital health, media health, pediatrics, social science, and sexual health. iKeepSafe also helps address cyberbalance concerns in the K–12 *Balance Curriculum Matrix*, a guide for building effective curricula that teach children the skills for maintaining *Life Balance* in media and online environments.

In order to begin implementing policies and programs that take cyberhealth (and other digital safety issues) into consideration, school systems and administrators need to promote conversation around these media-related issues among all parties playing a role in how education and technology intersect. In other words, leaders and administrators within educational communities should begin fostering discussion among all relevant education stakeholder groups.

Because the digital environment is so new and unfamiliar, many school districts and educational agencies currently employ a reactive framework in managing both usage of and incidents involving digital technology. That is, they can fall victim to a few key pitfalls, including:

- Lack of knowledge, planning, or preparation around digital issues
- Perceiving and engaging with technology as consumers, rather than as educators
- Responding to digital incidents as they would any other transgression occurring on campus

These mistakes indicate that educators are often still employing conventional techniques to meet entirely new and different needs of students in the 21st century. Cases involving sexting and cyberbullying, for example, are not being fully anticipated, prevented, and managed. Educators and school districts need to adopt a positive and *proactive* approach to develop and maintain cyberhealth, rather than simply a reactive approach.

The first step that can be taken to ameliorate these phenomena is the formation of a digital safety and privacy committee. Schools should open conversations among various stakeholders (e.g., teachers, curriculum directors, administrators, information technology [IT] directors, staff, community members) to address digital safety concepts, including cyberhealth. Doing so will begin fundamental discussion aimed at bridging institutional silos. Each of the groups participating has valuable insight relevant to developing a culture of cyberhealth; thus, forming a committee will empower school systems to take well-formed and effective steps toward fostering a positive digital culture.

Next, members of the designated committee can work collectively to establish cyberhealth and cybersafety goals and create policies for administrators and teachers regarding the proper use of technology in the curriculum. The committee will need to generate a list of procedures, to be shared with educators, that includes an explanation of strategies for minimizing screen addiction and imbalanced media usage. In order to most effectively prepare educators, they should receive proper teacher training in addition to receiving a packet of information with recommended policies and approaches. Such training will instruct educators on early detection of students who misuse media or technology, and proper strategies of intervention and communication with parents.

In addition to teacher training and instruction, the use of digital controls and filters is important in guiding students on the right path with their Internet usage. Through the application of firewalls, filters, and blocking of dangerous websites, students' navigation of the Internet can be monitored and limited to educational resources. These operations will help to keep students focused and prevent them from accessing harmful online material or websites.

Therefore, in implementing strategies to support cyberhealth and cyberbalance and reduce the incidence of uncontrolled media usage, it is recommended that schools generate a single program, initiative, and committee that uses a variety of strategies to target cyberhealth and ensure proper media usage. These strategies include software and computer controls, teacher and administrator training, and policies and procedures aimed at properly integrating technology and supporting early detection of unhealthy behaviors. This initiative will promote regulation and monitoring and ensure good cyberhealth, allowing students to maximize the benefits they receive from scholastic technology use.

CONCLUSION

Overall, it is important that educators give a concentrated and conscious effort toward ensuring children's health and wellness. Administrators should focus on teaching and fostering critical skills and competencies required to extend positive outcomes into a digital culture. The use of technology and digital tools today is ubiquitous and unavoidable; thus, it is important to harness the associated benefits and values while still protecting against related risks.

In addition, a reasonable level of deference to research in psychology, public health, and other sciences needs to be adopted. As the world of technology, particularly in education, is rapidly evolving and ever changing, cutting-edge scientific research is the best resource available to inform behaviors, policies, and practices. This information is especially useful in conjunction with context from legal experts, law enforcement, cyber security, digital literacy, and more. Because cyberhealth is an entirely new domain, we cannot rely on intuition alone when making key decisions surrounding technology use, content exposures, and digital communications.

Without a concentrated and well-structured plan, cyberhealth needs cannot be properly addressed. In order to minimize the negative effects of media usage and promote advantages and values, the main issues surrounding students' cyberhealth must be given active attention. Specifically, administrators and stakeholders, such as technology professionals, must come together and form a solid plan focusing on the six core pillars of BEaPRO: balance, ethics, privacy, reputation, relationships, and online security (iKeepSafe Team, n.d.).

Although the six foci of BEaPRO are based on credible and efficacious research aimed at preparing youth to thrive in digital culture, no prescriptive set of guidelines can guarantee complete protection, safety, or health. Therefore, it is important to both adhere to BEaPRO guidelines, but also to continue investing in the most up-to-date digital educational tools and security systems. Furthermore, it is important that professionals within the educational system stay alert and watchful for concerning behaviors among students such as overusage, inappropriate usage, and cyberbullying.

Although statistics have shown that excessive use of media can contribute to students receiving poor grades and having weak relationships with their parents, it in no way indicates that technology or the Internet does more harm than good. Rather, the results and outcomes of technology usage in the classroom are dependent on the environment and methods of integration. With proper incorporation of media and digital devices, the benefits of advanced technology are unprecedented, deepening the learning process and allowing students with different learning styles to thrive and excel. Although such benefits should be acknowledged, recognized, and lauded, safety measures and parameters must not be neglected or overlooked. Technology-related concerns must continue to remain a top priority in order to ensure student safety and success.

REFERENCES

Center on Media and Child Health. (2016, April 12). Michael Rich. Center on Media and Child Health. Retrieved from http://cmch.tv/about-us/our-team/michael-rich

Dempsey, A. G., Sulkowski, M. L., & Storch, E. A. (2010). Has cyber technology produced a new group of peer aggressors? *Cyberpsychology, Behavior, and Social Networking, 14*(5), 297–302.

Dowdell, E. B., Burgess, A. W., & Flores, J. R. (2011). Original research: Online social networking patterns among adolescents, young adults, and sexual offenders. *The American Journal of Nursing, 111*(7), 28–36.

Edutopia Team. (2008, March 16). Why integrate technology into the curriculum?: The reasons are many. *Edutopia*. Retrieved from http://www.edutopia.org/technology-integration-introduction

Federal Communications Commission. (2015, November 3). Children's Internet Protection Act. Retrieved from https://www.fcc.gov/consumers/guides/childrens-internet-protection-act

Finkelhor, D. (2011). The Internet, youth safety and the problem of "Juvenoia." Crimes Against Children Research Center. Retrieved from http://www.unh.edu/ccrc/pdf/Juvenoia%20paper.pdf

Hswen, Y., Rubenzahl, L., & Bickham, D. S. (2014). Feasibility of an online and mobile videogame curriculum for teaching children safe and healthy cell phone and Internet behaviors. *Games for Health: Research, Development, and Clinical Applications, 3*(4), 252–259.

Huang, Y.-Y., & Chou, C. (2010). An analysis of multiple factors of cyberbullying among junior high school students in Taiwan. *Computers in Human Behavior 26*(6), 1581–1590.

iKeepSafe. (n.d.). Cyberbalance in a digital culture. Retrieved from http://archive.ikeepsafe.org/cyberbalance

iKeepSafe Educators. (n.d.). Faux Paw the Techno Cat. Retrieved from http://archive.ikeepsafe.org/educators_old/fauxpaw

iKeepSafe Team. (n.d.). About BEaPRO™. Retrieved from http://archive.ikeepsafe.org/be-a-pro/info

Kim, J., LaRose, R., & Peng, W. (2009). Loneliness as the cause and the effect of problematic Internet use: The relationship between Internet use and psychological well-being. *Cyber Psychology & Behavior, 12*(4), 451–455.

Lam, L. T., Peng, Z., Mai, J., & Jing, J. (2009). The association between Internet addiction and self-injurious behaviour among adolescents. *Injury Prevention, 15*(6), 403–408.

Rich, M. (2016, April 12). How should clinicians diagnose patients with "Internet addiction"? Center on Media and Child Health. Retrieved from http://cmch.tv/diagnose-internet-addiction

Tokunaga, R. S. (2010). Following you home from school: A critical review and synthesis of research on cyberbullying victimization. *Computers in Human Behavior, 26*(3), 277–287.

INDEX

Printed in the USA
CPSIA information can be obtained
at www.ICGtesting.com
CBHW070958020424
6201CB00011B/60